THE AGADIR CRISIS

THE
AGADIR
CRISIS

BY

IMA CHRISTINA BARLOW
ASSOCIATE PROFESSOR OF HISTORY,
West Texas State Teachers College

ARCHON BOOKS
1971

ISBN: 0–208–01023–8
Library of Congress Catalog Card Number: 70–147380
Printed in The United States of America

PREFACE

During the early twentieth century, that dynamic imperialism which periodically darkened the international horizon had among its various fields of operation none more prominent than Morocco, whose material resources and strategical advantages excited the cupidity of her European neighbors. Struggle for control of this land attained international importance in the crisis of 1905; and, since the appeasement effected by the Algeciras conference lacked permanency, the conflict broke out again in 1911. In this imperialistic combat, France now won the prize—a victory, however, that meant not peace but a prelude to war.

The first Moroccan crisis and its resultant conference have been treated at some length;[1] but on the second conflict, the Agadir crisis, no intensive work has as yet appeared. The present inquiry surveys the incidents involved in that crisis and analyzes the motives of the various actors. It has, however, been necessary to narrow this study to those issues that endangered Franco-German relations and thereby threatened the peace of Europe. Spanish interests have therefore been treated only in so far as they inject themselves into the problem.

Pertinent German and British documents bearing on the origins of the war have been published. The French foreign office is bringing out gradually a similar collection in three series simultaneously; but apart from a few despatches in the first volume of the third series, official documentary material touching Morocco is as yet restricted to selections found in the *Livres jaunes*. These volumes of *Affaires du Maroc* are in themselves valuable and apparently complete on essential points. In fact, although the publication of all French documents relating to the crisis will probably clarify some details, it is doubtful if any startling disclosures will result.

---

[1] Eugene N. Anderson, *The First Moroccan Crisis.*

The University of Texas has all the material essential to a study of this problem except the files of foreign newspapers. This deficiency was supplied in part by means of photostats from the Library of Congress and in part by the kindness of Dr. Thad W. Riker who generously contributed the results of his research in London among newspapers published during the period of the crisis.

To the history faculty of the University of Texas and especially to Professor Thad W. Riker, who has patiently guided me through the labyrinth of European history and who, in this project, has given me inspiration and invaluable advice; to my brother, Edward Barlow, who by his criticism and unwearied assistance has kept me seeking the right phrase; to his wife, who has rendered indispensable aid in proof reading; and to my sister, Vivian B. Somerville, who has read the entire manuscript and offered many helpful suggestions, I owe a debt of deep gratitude. I wish to express my appreciation to Dr. L. F. Sheffy and the administrative staff of West Texas State College for their interest and coöperation. This book would never have been undertaken without the confidence and encouragement of my mother and my friends.

IMA CHRISTINA BARLOW

Canyon, Texas
July 15, 1939

CONTENTS

THE AGADIR CRISIS

Chapter **I**

MOROCCO: LAND OF PROMISE

Agadir! July 1, 1911. With dramatic suddenness, Germany focused the eyes of the world upon that isolated spot which to the general public was until then scarcely more than a name. The surprise was not so great among the chancelleries of Europe; for although the move Germany would take was unpredictable, they could have each joined with Aehrenthal when he said, "The interference of Germany in the Moroccan business has not surprised me in the least. . . ."[1] Germany had moved to Agadir by way of Algeciras, a route marked by many a piece of diplomatic or business bargaining, with each milestone leaving her more and more discontent. France's "peaceful penetration" had carried her along the same route but with far more success—a success that necessarily must appear as a challenge to the German people now newly saturated with an imperialistic spirit.

The nineteenth century saw the European powers march with bold strides across hitherto unknown lands and grab for their own delectation the luscious fruits with which a dauntless imperialism tempts its devotees. As choice bits were clutched by first one and then another of the imperialistic nations, insatiable hunger whetted by the decreasing reserve drove each nation to a fiercer determination to receive its share. Conflicting ambitions of European powers had thus far saved Morocco from the fate of her less fortunate neighbors, but as the struggle for empires became narrowed to fewer tracts, her strategic location and her promise of wealth decreed her doom. No longer could she hope to escape the plunderous rapacity of her European friends. Morocco, a land of forbidding and gaunt beauty, held the keys to many a diplomatic maneuver during the years immediately preceding the Great War. We find those keys juggled with the adroit legerdemain of France, the heavy swashbuckling of Germany, the almost occult tenacity

---

[1] Aehrenthal, private letter, July 4, 1911, *Österreich-Ungarns Aussenpolitik*, vol. III, no. 2554. (Hereafter cited as *Ö. U. A.*)

of Britain, and we are put to it to sift the truth from the chaff. But through every maneuver we find that the geography of Morocco with all it seemed to offer absorbed the attention of those clever gentlemen known as diplomats. Thus the geography of the land introduces one into that tangled maze known as the Moroccan question.

Sprawled across the northwest corner of Africa to the extent of some two hundred and twenty-five thousand square miles,[2] Morocco occupied a strategic position almost without parallel. Every interested power saw her as a sentinel, guarding or imperiling, according to its mood, the commerce of all the Mediterranean nations, and at times actually menacing the imperial position of some of them. Although firmly entrenched on the rock of Gibraltar, England looked across the straits with anxious eyes; for her Mediterranean route depended upon the strength of her position at the entrance of that sea. Her interest in the Atlantic littoral along the northwest corner of Africa was only slightly less intense than her interest in the Mediterranean coast. Today air and steamship lines from Europe to South America converge in the thriving modern harbor of Casablanca;[3] but at the opening of the twentieth century a port of call along the Atlantic coast of Morocco remained a dream full of potentialities, a dream, however, which disturbed the slumbers of many an astute diplomat whether he were British, French, Spanish, or German. A commercial harbor always holds the possibilities of a naval base, and such a unit created on the northwest coast of Africa could menace Britain's trade routes to various parts of the world and threaten her communications with her empire. The fate of her empire decreed that her statesmen keep the entire coast section of Morocco in the hands of her friends.[4]

---

[2] Augustin Bernard, *Le Maroc*, p. 7. Bernard, a professor of geography and colonization of North Africa, was a close student of Moroccan affairs and at times a member of the editorial staff of the *Bulletin du comité de l'Afrique française*. See p. 35 *infra*. (Hereafter cited as *L'Afrique française*.)

[3] Auguste Terrier, *Le Maroc*, p. 8.

[4] Francis R. Flournoy, *British Policy towards Morocco in the Age of Palmerston*, pp. 31-34, 53; Kurt Neumann, *Die Internationalität Marokkos*, pp. 213-216; Graham H. Stuart, *The International City of Tangier*, pp. 55-56; A. Bernard, *op. cit.*, p. 8; E. D. Morel, *Morocco in Diplomacy*, pp. 3-9.

Spain was also interested in the destiny which awaited the Sherifian empire. Her geographic affinity with the Berber kingdom accentuated her claims upon the land. The Riff and the Sierra Nevada, the Moroccan meseta and the Spanish meseta, indicate that the two lands were once one.[5] The ease with which General Franco has used Morocco as a military base strengthens Spanish contention that her existence depended upon keeping the Mediterranean littoral in her own hands. She could not meekly permit the northern part of Morocco to fall into the hands of an enemy, and in this she found an ally in England who could better trust her own fate to a weak power like Spain than to any of her stronger rivals.

Morocco, with the huge Atlas Range spread the full length of her eastern border, as though turning her back upon the African mainland, steadfastly gazed at the sea.[6] Thus arrogantly she defied any invasion from Algeria while at the same time she stood as a constant menace to that land. The configuration of her mountains was such that an enemy in possession of Morocco could threaten the entire North African empire, the prize colonial possession of France.[7] The French colonial empire, moreover, remained truncated unless she could win the coveted region. If she wished to maintain her position as a first rate imperialistic nation, France could not see Morocco in the hands of any nation other than herself.

When Germany entered the struggle for colonies, the finest fruits had already been picked. She, therefore, saw in Morocco her last chance to win a desirable portion for herself. She was also interested in the Sherifian land in the same manner as were the British. Germany was fast developing a world commerce to rival that of all other powers, and any point strategically located on the trade routes of the world would necessarily excite her interest. Her prestige as a power demanded that she be recognized as a

---

[5] Alan G. Ogilvie, "Morocco and its Future," in *Geographic Journal*, vol. XXXIX, p. 554; A. Bernard, *op. cit.*, pp. 12, 17; Stuart, *op. cit.*, p. 55; Victor Bérard, *L'Affaire marocaine*, p. 4; Jean Alengry, *Les Relations franco-espagnoles et l'affaire du Maroc*, pp. 9-11.   [6] A. Bernard, *op. cit.*, p. 7.

[7] *Ibid.*; Neumann, *op. cit.*, pp. 216-218; Thomas W. Balch, *France in North Africa*, p. 11; Pierre Noël, *Les Rapports de la France et du Maroc*, pp. 13-16; Stuart, *op. cit.*, p. 55; Morel, *op. cit.*, pp. 10-13.

nation worthy of consideration in the colonial bargains through
which the other powers were establishing their empires. In Morocco
lay a test not only of her ability to acquire colonies but of her
prestige as a power.[8]

The strategic value of Morocco made of her a prize worthy of
any imperialistic game, but added to that evaluation was her
potential economic wealth.[9] In fact, the German, Theobald Fischer,
believed that "Morocco was so rich and potentially important
that control over it by any one power would completely destroy
the economic and diplomatic balance of Europe. . . ."[10] Three
mountain chains sweeping across her eastern frontier saved her
from the effects of the desert and made west Morocco a desirable
place for European colonization. Of these chains the High Atlas
and the Middle Atlas, divisions of the same range, rose in the
northeast near Taza and, turning to the southwest, ran almost
the full length of the country to touch the Atlantic coast near
Cape Guir. They formed a barrier, though not an impassable one,
which separated Morocco from the rest of North Africa. The
Anti-Atlas broke off from the more northern range near Tamagurt
on the Dra and terminated on the Atlantic near Cape Ifni. These
ranges with their forested western slopes, especially the Middle
Atlas with its giant cedars, offered a fortune in timbered
wealth. In all their gaunt beauty, they intrigued with their promise
of mineral wealth and yet defied man to unearth their secrets.
The Riff, spread across the northern coast of the land, in the same
manner lured while it repelled those who wished to garner its
wealth.[11] The mountains alone were sufficient to excite the cupidity

[8] Neumann, *op. cit.*, p. 221; Herbert Feis, *Europe, The World's Banker,
1870-1914*, p. 413; Morel, *op. cit.*, pp. 16-24.

[9] S. H. Roberts, *History of French Colonial Policy*, vol. II, pp. 545-549;
Ogilvie, *op. cit.*, pp. 554-575; Theobald Fischer, "Morocco," in Smithsonian Institute *Annual Report*, 1904, pp. 355-372; Victor Piquet, *Le Maroc*, pp. 56-109;
A. Bernard, *op. cit.*, pp. 133-191; Budgett Meakin and K. A. Meakin, "Morocco,"
in *Encyclopedia Britannica*, 11th edition, vol. XVIII, pp. 850-860; J. M. Mac-
Leod, "The Achievements of France in Morocco," in *Geographic Journal*, vol.
LII, pp. 84-101; Bernhard Stichel, *Die Zukunft in Marokko*, pp. 16-38; Alfred
de Tarde, "The Work of France in Morocco," in *Geographical Review*, vol. VIII,
pp. 1-30. The *Comité du Maroc* in its journal *L'Afrique française* consistently
stressed the economic value of Morocco.

[10] Francis Torrance Williamson, *Germany and Morocco before 1905*, pp. 86-87.

[11] Terrier, *op. cit.*, pp. 30-36; A. Bernard, *op. cit.*, pp. 24-33; Élisée Reclus,

of imperialistic powers, but the true value of Morocco lay not in her mountains but in her plains and plateaus.

Of her three plateaus, the Sahara tableland, the Plateau of Shotts lying between the Middle and High Atlas, and the meseta, only the meseta offered promise of economic wealth. Triangular in shape, it lay between the coast and the Atlas, almost touching the coast at Mogador but shoved farther inland as the coast plain widened towards Rabat. Its general aspect was plain, but a plain cut with deep, impassable ravines and canyons which formed a serious obstacle to travel. Across this plateau the Oum-er-Rbia River cascaded its tumultuous way to the sea and offered no encouragement to commercial ventures. Nomads inhabited the land and combined their hostility with the natural obstacles to force all travel through the land from Marrakech to Fez from its most direct route into a detour which led the traveler from Marrakech to the coast, thence to Rabat, and then up the Sebou Plain to Fez. Even the sultan, whenever he changed his capital from the north to the south, had to follow this route. Yet this section was not without its value. Herds of cattle, sheep, and goats thrived on the steppes of the meseta and furnished the nomads of the land their means of barter with the more favored plain sections.[12]

Oasis cities relieved the drab barrenness of the meseta and presented gifts of olives, figs, quinces, oranges, almonds, and pomegranates. The red tower of Koutoubya, the watch tower of the ancient sultans, announced to the approaching traveler that he neared the capital of the south, Marrakech.[13] A true oasis city, surrounded by orchards and gardens, Marrakech formed the entrepôt for all trade from the Sous and from the Sahara. Men from Timbuctoo came here to barter their wares for the famous leather goods of the natives or for European goods brought in by adventurous traders from Mogador, the port for the entire south.[14]

Earth and Its Inhabitants, Africa, vol. II, pp. 348-353; Fischer, _op. cit.,_ p. 359; Ogilvie, _op. cit.,_ p. 554; Piquet, _op. cit.,_ pp. 7-12, 16-18, 57-59.

[12] A. Bernard, _op. cit.,_ pp. 18-20, 172; Fischer, _op. cit.,_ pp. 364-367; Terrier, _op. cit.,_ pp. 13-16, 80-91. See also the article by Ogilvie and the accompanying map, Ogilvie, _op. cit.,_ p. 557.   [13] Edith Wharton, _In Morocco,_ p. 127.

[14] _Ibid.;_ Fischer, _op. cit.,_ p. 367; A. Bernard, _op. cit.,_ pp. 24, 180; Reclus, _op. cit.,_ pp. 390-393.

Neither the mountains nor the plateaus of Morocco offered the immediate rewards which lay exposed upon her plains, and these rewards formed the core of French desire. Most important to the French empire was the famous Sebou-Moulouya Plain, a natural gateway which lay between the Riff and the Atlas and brought Algeria in touch with the Atlantic coast. Political and economic control of Morocco lay in the hands of any power that controlled this plain.[15] "Salé the white and Rabat the red frown at each other over the foaming bar of the Bou-Regreg" [16] and formed the old entrance from the coast inland into the Gharb, as the Sebou Plain was sometimes called. Here stood the tower of Hassan, the sultan's tower, which matched the Koutoubya of Marrakech as the watch towers of the old régime, fitting monuments of the past.[17] Yet it was not the ruins of the past with all their interesting tradition but the prospects for the future that excited the avarice of full-fledged imperialists. Their eyes were cast outside the old cities to the promise of the land beyond. A short distance to the north of the old port rose the mighty cork oak tangled in thick underbrush which marked the forest of Mamora, one of the most extensive and potentially one of the richest forests known in the world. Bound by the rivers Bou-Regreg on the south and Sebou on the north, the Mamora trees formed a veritable treasure house for that fortunate nation who might claim them as its own.[18]

The forested wealth of the region faded into insignificance before the agricultural possibilities of the land. The rich fertile fields which flecked the plain of Sebou from Rabat to Fez were admirably adapted to the cultivation of cereals, especially barley and wheat. Even under the primitive system of agriculture used by the natives, they richly rewarded their owners, and under a more advanced system presented unlimited possibilities.[19] Cotton was not produced by the natives in the early twentieth century but "the

[15] Terrier, *op. cit.*, pp. 37-39; Ogilvie, *op. cit.*, p. 561; Fischer, *op. cit.*, p. 364; A. Bernard, *op. cit.*, pp. 14-16.

[16] Wharton, *op. cit.*, p. 15.   [17] *Ibid.*, p. 31.

[18] A. Bernard, *op. cit.*, p. 47; Piquet, *op. cit.*, pp. 59-61; Terrier, *op. cit.*, p. 44; Tarde, *op. cit.*, p. 19; François Bernard, *Le Maroc, économique et agricole*, p. 183.

[19] Piquet, *op. cit.*, pp. 67-69; F. Bernard, *op. cit.*, pp. 150-171; Reclus, *op. cit.*, p. 383; Terrier, *op. cit.*, p. 54; A. Bernard, *op. cit.*, pp. 168-171.

old Moroccans remember having seen in their young days, great fields of cotton in the region of Quezzan. . . ." [20] In its western extremity, the part of the plain which lay between the Sebou and the Riff might be transformed into extensive fields of cotton. To the economic imperialist the venture was worth the trying. The Gharb was also justly famous for its pasturage. The best variety of sheep produced in the land was that which fed upon the grass of this region. Vast herds of cattle also dotted the plain and brought wealth to their owners,[21] while they excited the imagination and cupidity of the Europeans who desired the land.

On the road to Fez lay Meknez, the Versailles of old Morocco, built by Moulay Ismael in the time of Louis XIV.[22] The ostrich farm founded here over two hundred years ago by the sultans is still famous[23] and attracts as much attention as the ruins of the ancient palace of the ruler. Time had ruined the ancient edifice, but since the establishment of the French protectorate the discovery of oil in the nearby region[24] has completed the destruction. The city of royal pomp and ceremony has thus given way to a bustling oil town.

Fez, the key to northern Morocco, was its capital and was also in much the same sense as was Marrakech the entrepôt for the trade of its region. Almost in the center of the Sebou-Moulouya Plain, Fez had surrounding it all the production typical of the plains plus the fruitful orchards and gardens which clustered around its walls. Fez, like Marrakech, was famous for its olives, oranges, figs, and quinces and also for its weaving and embroidery of cloth, its manufacture of pottery, and more recently its distillation of brandy from the fruits of the area. The Jewish quarters, the famous mosques, the enchanting beauty of the mosaics which adorned the old buildings, the thriving bazaars where were bartered

---

[20] F. Bernard, *op. cit.,* p. 165. See also, Piquet, *op. cit.,* p. 75.

[21] Piquet, *op. cit.,* pp. 80-91; F. Bernard, *op. cit.,* pp. 172-182; A. Bernard, *op. cit.,* p. 172; Ogilvie, *op. cit.,* p. 561.

[22] Wharton, *op. cit.,* p. 58.   [23] F. Bernard, *op. cit.,* p. 182.

[24] Terrier, *op. cit.,* p. 185; Bernard Clarjean, "Petrole Nord-Africain et défense nationale," in *L'Afrique française, Renseignements,* Apr., 1937, pp. 37-40; René Hoffherr et Paul Mauchaissé, "Industrialisation minière et politique complementaire franco-marocaine," in *L'Afrique française,* 1934, pp. 234-239.

2

silks, rugs, mattings, pottery, native handicrafts in exchange
for the European wares which had come in from the coast, were
found behind the long line of ramparts and fortresses that mark
the approach to old and new Fez.[25]

Due east of Fez towered the mighty Atlas, but to the northeast
past Taza and Oudjda to the Algerian frontier extended the Plain
of Angad, the eastern extension of the Sebou-Moulouya Plain.
Drained by the Moulouya River into the Mediterranean Sea, this
section with its agricultural development similar to but less intensive than that of the Sebou Plain looked more to the east than
to the west for its economic life. Although tobacco was raised
in various parts of the empire, the Taza section had the most
abundant production. The development of the tobacco industry
was handicapped by the tobacco monopoly which permitted only
the favored few to participate in its cultivation.[26] Taza, located
on a high black rock, stood in the plain as a sentinel challenging
all who had passed Oudjda and dared to move on to the northern
capital, Fez.[27] The wealth embodied in the agricultural production of the Sebou-Moulouya Plain was sufficient to arouse the imperialistic ambitions of European powers, but—to reiterate—the
line that lay by way of Oudjda-Taza-Fez-Meknez to the Atlantic
coast touching at either Rabat or Casablanca was the route to
political and economic control of Morocco. France believed that
she must control this highway or face the destruction of her north
African empire.

The entrance into the heart of Morocco was by way of the bar
of Rabat-Salé instead of, as now, through the modern artificial
port of Casablanca. From Rabat southward to Mogador spread
the fertile coastal plain which formed the hinterland feeding the
city of Casablanca. The tirs, famous as the most fertile agricultural land of the world, covered the coastal plain and made of it a
veritable garden spot. Cereals of all kinds, but especially wheat
and barley, were produced in abundance. Orchards and gardens

[25] Piquet, *op. cit.*, pp. 92-95; A. Bernard, *op. cit.*, pp. 180-182; Wharton, *op. cit.*,
pp. 77-89; Reclus, *op. cit.*, pp. 378-381; Fischer, *op. cit.*, p. 367; Lawrence Harris, *With Mulai Hafid at Fez*, pp. 116-131; F. Ashmead-Bartlett, *The Passing
of the Shereefian Empire*, pp. 254-299.

[26] F. Bernard, *op. cit.*, p. 160; A. Bernard, *op. cit.*, p. 162; Reclus, *op. cit.*,
p. 378.   [27] Reclus, *op. cit.*, p. 378; A. Bernard, *op. cit.*, p. 16.

yielded their harvest of fruits and vegetables. Sheep and goat raising occupied the attention of many of the natives in the section; but to compete with the Gharb, the Chaouya, as the district around Casablanca was known, needed to improve the breed of its sheep and to develop more extensively its cattle raising. The chief difficulty which faced the agriculturist in the coastal plain was the lack of water. Springs were rare and, except for the large rivers from the interior like the Oum-er-Rbia and the Tensift, running water was lacking. The development of artificial means for securing water for the region has been one of the major problems facing France since the establishment of the protectorate.[28] Interest in the agricultural possibilities of the coastal plain and especially of the northern portion has been superseded by interest in the vast mineral wealth the district offers in its rich phosphate deposits.[29] This entire development has been, however, a post-protectorate one and did not attract the attention of economists or diplomatists prior to 1912.

The Sebou-Moulouya Plain of the north had its counterpart in the Sous Valley to the south. Reports of the wealth of southern Morocco, sheathed in that glamour with which adventurous souls present their tales, announced to patriotic nationals that in this region existed the raw materials needed to complement the industrial development of their country. The Sous, corseted between the High and Anti-Atlas and drained by the Sous River, held as its gateway the only good natural harbor on the Atlantic littoral— Agadir, the old port closed by an angry sultan in an effort to destroy its trade and make prosperous its rival, the dune-encircled Mogador.[30] Moreover, south Morocco offered agricultural possibilities equal to the more northern plains. Barley, some wheat, olives, figs, vines, and palms flourished. Horses, sheep, goats,

---

[28] Ogilvie, *op. cit.*, p. 561; Fischer, *op. cit.*, pp. 361-365; A. Bernard, *op. cit.*, pp. 19, 168-169; Reclus, *op. cit.*, pp. 387-390; F. Bernard, *op. cit.*, pp. 150-171; Piquet, *op. cit.*, pp. 36-45, 67-69; Tarde, *op. cit.*, p. 18; Terrier, *op. cit.*, pp. 54-56; Ladrette de Lacharrière, "Dans le Sud et L'ouest du Maroc," in *L'Afrique française, Renseignements*, 1912, p. 156.

[29] Terrier, *op. cit.*, p. 185; Hoffherr et Mauchaissé, *op. cit.*, pp. 234-239; G. Jacqueton, "Les Mines de L'Afrique française," in *L'Afrique française, Renseignements*, 1933, pp. 97-107, 170-178, 194-200.

[30] Paul Zeys, *Agadir*, p. 9; Reclus, *op. cit.*, pp. 393-395; Piquet, *op. cit.*, p. 249.

cattle, and mules grazed upon the plain and mountain slopes in only slightly less number than to the north.[31] The unique argan tree, which "presents more of a curiosity than of utility," thrived and provoked experiment in the hopes that its wood might be exploited for the construction of toys and other light objects.[32] Financiers, industrialists, and diplomats, only incidentally interested in the agricultural future of the Sous, saw visions of fortunes dug from the subsoil of this region; for in the early twentieth century southern Morocco was reputed rich in gold, silver, copper, precious stones, iron ore, and petroleum. Big industrialists urged their foreign offices to juggle their diplomatic balls adroitly; for the rich prize required clever tactics if it were not to slip from their grasp. This conflict has had an unusual sequel; for since the protectorate the Sous has not yielded up the mineral wealth accredited to it.[33] It is true that France has centered her attention

[31] Fischer, op. cit., p. 360; Zeys, op. cit., pp. 245-254; Reclus, op. cit., pp. 394-396; A. Bernard, op. cit., pp. 164-165; Lacharrière, op. cit., p. 40.

[32] Piquet, op. cit., p. 59; F. Bernard, op. cit., p. 185; Meakin, op. cit., p. 853; Ogilvie, op. cit., p. 562.

[33] As yet the potential mineral wealth of Morocco has not been developed and whether the visions of rich bonanzas will be transformed into realities remains a question for the future. Phosphates near Casablanca, oil near Meknez, manganese near Oudjda and Marrakech, and coal in paying quantities in the Oudjda section have been developed since French occupancy of the country, but of these only coal figured in the estimates prior to 1911.—Hoffherr et Mauchaussé, op. cit., pp. 234-239; Jacqueton, op. cit., pp. 97-107, 170-178, 192-200; Zeys, op. cit., p. 261; Louis Clariond et Paul Mauchaussé, "Le Charbon au Maroc," in L'Afrique française, Renseignements, 1934, pp. 199-205; Terrier, op. cit., p. 185; Clarjean, op. cit., pp. 37-40; George Chisholm, Handbook of Commercial Geography, pp. 566-567; George Hardy, "Le Maroc," in Gabriel Hanotaux, Histoire des colonies française, vol. III, p. 313.

The illusive mines of iron, gold, silver, and copper which loomed large in the diplomatic conflicts of the early twentieth century have not been unearthed in quantities of any appreciable value. Piquet mentions copper in the High Atlas and in the Sous, iron in the Atlas, gold near Taza, gold and silver near Tazeroult, phosphates near Casablanca, but concludes that "one still knows little about the mineral wealth of Morocco. . . ."—Op. cit., pp. 104-106. Ogilvie states that "The information with regard to minerals in the country is very scanty. . . . The mineral survey of Morocco is so little advanced, and so few results have been published that it is impossible at present to make any forecast as to the future of the country in this respect. . . ."—Op. cit., p. 569. Tarde confirms the opinion of Piquet and Ogilvie but inserts an interesting reason for the rumors. "The Moroccan subsoil is still little known. Its reputation of richness in all kinds of mineral wealth came from the notorious Mannesmann Brothers, who saw therein a means of drawing German interests to Morocco. . . ."—Op. cit.,

in the more northern districts and that little prospecting has been done in the south; but if the earlier speculations are true, it is surprising that France has left idle the financial return which the mineral development of the country might bring her. Yet the future may see the visions of the early twentieth century transformed into reality.

Economic imperialists saw in Morocco the possibility of exploiting rich timbered resources; of cultivating vast fields of wheat, barley, maize, and sorghum; of gathering from orchards a fortune in olives, figs, oranges, almonds, and dates; of supplying European markets with meat, leather, and wool from their herds of cattle, sheep and goats; and of delving into the subsoil of Morocco to bring forth the iron, coal, gold, silver, and copper which promised to them matchless wealth. Impassable roads and inadequate harbor facilities, which handicapped the economic development of the country,[34] could easily be overcome with European capital when the political destiny of the land had been settled, and in their minds formed no serious obstacle in their path. The strategic and economic importance of Morocco placed her in a position where she must cease being a backward nation or fall a prey to the imperialistic ambitions of more aggressive powers. At the beginning of the twentieth century the Sherifian empire was in no condition to save itself.

---

p. 21. François Bernard introduces his discussion of the mineral wealth of Morocco with the statement, "Mineral Morocco appears to us still a myth. . . . The legend built itself and will be difficult to demolish. . . . Hopes are great and nevertheless appear to be well-founded. . . ." He reports some iron in the Riff, in the neighborhood of Melilla, and in the Sous, copper at Taroudant and lead in the Middle Atlas, but none in valuable quantities. "Mineral Morocco is yet to be created . . . ," he concludes.—*Op. cit.*, pp. 190, 194. Augustin Bernard states that except for phosphates little mineral wealth had been found up to 1934.—*Op. cit.*, p. 468. Much more hopeful are the reports of Meakin and Stichel. Meakin announces that "mineral deposits of great value exist in Morocco there is little doubt. . . . In the Sus iron has long been worked. . . . Near Tetouan are mines, . . . but whether they furnished copper or lead authorities differ . . . lead and antimony are found south of the Atlas. . . ."—*Op. cit.*, p. 854. Stichel believes that the Riff and Sous are rich in gold, iron, precious stones, and silver; that silver also exists near Rabat, Tetouan, and in the Tadla, and copper in the Sous, Mamora forest, the Anti-Atlas, and near Tangier.—*Op. cit.*, p. 22. Davis states the popular belief that "The land was rich in minerals of every sort, iron especially. . . ."—W. S. Davis, *Roots of the War*, p. 403.

[34] A. Bernard, *op. cit.*, pp. 174-177.

A national consciousness did not exist in Morocco. Instead, Berber, Arab, Moor, and Jew inhabited the land as distinct elements with little or no tendency toward fusion. The Europeans living in the land could not be classified as forming part of the Moroccan people. In the eyes of the natives they were interlopers seeking to despoil them of their land. Estimates of their number varied. François Bernard states that early in 1907 there were between 250 and 300 Europeans in the country, but that as France extended her control the number increased until in 1912 there were 5,700 in Casablanca alone.[35] In a table quoted in *L'Afrique française,* the number in 1911 was placed at 9,890 in that portion of the empire that later fell under the dominance of France. The section that became the Spanish portion was omitted from the compilation. According to this table, Casablanca with its 6,000 was the favored spot, although none of the open ports was without its European element. Seventy-five were in Fez and sixty in Marrakech when the rebellion of 1911 destroyed the power of the sultan. The foreign element was distributed among the major interested powers in the following ratio: France, 5,370; Spain, 2,990; Italy, 665; Great Britain, 500; and Germany, 170.[36] Thus Germany ranked fifth in interest as displayed by the number of her nationals in the country. Of these ten were at Mogador and ten at Marrakech, but, as was true of all the other powers, the greatest per cent of her nationals was at Casablanca. As Agadir was a closed port and no European was supposed to live in the territory, it was not listed in the table.

Among the natives of Morocco, the pure Arab element was slight and traits distinctive to the race appeared largely among the Berbers with whom the Arabs had fused. The pure Arabs formed little more than a ruling class which in many sections was not even recognized. Their influence over the country as a whole was chiefly the influence of the cherifs who often exploited their origin and their so-called divine power in order to secure wealth and political influence. The cherifs of the tribe of Ouezzan became the richest landed proprietors of northern Morocco and,

---

[35] F. Bernard, *op. cit.,* p 198.

[36] "Population Européenne au 1er janvier 1911 et au 1er janvier 1914," in *L'Afrique française,* 1914, p. 95.

exempt from taxes, defied the authority of the sultan.[37]

From Spain came many Moors to add to the complex nature of the Moroccan population. Although immigration began as early as the eleventh century, the heaviest influx came after their expulsion from the Iberian Peninsula during the fifteenth century. The district between Salé and Meknez profited most from their coming.[38]

More important internationally than either the Arab or the Moor was the Jew. Various estimates have been placed on the number of Jews in the Sherifian empire. Cruickshank placed their number as between 200,000 and 300,000,[39] but Augustin Bernard restricted his estimate to 120,000.[40] Clustered in the coast and interior cities, they were largely interested in trade. Their life in nineteenth-century Morocco resembled that in medieval Europe or Nazi Germany. Before the middle of the century, international interference had secured some amelioration of their lot, but down to the time of the protectorate, their position was precarious because of the sporadic outbursts of religious fanaticism among Arab and Berber. At best they were subjected to discriminatory laws that required them to live in special quarters known as *mellahs* and to pay a special tax, the *dyezya*.[41]

Of the diverse elements entering into the racial complexities of the Sherifian empire, the Berber formed the majority among the approximately 2,500,000 natives.[42] Although some of them became thoroughly Arabized and a large number had both Berber and Arab traits, in general they retained their primitive character and spoke a language of their own. Naturally inclined to fanaticism in religion, these people found it easy to adopt Mohammedanism; but, curiously enough, they adapted this monotheistic religion to their native cults until it little resembled the religion

[37] Piquet, *op. cit.,* pp. 229-232; Ogilvie, *op. cit.,* p. 567; Fischer, *op. cit.,* p. 369; A. Bernard, *op. cit.,* p. 142. [38] Piquet, *op. cit.,* pp. 232-234.

[39] Earl F. Cruickshank, *Morocco at the Parting of the Ways,* p. 20.

[40] A. Bernard, *op. cit.,* p. 208.

[41] A. Bernard, *op. cit.,* pp. 208-210; Piquet, *op. cit.,* pp. 235-238; Reclus, *op. cit.,* p. 369; Cruickshank, *op. cit.,* pp. 20-28; L. Harris, *op. cit.,* pp. 190-203.

[42] The figure here cited is that of Williamson, *op. cit.,* p. 26. Estimates made prior to the French census of 1912 varied greatly. A. Bernard, *op. cit.,* pp. 132-135, gives some of these estimates.

of the Arab. Worship of saints, especially the cult of cherifs, alleged descendants of the Prophet, distinguished their faith from
that of their Arab neighbors.[43] The geography of the land largely
determined the life of the natives and made nomads of some while
others became sedentary. The fertility of the soil rather than a
difference in race marked the distinction; for Berber and Arab
elements were both found not only among the nomads of the mountains and steppes of the meseta but also among the settled tribes
of the plains.[44]

The disintegration that characterized the political composition
of Morocco was evident not only in the distinct racial differences
which distinguished Berber, Arab, Moor, and Jew, but also in the
minute independent or semi-independent tribal divisions which
marked the Berber race. On the whole, the Berbers were grouped
into three major divisions, Riffians, Berbers proper, and Cheleuh,
but each of these in turn was split into numerous tribes. The Riffians, as their name implied, lived along the northern strip of the
empire in the section now held by Spain. Representatives of the
Berbers proper were found in the north among the Beni M'Tir,
Zemmour, Beni M'Guild, and Zaer and in the south among the
Ait Atta, Ait Isdeg, and Ait Attab. The Glaoua, the most important and wealthiest of the southern tribes, in command of the
route from Marrakech to Tafilelt and in charge of the most of
the region east and south of Marrakech, was the outstanding tribe
belonging to the Cheleuh group. All these people possessed a strong
sense of independence, but the northern group, especially those
in the mountain sections, clung to their freedom with excessive
zeal. Within the tribe the chieftains of old Morocco occupied a
position comparable to the feudal lords of medieval Europe. They
built their castles in the form of fortresses on the most inaccessible
places in the mountains, often well guarded by narrow, steep
passes. Force could not dislodge them and only famine formed an
effective weapon against them. From these advantageous positions
they ruled their subjects and defied the authority of their liege

---

[43] A. Bernard, *op. cit.,* p. 197; Terrier, *op. cit.,* p. 59.

[44] A. Bernard, *op. cit.,* p. 142; Hardy, *op. cit.,* pp. 3-7. Ogilvie and Bérard hold
to the contrary view that Arabs were the nomadic and Berbers the sedentary
groups.—Ogilvie, *op. cit.,* p. 567; Bérard, *op. cit.,* p. 29.

overlord. Each petty division guarded the small section of fertile land and favored pastures which perchance it possessed while it waged almost constant warfare with its more fortunate neighbors in an effort to filch from them additional fruitful lands. Governors, or caids, sent out by the sultan to subdue the turmoil of the land met only mediocre success among the less aggressive people of the south and plains of the north and no success at all among the mountaineers.[45]

Natives of the land, in full recognition of the capricious nature of their ruler's authority, designated as the *Blad Maghzen* that portion of the land which recognized the temporal as well as the religious authority of the sultan and as the *Blad Siba* that which acknowledged only his religious headship. In the latter, neither the sultan nor his civil officials were permitted access to the land without the permission of the tribal chieftain in control of the district. If a section of the *Blad Siba* intervened between the sultan and his destination, he traveled by a circuitous route so as to avoid crossing the territory. Thus in going from Fez to Marrakech he went by way of Rabat, and in going from Fez to Oudjda he took the long detour back to the sea by way of Tangier and Oran and thence to Oudjda unless he could bribe the tribes to permit his passage. The *Blad Maghzen* fluctuated in size, expanded and contracted, according to the strength of the reigning sultan. Under a strong ruler like Moulay-el-Hassan (1873-1894) the power of the sultan spread over all the land except the inaccessible mountain sections, but under his successor, Abdul Aziz (1894-1908), the *Blad Maghzen* gradually shriveled to a narrow strip around Rabat and Casablanca. In general, however, the *Blad Maghzen* included the Houz of Marrakech, the coastal plain, and the Gharb, or Plain of Sebou. The sultan controlled Tangier, Tetouan, Ouezzan, Fez, Meknez, and Rabat in the north, and the tribes of the Chaouya and the Houz of Marrakech, but between Tangier and Rabat lived the independent Riffians and the semi-independent Zemmour, while between his capital at Fez and that at Marrakech lived the tribes of the meseta who recognized his authority only on those rare oc-

---

[45] Piquet, *op. cit.*, pp. 215, 245; A. Bernard, *op. cit.*, pp. 194–196, 229-326; Terrier, *op. cit.*, pp. 47-58; MacLeod, *op. cit.*, p. 89; Fischer, *op. cit.*, p. 371; Lacharrière, *op. cit.*, p. 40; Reclus, *op. cit.*, pp. 363-373; Ogilvie, *op. cit.*, p. 567.

casions when his military power was sufficiently strong to hold them in smoldering submission. The frontier of the *Blad Siba* might be pushed to the foothills of the mountains but no farther; for there the Atlas joined forces with the natives and successfully defied the authority of the sultan.[46] Morocco was not a unified nation but a disordered mosaic composed of minute particles.

As titular head of the Sherifian empire, the sultan theoretically possessed both religious and temporal control over his subjects, but in actual practice his power more nearly resembled that of a feudal suzerain than that of a national sovereign. To enforce his authority, a corps of officials, known in their entirety as the *maghzen*, had grown up around the sultan. A large number of these were sinecurists devoting their time to fulfilling the personal wishes of their lord in much the same manner as did the gentlemen of the chambers attached to the court of Louis XIV. The task of governing the land fell to the ministers who composed the administrative court. Functions of government were divided among them according to the European pattern of minister of foreign affairs, minister of war, minister of finance. Administration of the provinces was placed in the hands of governors, or caids, and *ouamanas*, tax-collectors, who were personal appointees of the sultan or by his authority appointees of the *maghzen*. Besides these, a host of minor officials swarmed in and around the court on personal duty bent in the guise of service to their lord.[47] The entire system was saturated with corruption.[48] As early as 1896 Sir Arthur Nicolson, later under-secretary in the British foreign office, described the situation as desperate and deplored the fact that it seemed impossible to "drill into their thick obstinate skulls that the longer they delay improving their country, the more hopeless becomes the future. . . ." Again in 1900 he wrote: "I do not be-

---

[46] MacLeod, *op. cit.,* p. 89; Alengry, *op. cit.,* pp. 142-158; A. Bernard, *op. cit.,* pp. 237-243; Lacharrière, *op. cit.,* p. 40; Fischer, *op. cit.,* p. 371; Neumann, *op. cit.,* pp. 28-31; Bérard, *op. cit.,* pp. 21-28.

[47] MacLeod, *op. cit.,* p. 89; Fischer, *op. cit.,* p. 371; Neumann, *op. cit.,* pp. 28-31; Piquet, *op. cit.,* pp. 238-245; A. Bernard, *op. cit.,* pp. 243-251, 257-261.

[48] Fischer, *op. cit.,* p. 371; Billy to Pichon, February 15, 1911, *Documents diplomatiques: Affaires du Maroc,* 1910-1912, no. 65 (hereafter cited as *Affaires du Maroc*); René Leclerc, "L'Année administrative marocaine en 1910," in *L'Afrique française,* 1911, pp. 96-99.

lieve that it is possible to reform this country from within. . . .
Self-interest is the only motive and the sole object of the governing
class. . . ." [49] The parasites who clung to the court and drained
it of its vitality needed to be torn loose; but the sultan, bound by
his financial and military weakness, could not defy the old order.

Like the feudal lords of old, the Sherifian emperor recruited his
army when in need by calls upon the tribal chieftains to bring their
contingents to his service. The response depended upon the will
of the chieftain and not upon that of the sultan. In the sixteenth
century the *maghzen* had created from more or less dissociated
groups the so-called *maghzen* tribes, who rendered military service to the sultan and received in return land and tax exemptions.
This practice continued into the twentieth century; but the
tendency was for each *maghzen* tribe as it grew more and more
wealthy to defy the sultan and refuse military service except when
it could be bartered for exceptional advantages.[50] In the rebellion
which threatened Fez in the spring of 1911, the sultan was not
able to retain the allegiance of these tribes and they renounced his
authority and joined the rebels.[51] A ruler with the armed forces
in the hands of his opponents is a travesty upon the name. Moulay-
el-Hassan recognized this fact, and in an attempt to render himself free from his military dependence on the tribes, called in
foreign instructors whose task was to organize and train for him
mehallas, or divisions of regular troops. His ambition was to establish his authority through the creation of a standing army
responsible directly to the sultan and not to the tribal chieftain.
In an agreement signed in 1877, France received the right to supply His Majesty with the instructors necessary for the performance of this task.[52] Although some progress had been made,
religious prejudices and financial weakness had proved to be in-
surmountable obstacles, and in the spring of 1911 Mulay Hafid,
besieged in the city of Fez, found himself forced to call upon a
foreign army for succor.[53]

---

[49] Harold Nicolson, *Portrait of a Diplomatist,* pp. 81, 95.

[50] A. Bernard, *op. cit.,* pp. 251-257; Piquet, *op. cit.,* p. 245.

[51] See Chapter VIII, *infra.*

[52] André Tardieu, *Le Mystère d' Agadir,* pp. 130-154; E. Dupuy, *Comment nous avons conquis le Maroc,* p. 33; Piquet, *op. cit.,* p. 307.

[53] See Chapter VIII, *infra.*

As military power and financial independence, the twin requisites of sovereignty, were lost to the Sherifian court, the sultan's power dwindled, and correspondingly his ability to collect taxes or to maintain an army decreased. In the field of finance the imperial régime depended upon an amazing array of taxes for its income, while it treasured the hope that some return from crown domain and *habous* might fill the gap which the increasing shortage in tax returns made ever larger. The sultans held as crown property land, markets, and buildings which they had taken from the tribes they conquered. This property was issued to other tribes who in turn were to have its usufruct and supply the *maghzen* with its needs. As the immediate needs of the court became pressing, the tendency of the sultans was to sell these rights with their eyes on the present rather than the future need of the court. As a result their income from this source gradually diminished. The *habous* were the non-free property, largely that set aside for religious purposes, the administration of which belonged to the sultan, who appointed nadirs to execute the function. Such offices were usually sold to the highest bidder and again present needs rather than efficient administration determined the sultan's decision and decreased his future income.[54] As a result administrative inefficiency forced the government to revert to foreign loans and consequently increased its dependence on the imperialistic powers who already coveted its lands.

Presumably the needs of the *maghzen* should have been amply supplied by the revenue from taxes, but such is mere presumption. Taxes on land, taxes on herds, taxes on sales, taxes on harbor rights, taxes on gates, taxes on opium, sulphur, and tobacco, taxes on Jews, not to mention a host of others, formed a hodge-podge of taxes levied and collected in a heterogeneous fashion which exploited the poor, set the wealthy to tax-dodging, and enriched the unscrupulous collector, but brought in only meagre returns to the imperial treasury.[55] An effort to reform the system after 1880 resulted in levying an additional tax, the *tertib*,[56] which

---

[54] Piquet, *op. cit.*, pp. 315-319; F. Bernard, *op. cit.*, pp. 32-45; A. Bernard, *op. cit.*, pp. 268-269.

[55] A. Bernard, *op. cit.*, pp. 261-264; Piquet, *op. cit.*, pp. 353-356; Feis, *op. cit.*, p. 397.   [56] Piquet, *op. cit.*, pp. 356-358.

only served to arouse the religious prejudices of the natives and
proved impossible to collect to any appreciable amount. Only the
customs duties were systematically and regularly collected and
these, as will be shown, were, by 1911, mortgaged to foreign
loans.[57] The little revenue that found its way to the treasury stuck
to the fingers of greedy officials and left the sultan with no means
of financing the reforms which his land desperately needed.

The weakness of the sultan's authority was further accentuated
by the extra-territorial power exercised by foreign nations. As
commercial privileges were granted to western powers, consular
jurisdiction over their nationals was also granted. The chief infringement of the sultan's sovereignty, however, arose in connection with the protégé system.[58] As consular and diplomatic offices
were established in Morocco, they were granted the privilege of
extending their protection over natives whom they employed in
their services. Commercial concerns found that they could better
conduct their business through natives, that they suffered loss unless
these natives in their employ were protected from the rapacity of
the imperial tax collector and the vengeance of their more fanatical religious brethren. They, therefore, asked and received the
right to extend their consular protection over their native employees. Until 1880, foreigners were not permitted to own land in
Morocco. For this reason, entrepreneurs, interested in agricultural
investments in the country, secured agricultural associates among
the natives who owned land, and garnered their returns in this
indirect fashion. Naturally they too sought to place their agricultural associates under the protection of their home government.
Natives thus protected were known as protégés, and their privileges, recognized as early as 1791, were codified in 1863. Two
classes of protégés were recognized, those attached to the various
legations and those attached to commercial concerns. Agricultural
associates and commercial employees, as factors, brokers, and
semsars, were granted exemption from taxes, especially the gate

---

[57] See Chapter VII, *infra*.

[58] A good discussion of all the points in the protégé system is given in Cruickshank, *op. cit.* See also Hugo C. M. Wendel, "The Protégé System in Morocco,"
in *Journal of Modern History*, vol. II, pp. 48-60; Neumann, *op. cit.*, pp. 246-250;
Noël, *op. cit.*, pp. 235-273; Stuart, *op. cit.*, pp. 23-31.

and agricultural taxes, and exemption from the jurisdiction of
the native courts. Thus arose a privileged class over whom officials
of the sultan dared not exercise authority for fear of infringing
upon their protégé rights and arousing the anger of some western
power.

The system in itself would tend to undermine the sultan's power,
but the irregularities and abuses that arose in its connection
acted as a locust plague upon the land. Unwarranted extension
of the right of protection exempted large numbers from the
authority of their caids and at the same time extended the political influence of the protecting nation. Natives, especially wealthy
agriculturists, bought protection in order to escape the sultan's
tax levies. A regular traffic in protégé certificates arose[59] and subjects of all nations seemed to have been guilty of the practice.[60]
Further difficulties arose over the system of naturalization practiced by several countries by which natives of Morocco lived a
short time in the foreign country, secured naturalization, and returned to Morocco with all the immunities of the foreigner.[61] The
capable Sir John Drummond Hay, who for forty-one years served
as British minister in Tangier, recognized the evils inherent in
the situation and in 1879 called a meeting of the diplomatic corps
in Tangier to discuss the problem. From this meeting resulted the
conference of Madrid of 1880 in which thirteen governments par-
ticipated, and the convention there adopted served to regulate the
protégé system until the establishment of the French protectorate.[62]

According to the Madrid convention, the number of protégés
attached to the various consular offices and those employed by
business concerns was limited, but the number of interpreters,
guards, and domestics attached to diplomatic offices was unlimited.
The right of protection was to extend only to the immediate
family of the protected person and not to the numerous relatives
and servants who sought immunity. Protégés were to be subject

---

[59] Wendel, op. cit., p. 54; Cruickshank, op. cit., pp. 32-50; L'Afrique française,
Jan., 1911, p. 42.

[60] One of the most flagrant offenders was the American consul, Felix A.
Mathews.—Cruickshank, op. cit., pp. 48-50.

[61] Ibid., pp. 34-35, 61-62, 83-85, 163-165.

[62] Ibid., pp. 97-174; Wendel, op. cit., pp. 55-60; Noël, op. cit., pp. 70-75.

to the civil jurisdiction of the Moroccan court but none was to be arrested without notification being sent to his patron. Agricultural associates were to pay the agricultural tax and tax on herds, but collection was to be through their consular agents. Irregular protection was forbidden and Moroccans naturalized to a foreign power were to be subjected to the law of the sultan when they returned. The sultan was to be furnished with a list of all subjects over whom a foreign power had spread its protection.[63] The reform appeared well on paper, but when efforts were made to put it into practice numerous difficulties arose over the matter of interpretation and ineffectiveness of enforcement. All efforts at reform seemed futile, and complaints of abuses within the system and of unwarranted extension of protégé rights were still being heard in 1911. Official lists of protégés, and the evaluation of property owned by and taxes due from them, were never accurate.[64] More and more the sultan's authority was undermined and his financial resources reduced by the exemptions to which the protégé system gave birth. In 1911 he could scarcely call himself master of his own house. The scene was set for clever diplomats, avid imperialists, and ardent patriots to play their game of saving the Sherifian empire from decay; but not the salvation of Morocco nor the peace of Europe but profits for themselves furnished the driving force motivating their performance.

[63] "Convention of Madrid, 1880," in *Documents diplomatiques, Question de la protection diplomatique et consulaire au Maroc*, pp. 271-273.

[64] *L'Afrique française*, January, 1911, p. 42; London *Times*, July 13, 1910 (Tangier correspondent); Cruickshank, *op. cit.*, pp. 200-201; Stuart, *op. cit.*, pp. 29-31.

Chapter II

FRENCH PENETRATION

French penetration of Morocco was not the result of a sudden outburst of imperialistic temper but a gradual development of economic and political interests progressing with varied tempo according to the state of affairs within France herself. Her interest in Morocco dated back at least as early as the twelfth century when Marseilles merchants looked upon that land as a fertile field for exploitation.[1] As France attained her national unity, the monarchy evinced its interest in and attempted to further the commercial relations between the two countries. Francis I won permission for his ships to enter the ports of the Sherifian empire[2] and a century later Richelieu secured additional commercial privileges, among them the right to establish consulates at certain designated places.[3] Louis XIV further advanced the cause of his merchants, and his treaty of 1682, renewed and modified from time to time, became the basis for Franco-Moroccan relations until the opening of the nineteenth century. According to this agreement, the sultan was to remain neutral in all conflicts between the Barbary pirates and the French nation, and was to extend French consular rights.[4] During the first half of the eighteenth century, however, French interest declined as British interest increased— a change that became marked during the closing years of that century and the first decades of the nineteenth. While the Revolution and the Napoleonic régime absorbed the attention and energy of the French people, British economic investments[5] reached first

---

[1] Piquet, *op. cit.*, p. 171.

[2] *Ibid.;* Noël, *op. cit.*, p. 22; G. H. Stuart, *French Foreign Policy from Fashoda to Serajevo, 1898-1914,* p. 138; Dupuy, *op. cit.*, p. 1; Bérard, *op. cit.*, pp. 49-50.

[3] Noël, *op. cit.*, pp. 22-26; Piquet, *op. cit.*, p. 172; Dupuy, *op. cit.*, p. 2; Bérard, *op. cit.*, p. 50.

[4] Piquet, *op. cit.*, p. 173; Noël, *op. cit.*, pp. 27-31; Dupuy, *op. cit.*, pp. 3-4; Bérard, *op. cit.*, pp. 51-52.

[5] Piquet, *op. cit.*, p. 174; Noël, *op. cit.*, pp. 42-46; Flournoy, *op. cit.*, p. 138; Bérard, *op. cit.*, pp. 52-54.

rank. Consequently, when she again entered the field, France found that much of her earlier advantages had disappeared.

In 1825 France revived her claims to economic consideration within the Sherifian empire in a new treaty that was in the main a reassertion of the privileges embodied in that of 1682 as later modified.[6] Franco-Moroccan relations, which up to this time had been largely economic in nature, were, however, soon to take on a definite political tinge. The change came as a natural result of French acquisition of Algeria whose western frontier lay coterminous with that of the turbulent state of Morocco. France recognized that her pacification of the newly acquired domain depended to a certain degree upon conditions in that region, a fact that soon forced itself upon her attention. In 1831 the important border town of Tlemcen that she claimed fell in Algerian territory was occupied by Moroccan troops. She consequently considered this an infringement of her rights and demanded that the sultan withdraw his troops. The affair was finally settled through the assistance of the British minister in Tangier, E. W. A. Hay, who, following his country's policy of keeping Morocco free from entanglements with European powers, urged the sultan to submit to French demands. Tlemcen thus became French,[7] but disturbances along the frontier were in no wise eliminated.

The people of Morocco sympathized with the Algerian chieftain, Abd-el-Kader, in his struggle to retain sovereignty over western Algeria and translated that sympathy into active aid, especially by supplying him with arms which the sultan permitted to be sent across his domain to the struggling warrior. Rumors that France intended to carry the conflict on to Moroccan soil brought forth border raids from that side of the frontier, and again France sought British aid in checking Moroccan activities. When assured by France that she had no aggressive designs upon Moroccan soil, Great Britain instructed her minister to do what he could to restrain the sultan. Hay warned His Sherifian Majesty of the dangers involved in his actions and secured the promise that arms transshipments into Algeria would be stopped. In 1842 it was

---

[6] Piquet, *op. cit.*, p. 174; Noël, *op. cit.*, pp. 47-48; Bérard, *op. cit.*, pp. 54-55.

[7] Flournoy, *op. cit.*, p. 50; Dupuy, *op. cit.*, pp. 21-22; Bérard, *op. cit.*, p. 55.

reported that all difficulties between France and Morocco had been settled; but if so, it was only a truce destined to be broken the next year.[8]

Abd-el-Kader, driven out of Algeria, took refuge in Morocco and busied himself with exciting the tribes to a Holy War. France pressed the sultan to stop these activities, but because of the intense sympathy that the Moors felt for the rebel, the sultan hesitated to act. Again France turned to England for aid and again Hay warned the sultan of the danger involved. Nevertheless, in April, 1844, a division of the French army, while constructing a fort at the border town, Lalla-Marnia, was attacked by Moroccan troops. The French ultimation to the *maghzen* was this time accompanied by an order for a French fleet to move to Tangier. Great Britain, fearful of French designs, also ordered a fleet to the troubled waters and instructed Hay to impress upon the sultan the necessity for submission. The Moroccan, however, interpreted British naval actions as indicative of support of his policy and remained obdurate until Hay journeyed to the southern capital, Marrakech, to persuade the obstreperous ruler to yield. Convinced that they could not depend on British aid, the ministers counseled prudence and the sultan submitted to French demands; but before Hay returned to Tangier, France had bombarded the town, and then followed this attack by the capture of Mogador. The sultan, now subdued, willingly signed the treaty of September, 1844.[9]

The treaty of September, 1844, and its corollary, the treaty of June, 1845, formed the basis for frontier relations between France and Algeria until they were modified by the agreements of 1901 and 1902. The first of these treaties provided that all hostilities between the two lands were to cease, that Moroccan chiefs involved in the recent aggression against France were to be punished, that the sultan was to give no refuge nor assistance to any enemy of France, that only a corps of two thousand men was to be stationed at Oudjda, and that a later convention was to delimit the frontier according to that which existed at the time of

---

[8] Flournoy, *op. cit.*, pp. 58-62; Dupuy, *op. cit.*, p. 22; Bérard, *op. cit.*, p. 55.

[9] Flournoy, *op. cit.*, pp. 71-111; Noël, *op. cit.*, pp. 51-57; Hardy, *op. cit.*, pp. 124-132; Dupuy, *op. cit.*, pp. 23-30; Piquet, *op. cit.*, p. 177; Bérard, *op. cit.*, p. 56.

Turkish control. All former treaties were recognized as of value and France was given the privileges of the most favored nation.[10] France asked no indemities for the recent disturbances—[11] a leniency she failed to observe in her later conflicts with the Sherifian government.

The treaty of June, 1845, complemented that of 1844 by delimiting the frontier. The two nations recognized the difficulty of drawing a geographic boundary and accepted the principle of delimitation according to tribes, which granted each nation juris- diction over any tribe that came within its territory.[12] Such an arrangement would necessarily lead to friction since the nomadic life of these people kept them constantly shifting from one juris- diction to the other. With these treaties as a basis, the two nations sought to maintain order along a frontier where the tribes gave no, or only meagre, submission to their liege overlord. Thus early, France had gained a measure of jurisdiction over the border tribes and had also gained a most-favored-nation position.

For the next few years, Franco-Moroccan relations improved. France secured the right to enlarge her consular establishments; a French company received the concession to work certain copper mines near Tetouan; and a Moor who held the concession for anti- mony mines in northwest Morocco agreed to associate with him French entrepreneurs.[13] Peaceful relations were again disturbed in 1851 when a French ship driven on the coast near Salé was pil- laged by the inhabitants. After the French retaliated by bombard- ing the city, the matter was adjusted and France was given the right to correspond directly with the sultan.[14]

During the period of the Second Empire, French interest in Morocco waned[15] while Great Britain, ably served by John Drum-

---

[10] "Convention à paix conclude à Tangier le 10 Septembre 1844 pour régler et terminer les differends survenus entre la France et le Maroc," M. de Martens, *Nouveau Recueil général de traités,* vol. VII (1844), pp. 378-381. See also Noël, *op. cit.,* p. 58; Marcel Dubois and August Terrier, *Les Colonies françaises,* vol. I, pp. 213-216; Flournoy, *op. cit.,* p. 108.

[11] Noël, *op. cit.,* p. 58.

[12] *Ibid.,* pp. 61-64, 143-149; Anderson, *op. cit.,* p. 11; Depuy, *op. cit.,* pp. 26-30.

[13] Flournoy, *op. cit.* pp. 112-136; Piquet, *op. cit.,* p. 177; Dupuy, *op. cit.,* pp. 30-31.

[14] Flournoy, *op. cit.,* pp. 136-146; Piquet, *op. cit.,* p. 177; Dupuy, *op. cit.,* p. 31.

[15] Bérard, *op. cit.,* p. 56; Noël, *op. cit.,* p. 69; Dupuy, *op. cit.,* p. 33.

mond Hay, who had succeeded his father in 1845,[16] attained a position of supremacy unrivaled until after 1880. Napoleon III, however, did throw open to commerce the full length of the Algerian frontier and strengthened French protégé rights in a new codified agreement in 1863.[17] Due to her most-favored-nation position, France also profited from the exceedingly favorable commercial treaty concluded between Morocco and Great Britain in 1856.[18] British interests continued to remain predominant during the decade from 1870 to 1880, although the Germans had begun to display their interest through scientific explorations.[19] The position of Sir John Drummond Hay was clearly shown by his influence with the sultan in calling the protégé conference at Tangier in 1879 and by his influence at the subsequent Madrid conference of 1880.[20]

The Madrid convention internationalized the Moroccan question. In addition to the agreement relative to protégés,[21] it gave subjects of all the signatory powers the right to buy property within the Sherifian empire under certain definite regulations, and it specifically guaranteed the open door.[22] France found her most-favored-nation position now merged into that sustained by all the signatory powers. Advancement of any nation to a position of predominance could easily infringe upon the rights guaranteed to the others by this convention, and the fact that henceforth any change in the status of Moroccan affairs would require consultation of the powers represented at Madrid became of utmost importance.

Heartened by the orderly régime of the strong sultan, Moulay Hassan, and by the opportunities opened through the internationalization of Morocco, subjects of various nationalities hastened to take advantage of the open door and to establish economic foot-

---

[16] Flournoy, op. cit., p. 102; Cruickshank, op. cit., pp. xv-xvi; Dictionary of National Biography, Supplement, vol. II, pp. 158-159.

[17] Bérard, op. cit., p. 56; Hardy, op. cit., p. 134; Piquet, op. cit., p. 178; Cruickshank, op. cit., p. 17; Noël, op. cit., pp. 69, 237, 247, 252-253.

[18] Piquet, op. cit., p. 178; Flournoy, op. cit., pp. 179-182.

[19] Bérard, op. cit., p. 57; Dupuy, op. cit., p. 33.

[20] See Chapter I, supra.   [21] See Chapter I, supra.

[22] "Convention of Madrid, 1880," in Documents diplomatiques, Question de la protection diplomatique et consulaire au Maroc, pp. 271-273.

holds in the Sherifian empire. The era from 1880 to the closing years of the century was marked by unusually peaceful relations between Morocco and her European neighbors and by an increase in foreign economic investments. Anglo-French rivalry continued intense, and a new industrial Germany also became interested in the economic possibilities of this fertile bit of Africa.[23] This era of relatively peaceful development was not to last long, for upon the death of Moulay Hassan the effeminate Abdul Aziz succeeded to the throne. So long as the capable grand vizier, whom he had inherited from his father, lived to continue his work, the orderly régime of the strong ruler held sway; but upon his death chaos reigned. The new sultan had not been trained to rule, and being interested solely in gratifying his personal tastes, which were slightly too European to please the religious susceptibilities of his people, he permitted the *Blad Siba* to engulf almost entirely the *Blad Maghzen*.[24] Chronic disorders, tribal warfare, and disrespect for imperial decrees became the order of the day. Such a situation must necessarily soon overflow into Algerian territory.

This return to a chronic state of disorder within the Sherifian empire synchronized with the accession to power of the ardent imperialist, Théophile Delcassé, to whom France entrusted control of her foreign policy from 1898 to 1905. He had long coveted Morocco as the capstone of French colonial expansion and for a time fate seemed to play into his hands. After he had successfully adjusted the ticklish Fashoda crisis,[25] he felt free to turn his attention to Morocco, and in a speech before the senate on July 5, 1901, he expressed the special interest of France in that land. He explained French occupation of the oasis Touat[26] the preceding

---

[23] Bérard, *op. cit.*, pp. 57-58; Stuart, *French Foreign Policy*, p. 139; Hardy, *op. cit.*, p. 143.

[24] Noël, *op. cit.*, p. 88; Stuart, *French Foreign Policy*, p. 139.

[25] For a discussion of this crisis see, Thad W. Riker, "British Policy in the Fashoda Crisis," in *Political Science Quarterly*, vol. XLIV, pp. 54-58.

[26] A. G. P. Martin, *Quatre siècles d'histoire marocaine*, pp. 356-357; Stuart, *French Foreign Policy*, p. 142; Anderson, *op. cit.*, p. 11; Note du département au Maroc, August 24, 1901, *Documents diplomatiques français, 1871-1914*, series 2, vol. I, no. 372. In June, 1900, Augustin Bernard explained the situation and advocated French occupation of Touat as a simple task for the Algerian police.—"Touat et Maroc," in *Questions diplomatiques et coloniales*, June, 1900, pp. 653-664.

year, and the installation there of a series of military posts as an
action dictated by the need to protect south Algeria from the
frequent border raids which distracted that region. France, he
averred, intended to maintain her treaty obligations, but due to
her frontier relationship she must secure respect for her people
and their property. He then proclaimed for France a singular
interest in the integrity of the Moroccan empire and in the maintenance of order along the eastern frontier.[27] Prior to this public
announcement, he had told Prince Radolin, German ambassador
in Paris, that "France, mistress of Algeria and Tunis," held a
special position relative to Morocco; to which statement Radolin
replied that everyone recognized that fact.[28] Delcassé had evidently
staked out Morocco for French exploitation, and conditions within
the Sherifian empire aided the progress of his policy of penetration.

Occupation of Touat alone could not solve the problem of
Algerian security, and continued attacks along the frontier gave
ample cause for further extension of French control in that
region. Nevertheless, Delcassé instructed Révoil, French representative in Tangier, to protest these attacks but not to use force
against the marauders west of a prescribed line. He also authorized him to accept the proposal of the *maghzen* for a Franco-
Moroccan commission to examine the situation and see if a better
adjustment than that made in 1845 could be effected.[29] At the
same time news spread that the sultan was sending a mission to
London and Berlin in order to secure aid in checking French
penetration.[30] Before anything was accomplished, the murder of a
French subject off the Riff coast led to French demand for reparation and to a naval demonstration in Moroccan waters.[31] Moroccan
missions were in London, Berlin, and Paris at the same time, and
while the first two accomplished nothing, the third secured a modifi-

---

[27] *Annales du senat,* session ordinaire de 1901, p. 647.

[28] Anderson, *op. cit.,* p. 14. See also Delcassé to Marquis de Noailles, June 23,
1901, *Affaires du Maroc,* 1901-1905, no. 18.

[29] Delcassé to Révoil, April 5, 1901, *Docs. dip. français,* series 2, vol. I, no. 175.

[30] Révoil to Delcassé, April 27, 1901, *Affaires du Maroc,* 1901-1905, no. 5;
Anderson, *op. cit.,* pp. 12-13.

[31] Delcassé to French ambassadors in Madrid, Vienna, St. Petersburg, Berlin,
Rome, London, May 24, 1901, *Docs. dip. français,* series 2, vol. I, no. 248; Stuart,
French Foreign Policy, p. 142; Noël, *op. cit.,* p. 102; Bérard, *op. cit.,* p. 70.

cation of the treaties of 1844 and 1845 regulating the Algerian frontier, and gave to France a stronger foothold in that region.

The protocol of July 20, 1901, supplemented the treaty of 1845. Morocco and France were to establish forts and customs posts along lines clearly recognized as falling within their respective territories. The tribes in the region were to choose the government under whose jurisdiction they wished to live; but a free movement of tribes was permitted between the two lines of forts, and they were privileged to continue the use of pasturages to which they had been accustomed. Each government was to designate two commissioners, one for the north and one for the south, who were to discuss and settle future border troubles.[32]

An effort to place this protocol into operation emphasized the fact that the chaotic conditions in Morocco stood as a constant menace to the security of Algeria. The assassination of two French officers in January, 1902, convinced Delcassé that France must secure a firmer control over the frontier tribes.[33] Consequently, additional protocols in April and May of that year further expanded the previous treaties and strengthened the position of France. These accords accepted the principle of Franco-Moroccan colloboration on the frontier in matters relating to customs, commerce, and police. In the section nearer the Mediterranean, a French and a Moroccan commissioner, one residing at Oudjda and the other at Lalla-Marnia, were to agree on measures of order and police in that region. In the more disturbed district from Teniet-el-Sasi to Figuig, the sultan was to have the coöperation of French troops in maintaining order. Both governments were authorized to establish markets and customs posts at designated places; but in the region from Teniet-el-Sasi to Figuig, France would pay the *maghzen* a fixed annual sum in lieu of customs duties. As the sultan was unable to maintain a semblance of order on the Algerian frontier,[34] France felt compelled to take such

---

[32] Delcassé to Martinière, July 20, 1901, *Affaires du Maroc,* 1901-1905, no. 20; Anderson, *op. cit.,* p. 15; Stuart, *French Foreign Policy,* p. 143; Noël, *op. cit.,* p. 103; Dupuy, *op. cit.,* pp. 47-48.

[33] Stuart, *French Foreign Policy,* p. 144; Anderson, *op. cit.,* p. 16; Bérard, *op. cit.,* pp. 73-77.

[34] Révoil to Delcassé, April 26, 1902, *Affaires du Maroc,* 1901-1905, no. 27, annex; Révoil to Delcassé, May 17, 1902, *ibid.,* no. 28, annex I; Anderson, *op. cit.,*

measures as were requisite to Algerian security; and these treaties gave to her a unique position, for she thereby gained the right, under the plea of maintenance of order, to move French troops on to Moroccan soil.

As a result of the protocols of 1901 and 1902 Delcassé further strengthened his country's position in the Sherifian empire by an expansion of the French military mission. That admirable ruler, Moulay Hassan, had realized that the imperial power could not be maintained unless the old feudal army of the sultan was reorganized on a more modern basis. As the first step in that direction he arranged with the French government to furnish him with instructors, part of whom were to direct and instruct the *mehallas* attached to his person and the other part to reside at Rabat. He also arranged for French officers to instruct divisions at Safi and Casablanca.[35] Although submissive to the influence of Caid Maclean and the *Times* correspondent, W. B. Harris,[36] Abdul Aziz had continued the policy of his father and had retained the French as his chief advisers in military affairs.

Moulay Hassan's dream of an effective fighting force had not been realized when in 1901 the need for a revision of the treaties of 1844 and 1845 arose. Late in that year the sultan approached the French government on the possibility of a reorganization of the military mission and requested that only those who spoke Arabic should be appointed for that service.[37] By the middle of the next year he had requested that instructors might be furnished for troops to be established at Figuig, Oudjda, and Adjeroud, or other points on the frontier where it might become necessary. Again he requested that only those who spoke Arabic should be appointed, and he also asked that when the *maghzen* had available sufficient trained native instructors the French officers should be recalled.

---

p. 16; Stuart, *French Foreign Policy*, p. 144; Noël, *op. cit.*, pp. 175-182; Hardy, *op. cit.*, p. 157; Dupuy, *op. cit.*, pp. 49-53; Bérard, *op. cit.*, pp. 79-83; Martin, *op. cit.*, pp. 364-366.

[35] Dupuy, *op. cit.*, p. 33; Tardieu, *op. cit.*, p. 130; Piquet, *op. cit.*, p. 307.

[36] Anderson, *op. cit.*, p. 3; Martin, *op. cit.*, pp. 389-395; Saint René Taillandier to Delcassé, Oct. 23, 1902, *Docs. dip. français*, series 2, vol. II, no. 454; A. W. Ward and G. P. Gooch, *Cambridge History of British Foreign Policy*, vol. III, p. 310.

[37] Martiniére to Delcassé, Dec. 6, 1901, *Docs. dip. français*, series 2, vol. I, no. 553.

He asked for one captain, a lieutenant, and two subordinates at this time. These were to be separate from the mission that accompanied the sultan and from that at Rabat, but were to be under the authority of the chief of the French military mission.[38] An arrangement upon this basis was accepted in July, 1902, and the *maghzen* agreed to allot ten thousand francs annually for expense of these officers.[39] By the end of 1902 France had won not only the right to assist the sultan with French troops but had secured the privilege of placing the Moroccan troops under French instructors at the most strategic points along the frontier.

Abdul Aziz, not unmindful of the fact that he might be purchasing French assistance at too costly a price, sent Caid Maclean to London to secure British protection against too great an expansion of French influence. The British government, however, was already interested in an Anglo-French accord and was, therefore, deaf to Maclean's pleas.[40] The sultan of necessity then turned back to France to extricate himself from the meshes of a confused and disorganized financial system which rendered futile all efforts to remedy the disordered state of his realm. Until he could secure the money requisite for the ordinary expenses of his government and sufficient additional sums to reorganize and pay his army, Abdul Aziz had little chance to subdue the numerous revolts that infested his land. Particularly serious was that led by a pretender to the throne who had established his power in and around Taza.[41] The necessity for a foreign loan was apparent. Delcassé came to the sultan's rescue and by his action advanced another step along his road to peaceful penetration.

The sultan's financial straits had already forced him to secure a loan from a French company in 1902, one from an English firm in April, 1903, and one from a syndicate of Spanish banks in July,

[38] Saint René Taillandier to Delcassé, July 22, 1902, *Affaires du Maroc*, 1901-1905, no. 29.

[39] Saint René Taillandier to Delcassé, Aug. 6, 1902, *ibid.*, no. 30, annex, Ben Sliman to Saint René Taillandier, July 30, 1902. See also Anderson, *op. cit.*, p. 17, and Dupuy, *op. cit.*, p. 33.

[40] Anderson, *op. cit.*, p. 17; Note communiquée par la section de renseignements de l'etat-major de l'armée, Oct. 7, 1902, *Docs. dip. français*, series 2, vol. II, no. 429; Paul Cambon to Delcassé, Oct. 23, 1902, *ibid.*, no. 456.

[41] Anderson, *op. cit.*, p. 18; Martin, *op. cit.*, pp. 395-409.

1903.[42] These loans served only as temporary measures of relief and in 1904 the financial condition of the sultan was, if possible, worse than ever. Delcassé, confident of the support of England, Italy, and Spain in his policy of predominance in Morocco, was now willing to negotiate an extensive loan with the *maghzen*. A group of eleven French banks, endorsed by the French government, drew up a contract with the Moroccan government for a loan of 62,500,000 francs bearing 5 per cent interest amortizable in thirty-five years. The loan was guaranteed by a mortgage on 60 per cent of all the customs revenues in all the open ports of Morocco, and, if this per cent were not sufficient, a larger portion could be allocated to meet the obligations on the loan. France was given the right to supervise the customs collections in each port. Two million francs were left on deposit with the *Banque de Paris et des Pays-Bas* to cover short payments. The outstanding loans held by French, English, and Spanish banks were to be redeemed, and no further loans guaranteed by the customs were to be contracted without the consent of the French banks, and in no case were loans to be contracted without giving preference to this consortium.[43] The political as well as the economic importance of this loan was clear to every European nation, and the full significance became clear to the Moroccans themselves when France established a controller of the customs in each port. In this manner the *maghzen* was made financially dependent upon France, and this dependence plus the position of French instructors in the *maghzen* army formed effective weapons for exercising pressure upon a recalcitrant sultan. Thus before the Conference of Algeciras France had two strong cards in her imperialistic game, and her interests in that land encouraged her to gain additional ones.

By the opening the twentieth century French business men had important economic investments among commercial, shipping, mercantile, and agricultural concerns in the Sherifian empire. A report to the minister of foreign affairs in September, 1902, stated that 6,500,000 francs of French capital had been placed in Morocco.[44] Camille Fidel asserts that this was too low an estimate and

---

[42] F. Bernard, *op. cit.*, p. 68; Anderson, *op. cit.*, pp. 17-18.

[43] *Affaires du Maroc*, 1901-1905, no. 170, annex II.

[44] According to this account, a statement of French investments abroad,

that 25,000,000 francs was nearer the true situation.[45] As much of the agricultural and mercantile business was carried on through protégés, and as the register of protégés was notably inaccurate in all the legations, estimates of the total amount invested in such enterprises are mere guesses. According to Fidel's computation, over one hundred and seventy-five French firms had establishments in Morocco in 1902. Of these, seventy-five were in Tangier, three in Melilla, three in Tetouan, seven in Larache, four in Rabat, thirty-one in Casablanca, four in Mazagan, three in Safi, twenty in Mogador, seven in Marrakech, and fifteen in Fez.[46] Billy, French agent in Tangier, reported to Pichon in 1911 that the value of immovable property owned by French subjects in the Chaouya alone reached the sum of 2,886,900 francs, despite the hostility of the natives toward foreigners' owning property and their reluctance to sell land to any outsider.[47]

The consular offices kept adequate accounts of foreign trade, and although statistics of the trade across the Algerian frontier were incomplete, commercial estimates were slightly more accurate than mercantile. In the tonnage of shipping in 1900 and 1903 England outranked France[48] and the two nations divided honors in commercial returns. The chief articles that Moroccans desired from their European neighbors were textiles, tea, and sugar. Great Britain had a virtual monopoly of tea importation and furnished the major portion of the textiles, but France ranked first in the importation of sugar.[49] This article occupied a position of great importance in the commercial exchanges between the two lands; and although for a time France feared the competition of Belgian firms, she was able to retain her superiority in this field. Even though sugar was the principal item of her trade, it did not

---

French capital in British Africa amounted to 1,592,000,000; in Egypt, 1,436,-000,000; in Tunis, 512,000,000; in Tripoli, 1,000,000; and in Persia, 2,000,000 francs. This report will be found in *Journal officiel de la Republique française,* Sept. 25, 1902.

[45] Camille Fidel, "Les intérêts français et les intérêts allemands au Maroc," in *L'Afrique française,* 1905, p. 258.   [46] *Ibid.,* pp. 258-261.

[47] Billy to Pichon, Jan. 26, 1911, *Affaires du Maroc,* 1910-1912, no. 52.

[48] Fidel, "Les intérêts français et les intérêts allemands au Maroc," p. 255.

[49] Williamson, *op. cit.,* p. 128; Dupuy, *op. cit.,* p. 40; Camille Fidel, *Les intérêts économiques de la France au Maroc,* pp. 30-31.

monopolize the attention of her entrepreneurs. France ranked second only to Great Britain in the importation of textiles, shipping to Morocco cotton, silk, and woolen goods. Construction materials, metal works, flour, and pastries formed other items of importance entering Moroccan ports from France.[50] In her export trade Morocco found France a good market for her wool, leather goods, almonds, and chick-peas. This was not all; for Algeria furnished an excellent market for Moroccan cereals, sheep, and cattle.[51] Algeria and France together absorbed a generous share of Moroccan products.

The total value of French trade with Morocco in 1900 was 19,447,560 francs, of which 10,439,703 francs were accredited to French articles sent into that land. According to this report, which included only the trade entering by way of Moroccan ports, Great Britain with a total of 34,330,931 francs almost doubled the value of French trade;[52] but Fidel would add to this report the trade by way of Algeria, by way of the Spanish presidios, and by way of the Sahara. According to his composite computation, French trade reached the sum of 35,000,000 francs while the British, who profited little from this interior trade, secured only a total of 34,-700,000 francs. The percentage shared by these two countries in 1900 was very close: 33.81 per cent for France, 33.60 per cent for Great Britain.[53] By 1903 French trade through Moroccan ports had reached the total of 23,527,520 francs, still surpassed only by the British.[54] In 1906 French commerce, including that by way of Algeria, represented 46 per cent of the Moroccan total and the British held only 29 per cent.[55] The percentage distribution in 1908 stood: France, 44.65 per cent of the total; England, 36.28 per cent.[56] By 1911 French trade through Moroccan ports amounted to 48,978,476 francs and, when that with Algeria was

---

[50] *Ibid.*, pp. 33-36; Fidel, "Les intérêts français et les intérêts allemands au Maroc," p. 255.

[51] Fidel, *Les intérêts économiques de la France au Maroc*, pp. 36-38.

[52] *Ibid.*, p. 26.   [53] *Ibid.*, p. 166.

[54] Fidel, "Les intérêts français et les intérêts allemands au Maroc," p. 253.

[55] Paul Deschanel, "Budget of Foreign Affairs," in *L'Afrique française*, May, 1912.

[56] C. René Leclerc, *Situation économique du Maroc*, 1908-1909, appendix, Statistiques du mouvement commercial & maritime du Maroc, année, 1908, p. 5.

added, rose to a total of 80,745,476 francs.[57] Commercial interests
were evidently sufficient in themselves to turn French eyes toward
the Moroccan shore.

France had other investments in Morocco. Mention has been
made of French concessions to operate copper mines near Tetouan
and antimony mines in the northwest. France had earlier secured
the right to construct a railroad from the Sahara to the oasis
of Figuig.[58] Two French cable lines, one from Tangier to Oran
and the other from Tangier to Cadiz, competed with the British
Eastern Telegraph from Tangier to Gibraltar. France, Germany,
England, and Spain had each their own postal service in the
Sherifian empire.[59] France also displayed her interest through
the establishment of dispensaries at designated places and
through the founding of schools, where stress was placed upon
the teaching of the French language. Natives so trained made admirable associates for French business and agricultural concerns.
By 1902 schools existed at Tangier, Tetouan, Larache, Fez,
Rabat, Casablanca, Mogador, and Marrakech.[60] These were, in
the main, private schools but encouraged by the French government, and not only encouraged but assisted by the *Comité de
l'Afrique française.*

The *Comité de l'Afrique française* had been organized in the late
nineteenth century by a group of prominent French citizens interested in the expansion of French African domain. This group
had through their *Bulletin* consistently sponsored the policy of
peaceful penetration of Morocco. They had also sponsored scientific explorations into that land.[61] By 1904 their interest had become so acute that they created a special *Comité du Maroc* as a
branch of the older organization. They stated the purpose of the
new *Comité* to be two-fold. It was to keep the French public informed of the influence of other powers in Morocco detrimental
to French interests, and to impress upon the French people the
value of that land. To accomplish this aim, the *Comité* planned to

[57] "Commerce en 1912 et 1911," in *L'Afrique française,* June, 1913, p. 243.
[58] Fidel, *Les intérêts économiques de la France au Maroc,* p. 177.
[59] Fidel, "Les intérêts français et les intérêts allemands au Maroc," p. 261.
[60] *Ibid.;* Terrier, *op. cit.,* pp. 131-132.
[61] Anderson, *op. cit.,* pp. 5-8; Dupuy, *op. cit.,* p. 71; *L'Afrique française,* 1891.

publish articles and books that would enlighten the public, to sponsor scientific missions and explorations into the Sherifian empire, and to pass on to the general public the results of these expeditions.[62] The *Comité de l'Afrique française* and its offspring the *Comité du Maroc* approved heartily of the program so far sketched by France's ambitious foreign minister.

Delcassé, however, recognized that any general plan of peaceful penetration could best be furthered if his country had the support of a coterie of friends. Although France had broken her isolation of 1871 when she won Russia as her ally, her colonial dreams required that she strengthen her position among the Mediterranean powers. Delcassé, as minister of foreign affairs, therefore labored hard to secure the favor of a group of powers that would support—or at the very least not oppose—his policy and thereby furnish a solid European basis for the pursuit of his imperialistic ambitions. Only the colonial bargains and expressions of friendships that formed the direct fruits of his labors, and not the long process by which they were secured, are pertinent to this discussion; but these fruits are important, for they changed the diplomatic alignments of Europe and, while they quieted the French cries of isolation, they provoked, instead, the German wail of encirclement.

Delcassé's first reward came in the agreements made with Italy in 1901 and 1902 according to which she granted France a free hand in Morocco in exchange for freedom of action in Tripoli.[63] When his first overtures to Spain in 1903 were blocked by Spanish reliance upon England to defend her interests,[64] he turned to Great Britain. That these two nations, historic rivals in the colonial field, could adjust their difficulties and establish grounds for mutual friendship was proof that there had now come into existence a force which appeared as a greater threat than the ancient foe. The humiliation of 1870 still rankled in French breasts; France courted any power that might serve her against Germany and looked upon her one-time rival across the Channel with her strong naval force as a potentially valuable friend. Al-

[62] *L'Afrique française,* 1904, p. 3.

[63] Anderson, *op. cit.,* pp. 19-34; Prinette to Barrère, July 10, 1902, *Docs. dip. français,* series 2, vol. II, no. 329.   [64] Anderson, *op. cit.,* pp. 35-40.

though she had retained her position of isolation, Great Britain had shown strong sympathy for the new progressive German nation and, until Fashoda, had viewed France as her chief colonial rival. This attitude changed during the early twentieth century. As German commerce came to compete with British in every section of the globe, as the Boer War demonstrated the danger of a too rigid policy of isolation, as the German naval program forced itself more and more into British consciousness, and as the settlement of the Fashoda crisis smoothed the way for something broader and more substantial, England listened attentively to the idea of an Anglo-French accord. After due diplomatic juggling, the two nations settled their differences and pledged their friendship in the agreement of 1904, the nucleus out of which grew the Anglo-French Entente. Although a treaty presumably settling colonial differences, this agreement was more important as a pledge of friendship; for France had here won British promise of support of her Moroccan program and this pledge might be stretched to more extensive fields.[65] The crises of 1905 and 1911 were to test the full strength of this agreement. In fact, Sir Edward Grey went so far as to state to the German ambassador that, according to his personal opinion, if France were attacked by Germany because of Morocco, public opinion would not permit England to remain neutral.[66]

In its relation to the colonial settlement, the published clauses of the Anglo-French treaty of 1904 recognized the predominant interest of France in Morocco and of England in Egypt, but stated that neither nation had the intention of altering the political or territorial status of the "backward country" acknowledged as its sphere of interest.[67] The secret clauses recognized the possibility of a change in that territorial status and arranged for a distribution of the estate. England was to have freedom in Egypt, France in Morocco, except for a section to the north conceded to Spain.[68]

---

[65] This treaty is published in various sources. The text here used is that found in *British Documents on the Origins of the War*, vol. II, no. 417. In article IX, the two governments pledged "one another their diplomatic support, in order to obtain the execution of the clauses of the present declaration regarding Egypt and Morocco."—*Ibid.*

[66] S. B. Fay, *The Origins of the World War*, vol. I, p. 205; Ward and Gooch, *op. cit.*, vol. III, p. 346.   [67] *Br. Docs.*, vol. II, no. 417.   [68] *Ibid.*

After the settlement with England, Spanish interests had still to be considered. Beginnings had been made in 1900 when the two nations adjusted the Rio de Oro boundary dispute[69] but the question of Morocco was left in abeyance. In 1902, however, they were on the verge of completing an accord when a change from a liberal to a conservative ministry in Spain defeated the project. The agreement as made by Delcassé and Leon y Castillo, Spanish ambassador in Paris, apparently contemplated partition when the sovereignty of the sultan should disappear,[70] and granted to Spain, upon that contingency, all the old kingdom of Fez and to France that of Marrakech as their respective shares.[71] Delcassé was evidently ruminating partition at this time; for, in a note of the department dated July 15, 1902, various possibilities involved in the question of a Franco-Spanish agreement over Morocco were analyzed; but it was decided that partition, since it might create more delicate international complications, was, for the time being, impracticable and the term "sphere of influence" would be more feasible.[72] Whatever may have been Delcassé's ambition, the proposed treaty was rejected by the Spanish conservatives despite its very favorable terms, because they feared that England might oppose the move, as in fact she did. On England's insistence (after being consulted) that she and Spain should act together on the question, the projected accord fell through.[73] Delcassé, as we have seen, then turned to Great Britain and closed

[69] *British Foreign and State Papers,* vol. XCII, pp. 1014-1017; Anderson, *op. cit.,* p. 37.

[70] Article II stated that in case the *status quo* could not be maintained, France and Spain should decide the limits in the interior in which each of them "would have the exclusive right to establish tranquility, to protect the life and property of persons, and to guarantee freedom of commerce. . . ."—Project de convention Franco-Espagnole relative au Maroc, Nov. 8, 1902, *Docs. dip. français,* series 2, vol. II, no. 473.

[71] *Ibid.;* Note pour le ministre, Nov. 23, 1902, *ibid.,* no. 501; Anderson, *op. cit.,* p. 38; André Tardieu, "France et Espagne, 1902-1912," in *Revue des deux mondes,* series 6, vol. XII, p. 636; *L'Afrique française,* 1911, pp. 450-451, especially the map, p. 451.

[72] Note du département, *Docs. dip. français,* series 2, vol. II, no. 333. Although the foreign office seems here to have contemplated partition, there was no continuity of program in French policy owing to the frequent change of ministries. See Chapter XV, *infra.*   [73] Anderson, *op. cit.,* pp. 38-40.

his deal with her before he attempted any further bargaining with Spain.

After the completion of the Anglo-French accord of April 8, 1904, Delcassé set to work to round out his program by a Franco-Spanish agreement. Spain now discovered that she had lost by relying on Great Britain but made the best of the situation and accepted the treaty of October 3, 1904, although the territory here assigned to her was less than that granted in 1902. Within this treaty was incorporated the provisions of the Anglo-French treaty as far as these related to Spanish interests. When the sultan ceased to exercise authority in the land, Spain was to have the right to extend her control over that territory bound by the Mediterranean, the Atlantic, the Moulouya River, and the heights on the right bank of the Sebou, and in addition the district around Ifni.[74] The French program was thus approved by Italy, England, and Spain, but the consent of Imperial Germany was still lacking. It is true that while Delcassé was engaged in negotiations with England, he seems to have put forth tentative feelers in the direction of Germany but met a rebuff.[75] At all events, failure to secure German approval proved the weak link in his policy and permitted his country to drift on to dangerous shoals.

Germany felt that she had reason to be concerned. Accordingly, in September, 1903, she informed Spain that in a division of Morocco she must be considered, and suggested that she be given "territorial compensation, for example in the region of the Sous, or elsewhere in the colonial world, perhaps by the cession of Fernando Po. . . ."[76] The Spanish minister acknowledged German right to a share[77] but there let the matter drop. As a result, when France completed her circle of friends in 1904, Germany was out-

---

[74] Convention between France and Spain, Oct. 3, 1904, *Br. Docs.*, vol. III, no. 59; Anderson, *op. cit.*, p. 123; Ward and Gooch, *op. cit.*, vol. III, p. 340.

[75] Anderson, *op. cit.*, p. 49; Mühlberg to Radolin, Aug. 18, 1902, *Die Grosse Politik der Europäischen Kabinette, 1871-1914,* vol. XVIII, no. 5882 (hereafter cited as *G. P.*); Schlözer to Foreign Office, Sept. 22, 1902, *ibid.*, no. 5883.

[76] Anderson, *op. cit.*, p. 137; Richthofen to Radowitz, Sept. 24, 1903, *G. P.*, vol. XVII, no. 5200.

[77] Anderson, *op. cit.*, p. 137; Radowitz to F. O., Sept. 29 and Oct. 4, 1903, *G. P.*, nos. 5203, 5205.

4

side, and French penetration of Morocco seemed on the way to completion without any regard for German interests.

German economic interests in the Sherifian empire were by no means negligible. As a matter of fact the remarkable industrial development of Germany during the late nineteenth century aroused both admiration and jealousy among the world powers; for a nation whose economy had expanded beyond the bounds of its national frontier would, of necessity, enter the hectic scramble for new markets, for raw materials, and ultimately for colonies. With the constantly diminishing area of available lands where imperialism could glut its appetite, the struggle became more intense and the entrance of a new arrival was viewed with alarm. Germany had entered late but had managed to secure for herself a few choice morsels. Encouraged by her success, the colonial and Pan-German leagues preached a doctrine of German expansion satisfying to the national ego of her people and fixed her eyes on the few remaining bits of African territory and the vast possibilities of the Near East. Especially did the Pan-Germans expound upon the potential wealth hidden in Morocco—a wealth that the virile German people should win as a supplement to their great industrial growth.

The twentieth century opened with Germany ranked a weak fourth[78] in her economic investments within the Sherifian empire. England, France, and Spain all outstripped her; yet her capitalists had gained a foothold. The chief interests of Germans were trade, commission business, and shipping.[79] Although the number of ships was less, the tonnage of German ships surpassed the French in 1900;[80] but in 1903 the French had forged ahead with a tonnage of 265,612 to the German 221,385.[81] Germany consistently exported more from Moroccan ports than she imported to them. She sold metalware, nails, perfumes, porcelain, and china-

---

[78] For German interests see the reports of the German representatives in Morocco in *G. P.*, vol. XXIV.

[79] Williamson, *op. cit.*, p. 131; Saint René Taillandier to Delcassé, Jan. 27, 1903, *Docs. dip. français*, series 2, vol. III, no. 44.

[80] Fidel, *Les intérêts économiques de la France au Maroc*, p. 27.

[81] Fidel, "Les intérêts français et les intérêts allemands au Marco," p. 255. Sir Thomas Barclay states that Germany still had a greater tonnage than France in 1901.—*Thirty Years, Anglo-French Reminiscences, 1876-1906*, p. 276.

ware; and purchased almonds, wax, olive oil, hides, woolen felt, and grain.[82] In 1900 she imported from Morocco goods to the value of 7,764,146 francs, while her exports into that country were evaluated at only 3,768,765 francs.[83] The total value of her trade in 1903 was slightly less than it had been in 1900.[84] By 1906 the German part of Moroccan trade was only 9 per cent of the total;[85] in 1908, from 9.47 per cent[86] to 10.9 per cent;[87] and in 1910, was still only 13 per cent.[88] During these same years, France held almost 50 per cent of the total trade.[89] In 1911 the total value of German trade with Morocco had reached 25,289,042 francs as compared with 80,745,476 francs for France and 44,965,310 francs for England. If the trade through Algeria were omitted from the calculation, the value of exports sent from Morocco to Germany in 1911 surpassed that sent to France by approximately 2,000,000 francs.[90] Casablanca was in general the most important port with Tangier a close second; but German trade was centered at Safi and Mogador, and at Mogador her exportation surpassed that of any other country.[91] Although Germany continued to rank third among the powers interested in the commerce of the Sherifian empire, the value of her commerce was increasing each year. It was not the present situation that caused her worry but the fear of the extent to which French "peaceful penetration" would prevent further development of her economic interests.

Despite the apparent friendliness with which he had first received the Anglo-French Accord,[92] Chancellor von Bülow had no intention of sacrificing the future of German economic interests;[93]

---

[82] Williamson, *op. cit.*, p. 129.

[83] Fidel, *Les intérêts économiques de la France au Maroc*, p. 26.

[84] Fidel, "Les intérêts français et les intérêts allemands au Maroc," p. 253.

[85] Deschanel, *op. cit.* [86] René Leclerc, *op. cit.*, p. 5.

[87] J. Ellis Barker, "Germany, Morocco, and the Peace of the World," in *Fortnightly Review*, vol. XCVI, p. 230.

[88] Billy to Selves, Sept. 13, 1911, *Affaires du Maroc*, 1910-1912, no. 546.

[89] See p. 34, *supra*. [90] *L'Afrique française*, June, 1913, p. 243.

[91] Billy to Selves, Sept. 13, 1911, *Affaires du Maroc*, 1910-1912, no. 546; Barclay, *op. cit.*, p. 276.

[92] Memorandum of Bülow, April 9, 1904, *G. P.*, vol. XX, no. 6374 and editor's footnote.

[93] The German chargé d'affaires at Tangier, Kühlmann, was aggressive in pushing German interests. See his reports in *G. P.*, vol. XX, part I, especially no. 6540. The French minister in Tangier, Saint René Taillandier, protested

nor did he have any intention of permitting French absorption of the Sherifian empire with all the added prestige and power that such a victory would bring her. Moreover he felt that he could not afford to surrender silently German interests in Morocco because other powers, encouraged by an easy victory, might disregard German rights in even more important questions. The time seemed propitious. Russia, weakened by the Russo-Japanese War, could not offer effective aid to France; and the new Anglo-French Entente was still a fledgling that knew not its own strength. He, therefore, maneuvered the Kaiser's visit to Tangier as a protest to the French program and an assertion of German right to be consulted in colonial bargains of such a nature. The Kaiser's visit abruptly announced that France must settle with Germany before she could proceed with her absorption of the Sherifian empire.[94] The first Moroccan crisis was thus precipitated; and Delcassé was forced out of office by the fear of the premier, Rouvier, that, without some outward sign of conciliation, a brush was certain. Germany, however, rejected Rouvier's overtures for a general settlement of colonial difficulties by direct negotiations with France and perhaps lost her opportunity to secure favorable compensations. Bent on pulling off a diplomatic victory and mindful of the legal position of the great powers as envisaged in the Madrid convention, Bülow pressed, instead, for an international conference and virtually forced France to agree to the meeting at Algeciras.[95]

---

against Kühlmann's actions and accused him of purposefully embarrassing French policy. He charged that the German chargé incited his compatriots to acts certain to provoke native resentment against foreigners while France tried to prevent such incidents occurring.—Saint René Taillandier to Delcassé, Feb. 27, 1905, *Docs. dip. français,* series 2, vol. VI, no. 120.

[94] The Kaiser asserted that "he visited the Sultan as an independent ruler, and that he hoped that under the authority of the Sultan a free Morocco would be opened to the peaceful competition of all nations without monopoly or exclusion . . ." and that to protect German interests he "would enter into direct relations with the Sultan, whom he regarded as an independent ruler. . . ." —Quoted in Anderson, *op. cit.,* pp. 193-194; Ward and Gooch, *op. cit.,* vol. III, pp. 338-339; Fay, *op. cit.,* vol. I, p. 184.

[95] For a discussion of the first Moroccan crisis and the Algeciras conference see Anderson, *op. cit.* (the fullest account); Morel, *op. cit.;* Bérard, *op. cit.;* Fay, *op. cit.,* vol. I; G. P. Gooch, *Franco-German Relations, 1871-1914;* Erich Brandenburg, *From Bismarck to the World War;* Heinrich Friedjung, *Das Zeitalter des Imperialismus,* vol. II; Dupuy, *op. cit.;* Stuart, *French Foreign*

Here, indeed, was staged the first of a series of struggles between the two powers; and Morocco was presumably to fall as the prize to the winner!

Policy; Ward and Gooch, *op. cit.,* vol. III; G. P. Gooch, *Before the War, Studies in Diplomacy,* vol. I; and others.

Chapter III

ALGECIRAS AND ITS AFTERMATH

The Algeciras conference, called to solve the Moroccan problem, proved to be only one scene in a long drama of envenomed rivalries. The summoning of the conference was a definite victory for Germany, a recognition of her right to be consulted in the family of nations when the fate of backward countries was under discussion. But the conference itself showed the international weakness of the German Empire, as the fidelity of France's friends stood forth in marked contrast to the weakness of the Triple Alliance. In fact, Germany stood almost alone. Her ally, Austria, with the United States and Italy, served as mediator, while France had the whole-hearted support of England and Spain and the sympathy of Russia. German action had been interpreted as a challenge to the Entente and to this challenge the British government had responded in almost clarion tones. Not for a moment did British support of France waver, and Germany, faced with a united opposition, compromised on every point.

When the conference met, the delegates discussed the less controversial issues first and adjusted them without much friction. They then picked up the more difficult problems. Two of these, the police and the Moroccan State Bank, were in themselves sufficiently controversial to disrupt the conference. Germany came to the meeting convinced that an international police force should be established in which she would be represented at least in the Atlantic ports. France was determined that control of the police should be in her hands, except in so far as she was willing to permit the co-operation of Spain. The distribution of shares in the Moroccan State Bank with the resultant distribution of control was an equally disturbing issue. Over these two problems the conference wrangled for almost three months; but with the firm support of Great Britain, France saw no need to yield on essentials. The work of the conference finally culminated in the Act of Algeciras, which attempted to harmonize the idea of internationalization of the Moroccan empire with recognition of the predominant interest of France and Spain within that land. The result was a curious hybrid fated to live only so long as Moroccan welfare and French interest ran parallel.

The Act of Algeciras recognized the integrity and independence of the Sherifian empire; but acknowledging the preponderant interest of France and Spain in the maintenance of order within that empire, it distributed between those two nations the right to organize a police force composed of Moroccans. French instructors were to be in charge in Safi, Mogador, Rabat, and Mazagan, Spanish in Larache and Tetouan, and a mixed French and Spanish force in Casablanca and Tangier; but the entire staff was to be supervised by a Swiss inspector. France and Spain were also given the power to direct the suppression of contraband trade. The power thus entrusted to France and Spain gave them a preponderant political position capable of far-reaching expansion. If disorders surrounding an open port threatened the city, were France and Spain empowered to quell the disturbances? If so, how far inland did the police power granted to them extend? If the native police was not able to handle the situation, were they empowered to use foreign troops? If so, who was to be the judge of the emergency, and who was to determine when and where such troops were to be employed? All these questions arose to plague the powers as French leaders sought to mold the Act of Algeciras to their program.

The conference also took cognizance of the economic condition of Morocco and arranged for international control in an effort to establish equality of trade for all interested powers. A state bank whose capital was to be secured from the participating powers, whose directors were to be appointed by those shareholders, and whose operation was to be supervised by international censors, was given control of the financial affairs of the Moroccan government. A scheme for a reform of the tax system and the organization of an international committee for supervision of the customs were established, in an effort to bring forth revenue for the depleted Sherifian treasury. In all these international commissions France occupied a position of prominence. She could, there-

fore, watch after the economic interests of her subjects while she
guarded her political prestige.

In an effort to prevent the absorption of the economic resources
of the country by one power, the conference established the principle of public adjudication for all concessions relating to public
works. It was provided that concessions were to be awarded only
after due publicity had been given the proposed enterprise and
only according to open bids. No one nationality was to receive a
privileged position in any field of economic development. In addition, the sultan was instructed to form a mining law conformable
to western usage in order to prevent complications in awarding
mining concessions. Political instability within the Sherifian empire
and disputes between the interested imperialistic powers served to
handicap economic progress, as each question of concession became involved in the larger problem of political control. The Act
of Algeciras[1] was a futile effort to internationalize Morocco, but
it only inaugurated a series of events finally culminating in the
Agadir crisis and a French protectorate for the ancient empire.
During the period from 1906 to 1911, the fundamental principles
of the Act were gradually worn away until only a bare skeleton
remained to be scrapped in 1911.

The period of intense strain which accompanied the first Moroccan crisis and the resultant Algeciras conference had held before
each power the danger of war. Adjustment of the Moroccan difficulty was subsidiary to the larger problem of maintaining the
peace of Europe and of strengthening the system of alliances which
each nation sought to build up as a guarantee of her position.
Thoroughly distrustful of Germany, England settled her differences
with Russia; and the Anglo-French Entente, welded into closer
bonds by German tactics, now grew into the Triple Entente. Ill
feeling and distrust throve, while each power labored to increase
its defenses. Germany became more and more suspicious of the
encirclement policy of her rivals and strove to defeat their program. Smarting under the humiliating blow administered her at
Algeciras, she watched French penetration of Morocco continue

---

[1] The Act of Algeciras may be found in many sources. The copy here used is
that published in *Affaires du Maroc*, 1906, no. 37.

under the cover of the Algeciras Act, and, jealously mindful of British support of that expansion, she awaited an opportunity to assert her rights. As each example of French activity aroused her to action, she unfortunately varied her tactics with every move and in each instance weakened her own case.

The seriousness of the crisis that had its outcome in the Act of Algeciras, however, tended for a time to restrain the French government in its forward policy. This check was not due to the restrictions in the Act itself so much as to the marked anti-colonial feeling in France. Although the conference had recognized French special interests in Morocco, it retarded French progress in her plan of "peaceful penetration" through the creation of agencies of international supervision. A more effective restraint was the fact that in 1906 public opinion, led by Jaurès, and the French government dominated by Clemenceau, opposed colonial projects and insisted on a strict enforcement of the Algeciras Act. Nevertheless, opinion as to the degree to which this Act formed a real hindrance to France differed on the two sides of the Rhine. Circles in France interested in French expansion complained of the utter inertia of the French government from 1906 to 1909 and of German exaggeration of her rights.[2] From the other side, almost before the Act was signed, came complaints of French expansion, which, if it did not break, at least strained, the agreement made at Algeciras. These complaints, in general, arose in protest to French actions that were called forth by the disordered condition of Morocco.

Every time the situation seemed to settle down, minor incidents arose to harass the nationals of both countries and to try the patience of their foreign offices. In 1906 a Frenchman was assassi-

---

[2] Lowther to Grey, Dec. 4, 1907, *Br. Docs.*, vol. VII, no. 87; Roberts, *op. cit.*, p. 552; Joseph Caillaux, *Agadir, ma politique extérieure*, p. 27; Tardieu, *op. cit.*, pp. 7-10; Hardy, *op. cit.*, p. 178. Hardy comments that France tried scrupulously to carry out the provisions of the Algeciras Act, while Germany played her cards less frankly. "She [Germany] sent to Morocco a diplomat already known for his anti-French sentiments and his spirit of chicanery, Dr. Rosen, who immediately posed as the champion of the independence of Morocco and succeeded in giving many discreet strains to the Act of Algeciras to the profit of Germany; nomination of German engineers in Morocco, concessions of public works to German enterprises. . . ."—*Op. cit.*, p. 178.

nated at Tangier. France secured the promise of satisfaction only after sending ships of war.[3] In 1906 the bandit, Raisouli, became caid of the outskirts of Tangier and inflicted numerous vexatious trials on the Europeans, which led to a French and Spanish naval demonstration.[4] In 1907 Dr. Mauchamp, in charge of the French dispensary at Marrakech, was assassinated.[5] French troops then moved from Algeria and occupied the village of Oudjda in order to force the sultan to maintain order.[6] Consequently, when in 1907 occurred the bombardment of Casablanca, Germans began to express opposition to French policy.

Casablanca is today a key position on some of the air and steamship lines uniting Europe and Brazil and the outlet through which debouch the rich phosphates and agricultural products of the Tadla and Chaouya. Thirty years ago, dreams of its commercial importance stimulated great interest in the harbor improvements for which a French company had secured the concession in February, 1907.[7] To expedite the project, the company had built a railroad from the seafront to a short distance beyond the town. Objections arose especially among the Arabs because the railroad skirted the old Moorish cemetery. Discontent at the weakness of Abdul Aziz had been growing since the French loan of 1904 and increased with the organization of the customs under French officials. The construction work at Casablanca, and particularly that of the railroad, was, consequently, interpreted by the discontented elements as proof that Abdul Aziz had sold their country to the foreigner. Disturbed conditions had existed in and around Casablanca for several days but seemed to be controlled by the local officials until, on July 30, a mob attacked a group of workers and killed nine Europeans. France believed she must take some action to punish the offenders.

Although the consul advised delay until the cruiser, *Du Chayla*,

---

[3] *Affaires du Maroc,* 1906-1907, nos. 9, 11, 16, 21, 22, 25.

[4] *Ibid.,* nos. 72, 73, 77, 80, 90, 100, 101, 102, 103, 114, 134, 154.

[5] *Ibid.,* no. 214. This incident is dramatically described in "Le Drame de Marrakech," in *L'Afrique française,* 1907, pp. 129-139.

[6] *Affaires du Maroc,* 1906-1907, nos. 219, 234. France claimed the right to occupy this territody under her treaty made with Abdul Aziz in 1902 according to which France and Morocco were to coöperate in maintaining order on the frontier. See p. 29, *supra.*   [7] *Affaires du Maroc,* 1906-1907, no. 194.

arrived from Tangier, the commander of the French ship, *Galilée*, which appeared in the harbor on August 1, permitted the pressure of events to force him to premature action. Now since the caid in charge of the Chaouya was coöperating with the Europeans in an effort to quell disturbances and to arrest the guilty, and since the consular offices feared that if only a small party attempted to land it would not be able to control the fanaticism that was likely to break loose, they insisted that the commander of the *Galilée* act with circumspection. Nevertheless he authorized the landing of a small party, and when a struggle broke out between the party and a group of natives at the gates, the *Galilée* bombarded the town, killed many natives, and laid waste the city. Later in the morning the *Du Chayla* appeared, and Manzin, the French commander of police, took charge of the town. On the seventh, the French squadron arrived, and under General Drude the work of pacification of the district was begun.[8]

In this work Spain coöperated with France, though she considered that French action had made the situation more complicated.[9] The two countries under the aegis of the Algeciras Act then organized an effective police but continued to retain troops in the district. France agreed to the creation of an international commission on claims, whose function was to adjust the claims of the citizens injured during the bombardment or during the pillaging that followed.[10] The entire cost of the expedition was presented to Abdul Aziz. But the negotiations that Regnault, French representative at Tangier, undertook in order to adjust the claims of France against Morocco because of the incident fused into the negotiations for the loan of 1910.

Criticism of French action was widespread. Ashmead-Bartlett, a

---

[8] Ashmead-Bartlett, *op. cit.*, pp. 20-54. The report given by Carl Ficke agrees in essentials with the account given by Ashmead-Bartlett. Ficke's report is enclosed in a despatch of Langwerth to Bülow, Aug. 19, 1907, *G. P.*, vol. XXIV, no. 8286. The French account given in *Affaires du Maroc*, 1906-1907, is substantially that given above.

[9] Daeschner to Pichon, Aug. 3, 1907, *Affaires du Maroc*, 1906-1907, no. 353; Lascelles to Grey, Sept. 11, 1907, *Br. Docs.*, vol. VII, no. 78.

[10] Pichon to French representatives in London, Berlin, St. Petersburg, Lisbon, The Hague, Brussels, Oct. 11, 1907, *Affaires du Maroc*, 1906-1907, n. 519. Herbeau to Pichon, Jan. 7, 1910, *ibid.*, 1908-1910, no. 365 gives a report of the commission as to the amount due to the nationals of each country.

British journalist in Casablanca at the time, was rather cynical in his denunciation of the commander of the *Galilée*. Baron Greindl, Belgian chargé d'affaires to Berlin, was quoted as saying, "Immediately after the assassination of its subjects at Casablanca and without having any reason to believe that the Moroccan government would neglect to seek out and punish the guilty, the French government replied by a proceeding more odious still than that of the assassins, bombarding of an open town, massacring the women and children, ruining inoffensive merchants. . . ." [11] Criticism of French action always carried with it inquiry into French motives. Greindl believed that Paris realized such a ruthless action would stir up fanaticism throughout the Musulman world and would furnish the necessary pretext for occupation "qualified officially as temporary but which they proposed evidently to render permanent. . . ." [12]

From the German side came severe accusations. Carl Ficke, a German merchant and newspaper correspondent in Casablanca, [13] accused France of deliberately stirring up the natives by an utter disregard of their prejudices in order to create a situation justifying expansion of French power in the territory. [14] German newspapers gave great prominence to the incident and blamed France for the entire affair since she had neglected to organize an effective police in the city. Several papers reminded their readers that after the murder of Dr. Mauchamp the French occupied Oudjda, and warned the public that the death of nine Europeans,

---

[11] Baron Greindl to Davignon, May 6, 1908, *Belgische Aktenstücke, 1905-1914*, no. 44. Also quoted in a footnote in *G. P.*, vol. XXIV, no. 8281. It is interesting to note that Grelling speaks of Greindl as a Pan-German.—*Belgian Documents*, vol. IV, p. 21.

[12] Greindl to Davignon, May 6, 1908, *Belg. Akt.*, 1905-1914, no. 44.

[13] Ficke served as the agent for the German Moroccan committee.—White to Grey, Oct. 4, 1908, *Br. Docs.*, vol. VII, no. 122. Ficke was active in intrigues against France and in stirring up the natives against French control. He was also accused of engineering desertions from the French foreign legion. After the outbreak of the World War he was arrested, tried by a French military court, and executed on the strength of documents found in his home.—*Revue des deux mondes*, series 7, vol. XIII, p. 317; L. B. Maurice, *La Politique marocaine de l'Allemagne*, p. 76.

[14] Ficke's report included in Langwerth to Bülow, Aug. 19, 1907, *G. P.*, vol. XXIV, no. 8286.

three of whom were French, would surely be followed by further territorial occupation.[15] The reports of Germans living in Morocco, both business men and official representatives, were full of complaints that did not stop with criticizing France for bombarding the city but charged her with conscious effort to destroy German interests. Discontent with the support given them by the Berlin office found expression in such phrases as that German business had been left "strongly in the lurch" by the policy of the government.[16] Tattenbach, German chargé d'affaires in Lisbon, wrote to Tschirschky, acting secretary of state for foreign affairs, that "German interests in Casablanca are really very great and with calm development of things would have had a yet greater future. . . . Through the advance of the French, the commercial people in Casablanca have suffered not only serious loss . . . but must renounce any further future. . . ." [17]

The French bombardment rested on the hasty decision of the commander of the *Galilée,* but the government upheld his action. The defense of French action rested upon her belief that the disorders which surrounded the city necessitated drastic action if her subjects were to carry out their work within the district. Concessionaries could not operate if they were constantly endangered by threats of fanatical riots. Protection of nationals is held by every nation as a fundamental principle of foreign policy, but France added to that principle the power granted her by the Act of Algeciras to direct the police force in certain open ports. Casablanca was one of the ports allotted to the coöperative work of France and Spain, and Spain soon joined her in the work of pacifying the city. As she had no faith in the sultan's good will nor in his power to seek out and punish the culprits, France believed that her retaliatory action would increase French prestige among the natives and force them to respect the rights of her

---

[15] Lascelles to Grey, Aug. 4, 1907, *Br. Docs.,* vol. VII, no. 65.

[16] Ficke's report included in Langwerth to Bülow, Aug. 19, 1907, *G. P.,* vol. XXIV, no. 8286.

[17] Tattenbach to Tschirschky, Aug. 30, 1907, *ibid.,* no. 8287. Tattenbach also enclosed a letter from a German protégé in Casablanca, which complained of the death of German business in the city. Many such examples can be cited from the reports given in *G. P.,* vol. XXIV, chapter CLXXIX.

subjects. She was convinced that in dealing with a backward people a show of force was necessary. Nevertheless, her hasty and
ruthless action weakened her position in the eyes of the world and
left her open to justified criticism. The heartless bombardment of
the city was a punishment unnecessarily severe for the offense committed. There was no immediate danger of a renewed outbreak and
punishment inflicted after a calm investigation of the situation
would have been less open to criticism. The German charges, however, that France had deliberately perpetrated the incident in
order to injure the business of her rivals have no foundation.

Notwithstanding the complaints of its subjects, the German
government offered no difficulties to France for her action. On
August 6, 1907, Jules Cambon, French ambassador to Berlin,
presented to the German foreign office his government's official
notification of the events that occurred in Casablanca and its
action taken in response thereto. Tschirschky replied that "France
had all our sympathies in her work of chastisement in order to
safeguard the interests and guarantee the security of all the
Europeans. . . ."[18] Spain reported that Germany had stated that
she accepted her explanation and that of France for their action,
but that French and Spanish troops in Moroccan ports were "an
infringement of the Act of Algeciras which contemplated the creation of a police force composed of Moors. . . ."[19] Carrying out her
friendly policy, Germany sent instructions to her officials in
Morocco not to oppose French and Spanish military action that
had resulted from the Casablanca affair.[20]

Nevertheless, by the end of the year the German government
was worried over the position of France in Morocco and began to
ask to what extent her Gallic neighbor intended to compensate
herself for the incident of Casablanca. By April 4, 1908, Prince
Radolin, German ambassador to Paris, reported to Bülow that he
had talked to Stephen Pichon, minister of foreign affairs, and
had called his attention to the fact that there was danger that

---

[18] Note of Tschirschky, Aug. 7, 1907, *ibid.*, no. 8287; Lascelles to Grey, Aug. 8,
1907, *Br. Docs.*, vol. VII, no. 70; Carbonnel to Pichon, Aug. 6, 1907, *Affaires du
Maroc*, 1906-1907, no. 476.

[19] Lascelles to Grey, Sept. 11, 1907, *Br. Docs.*, vol. VII, no. 78.

[20] Tschirschky to Langwerth, Aug. 21, 1907, *G. P.*, vol. XXIV, no. 8284; Grey
to Bertie, Aug. 22, 1907, *Br. Docs.*, vol. VII, no. 73.

the situation might bring on strained relations with Germany.[21] Bülow considered the situation sufficiently grave to justify his instructing Schoen, secretary of state for foreign affairs, to consult with Cambon in an effort to secure from France a definite statement of her plans.[22] Schoen, accordingly, discussed with Cambon the entire Moroccan question, let him understand that Germany did not argee that France had exercised a European mandate as Pichon claimed, and urged French withdrawal from the Chaouya.[23] Cambon insisted that France had not exceeded the provisions of the Act of Algeciras and would withdraw as soon as order was restored.[24] Early in 1908 the question of French occupation of the Chaouya became entangled in the contest for the throne of the Sherifian empire, a conflict which intensified the friction between Germany and France.

At no time had Abdul Aziz proved himself to be a strong ruler, and the continued subservience to France served to weaken him even more among his subjects. August 16, 1907, soon after the disastrous Casablanca bombardment, Mulay Hafid, his elder half-brother, was proclaimed sultan at Marrakech.[25] Mulay Hafid, as governor of the Marrakech district, gave promise of being a strong ruler and to many of the Moroccans seemed to be their one hope of saving their country from foreign domination. His revolt against his brother and lawful sovereign spread rapidly over the entire south. Rumors of the savagery of the pretender kept the Europeans in the coast cities in a constant state of alarm; but the rumor that Mulay Hafid had proclaimed a Holy War, a rumor that he consistently denied, excited terror among them.[26] France was urged by her nationals and protégés to prevent his passage to the north,

---

[21] Radolin to Bülow, April 4, 1908, *G. P.*, vol. XXIV, no. 8323.

[22] Bülow to Schoen, April 24, 1908, *ibid.*, no. 8327. Schoen had returned and taken over the foreign office; Tschirschky had gone to Vienna as German ambassador.

[23] Note of Schoen, April 28, 1908, *ibid.*, no. 8329; Cambon to Pichon, April 29, 1908, *Affaires du Maroc,* 1907-1908, no. 250. Although dated one day later this seems to be a report of the same conversation as that given in Schoen's report.

[24] Cambon to Pichon, April 29, 1908, *Affaires du Maroc,* 1907-1908, no. 250.

[25] Langwerth to F. O., Aug. 24, 1907, *G. P.*, vol. XXIV, no. 8288; Saint-Aulaire to Pichon, Aug. 19, 1907, *Affaires du Maroc,* 1906-1907, no. 413.

[26] As examples, see *Affaires du Maroc,* 1906-1907, nos. 428, 449, 354, 355; *ibid.*, 1907-1908, no. 1; Tardieu, *op. cit.,* p. 90.

but she refused to do more than maintain order within the Chaouya district.[27] The position of France became complicated by the action of Abdul Aziz when he decided to move from Fez to Rabat, under the plea that he would then be in a better position to call the southern tribes back to their allegiance. When it is recalled that the French were in possession of Casablanca, only a short distance from Rabat, the inadvisability of this move becomes clear. Nevertheless, on September 21 Abdul Aziz entered Rabat,[28] and charges that he had sold out to the French gathered momentum to such a degree that he found himself master only of Rabat and the Chaouya district. Early in January, 1908, Mulay Hafid was proclaimed sultan at Fez, and he began his triumphant march to the northern capital,[29] entering there in June.

Meanwhile the play of international politics had entered into the question. When Abdul Aziz took refuge in Rabat, charges that he had done so in order to secure French military protection were spread not only among the Moroccans but among the diplomatic courts of Europe. These charges were accentuated when Regnault, French minister at Tangier, became his closest adviser.[30] France maintained that as Abdul Aziz was the legally recognized sultan, her actions did not exceed recognized diplomatic procedure and that her maintenance of order in the Chaouya district was a result of the Casablanca affair and not of the struggle for the throne.[31] Charges that France was aiding Abdul Aziz, Pichon denied, but insisted that Mulay Hafid must prove his power before being recognized.[32] In the eyes of the Moroccans Abdul Aziz was

---

[27] *Affaires du Maroc,* 1907-1908, no. 430.   [28] *Ibid.,* no. 494.

[29] Rosen to Bülow, Jan. 14, 1908, *G. P.,* vol. XXIV, no. 8309; Saint-Aulaire to Clemenceau, Jan. 14, 1908, *Affaires du Maroc,* 1907-1908, no. 92.

[30] Wangenheim to F. O., Aug. 12, 1908, *G. P.,* vol. XXIV, no. 8355; Bunsen to Grey, Sept. 7, 1908, *Br. Docs.,* vol. VII, no. 101; White to Crowe, Feb. 23, 1908, *ibid.,* no. 91; Regnault to Pichon, Dec. 9, 1907, *Affaires du Maroc,* 1907-1908, no. 50. Suggestions that France remove Regnault and that Germany remove Rosen crop out frequently during these years. Note of Schoen, Sept. 18, 1908, *G. P.,* vol. XXIV, no. 8439; Lancken to Bülow, Oct. 14, 1908, *ibid.,* no. 8460.

[31] Pichon to Cambon, Oct. 2, 1907, *Affaires du Maroc,* 1907-1908, no. 507; Pichon to Paul Cambon, Oct. 5, 1907, *ibid.,* 1906-1907, no. 517; Cambon to Pichon, Jan. 16, 1908, *ibid.,* 1907-1908, no. 104; Pichon to Saint-Aulaire, Jan. 21, 1908, *ibid.,* no. 110.

[32] Lancken to F. O., Aug. 26, 1908, *G. P.,* vol. XXIV, no. 8411; Pichon to

the claimant supported by France; and when, lacking French support, he was forced to abdicate, French prestige suffered. For this reason, Pichon was severely criticized in France for his failure to support the sultan effectively.

Jules Delafosse, speaking in the chamber of deputies January 15, 1909, delivered a biting criticism against the policy of Pichon and explained the international complication by his statement that the success of Mulay Hafid was a defeat for France because "Mulay Hafid was other than a Moroccan pretender and his cause was not a purely Moroccan affair; he was the candidate, the pretender of a foreign power and the cause of this foreign power was intimately tied to his. . . . The truth is that the Moroccan question is a rivalry of influence between France and Germany; it is even only this, and if it were not this, it would not exist. . . ." [33] Wangenheim, German chargé d'affaires at Tangier, as early as August 27, 1908, had expressed similar sentiments, agreeing that a defeat of Abdul Aziz would mean a defeat of France because of the close tie existing between the two. The people of Morocco had come to believe that defeat of Abdul Aziz would mean ridding Morocco of the French; consequently, Wangenheim urged upon his foreign office to take advantage of the situation and increase German power in Morocco.[34] The degree to which Germany aligned herself on the side of Mulay Hafid, therefore, became an important question.

When the struggle between the two claimants to the throne first broke out, the German foreign office consistently instructed its representatives to maintain strict neutrality,[35] and at first even the German merchants seemed to believe that neutrality would be best.[36] But as more and more of the country swung to the side of

---

French ambassadors in London, Berlin, St. Petersburg, Lisbon, The Hague, Brussels, Aug. 26, 1908, *Affaires du Maroc,* 1907-1908, no. 403.

[33] *Annales de la chambre des députés,* session ordinaire, 1909, vol. I, p. 20.

[34] Wangenheim to Bülow, Aug. 27, 1908, *G. P.,* vol. XXIV, no. 8423. The Belgian minister at Tangier to F. O., Jan. 18, 1908, *Die Belgischen Dokumente zur Vorgeschichte des Weltkrieges,* vol. IV, no. 3, states, "The final triumph of Abdul Aziz is necessary to the success of French policy. . . ."

[35] Tschirschky to Langwerth, Aug. 26, 1907, *G. P.,* vol. XXIV, no. 8289; Tschirschky to Rosen, Oct. 11, 1907, *ibid.,* no. 8300; Schoen to Rosen, Jan. 18, 1908, *ibid.,* no. 8311.

[36] Rosen to F. O., Jan. 18, 1909, *ibid.,* no. 8313. However, charges that Mulay

Mulay Hafid, German commercial interests began to urge upon the Berlin office that a more aggressive policy be taken.[37] They also increased their complaints of the activities of Regnault, whom they suspected of holding out to Abdul Aziz hopes of French military aid, while demanding from him recognition of a "virtual French protectorate." [38] The German claim that if French troops were withdrawn, Mulay Hafid would immediately be proclaimed sultan throughout the land and the internecine strife so disastrous to German economic interests would be quelled, was justified. Even France, by May, 1908, seemed to realize that the throne must go to the elder brother, and the question of recognition of Mulay Hafid became the burning issue.

On May 28, 1908, Cambon stated to Schoen that France was willing to recognize Mulay Hafid, but such recognition should come only after an agreement of the powers signatory to the Act of Algeciras. Schoen at this time expressed his willingness to wait on

---

Hafid secured funds from the Mannesmann Brothers while he was still in the south have been made. Tardieu and Staley state that Mulay Hafid, in return for funds received from the Mannesmann Brothers, granted them concessions as early as October, 1908.—Tardieu, *op. cit.*, p. 46; Eugene Staley, "Mannesmann Mining Interests and the Franco-German Conflict over Morocco," in *Journal of Political Economy*, vol. XL, p. 59. See also, Hardy, *op. cit.*, p. 207.

[37] Schoen stated he had received reports from the German residents in Morocco to the effect that Mulay Hafid's chances were as good as those of Abdul Aziz and that it "would be little short of a calamity if the port of Saffi were to be recaptured for Abdul Aziz." Cambon replied that "It was perfectly natural that the German residents should have reported in this sense. They were all traders. . . . And as long as that port was in the possession of Mulay Hafid, no customs dues were levied. . . ."—Lascelles to Grey, May 6, 1908, *Br. Docs.*, vol. VII, no. 93.

[38] Wangenheim to F. O., Aug. 12, 1908, *G. P.*, vol. XXIV, no. 8355; White to Crowe, Feb. 23, 1908, *Br. Docs.*, vol. VII, no. 91. White reported that Regnault had obtained from the sultan an agreement as follows:

"1. The French should administer the finances of the Moorish Government for a certain number of years.

"2. The Sultan's army to be trained by Frenchmen only, the two German Officers in the Moorish service to leave; also a force of three to four thousand men to be formed at Tangier and to be trained by Frenchmen only, not by Spaniards.

"3. The control of the contraband of arms to be entirely in the hands of the French.

"4. The lighter service of the ports to be in the hands of the French. . . ."— Regnault to Pichon, Dec. 19, 1907, *Affaires du Maroc*, 1907-1908, no. 50 is the official report of the agreement secured by Regnault.

French wishes in the matter.[39] The French plan was for France
and Spain to agree upon a note to be sent to Mulay Hafid in which
was to be stated the conditions upon which the powers would
recognize the new sultan. The note was to be presented to Mulay
Hafid by the dean of the diplomatic corps at Tangier after being
approved by the powers. The recognition of Mulay Hafid was in
this manner delayed due to the slowness of diplomatic action. As
a result, German representatives in Morocco became more and
more suspicious of French motives and warned the Berlin office
that the French plan was detrimental to German interests. Stemrich, acting state secretary of foreign affairs, summed up the
German view of the situation in the following report sent to Bülow.

Stemrich believed that France wished "to prolong the recognition of Mulay Hafid by the Conference Powers, in order then,
under the nominal assistance of Spain, to treat with Mulay Hafid
as representative of the other Powers about the recognition and
thereby first of all to assure her [France's] special interest as a
preliminary condition. . . . The mandate as representative of
Europe always striven for by France which we have restricted in
Algeciras with such trouble to a mere . . . police mandate, would
acquire thereby the general and very extended meaning desired in
vain up to now by France. . . ." France wanted the power to recognize Mulay Hafid alone and to that Stemrich thought Germany
should not agree. He did not believe that Schoen's earlier statement[40] bound his government to agreement with French plans, and
he continued his report by insisting that the question was only
"whether we should not now recognize Mulay Hafid alone. . . ."
Perhaps that would not be advisable, but it was to German interest
that a German consular official "should be sent to Fez, in order to
apply himself to our interests there amounting to several million
and at the same time maintain such relations with Mulay Hafid
that the expected French intrigue be crossed if possible. . . ."[41]

The request that a German consular agent be sent to Fez

[39] Schoen to Rosen, May 29, 1908, *G. P.*, vol. XXIV, no. 8340. Schoen informed
Rosen that he had expressed to France "our willingness to recognize Mulay
Hafid; yet we were willing to wait in this matter on French wish until the other
Conference Powers were also ready to recognize. . . ."

[40] See footnote 39.

[41] Stemrich to Bülow, Aug. 27, 1908, *G. P.*, vol. XXIV, no. 8412.

appeared in the report of Wangenheim dated August 26 and that
of the German consul at Tangier, Rosen, dated August 27.[42] Dr.
Vassel, former consul at Fez, was recommended by both, as the
man most fitted for the task. Among the interests he was to secure
for Germany was approval of the concessions granted by Abdul
Aziz for a port construction in Larache and Tangier. This must
be done before "French intrigue takes hold." [43] On August 28
Stemrich reported to Bülow that Rosen had informed him that
France had sent a messenger to Fez to begin the negotiations for
recognition but that he was riding a "mule, so that he can scarcely
enter Fez for ten days. . . ." A more rapid traveler could make the
trip in three or four days. Stemrich urged haste upon the government in dispatching Vassel to Fez.[44] Apparently now convinced,
Bülow, August 29, telegraphed the foreign office to send Vassel
and to instruct him to secure the desired concessions.[45] Bülow also
ordered the foreign office to notify France of the action taken.[46]
On August 31 Stemrich sent Lancken, German chargé d'affaires in
Paris, instructions to present the situation to the government of
France.[47]

---

[42] Wangenheim to F. O., Aug. 26, 1908, *ibid.*, no. 8409; Note of Rosen, Aug.
27, 1908, *ibid.*, no. 8410.

[43] Wangenheim to F. O., Aug. 26, 1908, *ibid.*, no. 8409. Further proof of
German suspicion of French motives is given by Bunsen, who reported to Grey
that "Radowitz has returned to Spain in a highly irritable frame of mind. . . ."
To Bunsen's remark that he could not understand German action, Radowitz
replied that "Germany's stock of patience was at an end, that she could no
longer tolerate the interruption of her trade with Morocco, and that the policy
of France in that country was very offensive to Germany. . . ."—Bunsen to Grey,
Sept. 7, 1908, *Br. Docs.*, vol. VII, no. 101.

[44] Stemrich to Bülow, Aug. 28, 1908, *G. P.*, vol. XXIV, no. 8414.

[45] Bülow to F. O., Aug. 29, 1908, *ibid.*, no. 8415.

[46] Bülow to F. O., Aug. 29, 1908, *ibid.*, no. 8416.

[47] Stemrich to Lancken, Aug. 31, 1908, *ibid.*, no. 8421. Stemrich's instructions
were to present orally the following:

"In view of the turn which things in Morocco have taken lately, the Imperial
Government considers it should point out to the Powers that it lies in the interest of final pacification of Moroccan relation, of final maintenance of peace,
and of final return to the pledges taken in Algeciras, now to proceed to recognition of Mulay Hafid. . . ."

"We solely for the settlement of claims pending for a long time which in the
face of complaints of the interested parties a further delay could not endure,
sent back our consul in Fez to his post, a special political purpose is not connected with this mission. . . ."

As was to be expected, France was highly irritated at the news, but excitement in England also reached a high pitch. In general the British newspapers opposed the German move and suspected German motives.[48] The foreign office was only slightly less vigorous in its disapproval. The notes of the senior clerk, Sir Eyre Crowe, always breathing hostility to Germany, spoke of this as "a piece of sharp practice on the part of Germany. She wishes to be first in with Mulay Hafid. . . ."[49] Regretful of the tension that had developed, he urged the powers supporting France to be "most careful to make no mistake and to do strictly what is right internationally. So far it looks as if Germany would again place herself technically in the wrong. . . ."[50] To this note Grey added, "I should say Germany had already placed herself in the wrong; she ought not to have sent her Consul back to Fez without any consultation with the Powers interested, and she ought surely before launching and publishing her proposal to recognize the new Sultan to have sounded the French and Spanish Gov[ernmen]ts. . . ."[51] English opposition was not unexpected by Germany, but Bülow hoped by stating that no political motives were involved to ward off the full force of English wrath.[52]

The other powers gave to the French viewpoint varying degrees of support. Spain, coöperating with her in her negotiations with Mulay Hafid, officially supported France; but the action of Germany did not cause "in Spain the irritation which is so apparent in the press of all the principal countries outside Germany and even in some of the German newspapers. . . . The reason, no doubt, is that the German view of the situation is more to the liking of Spain than the French view. . . ."[53] Even Germany's allies agreed with France that recognition should not be "one-sided by one power but only by reason of an agreement determined by the collective signatory Powers of the Conference of Algeciras. . . ."[54]

[48] Stumm, German chargé d'affaires, to Bülow, Sept. 8, 1908, *ibid.*, no. 8428.

[49] Note of Crowe to despatch, White to Grey, Aug. 31, 1908, *Br. Docs.*, vol. VII, no. 95.

[50] Note of Crowe to despatch, Bertie to Grey, Sept. 8, 1908, *ibid.*, no. 96.

[51] Note of Grey to despatch, Bertie to Grey, Sept. 8, 1908, *ibid.*, no. 96.

[52] Bülow to F. O., Aug. 29, 1908, *G. P.*, vol. XXIV, no. 8417.

[53] Bunsen to Grey, Sept. 7, 1908, *Br. Docs.*, vol. VII, no. 101.

[54] Note of Aehrenthal of a conversation with Tittoni, Sept. 5, 1908, *Ö. U. A.*, vol. I, no. 67.

The German program not only excited the disapproval of her allies but also ultimately created an atmosphere of tension that darkened her friendship with Austria. Loehr, a German subject who had been for a long time a merchant in Fez, had served as Austrian consul there and was anxious to return to the city, but his request was refused by the Austrian chargé d'affaires at Tangier who told him that if he went anyhow, he would lose his consular powers. Stemrich telegraphed the German chargé d'affaires in Vienna to call upon Aehrenthal and point out to him "how unfriendly such a disavowal, which our closest confederate gives thereby to our sending of Vassel, must work at present . . . ," and persuade him to instruct the officials at Tangier to grant Loehr's request.[55] The chargé, Brockdorff-Rantzau, carried out the instructions of his superiors, but with no success; for Aehrenthal refused to countermand the orders and insisted that if Loehr went to Fez, he must renounce his consular functions. Brockdorff-Rantzau emphasized the point that as Loehr was a subject of the German Empire as well as Austrian consul, for him to lay down his consular functions at this time would necessarily be construed in public as a disavowal of the German act in sending Dr. Vassel.[56] Bülow advised his agent to proceed with caution, as Germany was not "trying to dictate to Austria," but urged him to secure Aehrenthal's consent to the trip.[57] September 19, 1908, Aehrenthal agreed to Loehr's making the trip on the condition that he would not enter into official communication with the government of Mulay Hafid until recognition had been fully granted.[58] Aehrenthal remained firm in his decision that recognition should come by acceptance of the French procedure, although he promised Germany to examine the details of the Franco-Spanish note with German interests in mind.[59]

France, as the power most interested, expressed in her official response her displeasure and her surprise. In the official conferences at Paris and Berlin, the French representatives not only stated the protest of their country, but also explained French plan

[55] Stemrich to Tschirschky, Sept. 17, 1908, *G. P.,* vol. XXIV, no. 8437.

[56] Brockdorff-Rantzau to F. O., Sept. 18, 1908, *ibid.,* no. 8440.

[57] Bülow to Brockdorff-Rantzau, Sept. 19, 1908, *ibid.,* no. 8441.

[58] Brockdorff-Rantzau to F. O., Sept. 19, 1908, *ibid.,* no. 8442.   [59] *Ibid.*

of procedure. France was not claiming an international mandate, but merely attempting to expedite matters by arranging with Mulay Hafid concrete proposals to present to the powers for acceptance before recognizing the pretender. Recognition of Mulay Hafid should be made dependent upon his acceptance of the Act of Algeciras and the international obligations which resulted therefrom.[60] Berckheim, the French chargé d'affaires in Berlin, wished to secure from Stemrich a statement that Germany did not consider that France had violated the Act of Algeciras but only succeeded in drawing from him the qualified statement that he "did not doubt Pichon and Clemenceau's good will but that many officials in Morocco had violated the spirit of the Algeciras Act. . . ."[61] It was evident that Germany did not trust France to limit her demands upon Mulay Hafid to matters of international interest but suspected her of pressing undue claims upon him for the benefit of France alone.[62] Nevertheless, the negotiations between France and Spain on the one side and Mulay Hafid on the other proceeded with some dispatch, and, on September 14, 1908, the joint French and Spanish note was presented to the signatory powers.[63]

According to this note, Mulay Hafid was to accept the Act of Algeciras and all the laws of application resulting from it, accept all other treaties and engagements concluded by his predecessors, assume the debts of Abdul Aziz, grant to France and Spain the right to supervise contraband trade, submit the question of damages due from the Casablanca incident to an international commission, and agree to maintain order. Moreover, each power reserved the right to negotiate separately with Mulay Hafid on matters that touched their interests exclusively. This last provision

---

[60] Lancken to F. O., Sept. 3, 1908, *ibid.*, no. 8425; Note of Stemrich, Sept. 3, 1908, *ibid.*, no. 8426; Bertie to Grey, Sept. 13, 1908, *Br. Docs.*, vol. VII, no. 104; Pichon to French representatives in London, Berlin, St. Petersburg, Lisbon, The Hague, Brussels, Sept. 1, 1908, *Affaires du Maroc*, 1907-1908, no. 419; Berckheim to Pichon, Sept. 3, 1908, *ibid.*, no. 430.

[61] Note of Stemrich, Sept. 3, 1908, *G. P.*, vol. XXIV, no. 8426.

[62] Wangenheim to Bülow, Sept. 7, 1908, *ibid.*, no. 8431.

[63] Franco-Spanish note, Sept. 14, 1908, *ibid.*, no. 8433; Bunsen to Grey, Sept. 7, 1908, *Br. Docs.*, vol. VII, no. 101. *Affaires du Maroc*, 1907-1908, nos. 445-456 give reports of French representatives in presenting the note to the various chancelleries.

left open to France and Spain the right to secure reimbursement for their expenses in the military actions undertaken around Casablanca.[64] All the signatory powers, Germany included, accepted the note by November 12, 1908,[65] and it was then transmitted to Mulay Hafid, who accepted December 6, 1908.[66] This did not mean, however, that Franco-German tension over Morocco was now over. On the contrary, since September their relations had been strained to the breaking point by the Casablanca deserters affair which, though settled at approximately the same time as the Mulay Hafid case, had aroused such popular excitement that repercussions continued for some time.

Usually historians list the Kaiser's visit to Tangier as the first Moroccan crisis and the *Panther's* stay at Agadir as the second Moroccan crisis; but some would call the latter the third and number the Casablanca deserters affair as the second crisis. The seriousness of the situation was indeed only slightly less grave for a few days in November, 1908, than in either 1905 or 1911. The crisis arose in this fashion. Six deserters from the French foreign legion, assisted by the German consul Lüderitz and his aide, were attempting to reach a German vessel anchored in the harbor and make good their escape. The French officials learned of the venture in time to appear at the docks before the boat shoved off and prevent the departure of the deserters. When the German consul attempted to protect the deserters, a French officer threatened him with a pistol. Though the German officials formally demanded the release of the prisoners, the French military authorities retained them in custody.[67]

Necessarily, the question immediately entered the diplomatic channels. Pichon, on September 28, expressed his regret at the incident and hoped that the matter would be solved satisfactorily. The divergence in the French and German viewpoint appeared even in this early conference. According to the German point of view, the fact that a subject of the German Empire had taken

[64] Franco-Spanish note, Sept. 14, 1908, *G. P.*, vol. XXIV, no. 8433.

[65] Schoen's note, undated, *ibid.*, no. 8446; *Affaires du Maroc, 1908-1910*, no. 33.

[66] Saint-Aulaire to Pichon, Dec. 6, 1908, *Affaires du Maroc, 1908-1910*, no. 50.

[67] Wangenheim to F. O., Sept. 28, 1908, *G. P.*, vol. XXIV, no. 8362; Bertie to Grey, Sept. 28, 1908, *Br. Docs.*, vol. VII, no. 119. The French *Yellow Books* give no account of this affair.

service in a foreign army did not deprive him of his German nationality, and consequently the German consul was within his rights in protecting him. For a French officer to threaten a German official with a pistol was intolerable. Desertions had been going on for sometime, and France should have first discussed the matter instead of taking the law into her own hands. France maintained that in international right German jurisdiction did not cover German subjects in a foreign army, and that desertion was always considered as a crime punishable by the proper military authorities.[68] Germany's arguments were weakened by the fact that of the deserters only three were Germans, one being an Austrian, one a Swiss, and one a Russian Pole. The French case was weakened by the action of her agent in threatening the German official.

Although all the elements of a severe crisis lay embedded in the situation, there was every chance for a peaceful adjustment since both France and Germany seemed anxious to settle the matter and presented tentative proposals.[69] Schoen proposed that France express her regrets for the acts committed by her agents against the prerogatives of the German consul and on persons protected by the German consul; that Germany express her regrets for the consul's giving safe conduct to persons to whom he did not have the right to extend that privilege; and that the solution of the question of right be left to arbitration.[70] France was willing to submit the question to arbitration and understood that the question of apology was not to arise until after the decision by the arbiter.[71] Though the negotiators had not reached a settlement of the difficulty, discussion was progressing in a relatively calm fashion until October 29, when Schoen informed Cambon that the question of the German consul's right and authority could not come into

[68] Lancken to F. O., Sept. 28, 1908, *G. P.,* vol. XXIV, no. 8363; Bertie to Grey, Sept. 28, 1908, *Br. Docs.,* vol. VII, no. 119; White to Grey, Oct. 7, 1908, *ibid.,* no. 123. White quotes Wangenheim for the German and Regnault for the French view.

[69] Lancken to F. O., Oct. 15, 1908, *G. P.,* vol. XXIV, no. 8378; Schoen to Radolin, Oct. 15, 1908, *ibid.,* vol. XXIV, no. 8377; Lascelles to Grey, Sept. 30, 1908, *Br. Docs.,* vol. VII, no. 121.

[70] Schoen to Radolin, Oct. 19, 1908, *G. P.,* vol. XXIV, no. 8381.

[71] Grey to Bertie, Nov. 3, 1908, *Br. Docs.,* vol. VII, no. 128; Bertie to Grey, Nov. 4, 1908, *ibid.,* no. 129; Count de Salis to Grey, Nov. 6, 1908, *ibid.,* no. 137.

the arbitration discussion.[72] This move was immediately followed
by the action of Bülow, who, considering that France had been
dilatory in meeting German proposals, instructed Radolin on
October 30 to demand of the French government the immediate
release of the three German deserters and proper satisfaction for
the mistreatment of the two German consular officials.[73] As the
ministers were out of town, Radolin presented the demands to
Georges Louis, who replied that "It would be impossible for the
French government to give the wished for satisfaction . . . ," but
that if the arbitration court declared France guilty, she "would
then be ready to make the demanded apology. . . ." [74]

The official circle of France upheld the position assumed by
Georges Louis. Radolin had made an informal presentation of the
demands to Louis on October 31, and then rendered them formally
on November 1.[75] The *Daily Telegraph* interview had been published on October 28. The natural tendency was to tie the two
together.[76] Cambon declared that France might have granted
some concessions but, after the publicity given the affair, conces-

---

[72] Note of Schoen, Oct. 29, 1908, *G. P.,* vol. XXIV, no. 8383.

[73] Bülow to Radolin, Oct. 30, 1908, *ibid.,* no. 8384.

[74] Radolin to F. O., Oct. 31, 1908, *ibid.,* no. 8385; Bertie to Grey, Nov. 4, 1908,
Br. Docs., vol. VII, no. 129.

[75] Radolin to F. O., Oct. 31, 1908, *G. P.,* vol. XXIV, no. 8385; Radolin to F. O.,
Nov. 1, 1908, *ibid.,* no. 8386.

[76] In an interview published in the *Daily Telegraph,* the Kaiser discussed freely
German foreign policy, and although he assured England of his own friendship,
he stated that there was a strong anti-British feeling in Germany. His indiscreet
comments aroused a furor in both countries and provoked open criticism in
the Reichstag. Feeling in France was equally high. "The interview . . . stiffened
France's attitude in regard to the Casablanca incident. . . . In search, apparently,
of a diversion for the impending crisis at home, Bülow proceeded to revive the
Casablanca incident in an exaggerated form. . . ."—E. M. Carroll, *French Public
Opinion and Foreign Affairs,* p. 227. Pichon thought, "the demand might have
been made as an attempt to divert attention in Germany from the stir created
by the publication of the interview with the Emperor. . . ."—Grey to Bertie,
Nov. 3, 1908, *Br. Docs.,* vol. VII, no. 128. Isvolski concurred in this view.—
Nicolson to Grey, Nov. 6, 1908, *ibid.,* no. 135. Radolin reported "the French
think Germany changed her attitude on the Casablanca affair because of the
inner trouble of the *Daily Telegraph* and resented Germany's making difficulties
for France for internal politics. . . ."—Radolin to Bülow, Dec. 24, 1908, *G. P.,*
vol. XXIV, no. 8472. Bülow denied that Germany had changed her attitude on
the Casablanca affair because of internal politics and pointed out that Germany
had agreed to the Hague arbitration at the time of the internal storm.—Bülow
to William II, Dec. 29, 1908, *ibid.,* no. 8473.

sions would not be possible.[77] Pichon's reply was a refusal and pointed out that France had already accepted the plan of arbitration and that he could not ask an apology from the French officers.[78] The statement that Premier Clemenceau, when Radolin reported the demands to him, "made a move to open one of the drawers of his desk and said to the ambassador: 'Do you wish your passports . . .' "[79] is not proven; but that Clemenceau was obstinate in his determination not to yield beyond the offer already made by France is substantiated.[80] He considered the danger to lie in "the impossibility of depending on the German Emperor from one day to another . . . ," and especially referred to the *Daily Telegraph* interview.[81] As Germany insisted on her demands and France refused to yield, a situation of extreme tension resulted.[82] Schoen was frankly worried and feared that "we must now perhaps bring up the heavy artillery and with disturbance in the diplomatic relations perhaps even threaten with sending of ships to Casablanca. . . ." [83] Schoen was sincerely anxious to avoid a break and, working with Cambon, he labored to effect a settlement.[84]

The action of the other powers unquestionably had a great deal to do with his success. England unhesitatingly supported

---

[77] Note of Flotow, Nov. 1, 1908, *G. P.*, vol. XXIV, no. 8387.

[78] Grey to Bertie, Nov. 3, 1908, *Br. Docs.*, vol. VII, no. 128.

[79] Pierre Albin, *La Querrelle franco-allemande, Le "Coup" d'Agadir; origines et developpement de la crise de 1911*, p. 115.

[80] Bertie to Grey, Nov. 4, 1908, *Br. Docs.*, vol. VII, no. 129.

[81] *Ibid.*

[82] See the two reports of Nicolson to Grey, Nov. 6, 1908, *ibid.*, nos. 133 and 135. Russia seemed especially worried over the situation. Crowe in the note of the first document suggested that Germany might be "trying to frighten Russia so as to persuade her to put pressure on her ally France, to yield to German demands. . . ."—Note of Crowe to despatch, Nicolson to Grey, Nov. 6, 1908, *ibid.*, no. 133.

[83] Note of Flotow, Nov. 1, 1908, *G. P.*, vol. XXIX, no. 8387, marginal note of Schoen.

[84] Schoen carried on the negotiations until November 7, when he became ill and was forced to turn the matter over to Kiderlen. The final adjustments were arranged between Kiderlen and Cambon, but Kiderlen's claim that sole honor for settling the difficulty should be his, is unjustified.—Ernest Jäckh, *Kiderlen-Wächter, der Staatsmann und Mensch*, vol. II, pp. 13-16. The official report of the facts in the case, which arrived November 7, had much more to do with effecting a settlement than a change of officials.

France, as was to be expected,[85] but again, as in the question of the recognition of Mulay Hafid, Austria was more in sympathy with France than with Germany. Franz Joseph in conversation with William II, November 6, "in a very pressing manner spoke the urgent wish that Germany do as much as possible in order to come to an understanding with France in the Casablanca affair. . . ." [86] Operating as an additional aid toward settlement was the French official report of the facts in the case prepared by the French police commissioner, Durde, delivered to Germany on November 7.[87] The air began to clear on November 7, and by November 10 Bülow was to telegraph the Emperor that the formula for an agreement had been reached.[88] The dispute over the

[85] Grey was worried over the situation, and favored arbitration.—Grey to Bertie, Nov. 5, 1908, *ibid.*, no. 132. Grey wrote to McKenna:

"I do not like the way in which the Germans have revived the Casablanca difficulty with France. A fortnight ago, Bülow himself said it was practically settled.

"It certainly will not do for us to make any preparations or movements of ships which are noticeable; that might precipitate a quarrel between Germany and France, which might not otherwise occur; for any hostile movement on our part would be construed as an unjustifiable menace at this stage, and would influence German opinion.

"But I think the Admiralty should keep in readiness to make preparations in case Germany sent France an ultimatum and the Cabinet decided that we must assist France."

[86] Tschirschky to F. O., Nov. 7, 1908, *G. P.*, vol. XXIV, no. 8399. Note also the editor's note to this document. The earlier protest of the Austrian vice consul at Tangier to French action was immediately disavowed by his superiors. —White to Grey, Oct. 7, 1908, *Br. Docs.*, vol. VII, no. 123; White to Grey, Oct. 16, 1908, *ibid.*, no. 124; White to Grey, Oct. 31, 1908, *ibid.*, no. 127.

[87] Bülow to Jenisch in the Imperial retinue, Nov. 7, 1908, *G. P.*, vol. XXIV, no. 8400. French dilatoriness in preparing and delivering this report provoked criticism and formed the basis for German charges that France was not sincere in her efforts to settle the case. To this degree France must bear a share of the responsibility for the crisis.

[88] Bülow to Jenisch, Nov. 10, 1908, *ibid.*, no. 8403. The formula ran thus:

"The French and German Governments regretting the events which arose at Casablanca last September 25, and which led some subordinate agents to violence and to aggressive acts, decided to submit the entire question raised by the subject to arbitration. By mutual agreement each of the two Governments bind themselves to express their regrets at the conduct of its officials according to the decision which the arbiter shall give on the question of fact and of law. . . ."

The decision of the arbitral committee was handed down May 23, and the protocols signed by France and Germany, May 30, 1909.—Auguste Gauvain, *L'Europe au jour le jour,* vol. II, pp. 379, 386; Editor's note, *Br. Docs.*, vol. VII, no. 130.

recognition of Mulay Hafid and the question of the deserters were settled within the same month, but the greater problem of Franco-German relations in Morocco was as yet unsettled.

The sum total of events in the years since Algeciras had left France in possession of the village of Oudjda in the east and Casablanca and the Chaouya in the west. But the German-supported claimant to the throne ruled in Fez. The events of these years had taught German and French diplomats that the interests of both countries were being injured by the constantly recurring crises, and that some kind of mutual agreement was necessary to prevent that powderkeg known as Morocco from exploding and destroying the profits of both German and French nationals.

Chapter IV

THE FRANCO-GERMAN ACCORD, 1909

The disorders that accompanied Mulay Hafid's struggle for the throne had proved disastrous to foreign as well as to native interests. Projects for public works, especially port improvements, such as the concessions to German companies at Larache and Tangier, were discontinued; the Casablanca indemnity question could not be adjusted; commerce with the interior was practically cut off; and the fields of agricultural associates were often pillaged.[1] To these local disturbances was added the international situation, which grew tense whenever Morocco, wasp's nest to diplomats, was mentioned. A solution of the international aspects of the problem was dependent upon a rapprochement between France and Germany. Germany had seen the powers of Europe support France in every dispute arising over Morocco, and in the crises of 1908 saw even her ally, Austria, align herself on the side of France. If Germany were to improve her general diplomatic position,[2] if she were to secure for her nationals a share in the exploitation of Morocco,[3] she must adjust her difficulties with France. If, on the other hand, France were to guard her Algerian frontier, if she were to extend her economic penetration, if, in sum, she were to profit to the fullest from her diplomatic arrangements with England, Spain, and Italy, she must come to terms with Germany.[4] Both Germany and France realized these

---

[1] Piquet, *op. cit.*, p. 199; *Affaires du Maroc*, 1907-1908.

[2] Tardieu gives this as the main reason for German action.—*Op. cit.*, p. 4. German officials in London had warned Germany that "a solution of the Moroccan problem appears therefore as the first preliminary condition for . . . a settlement with England."—Stumm to Bülow, Sept. 8, 1908, *G. P.*, vol. XXIV, no. 8428. Bertie reported Pichon as stating that Germany wanted an agreement with France in order to draw her from the English orbit.—Bertie to Grey, Sept. 3, 1908, *Br. Docs.*, vol. VII, no. 98.

[3] Schoen to Rosen, Feb. 25, 1909, *G. P.*, vol. XXIV, no. 8499; Note of Wangenheim, Jan. 9, 1909, *ibid.*, no. 8476.

[4] Tardieu, *op. cit.*, pp. 5, 7; Caillaux before the chamber of deputies, *Annales de la chambre des députés*, séance 18 decembre, 1911; Ribot before the senate,

facts, and evidence of a desire on the part of both to remove Morocco from the field of international conflict appeared as early as 1907.

A conversation took place between the French and German chargés d'affaires in Tangier in August, 1907, in which the possibility of an agreement on economic and financial affairs as relating to Morocco was discussed. When this was reported to Paris, the foreign office expressed interest, and Bülow annotated Radolin's report from Paris with a question as to the form such an agreement might take.[5] A few days later, Grey informed France that Bülow "was most anxious for an improvement in the relations between France and Germany. He thought this could be effected by a display of tact on both sides, especially on the part of the local representatives of the two Powers. . . . He gave most formal assurances that Germany had no intention of attacking France, nor of creating difficulties for her in Morocco. . . . All Prince Bülow wanted was that German traders and merchants should not be unfairly treated by the French authorities and should not be excluded from fair competition. . . ."[6] Germany displayed her interest further by wiring Langwerth, German representative in Tangier, September 2, 1907, for his opinion of what compensation in Morocco Germany could ask for "attainment of an arrangement with France. . . ."[7] Tschirschky, however, soon decided that when "the cannons speak in Morocco, is a bad time for diplomacy" and that compensation outside of Morocco "we could . . . not draw into consideration . . ." and wrote Bülow to that effect.[8] The matter was apparently dropped for the time being, but was revived the next fall when, on September 18, 1909, Schoen stated to Jules Cambon that Germany had "no intention to create difficulties for France, whose special interest we fully recognize. . . . An understanding, namely on the economic field, perhaps under the neutralization of the Moroccan market, appears to me not too

---

Annales du senat, séance 9 février, 1912; and Pichon before the senate, *ibid.,* séance 8 février, 1912.

[5] Radolin to Bülow, Aug. 10, 1907, *G. P.,* vol. XXIV, no. 8280; Caillaux, *op. cit.,* p. 31.

[6] Grey to Bertie, Aug. 22, 1907, *Br. Docs.,* vol. VII, no. 73.

[7] Tschirschky to Langwerth, Sept. 2, 1907, *G. P.,* vol. XXIV, no. 8292.

[8] Tschirschky to Bülow, Sept. 4, 1907, *ibid.,* no. 8294.

difficult. . . ." [9] Later in the month, after the Casablanca deserters incident, Cambon asserted his desire to solve the affair peacefully, and also spoke of the wish to bring Germany and France into a more harmonious relation.[10]

Before any progress could be made from these tentative moves, the Bosnian crisis[11] crashed into the European scene and drove the Moroccan question into the background. This crisis emphasized again the danger underlying the European structure and the need for removing points of friction wherever possible. In France especially, a renewed impetus was thus given to the idea of a Franco-German agreement on the troublesome question of Morocco, which led to repeated attempts to interest Germany. Germany at this point began to act hesitant and cautious whenever approached on the subject. Lancken, German chargé d'affaires in Paris, described the feeling that existed after the Bosnian crisis as definitely favorable to an agreement "even in spheres . . . which earlier opposed us in every circumstance. . . ." He quoted in this connection a statement of Tardieu's to the effect that "Germany and France through the force of things would be compelled to support each other in the Orient, and . . . that Germany and France should have the courage to make an end for all time to the return of dissension in the Moroccan affair. . . ." According to Lancken, Tardieu considered the friendly atmosphere created by the Eastern crisis a favorable opportunity for establishing an understanding about Morocco, which "must be within the framework of the Algeciras Act. . . ." Lancken replied to Tardieu's overture by the warning that "it was not the time to bring the Moroccan question upon our heads. . . ." [12]

Nevertheless, France persisted in her efforts and on October 28 Cambon pointed out to Schoen that the mutual interests of

---

[9] Note of Schoen, Sept. 18, 1908, *ibid.*, no. 8439.

[10] Stemrich to Bülow, Sept. 29, 1908, *ibid.*, no. 8365. Stemrich, in reporting the conversation, stated that "Cambon has often wished to offer us compensation in Turkey for Morocco. . . ."

[11] In 1908 Austria annexed Bosnia and Herzegovina and thereby precipitated an international crisis over the Balkan question. Russia supported Serbia in her protest until, convinced by France and England, she gave way and accepted the annexation.

[12] Lancken to Bülow, Oct. 14, 1908, *G. P.*, vol. XXIV, no. 8460; Caillaux, *op. cit.*, p. 33.

Germany and France in the Eastern question made it desirable for the two nations to come to an understanding about Morocco. Schoen declared that "in general he was ready to come to an understanding on the general line of the Algeciras Act. . . ." [13] A month intervened before further overtures were made, but on December 14, Joseph Caillaux, at that time minister of finance, stated (so Lancken reported to Bülow) that "it is absolutely essential that Morocco be removed as an eventual object of strife in our relations. If this does not happen, we move towards a conflict with certainty. For for France it is a life question to maintain a far-reaching political position in Morocco. . . ." To this statement Lancken retorted that Germany only wanted the open door in Morocco, but that French actions made her highly suspicious that France wished to force her out entirely. Caillaux then asked what economic guarantees Germany wanted, to which Lancken countered by the statement that "it would be the business of France to come forth with proposals. . . ." Caillaux replied that he thought France would be willing to do so.[14]

Nothing apparently came of this interplay, and the question rested until December 24, when Prince Radolin described conditions in general to his foreign office. He pointed out that every act of Germany's was interpreted in France as indicative of an active hostility against her and that many circles in France believed a war with Germany was inevitable. The fact that Regnault's policy in the sultan strife had culminated in a fiasco, Radolin thought, explained the French wish to form an agreement with Germany; yet the Oriental crisis had certainly strengthened this wish. He believed that the moment was not favorable for a rapprochement, but that a period of quiet should first intervene. Moreover, any agreement that might be made must be formed on the basis "that France guarantee us there absolutely the open door for which we could leave them great political freedom of action. . . ." To this last statement William II attached a laconic "Right; I have emphasized it over and over again. . . ." [15]

Although as late as December 29, 1908, Bülow wrote to William

---

[13] Note of Schoen, Oct. 28, 1908, *G. P.*, vol. XXIV, no. 8463.

[14] Lancken to Bülow, secret, Dec. 14, 1908, *ibid.*, no. 8471.

[15] Radolin to Bülow, Dec. 24, 1908, *ibid.*, no. 8472.

II that a period of quiet must take place before any agreement could be established with France,[16] it is evident that Germany was definitely considering the step by January 5, 1909.[17] Wangenheim, who was in Berlin on leave from his post at Tangier, was asked to write his opinion of the Moroccan situation. His note, dated January 5, 1909, related the conflict of interests of the two nations within Morocco that was bound to result in disaster for German interests. Sooner or later Mulay Hafid, as had Abdul Aziz, would fall under the influence of Regnault; and then the French legation at Tangier would be the real center of the Moroccan government. German influence would then disappear and German business suffer. "At best German merchants would be able to vegetate in Morocco only by the grace of France. . . ." The Germans who lived in Morocco believed that if Germany did not want a war with France to arise from these difficulties, an agreement should be made as soon as possible. If France were granted the right to establish French military and financial control, which was her ambition, the real "Tunisfication" of this territory would begin; yet he agreed that the Sherifian government without energetic assistance from a foreign power could not solve its own problems. "In a Morocco administered by France the chances for an economic development of Germany doubtless would be infinitely much greater than in the Morocco of today which stands bound by the all-paralyzing Algeciras Act. . . ." In the light of these facts, Wangenheim recommended to his government that an agreement which assured German economic interests and which did not

---

[16] Bülow to William II, Dec. 29, 1908, *ibid.*, no. 8473.

[17] The reason for the change in German viewpoint at this time probably lay in the domestic situation. Bülow was facing a hostile Reichstag and he had already lost the confidence of the Kaiser, because of his failure to give him unqualified support in the *Daily Telegraph* affair. Paul Cambon explained the situation to Hardinge in this manner: Bülow was "in a very bad position in the Reichstag where he is being strongly attacked as disturber of the peace. Prince Bülow was anxious, therefore, to do something to show that he is a pacifist. . . ." —Grey to Bertie, Feb. 11, 1909, *Br. Docs.*, vol. VII, no. 157; also Grey to Bertie, Feb. 9, 1909, *ibid.*, no. 153. The official communiqué issued in Paris, February 9, 1909, as quoted by the London *Times*, Feb. 10, 1909, stated that the agreement was "due to the initiative of Germany. . . ."—London *Times*, Feb. 10, 1909. See also Kiderlen's statement, p. 79, *infra*.

violate her pledge to the Algeciras Act should be formed with France as soon as possible.[18]

The German foreign office continued its study of the project and through its counsellor, Erkert, further elaborated its views. Erkert criticized the alternating advances and retreats that characterized German Moroccan policy, but concluded that since "in every little situation in Morocco, Germany is faced with the decision to let it go or defend German viewpoint, in which case Germany is accused of wanting to use Morocco as an excuse for war. . . . We must seek to find a new basis for our Moroccan policy. . . ." He considered two proposals. Germany might simply give up her position and "silently look on as all other powers do, leave the French alone as they destroy the Algeciras Act and carry through their penetration. . . ." Erkert was opposed to this, for it would destroy respect for Germany and would not result in any improvement in Franco-German relations. She might exchange her position for some other object, "a French colony or something else . . . ," but it would be difficult to evaluate "an influence against something as a territory." Even this would damage German prestige. He proposed instead of either of these suggestions that Germany grant France political preponderance in return for assurance for her trade. The main questions were control of the finances and assurances for commerce. As a solution for the first, he proposed French control through some sort of an international organization as a state bank for Morocco. Formation of one or more syndicates of German and French companies in which France might have the main share so long as German creditors were treated on an equal basis with the French in all financial syndicates was his suggestion for solving the economic question. He naïvely thought that all of this could be accomplished without renouncing the Algeciras Act;[19] but the manner by which he expected to harmonize the internationalization planned by this Act with French political and Franco-German economic preponderance is not clear.

These two memoranda seemed to have formed the basis for

---

[18] Note of Wangenheim, Jan. 5, 1909, *G. P.*, vol. XXIV, no. 8476.

[19] Note of Erkert, Jan. 8, 1909, *ibid.*, no. 8478.

German action in beginning negotiations on January 9. On that date, Schoen reminded Cambon that he had often expressed the desire to discuss the Moroccan question and that he, Schoen, had encouraged him, although Cambon had never presented concrete proposals. Germany was "ready now as ever to enter into an exchange of ideas. . . ." Cambon acknowledged that France wished to form an agreement and asked Schoen if he had a formula or a program to propose. Schoen replied that "a formula which would form a political program so precise that misunderstanding in meaning would be excluded, would be very difficult to find. . . ." He thought that an understanding "about individual practical questions," such as French and German coöperation in financial matters with a "considerable preponderance to France," would be easier. Cambon was impressed and, as he was going to Paris, promised to take the matter up there.[20]

By January 26 the two governments had progressed to the stage of proposals and counter-proposals.[21] The formation of a formula by which Germany was to acknowledge French political preponderance in Morocco created difficulty.[22] Cambon's draft, which read, "The Imperial Government resolves not to oppose anything to the political action of the French Republic . . . ," was altered by Schoen so as to read, "The Imperial German Government decides

[20] Note of Schoen, Jan. 9, 1909, *ibid.*, no. 8479. A "very secret" despatch of Schoen to Rosen presented an interesting sidelight. Schoen informed Rosen of the negotiations under way, and continued, "there exists the danger that Mulay Hafid, if he . . . hear of it through the French, gain the idea that we have dropped him. Thereby our influence on him as a compensation object before the French would be prematurely cut out. . . ." Consequently he urged Rosen to instruct Vassel to convince the sultan that German action was due to the wish to strengthen economically the government of Mulay Hafid and that this could best be done by coöperation between Germany and France.—Schoen to Rosen, Jan. 9, 1909, *ibid.*, no. 8480.

[21] Cambon to Pichon, Jan. 26, 1909, *Affaires du Maroc,* 1908-1910, no. 98; Cambon to Pichon, Jan. 28, 1909, *ibid.*, no. 100.

[22] Kiderlen served as an adviser in the foreign office, November, 1908 to March, 1909.—Jäckh, *op. cit.*, vol. II, p. 6. He was now conducting most of the negotiation with Cambon, although Schoen was also active. Evidently the negotiation was being carried on by the three; for Cambon expressed the wish that "we will succeed, M. de Schoen, M. de Kiderlen, and I, in finding a formula to which the two parties would be able to accede. . . ."—Cambon to Pichon, *Affaires du Maroc,* 1908-1910, no. 104.

to pursue in Morocco only economic interest. . . ." [23] The greater value of the first to France in her program of peaceful penetration is obvious. Despite this divergence in view, the negotiators moved rapidly to a settlement and notified their respective governments on February 7 that an agreement had been reached.[24] On February 8 copies of the agreement were transmitted to the various foreign offices of Europe[25] and, on February 9, the news was released to the press.[26] In this manner was launched the Franco-German Accord of 1909, upon whose success or failure hung the hopes of Europe for a peaceful solution of the delicate Moroccan problem.

The years that had intervened since the creation of the Act of Algeciras had seen Morocco seared by civil war, had watched the destruction of foreign economic investments, and had listened to the rumblings of international conflict. This Act had accomplished little in the task of removing Morocco from the field of international friction or in that of saving it from its decadent state. It seemed to Germany that only the tempo of French absorption of the land had been checked and in no way had her program been deflected from its original path. To France, it seemed that her entire program was blocked by the malicious spite of her neighbor across the Vosges. Each side was able to checkmate the other, but, as neither was able to win the game, a change of policy seemed advantageous to both powers. The European situation in 1908 favored a policy of conciliation as a substitute for one of friction. The Bosnian crisis had brought the powers dangerously near to war, an eventuality that none of them wanted

---

[23] Schoen to Radolin, Feb. 4, 1909, *G. P.,* vol. XXIV, no. 8485, and editor's footnote, p. 486.

[24] Bülow to William II, Feb. 7, 1909, *ibid.,* no. 8487; Cambon to Pichon, Feb. 9, 1909, *Affaires du Maroc,* 1908-1910, no. 117. Copy of the agreement had been sent earlier. See footnote 25, *infra.*

[25] Pichon to French representatives in London, St. Petersburg, Madrid, Rome, and Vienna, Feb. 8, 1909, *Affaires du Maroc,* 1908-1910, no. 114.

[26] London *Times,* Feb. 10, 1909; Bülow to William II, Feb. 7, 1909, *G. P.,* vol. XXIV, no. 8487. Bülow told the Kaiser that the agreement would be published on the ninth so that in this manner "will be prevented every thought that the agreement was dependent on the coöperation of King Edward. . . ." Edward VII was to arrive in Berlin on the ninth.

but that they each feared might arise if the various fields of friction were not removed. The domestic uproar which resulted from
the *Daily Telegraph* interview had made the German foreign office anxious to present a peace offering to its critics. In the light
of their own self-interest, both powers were maneuvering for an
advantageous position and in their judgment the situation now
called for a change of tactics. As neither had gained by a policy
of enmity, they now set forth to solve the Moroccan problem as
partners; but, as future events were to show, the change was one
of tactics and not a fundamental alteration of policy.

As the Accord of February, 1909, formed the basis for Franco-
German relations during the eventful years of 1909, 1910, and
early 1911, and as these relations led finally to the crisis of 1911,
quotation in full of the Accord and the explicative letters, which
accompanied it, is here necessary. The Accord reads:

> The Government of the French Republic and the German Imperial
> Government, animated by an equal desire to facilitate the execution
> of the Act of Algeciras, have agreed in stating the import which
> they attach to the clauses, in view of avoiding all cause of misunder-
> standing between them, in the future.
>
> In consequence,
>
> The Government of the French Republic, firmly attached to main-
> taining the integrity and the independence of the Sherifian empire,
> resolved to safeguard there economic equality, and consequently,
> not to hinder German commercial and industrial interests there,
>
> and the Imperial German Government, pursuing only economic
> interests in Morocco, recognizing on the other hand that the special
> political interests of France are there closely tied to the consolidation
> of internal peace and order, and resolving not to interfere in these
> interests,
>
> declare that they will not pursue nor encourage any measure of a
> nature to create in their favor or in favor of any power whatsoever
> an economic privilege and that they will seek to associate their
> nationals in the affairs for which they may obtain the contract.[27]

The explicative letter, written by Cambon to Schoen and ac-

---

[27] Pichon to French representatives at London, St. Petersburg, Madrid, Rome,
Vienna, Feb. 8, 1909, *Affaires du Maroc,* 1908-1910, no. 114; Franco-German
Accord, *G. P.,* vol. XXIV, no. 8490.

knowledged by Schoen, who quoted the entire letter and added, "I am entirely in agreement with you," follows:

> In order to avoid all misunderstanding on the meaning of our arrangement of this day on the Moroccan affairs, Your Excellency will permit me to specify that the political disinterest of Germany does not carry injury to the situations already acquired by her nationals, but implies the non-candidature of her subjects to functions of directors or of technical counselor of Moroccan public services having or susceptible of having a political character or of instructors in these services.
>
> On the other hand, it is understood that in the affairs which will admit of an association of German and French interests, it will be taken account in the measure possible, of the fact that French interests in Morocco are more important than German interests.[28]

The initial reception accorded the agreement by the public belied the dangers involved in the economic and political clauses of the treaty; for the treaty was received with general rejoicing. Tardieu stated that French public opinion saw in the Accord the moral value of the lack of German political opposition and paid no attention to the details of the economic clauses.[29] The London *Times* asserted that Clemenceau was not able to conceal his satisfaction that the "agreement was no more or less than Germany's withdrawal from Morocco and the end of the policy of pinpricks. . . ." [30] Comments in the Reichstag showed that the public men of Germany welcomed the relaxation of tension between Germany and France.[31] The London *Times* commented editorially on the universal rejoicing over the fact that France and Germany had healed their wounds, and on the pleasure that England took in seeing the success of the Entente policy. "The coincidence of the visit of the King and Queen to Berlin with the publication of the Franco-German agreement on Morocco is indeed happy . . . ," for a rapprochement between England and Germany would now

---

[28] Cambon to Schoen, confidential, Feb. 9, 1909, *G. P.*, vol. XXIV, no. 8491; Schoen to Cambon, Feb. 9, 1909, *ibid.*, no. 8492. These letters were not published, nor were they sent to the various chancelleries of Europe.

[29] Tardieu, *op. cit.*, p. 11.

[30] London *Times*, Feb. 10, 1909, report of Paris correspondent. For further discussion of reaction in France see Gauvain, *op. cit.*, vol. I, pp. 334-340.

[31] *Stenographishe Berichte des Reichstags*, vol. 236, March 29, 1909.

be more easily attained.[32] In general the press of Europe greeted the Accord as a definite step towards international peace.

Except for Spain, the doubting Thomas, the chancelleries of Europe took a few precautionary measures and then accepted the Accord with congratulations to the two interested parties. England asked if the economic clauses would be construed to mean that Franco-German coöperation excluded nationals of other powers. Upon being assured that no such interpretation was intended, Grey approved the agreement.[33] Aehrenthal, Austrian foreign minister, and Tittoni, Italian minister of foreign affairs, delighted in the fact that Germany and France had settled their difficulties.[34] Spain, however, let it be known "that she does not appreciate the Accord" and expressed a desire to open negotiations with Germany on the issue. Germany assured her that the agreement lay within the provision of the Act of Algeciras, and that, as there was no point of friction between Germany and Spain, there was no need for negotiations.[35] Spain, always suspicious that France would deprive her of her share of Morocco, feared that the Franco-German agreement ignored her interests. She may also have regretted any agreement between France and Germany, since Franco-German rivalry was of advantage to her in her Moroccan program.[36]

---

[32] London *Times*, Feb. 10, 1909.

[33] Grey to Bertie, Feb. 9, 1909, *Br. Docs.*, vol. VII, no. 153; Paul Cambon to Pichon, Feb. 10, 1909, *Affaires du Maroc*, 1908-1910, no. 122. In a note attached to a despatch of Bertie's to Grey, Grey shows his views of the entire question. He wrote:

"Politically it is a great advantage that France and Germany should agree not to quarrel about Morocco.

"Commercially I fear other people must lose by an entente between them, though the open door must be preserved on paper.

"As long, however, as the independence and integrity of Morocco are preserved, the Government and condition of that country will be so bad that there will not be very valuable commercial development for anybody. . . ."—Bertie to Grey, Feb. 6, 1909, *Br. Docs.*, vol. VII, no. 149. See also Grey to Bertie, Feb. 11, 1909, *ibid.*, no. 157.

[34] Crozier to Pichon, Feb. 10, 1909, *Affaires du Maroc*, 1908-1910, no. 123; Barrère to Pichon, Feb. 20, 1909, *ibid.*, no. 135.

[35] Schoen to Graf von Tattenbach, Feb. 9, 1909, *G. P.*, vol. XXIV, no. 8493.

[36] Lister stated, "The person who will not be pleased is the Spanish minister . . . whose principal trump card was German hostility to France. . . ." Lister to Grey, Feb. 9, 1909, *Br. Docs.*, vol. VII, no. 151.

The pleasure that this Accord produced caused the men connected with its formation to be honored in many ways.[37] The Emperor sent a congratulatory telegram to Radolin, and Radolin and Schoen both received the cross of the legion of honor. Rival claims for the glory of having formed the treaty present a rather amusing picture. Kiderlen wrote to his friend that "I am able to say to you, just between us, that I all alone with the French ambassador, Cambon, made it . . . ," and complained that Radolin, "the good Radolin who knew of the negotiations only when all was finished and ready for signature . . . ," had received the honors. He spoke with pleasure of the fact that "Cambon, who knew well with whom he had worked, had given to me by the President of the Republic two magnificent pieces of Sèvres . . . which are certainly more than a red ribbon. . . ."[38] William II, later in the year, wrote, "The Moroccan Accord is my own personal work, carried through by me in spite of the deception and pusillanimity of my officials. . . ."[39]

The initial joy was short-lived, and soon doubts began to be expressed.[40] The official statements of the two foreign offices had

[37] Jäckh, op. cit., vol. II, p. 24.

[38] Letter from Kiderlen written March 7, 1909, probably to Marina de Jonina, quoted in Jäckh, op. cit., vol. II, p. 24. Radolin on February 5 had presented two possible changes to the proposed treaty, if it were not too late. These were that Germany should share in the financial control of Morocco and that a definite mutual pledge relative to the per cent each was to share in the business undertakings should be included. Both of these proposals were apparently ignored by the Berlin office.—Radolin to F. O., Feb. 5, 1909, G. P., vol. XXIV, no. 8486.

[39] Marginal note of William II to the despatch Bethmann Hollweg to William II, Nov. 25, 1909, G. P., vol. XXIX, no. 10485. Brandenburg states that "For this easy and unexpected success the French really had to thank the Kaiser, who was anxious to liquidate the old Morocco policy and thought this a favorable time, when Germany was endeavoring jointly with France and England to maintain peace in the East. . . ."—Op. cit., p. 342.

[40] Of course there was a minority who opposed the treaty from the time of its publication. For example, the London Times, Feb. 16, 1909, quoted Hannotaux as saying, "Let us frankly acknowledge that in this regard Germany has obtained even more than she demanded at the outset. She has not only prevented the 'Tunisification' of Morocco; she is admitted to a privileged competition in its markets." The Times correspondent added that Hannotaux's "interpretation . . . is manifestly at variance with the Act of Algeciras and the whole series of other international conventions regarding Morocco. . . ."

Rosen received the news with "bad grace."—Lister to Grey, Feb. 9, 1909, Br. Docs., vol. VII, no. 151. Rosen admitted that "As French political pre-

something to do with this changed viewpoint. On March 29 Bülow, in a speech before the Reichstag, answered the criticism that Germany had pursued an inconsistent Moroccan policy by the statement that such charges rested on a "false conception of our task in Morocco. Should we really aim in a land where we have no political interest and have never claimed political interest, to prepare continued difficulties for France who there possesses very natural and considerable political interests? . . . The German people is strong and great enough to carry out an open, a clear, a just policy, and the Accord that I have concluded with the French government about Morocco, is, moreover, the outcome of such a policy. . . ." [41] Radolin reported to his foreign office that the reception accorded Bülow's speech was in general favorable, but that several saw in it German boasting of power.[42] Within a year other sentences in his speech drew more attention. The culpable sentences, taken from his instruction to Rosen, ran, "It [the Accord] assures France . . . a not unjustified political influence, without giving it the possibility to appropriate to itself that land in any form. The Accord assures Germany the free participation in commerce and trade in an independent Morocco. . . ." [43] Pichon's speeches did nothing to clarify the situation. Speaking in the chamber of deputies, November 23, 1909, he extended "homage to the loyalty with which our Accord is practiced by the government of Berlin," applauded the détente which had resulted, and affirmed that French policy had not changed and that "We have never intended,

---

ponderance will be united to the general economic equality," the Accord "may be a new nut which he would have to crack. . . ."—Michael Bukuwky to F. O., *Ö. U. A.*, vol. I, no. 986. Rosen remained stationed at Tangier until 1910, even if he may have had a desire to be transferred as Bukuwky believed.—*Ibid.*

[41] *Stenographische Berichte des Reichstags,* vol. 236, p. 7800.

[42] Radolin to Bülow, Mar. 30, 1909, *G. P.*, vol. XXIX, no. 10457.

[43] Schoen to Rosen, Feb. 25, 1909, *G. P.*, vol. XXIV, no. 8499; *Stenographische Berichte des Reichstags,* vol. 236, p. 7800. In these instructions was also included the statement that "The first condition for it, that the Accord show the hoped for fruit, is naturally its loyal maintenance by both sides. . . ." To which Rosen replied that he was ready to carry out these instructions, but that Germans in Morocco were afraid of what France might claim under the Accord especially if Regnault remained.—Rosen to Bülow, Mar. 3, 1909, *G. P.*, vol. XXIV, no. 8500.

we do not intend to go beyond the limits fixed by the Act of Algeciras." [44] But, on December 27, he was forced to answer before that same body charges that the Accord had been extended to include non-Moroccan affairs, for example, the Bagdad railway. He denied all such charges and affirmed that there had been "in the Accord between Germany and us only question of Moroccan affairs. . . ." [45]

Criticism of this diplomatic experiment increased for the next two years, and the final judgment of the critics was one of mixed good and evil. Caillaux granted that the Accord was fortunate "because it inaugurated an era of direct transactions between France and the only power who had made opposition to her action in Morocco"; but it was an "incomplete Accord, because, conceived in vague terms, it did not state precisely any of the consequences of political liberty which appeared to be conceded to France, because it left us political influence but it did not give to us political action; incomplete Accord too, because . . . we formed a sort of economic mortgage on Morocco from which it was visible that one day or other it would be necessary to free ourselves. . . ." The chief gain, according to Caillaux, was the fact that Germany had proclaimed that "Morocco is for her only an object of trade

[44] Annales de la chambre des députés, session extraordinaire de 1909, vol. I, pp. 735-741; Radolin to F. O., Nov. 23, 1909, G. P., vol. XXIX, no. 10482. Schoen in a marginal note to this despatch recommended that Radolin express to Pichon thanks for "his declaration about our loyalty." Bethmann Hollweg added "Ja." —Radolin to F. O., Nov. 23, 1909, G. P., vol. XXIX, no. 10482. Pichon, speaking before the senate, June 24, 1909, on the question of the negotiations for a loan to Morocco, replied to newspaper charges that he was planning a new undertaking in Morocco with the statement, "our interests and our rights in this country are today that which they were yesterday. We intend to maintain and defend them."—Annales du senat, session ordinaire de 1909, vol. LXXV, p. 636. Caillaux quoted the statement to substantiate his charges that the Accord did not grant to France any advantage.—Caillaux, op. cit., p. 37. The statement taken from its context was given a greater force than when read in its original setting. In the entire speech of Pichon, the Franco-German Accord was not directly mentioned.

[45] Annales de la chambre des députés, session extraordinaire de 1909, vol. I, pp. 1904-1905. Pichon later made the statement that "In a conversation with our ambassador, the Chancellor [Bülow] summed up his thoughts thus: 'We have disinterested ourselves politically from Morocco; you will certainly bring to an end that which French policy pursues there. We only ask you to be patient!' . . ."—Annales du senat, session ordinaire de 1912, vol. LXXXI, p. 229 (Feb. 8, 1912).

[bargain]."[46] Tardieu considered that as a result "the Act of Algeciras passed to second plane and it passed thereto without assent. . . ."[47] By 1912 Pierre Baudin, a prominent member of the senate, expressed regret that the French government had in this manner become involved in business deals which should have been conducted as private negotiations.[48] One of his colleagues, Ribot, was convinced that the idea back of the economic coöperation was excellent but its practical application was bound to lead to misunderstanding.[49] As a result of the ineffective operation of the Accord, the jubilation with which it had been welcomed gradually died away, and to be connected with the negotiations ceased to be an honor and became a stigma.

It was not surprising that the Accord proved inoperative, for the vagueness of its terms gave it little promise of success and scarcely justified the exuberance with which it had been greeted. It had left too many major problems unsettled. For example: To what extent had Germany conceded to France political control in the Sherifian empire? To what extent had France pledged herself to secure economic concessions for Germany? British and German economic rivalry within the Sherifian empire might place France in the dilemma of choosing between her staunch British friend and her new German partner. In such a case, France would be compelled to consider the general European situation as more important than the colonial; for, so long as the question of the Rhine remained a thorn in her side, she must cling to England. Moreover, she would be inclined to limit her obligations under the economic clause, considered by Germany as all important, while she stretched to its maximum extent the political clauses. When faced with the practical task of solving concrete problems in the Moroccan imbroglio, the powers read into the agreement the interpretation best adapted to further their own national interests with little regard for their other partner or for the other powers in general. Furthermore, neither power in 1909 seemed disturbed

---

[46] Caillaux before the chamber of deputies, *Annales de la chambre des députés,* session extraordinaire de 1911, vol. I, p. 1468; Caillaux, *op. cit.,* pp. 37, 41.

[47] *Op. cit.,* p. 11.

[48] *Annales du senat,* session ordinaire de 1912, vol. LXXXI, pp. 217-220.

[49] *Ibid.,* pp. 244-253.

by the fact that it could not harmonize the privileged position created by the Accord of that year with the international program laid down by the Act of Algeciras. The conflicting obligations involved in these two agreements and the indefiniteness of the Accord of 1909 were sufficient in themselves to wreck every attempt at economic coöperation. But optimistically the two powers set to work to place their Accord into operation. It thus became entangled in a mass of financial, business, and diplomatic threads which finally strangled it. A discussion of the attempts at economic coöperation will bring out the truth of this statement.

Chapter V

QUARRELSOME PARTNERS

Mines, public works, railroads, and loans formed the major projects for associating French and German nationals in common enterprises. Each of these demands a detailed discussion, but in addition several relatively minor incidents entered as disturbing factors into the allegedly peaceful scene. The mutual mistrust and suspicion that existed between the French and German representatives in Morocco formed a constant source of friction. Rosen had never approved the Accord,[1] and his reports formed one long wail against French aggression and the indifference of the German foreign office.[2] Schoen found it frequently necessary to curb the restlessness of the consul and to calm his repeatedly expressed fears. For example, March 20, 1909, Schoen advised him to give up his plan to go to Fez as such a trip might produce misunderstanding over German interpretation of the February Accord.[3] On July 12, Lancken reported that Dr. Muehlon, who, as representative for the Krupp interests, had spent some months in Morocco, found that German business was in a poor condition and that France was, and always would be, aggressive in her encroachments. Rosen was resigned and ceased to report much that happened to the German foreign office, since Berlin "would not listen to complaints of French conduct." Muehlon thought that as a consequence Germany was losing prestige in Morocco. Lancken said that "naturally the French in Morocco act as masters of the land," but that the German consul should report each act of aggression to Berlin. Muehlon also reported that Mulay Hafid, through Vassel, had informed Rosen that Mokri, Moroccan minister in Paris, had to give up his trip to Essen because France gave him to understand that she did not wish it. Nevertheless, Rosen did not think it worth while to report this piece of informa-

---

[1] See footnote 40, p. 79, *supra*.

[2] See any of Rosen's reports in *G. P.,* vol. XXIX.

[3] Schoen to Rosen, Mar. 20, 1909, *ibid.,* no. 10455.

tion to Berlin. Lancken called Pichon's attention to the report, and Pichon flatly denied that he had interfered with Mokri's trip to Essen. He urged Lancken to report all such rumors so that they might be corrected and acknowledged that some of the French in Morocco were too enthusiastic and went beyond the intentions of the French government.[4] This note plus a German newspaper item complaining of encroachment on German interests in Morocco provoked a reprimand from Schoen to Rosen requesting him to report all points of friction to his superiors. Schoen also assured him that Pichon was sincerely desirous to carry out the Accord of 1909.[5] But Rosen's complaints continued. On November 6, 1909, we find him asking about the rumor of "the alleged extension of French occupation in the Chaouya territory," [6] and on March 1, 1910, warning his government just as France had occupied Oudjda, Casablanca, and the Chaouya "the advance of the French against Taza and against Fez is likewise only a question of time. . . ." [7]

Rosen was not the only German official to warn the government against the gradual encroachment of the French, and these warnings increased as the years advanced to May, 1911. In 1910 reports of French activities became so frequent that they led to inquiries from the German foreign office and to official denials on the part of France.[8] The ambitious program of local French agents frequently caused a flurry in the foreign offices until official disavowal was issued. One such incident was provoked by General d'Amande's criticism of a Spanish advance into the Riff and his proposal that French troops be despatched to meet the Spanish. Pichon issued a quick denial, which Germany thought indicated his wish not to open again the Moroccan question.[9] Saint-Aulaire, Regnault's ardent second, made an enthusiastic speech on the

---

[4] Lancken to Erkert, July 12, 1909, *ibid.*, no. 10460.

[5] Schoen to Rosen, July 18, 1909, *ibid.*, no. 10461; Langwerth to Lancken, July 21, 1909, *ibid.*, no. 10462.

[6] Rosen to Bethmann Hollweg, Nov. 6, 1909, *ibid.*, no. 10481.

[7] Rosen to Bethmann Hollweg, Mar. 1, 1910, *ibid.*, no. 10507.

[8] Rotenhan to Bethmann Hollweg, July 29, 1910, *ibid.*, no. 10512; Kiderlen to Lancken, Aug. 5, 1910, *ibid.*, no. 10513; Lancken to Bethmann Hollweg, Aug. 16, 1910, *ibid.*, no. 10514.

[9] Editor's footnote to note, unsigned and undated, *ibid.*, no. 10476.

future of France in Morocco and stated that "France finds itself
in spite of the Algeciras Act and the Moroccan Accord 'on the way
to full sovereignty in Morocco.' "[10] This speech called forth a
protest from the Berlin foreign office, to which Pichon replied that
Saint-Aulaire "had received a sound rebuke. . . ."[11] Regnault remained as a constant source of irritation to the German officials,
though the hope that he might be recalled revived again and again.

According to the official reports, more confidence existed between the foreign offices of the two nations than between their local
representatives. Pichon in his public utterances repeatedly expressed his confidence in Germany's desire to uphold the Accord
with all loyalty.[12] Despatches of Lancken, Radolin, and Schoen
reiterated faith in French desire to keep matters quiet.[13] In at
least one instance, French faith in German loyalty seemed to be
justified. Mulay Hafid approached Germany with the offer of "a
coaling station on the Atlantic coast," because his country realized
that it could not stand alone against the pressure of western powers and that "a foreign power could only have more than words
for Morocco if its interest in Morocco" was more than commercial.
As to this proposal Schoen commented, "An awkward attempt of
the Sultan's to interest us again politically and to play us out
against France."[14] In a lengthy note prepared for Bethmann
Hollweg, he stated various reasons why Germany would not consider such a gift. It would be "against the integrity of Morocco
guaranteed by the Algeciras Act; . . ." It would be "against our
Moroccan Accord with France. . . . The acquisition of a coaling
station would be considered in France as disloyal conduct and

---

[10] Radolin to Bethmann Hollweg, Feb. 10, 1910, *G. P.,* vol. XXIX, no. 10497.
The speech was printed in the Tangier *Dépêche Marocaine,* Jan. 2, 1910.

[11] Schoen to Radolin, Jan. 25, 1910, *G. P.,* vol. XXIX, no. 10493; Radolin to
Bethmann Hollweg, Feb. 10, 1910, *ibid.,* no. 10497.

[12] See p. 80, *supra.*

[13] Lancken to Bethmann Hollweg, July 28, 1909, *G. P.,* vol. XXIX, no. 10463;
Schoen to Tschirschky, Nov. 3, 1909, *ibid.,* no. 10479; Radolin to Bethmann
Hollweg, Sept. 21, 1910, *ibid.,* no. 10515. According to Radolin, President
Fallières stated that "if we [Germany] today were in a position to offer him
the entire Morocco, he would refuse the gift decisively, because he did not
wish to puncture the wasp nest. . . ."—*Ibid.*

[14] Schoen's marginal note attached to the despatch, Rosen to F. O., Dec. 12,
1909, *G. P.,* vol. XXIX, no. 10488.

as a breach of our Accord. . . . The entire work of the Accord of February 9, 1909 would, through an acceptance of the offer of the sultan's about the port, be thrown over and our relations with France . . . be worse than they were at any time during the Moroccan crisis. . . ." [15] He instructed Radolin to inform Pichon, "very confidentially and only for his personal information," of the offer and the rejection.[16] The practical application of the economic clauses of the Accord of 1909 proved too great a strain, and whatever confidence and loyalty may have existed between the two foreign offices turned to mutual suspicion and mistrust.

One of the greatest contributive factors to the break-down of the Accord was the financial status of the sultan. The loan of 1904 had saddled upon the Moroccan government a debt of 62,-500,000 francs and had mortgaged 60 per cent of the customs revenue as guarantee for the payment of the service charges. The internal disorders that accompanied the struggle of Mulay Hafid for the throne had rendered collection of the internal taxes almost impossible. Consequently, Mulay Hafid found himself without funds to carry on the ordinary expenses of the government or to meet the demands of the concessionaires for payment on constructions in progress, not to mention the Casablanca indemnities nor the compensation due to France and Spain for their military expeditions. Germany, as well as France and Spain, recognized the need for a loan to the sultan;[17] and Mulay Hafid realized that if he

---

[15] Schoen's note for Bethmann Hollweg, Dec. 14, 1909, *ibid.*, no. 10489.

[16] Schoen to Radolin, Dec. 14, 1909, *ibid.*, no. 10490. The plea for secrecy Pichon evidently did not respect, for Lister, a member of the British embassy in Tangier, reported to Grey that "The French Minister told me today that there was no doubt that the Sultan had been doing all in his power during the last few months to induce the German Government to save him from the French; in return for this he had gone so far as to offer them a coaling station. The German Government, however, had resisted even that temptation . . . and had told His Shereefian Majesty that by their arrangement with France they had abandoned all political interest in Morocco. . . ."—Lister to Grey, Feb. 9, 1910, *Br. Docs.*, vol. VII, no. 163.

[17] Note of Wangenheim, Jan. 6, 1909, *G. P.*, vol. XXIV, no. 8477. Wangenheim stated that "we have the greatest interest in it, that as soon as possible Morocco receive a loan. If this does not succeed, German creditors who have furnished Morocco some 20,000,000 marks will not be able to be paid. . . ." He recognized that Morocco needed a loan and that the only thing she had to pledge was her internal taxes which would be worth nothing unless she had troops to collect

were to establish an orderly government he must solve the pressing problem of finances. Even before his recognition he had notified Regnault that he admitted the principle of French compensation for expenses of the military expedition in the Chaouya and asked Regnault to come to Fez to complete the negotiations. Regnault agreed to go after Mulay Hafid signed the Franco-Spanish recognition note.[18]

In December, 1908, Pichon approved the trip and instructed Regnault "to do nothing that is able to be interpreted as being in contradiction with the text and the spirit of the international conventions that bear our signature . . ."; to respect the independence of the Moorish empire and not let an idea arise that France was trying to establish a protectorate; to preserve economic equality but to take into consideration the special interests of France; to discuss the question of indemnity due to French nationals and compensation to France for military expenses; to settle the question of the occupation of the Chaouya and the Algerian frontier on the basis of a guarantee of Mulay Hafid for the maintenance of order.[19] Regnault went to Fez to open up negotiations while Mokri, as representative of his sultan, went to Paris to arrange for a loan.[20]

The chief points of difference arose over adjustment in the Chaouya and Oudjda sections. Mulay Hafid wished a rapid withdrawal of troops from Moroccan soil, while France insisted upon gradual withdrawal based upon effective restoration and adequate guarantee for the maintenance of order. Among these adequate guarantees was the gradual replacement of French troops by native divisions, trained and officered by French instructors. This

---

them. Germany recognized that France as the main creditor had the greatest interest, but Germany could not grant to France the right to control the finances and military organization of Morocco. He recommended an international organization, yet he was willing for France to have the major share in this organization. Notice that this note was written before the February Accord was negotiated.

[18] Regnault to Pichon, Nov. 15, 1908, *Affaires du Maroc,* 1908-1910, no. 38.

[19] Pichon to Regnault, Dec. 28, 1908, *ibid.,* no. 78.

[20] Regnault to Pichon, Jan. 31, 1909, *ibid.,* no. 107; Regnault to Pichon, Feb. 13, 1909, *ibid.,* no. 129; Saint-Aulaire to Pichon, April 13, 1909, *ibid.,* no. 171.

would mean the extension of the French military mission to wide sections of Morocco.[21] The sultan remained so obdurate that Pichon complained to the courts of Europe that Mulay Hafid was not even trying to carry out the Act of Algeciras.[22]

Settlement of the demands of France was a preliminary condition to any grant of a loan, and the continued delay of the sultan caused irritation among the foreign colonies in Morocco. A German firm, Renschausen, expressed its irritation in a forceful manner. Renschausen, who claimed he would be ruined if he were not paid, accompanied by a dragoman of the German legation, demanded payment for the work done on the port at Tangier and threatened to take possession of the works and seize funds of the Moroccan State Bank sufficient to satisfy his claims. To emphasize his demands, he raised the German flag over the jetty under question. Immediately the German legation ordered him to lower it.[23] Saint-Aulaire, in reporting the incident, commented that this would probably be followed by many acts of the same nature as it was "proof of the extreme irritation caused to foreigners by the attitude of the sultan. . . ." [24] When the Renschausen claims were submitted to the German foreign office, the German government instructed Radolin to discuss with France means for adjusting the claim.[25] Mulay Hafid told Guebbas, his minister of foreign affairs, to arrange with Renschausen about the debt;[26] and the matter was settled by an arrangement made by Mokri and a French bank, the *Credit Foncier et Agricole d'Algérie*, for the bank to pay an advance of six hundred thousand francs and take as security the lands which constituted the pledge of the Renschau-

---

[21] Regnault to Pichon, Mar. 4, 1909, *ibid.*, no. 144; Regnault to Pichon, Mar. 6, 1909, *ibid.*, no. 145; Regnault to Pichon, Mar. 14, 1909, *ibid.*, no. 150; Regnault to Pichon, Mar. 23, 1909, *ibid.*, no. 161; Pichon to Regnault, Mar. 28, 1909, *ibid.*, no. 164; Pichon to Saint-Aulaire, Nov. 6, 1909, *ibid.*, no. 333.

[22] Pichon to French representatives in London, Berlin, St. Petersburg, Vienna, Rome, Washington, Madrid, Lisbon, Brussels, and The Hague, Apr. 21, 1909, *ibid.*, no. 174.

[23] Saint-Aulaire to Pichon, Apr. 25, 1909, *ibid.*, no. 179; Cambon to Pichon, Apr. 26, 1909, *ibid.*, no. 180.

[24] Saint-Aulaire to Pichon, Apr. 25, 1909, *ibid.*, no. 179.

[25] Cambon to Pichon, Apr. 26, 1909, *ibid.*, no. 180.

[26] Saint-Aulaire to Pichon, May 1, 1909, *ibid.*, no. 184.

sen contract.[27] Germany expressed her appreciation for French help in settling the matter.[28] But the complaints of the foreign colonists increased every day.[29]

The French foreign office was besieged with complaints from its own as well as from German nationals. In a letter dated October 8, 1909, Regnault listed twenty-four grievances that French subjects had against the sultan. Among these were pillage of property belonging to French companies, arrests of French subjects and agricultural associates, forced collections of taxes to which French subjects and protégés were exempt by treaty rights, pillage of caravans, appointment to positions of caid of those known to be hostile to France, and violation of engagements taken to the Jews in Fez. France could add to her list of grievances the fact that Mulay Hafid had not returned to Abdul Aziz the personal jewels due him and had not paid his pension as he had agreed; and as these promises were guaranteed by France, Mulay Hafid's neglect only served to irritate her more.[30] By November 6, 1909, Pichon had lost patience to the extent of threatening to break off negotiations.[31]

While the negotiations were continuing their slow, tedious course, conditions in Morocco grew worse, banditry continued, and rumors of Mulay Hafid's barbarity in treatment of his recalcitrant subjects called forth an interpellation in the French chamber of deputies. On November 22, 1909, Émile Merle urged the government to undertake more aggressive action against Mulay Hafid.[32] Jaurès, socialist deputy, thereupon, delivered an attack on the entire Moroccan policy of the government and opposed any aggressive measures, since the conditions in Morocco were largely due to the action of the French government in pressing on the sultan a loan the conditions of which would discredit him in the eyes of his people. He stressed the fact that Mulay Hafid could not main-

[27] Pichon to Saint-Aulaire, May 5, 1909, *ibid.*, no. 188; Pichon to Berckheim, Aug. 5, 1909, *ibid.*, no. 242.

[28] Berckheim to Pichon, Aug. 8, 1909, *ibid.*, no. 244.

[29] Saint-Aulaire to Pichon, May 1, 1909, *ibid.*, no. 184.

[30] Regnault to Pichon, Oct. 8, 1909, *ibid.*, no. 314.

[31] Pichon to Saint-Aulaire, Nov. 6, 1909, *ibid.*, no. 333.

[32] *Annales de la chambre des députés,* session extraordinaire de 1909, vol. I, pp. 686-695.

tain order unless he could free his land from foreign troops and that the indemnity question would mean continued occupation and destruction of the sultan's power.[33] The next day Pichon answered his critics by explaining that all the powers were interested in the loan and that the nationals of all governments protested "with vehemence and demand with vivacity the reimbursements of sums which, for a long time, are due them. . . ." The loan could not be delayed longer, he stated, and "It would not be without peril for the Moroccan government to have illusions on this point. . . ." [34]

The formula for an agreement had been worked out as early as August 16, 1909,[35] and was accepted on January 15, 1910, by the Moroccan representatives in Paris;[36] but when the agreement was sent to Mulay Hafid for ratification he refused to sign.[37] On January 28 Radolin informed the foreign office that Tardieu had remarked that France would have to use energetic measures to force the sultan to accept the loan.[38] Schoen, thereupon, replied that he feared that if France used force to secure ratification renewed disorders would break out in Morocco. He recommended that France, "before undertaking measures of force would lay before the signatory Powers, who, so much as is known here, are interested collectively in the quick completion of the loan, the proposal, through their embassies in Tangier, to press urgently on the sultan in the interest of the loan. Consuls in Fez must support the démarche. Should the sultan not yield to their pressure, contrary to expectation, then the use of force would appear before public opinion of Europe far more plausible. . . ." [39] Pichon replied that Tardieu was always wanting to undertake military measures, but that he, Pichon, had no idea of doing so, for he believed Mulay Hafid would sign the loan.[40]

---

[33] *Ibid.,* pp. 695-702.   [34] *Ibid.,* pp. 735-741.

[35] Pichon to Saint-Aulaire, Aug. 16, 1909, *Affaires du Maroc,* 1908-1910, no. 249.   [36] Pichon to Saint-Aulaire, Jan. 15, 1910, *ibid.,* no. 371.

[37] Pichon to Regnault, Feb. 10, 1910, *ibid.,* no. 380; London *Times,* Feb. 12, 1910 (Paris correspondent).

[38] Radolin to F. O., Jan. 28, 1910, *G. P.,* vol. XXIX, no. 10494.

[39] Schoen to Radolin, Jan. 29, 1910, *ibid.,* no. 10495. German interests in the loan were summarized in the London *Times,* Jan. 8, 1910 (Berlin correspondent).

[40] Radolin to F. O., Jan. 31, 1910, *G. P.,* vol. XXIX, no. 10496.

A month had passed and still the sultan delayed ratification. On February 16 Regnault proposed to Pichon that the sultan be instructed to ratify in forty-eight hours or the French colony in Fez would be recalled. He thought it advisable to include in this ultimatum demands for satisfaction of claims of French nationals injured by the disorders of the past year, provisions for the execution of the agreement of January 15, and explicit demands for the dismissal of Turkish instructors in the Moorish army.[41] Pichon wired Regnault, February 17, that the council of ministers approved his propositions and authorized him, if he did not receive official ratification by the next morning, to send to the sultan the ultimatum relative to the treaty.[42] Not until the eighteenth did Pichon reply to Regnault's suggestions for additional demands. He then authorized him to inform the sultan that the French military mission would not resume its work until the Turkish instructors were dismissed. Other questions were to be discussed later.[43] Regnault had included all his demands in his original instructions to Gaillard, French consul at Fez,[44] but then modified them in accordance with Pichon's letter.[45]

It seems that Pichon had notified the powers of Europe, on February 17, of the action taken by France and asked the governments to agree that their nationals leave Fez at the same time as the French. To this note he added, "the Government of the Republic will not recoil, if it need be, before employing coercive means in order to assure the respect of its rights by the *maghzen*. . . ."[46] The response of the powers was sympathetic with France. Spain

---

[41] Regnault to Pichon, Feb. 16, 1910, *Affaires du Maroc,* 1908-1910, no. 391. Due to the danger attached to the service of French instructors in the *mehallas* of the sultan, Pichon had instructed General Mangin, in command of the mission, to prevent French officers accompanying the *mehallas* on their campaigns. At that time the sultan was faced with insurrection of the tribes and to supply the deficiency had employed a Turkish captain and ten subordinate officers.—Tardieu, *op. cit.,* pp. 130-154.

[42] Pichon to Regnault, Feb. 17, 1910, *Affaires du Maroc,* 1908-1910, no. 394; London *Times,* Feb. 21, 1910 (Tangier correspondent).

[43] Pichon to Regnault, Feb. 18, 1910, *Affaires du Maroc,* 1908-1910, no. 398.

[44] Regnault to Pichon, Feb. 17, 1910, *ibid.,* no. 396.

[45] Regnault to Pichon, Feb. 18, 1910, *ibid.,* no. 399.

[46] Pichon to the French representatives in Berlin, London, Rome, St. Petersburg, Vienna, Madrid, Washington, Brussels, The Hague, Lisbon, Stockholm, Feb. 17, 1910, *ibid.,* no. 395.

instructed her consul at Fez to work in concert with his French and English colleagues, and if the French colony withdrew, he was to inform the *maghzen* that he considered that security was not sufficiently guaranteed and that he would leave Fez with his colony.[47] Italy replied that she was instructing her consul to work in concert with the French.[48] Aehrenthal received the communication of the French ambassador in a sympathetic manner and expressed confidence in France's not surpassing her rights as conceived in international agreements.[49] The British government submitted the question of withdrawal of the British colony to the judgment of its local representative at Tangier,[50] and upon his advice instructed the British consul at Fez to support his French colleague and leave Fez "if the sultan proves obdurate and a similar step is taken by the other Powers. . . ."[51] Bethmann Hollweg stated that according to the Accord of 1909, Germany was not politically interested and would make no difficulty for France in her move in Morocco, especially as an early conclusion of the loan would be of advantage to Germany.[52] Berckheim, French chargé d'affaires in Berlin, reported that Schoen had expressed his personal opinion that the German colony "ought to leave Fez in the case where all the other colonies did so";[53] but Schoen's instructions to Rosen were less emphatic. He ordered Rosen to instruct Vassel "to stress

---

[47] Révoil to Pichon, Feb. 19, 1910, *ibid.*, no. 409. Bunsen reported the Spanish foreign minister as saying that Spanish withdrawal "would be represented rather as an act of prudence in case of possible native resentment against Europeans than as a political demonstration against the Sultan. . . ."—Bunsen to Grey, Feb. 19, 1910, *Br. Docs.*, vol. VII, no. 164.

[48] Barrère to Pichon, Feb. 19, 1910, *Affaires du Maroc*, 1908-1910, no. 406.

[49] Crozier to Pichon, Feb. 19, 1910, *ibid.*, no. 407.

[50] Grey to Lister, Feb. 19, 1910, *Br. Docs.*, vol. VII, no. 165; Cambon to Pichon, Feb. 19, 1910, *Affaires du Maroc*, 1908-1910, no. 400.

[51] Grey to Lister, Feb. 21, 1910, *Br. Docs.*, vol. VII, no. 167. Lister had quoted Regnault as saying that he "considered it imperative that the Sultan should be made to realize that complete solidarity existed amongst the Powers: moreover, he thought a general exodus advisable on grounds of prudence, should the Sultan remain obdurate. Were any Europeans to remain in Fez he considered it not improbable that the Sultan might excite popular fanaticism and cause a disaster. . . ."—Lister to Grey, Feb. 21, 1910, *ibid.*, no. 166.

[52] Bethmann Hollweg to William II, Feb. 19, 1910, *G. P.*, vol. XXIX, no. 10502.

[53] Berckheim to Pichon, Feb. 19, 1910, *Affaires du Maroc*, 1908-1910, no. 403.

anew urgently, before the sultan . . . our interest in a quick completion of the loan. . . ." [54]

To this, Rosen replied in a typically Rosen style. "I regret the suddenness of the French proceedings that places us before a *fait accompli* in case Mulay Hafid does not readily yield. A general exodus of Europeans from Fez injures only the Germans, since they alone are seriously represented in the commerce of that place. On the other hand, the démarche of the French consul, if from the beginning it could have been supported by the other three consuls, would have had the greatest possibility of success. . . ." He reported, however, that he had carried out Schoen's instructions.[55] The threatened withdrawal of the French colony was evidently sufficient pressure, for on February 21 Mokri announced that he had been empowered to ratify the treaty.[56]

For over a year, Regnault had worried with the task of adjusting the financial needs of the *maghzen* and of settling the outstanding grievances that hampered friendly relations between the two countries. The final culmination of his work seemed at hand; but he feared that the dilatory policy adopted by the sultan might be repeated and ultimately destroy all that he had attained. He, therefore, on February 21, repeated his plea that ratification should not take place until certain measures that would render the treaty effective—as for example, provisions for auditing the debt of the *maghzen* and for establishing control of the mortgaged revenues—were accepted, and until the question of the Turkish military instructors was settled.[57] Pichon, now convinced, instructed Gaillard to carry out Regnault's suggestions[58] and informed the powers of Europe of the situation.[59] The sultan naturally wished some explanation for the additional de-

[54] Schoen to Rosen, Feb. 19, 1910, *G. P.,* vol. XXIX, no. 10501. Note of Erkert, Feb. 23, 1910, *ibid.,* no. 10504 also stressed the interest of Germany in the completion of the loan.

[55] Rosen to F. O., Feb. 20, 1910, *ibid.,* no. 10503.

[56] Pichon to Regnault, Feb. 21, 1909, *Affaires du Maroc,* 1908-1910, no. 412.

[57] Regnault to Pichon, Feb. 21, 1910, *ibid.,* no. 413.

[58] Pichon to Regnault, Feb. 22, 1910, *ibid.,* no. 414.

[59] Pichon to French representatives in London, St. Petersburg, Rome, Vienna, Madrid, Berlin, Washington, Brussels, The Hague, Lisbon, Stockholm, Feb. 22, 1910, *ibid.,* no. 415.

mands since he had ratified the treaty,[60] but with no outside support to aid him he was forced to give way. On March 1, 1910,
Pichon announced that the sultan had agreed to all the points asked
for by France. "All the questions which had made the object of the
ultimatum carried to Fez are solved to our entire satisfaction.
. . ." [61] On March 4, 1910, the Accord was signed.[62]

The treaty consisted of three distinct parts. The first dealt
with the Chaouya. France agreed to evacuate the Chaouya when
the *maghzen* had installed in this region a Moroccan force of
fifteen hundred men, formed and instructed under the French
military mission, for the maintenance of order. The *maghzen*
agreed to keep up the telegraphs, bridges, and other public works
begun by France. A penalty of two and one-half millions was imposed on the tribes of the Chaouya for their attitude in the Casablanca affair, the money to be used for improvements in the port
of Casablanca. France expressed willingness for taxes for this
penalty to be levied on her protégés if the other governments
would permit such a levy on theirs.[63] The *maghzen* was to pay
the expense of the French military occupation of the Chaouya.
France stated that she "had never ceased considering the city of
Casablanca as Moroccan territory and does not have the intention
of exercising there definitive occupation . . . ," but that she
would withdraw when she considered that the organization of the
Chaouya would assure maintenance of order and when the expense of the military occupation had been paid.

The second division treated of the Algerian frontier. France
agreed to evacuate Oudjda, Beni-Snassen, Bou Anane, Bou Denib,
but would hold Doui Menia, Oulad-Djeru, and Berguent. In this
manner, French troops were to be withdrawn from the entire
northern section of the frontier and most of the southern. A Mo-

[60] Regnault to Pichon, Feb. 26, 1910, *ibid.*, no. 420, enclosure Gaillard to Regnault, Feb. 23, 1910.

[61] Pichon to French representatives in London, Madrid, Berlin, Rome, St.
Petersburg, Vienna, Washington, Lisbon, Brussels, Stockholm, The Hague, and
Berne, Mar. 1, 1910, *ibid.*, no. 423.

[62] Pichon to Regnault, Mar. 4, 1910, *ibid.*, no. 426.

[63] France took no active measures in this respect, and the proposal died of
inertia, which leaves the impression that France was only making a courteous
gesture.

roccan high commissioner was to associate with the French to
carry out the accords of 1901 and 1902 relative to joint action
for the maintenance of peace on the frontier. The evacuation of
Bou Denib and Bou Anane was to take place as soon as the sultan could guarantee the safety of the caravans.

The third section dealt with the Moroccan loan. Morocco
owed 80,000,000 francs to various creditors and 70,000,000
francs to France for military expenses. France proposed to secure
for the sultan a loan of 80,000,000 francs by means of an annuity
of about 4,660,000 francs for seventy-five years. France would
not include the entire sum due her but only an annuity of 2,740,-
000 francs. The resources to be used to guarantee the loan were
the customs, after the expense of administration and the amount
reserved for the loan of 1904 were deducted, a monopoly of tobacco, the taxes on markets and the income tax in the cities on the
coast, half the tax on property in the cities, and returns from
the royal property. The details of the loan were to be worked out
later and Mokri was to receive the necessary authorization for
this function.[64]

On March 21 Pichon reported that the loan had been completed.
The Moroccan State Bank was to lend the government 90,000,000
francs bearing 5 per cent interest, amortizable in seventy-five
years. This loan was to liquidate all engagements contracted by
the *maghzen* prior to June 30, 1909, to pay the Casablanca indemnities, the credits due the Mendelsohn Bank and the French consortium, advances due to the Moroccan State Bank, public works
executed or in course of execution in the ports of Tangier, Casablanca, and Safi, works proposed for Larache, indemnities for
expropriating the tobacco monopoly, the loans on the crown jewels, and the semi-annuity on the loan of 1910. The guarantees
were the customs, except the 5 per cent reserved to the sultan,
rent from the tobacco and sulphur monopoly, income tax and tax
on markets, revenues from the domain property in all ports and

---

[64] Pichon to Regnault, March 4, 1910, *Affaires du Maroc,* 1908-1910, no. 426;
Pichon to Saint-Aulaire, Aug. 16, 1909, *ibid.,* no. 249; Pichon to Saint-Aulaire,
Dec. 25, 1909, *ibid.,* no. 360; Pichon to Saint-Aulaire, Dec. 26, 1909, enclosure
Moroccan ambassador to Pichon, *ibid.,* no. 361.

in a radius of ten kilometers outside the ports, and that part of the urban taxes that went to the central government. The control of the customs was the same as agreed to in 1907 and was now extended to include collection of all taxes mortgaged for the loan.[65] On May 13, 1910, Pichon reported that the contract for the loan was signed by El Mokri and the Moroccan State Bank.[66] In addition to the treaty itself, France, carrying out the suggestions of Regnault, secured the dismissal of the Turkish instructors in the army, the promise of Mulay Hafid that none other than French instructors were to be employed and that the French commander was to become the instructor-in-chief of the empire, and the appointment of a French counselor to advise the minister of finance in all matters relating to public works, mines, and sanitation projects.[67]

The Franco-Moroccan agreement of 1910 was subjected to criticism from the time of its conception. Jaurès had consistently fought the measures in the chamber of deputies and again repeated his warnings to the government on the day Pichon announced the completion of the treaty. Jaurès opposed imperialism in all its forms and he saw only too clearly that as Mulay Hafid became more and more entangled with foreign powers, his people would revolt against him as they had against Abdul Aziz, and France would be led into a situation from which she could not extricate herself without taking aggressive action. He also warned the government that any move of France would be countered by one from Spain.[68] Opposition to the treaty was expressed in the Reichstag, even before it was completed, on the grounds that the conditions attached to the loan overstepped the Algeciras Act and infringed

---

[65] Pichon to Regnault, Mar. 21, 1910, *ibid.,* no. 439; Piquet, *op. cit.,* pp. 347-352; Tardieu, *op. cit.,* pp. 119-129.

[66] Pichon to M. de Billy, chargé d'affaires in Tangier, May 13, 1910, *Affaires du Maroc,* 1908-1910, no. 458.

[67] Pichon to French representatives in London, Madrid, Berlin, Rome, St. Petersburg, Vienna, Washington, Lisbon, Brussels, Stockholm, The Hague, and Berne, Mar. 1, 1910, *ibid.,* no. 423.

[68] *Annales de la chambre des députés,* session ordinaire de 1910, vol. I, pp. 2101-2107. Spain completed her agreement with Morocco November 19, 1910, by which she secured sixty-five millions of pesetas against mining returns.—*Affaires du Maroc,* 1910-1912, no. 21.

on the sovereignty of the sultan.[69] From the opposite side of the Rhine came the criticism that the treaty failed to uphold the rights of France, that it was a sign of weakness and was so interpreted by the sultan.[70] Tardieu criticized severely the part of the treaty that dealt with the Algerian frontier. General Lyautey had presented a detailed program for the pacification of the area and had recommended the establishment of advanced posts in the Oudjda district.[71] Instead of following his recommendation, Pichon had arranged to evacuate the posts then held by France. Ever since her treaty of 1902, France, conjointly with Morocco, had had the right to maintain peace on the frontier,[72] and this evacuation was, so Tardieu believed, "indicative of feebleness and so interpreted by the Sultan. . . ." France "had under diverse conditions engaged to evacuate Chaouya, where she did not possess title to stay; the north zone of the Algerian frontier where it was not established that she ought to leave; the south zone of this frontier, where it was certain that she had, in virtue of the accords of 1902, the right to stay. France, on the other part, granted to the Sultan a loan which ought to permit of liquidation of the past but not of organizing for the future. . . ." [73] Viewed from the standpoint of French imperialism, the promise to evacuate territory once secured seemed a retreat which would renounce the work of French officials in Morocco; and to some it was a sign of failure to profit by the political provisions of the Accord of 1909.[74]

Viewed from the standpoint of Morocco, the treaty gave to her the promise of ultimate withdrawal of French troops, but a promise based on the organization of an effective system of police. That condition Morocco could not fulfil unless she had the means to pay her troops and the force with which to collect the internal taxes. The conditions attached to the loan mortgaged the resources of the sultan to such an extent that it is impossible to see how one could expect the sultan to meet the contingencies of his government. The past debts of the *maghzen* were to be paid, but there was no provision for future obligations. Although the contract for

[69] Kanitz before the Reichstag, *Stenographische Berichte des Reichstags,* vol. 260, p. 2130.   [70] Tardieu, *op. cit.,* p. 96; Caillaux, *op. cit.,* p. 44.
[71] Tardieu, *op. cit.,* p. 107.   [72] See p. 29, *supra.*   [73] *Op. cit.,* pp. 95-100.
[74] *Ibid.,* pp. 119-129, 156; Caillaux, *op. cit.,* pp. 43-45.

the loan was not signed until May 13, 1910, by the following November Mokri was again in Paris trying to secure a new loan to relieve the government from the pressing demands for funds, especially funds with which to pay its troops. El Mokri was handicapped in his negotiation for this loan by the general revolt raging in Morocco and by German opposition to the loan. Germany had accepted the loan of 1910 and had aided France in her efforts to secure its ratification, but she opposed the loan of 1911. She objected to the new loan on the ground that it would burden Moroccan finances too heavily. Unquestionably this fact influenced her decision; but it is also true that Germany approved the loan of 1910 because her nationals benefited directly through payments made to German concessionaires and because she hoped to share in a lucrative economic program after Moroccan finances had been adjusted. By 1911 her expectations had been shattered, for the many efforts to turn to practical account the economic clauses of the Accord of 1909 had failed.

When the February Accord of 1909 was signed, Germany suggested a technical negotiation to put it into practical application. France agreed and selected as her representative M. Guiot, director of the Moroccan State Bank and controller of Moorish customs, while Germany appointed Erkert and Langwerth of the foreign office to conduct the negotiations for her. The negotiations lasted from March 24 to April 1, 1909, and formed the basis for the *aide mémoire* submitted to France by the German government in early June.[75] Guiot stated that he placed the interview on the basis not of "the preponderance of our political interest but on that of the political renunciation of Germany," and that Erkert

---

[75] Tardieu, *op. cit.*, pp. 27, 42; Caillaux, *op. cit.*, p. 47; Antonin Débidour, *Historie diplomatique de l'Europe depuis le Congrès de Berlin jusqu'à nos jours*, vol. II, p. 138. Tardieu and Débidour give the date of the presentation of the German note as June 2; Caillaux gives it as June 9. The only mention of Guiot's mission given in *G. P.* is in a footnote to a despatch, Stemrich to Rosen, May 17, 1909, *G. P.*, vol. XXIX, no. 10458. In this footnote, the editors stated that the negotiations took place between March 24 and March 27 and that they led to a far-reaching understanding, but, of course, not to a formal agreement about economic matters. The financial question was not discussed in this footnote, and the matter of economic concessions other than mining concessions was mentioned only slightly. Instead the mining concessions occupied almost the entire attention of the editors. The mining situation will be discussed later.

made no changes dealing with such terms as "political disinterest," and "political renunciation." [76]

Guiot's mission involved a discussion of financial questions, administration of revenues, public works, and later a mining law. One of the first points discussed was the question of the loan then under negotiation between France and Morocco. According to Tardieu, Germany presented a list of Moroccan debts, but omitted from the list the war indemnities demanded by France and Spain for their respective expeditions into the Chaouya and Riff territories. At the same time she asked preferential treatment for the claims of the Renschausen firm. Germany recognized that the war indemnities should be paid, but claimed that all other debts should be paid first. Tardieu considered that Germany granted to France a very valuable concession in regard to the loan in that she recognized the preponderant interest of France in the financial and political order of Morocco and agreed that France might either guarantee the loan or hold a majority share in any international organization issuing the loan. Germany was willing to concede this point even though she recognized that a French guarantee of a Moroccan loan would inevitably lead to increase of French political power within the Sherifian empire.[77] One of the chief criticisms Tardieu made against the Franco-Moroccan loan of 1910 was the fact that France did not take this opportunity to guarantee it, although he considered that the control of the customs guaranteed in it did grant France a basis for political action.[78]

More important in its immediate application than the financial agreement was the negotiation relative to economic concessions. In this field Germany wished to substitute private contract for the system of adjudication established by the Act of Algeciras. In this manner syndicates composed of German and French firms would have the greater chance of securing concessions. France wished to admit into the syndicates thus formed English and Spanish firms. Germany was willing to consent to this on the condition that the share allotted to English and Spanish firms would be taken from the French quota. The German note was presented

---

[76] Pichon before the senate, Feb. 8, 1912, *Annales du senat*, session ordinaire de 1912, vol. LXXXI, p. 230.

[77] Tardieu, *op. cit.*, pp. 27-34.   [78] *Ibid.*, p. 33.

to France in early June and France did not answer until October 14, and then her answer was evasive, especially as regards the economic concessions. The German note stated that Germany wished to see formed syndicates of German and French firms to bid for large "concessions with the certitude of obtaining them," while the French response read that "They would see with favor some groups forming themselves . . . between entrepreneurs of different nationalities . . . and notably between French and German houses. . . ." The German note continued, "The French government would have the faculty of associating in an enterprise in Morocco . . . also English and Spanish. . . . But this association would be at the expense of the French quota. . . ." The French reply stated, "The French government desires, moreover, as the German note mentioned, in as large measure as possible, to have English and Spanish industrials take part, the determination of the part of each nationality . . . being left to interests. . . ." There was to be joint action of the two legations in Tangier in order to secure their mutual interests.[79]

Tardieu and Caillaux agreed that this arrangement was the establishment of an economic condominium between France and Germany. As Tardieu expressed it, third parties might be invited to the feast, but they were to receive the crumbs, while only France and Germany were to sit at the table.[80] Caillaux stated that "Deliberately we had bound ourselves on the ground of privilege and monopoly. . . ." [81] Tardieu considered that "Politically it [the agreement] did not offer us a serious advantage other than the possibility of guaranteeing the Moroccan loans . . . not excluded . . . in the Act of Algeciras, but which had been, without agreement with Germany, of difficult utility. . . . Economically it placed before the French government . . . the question of the future rule of Morocco on the basis of a general and exclusive association of French and German interests. . . ." Tardieu pointed out that the association of the two legations before the *maghzen* was political in nature and might lead to a Franco-German political condominium.[82] France recognized the preferential position of the Renschausen claims and the Larache port

---

[79] *Ibid.*, pp. 33-43; Caillaux, *op. cit.*, pp. 47-50; Débidour, *op. cit.*, vol. II, p. 138.   [80] *Op. cit.*, p. 29.   [81] *Op. cit.*, p. 50.   [82] *Op. cit.*, p. 35.

expenses in the Franco-Moroccan loan; and Germany was willing
to renounce any claim to share in the works at Larache and
Tangier.[83] But the main details of economic concessions were not
completed, and direct negotiations between business firms working
with the approval of their respective governments resulted finally
in the formation of two important syndicates.

A Society for the Monopoly of Tobacco was formed with France
holding 36½ per cent of the stock, Germany 17 per cent, Spain
17 per cent, and all others 5 per cent; and to this Society the monopoly of tobacco was granted December 3, 1910. The more important syndicate was the Moroccan Society of Public Works
formed February 17, 1910, with France holding 50 per cent of the
stock, Germany 26 per cent, England 6½ per cent, Spain 5 per
cent, Italy 2½ per cent, Belgium 2½ per cent, Sweden 2½ per
cent, Portugal 1½ per cent.[84] The board of directors was composed of six Frenchmen, four Germans, one Englishman, and one
Spaniard. The presiding officer was French and was to hold a deciding vote. The purpose of the Society was to study in Morocco
all concessions of public works and of business related directly or
indirectly to them. "The obtaining, the exploitation, the cession
or the share, in whole or in part . . . of all concessions or enterprises of work or public services in Morocco, notably in that which
concerns the ports, roads, canals, railroads . . . and all that
which is attached directly or indirectly to it . . ." was listed as
the scope of the work of the Society. The division of the work between the participating firms was to be placed by the Society in
adjudication. The important and secondary works would be
awarded in proportion to the capital invested by each nationality
and in so far as possible according to the national interest in the
district where the work was to be.[85]

The Moroccan Society of Public Works studied various projects such as water concessions, tramways in Tangier, installations
of lighthouses on the Moroccan coast, and the organization of a

---

[83] For the recognition of the Renschausen and Larache port claims, see pp.
89-90, 96, *supra*. For German concessions, see editor's footnote, Stemrich to
Rosen, May 17, 1909, *G. P.*, vol. XXIX, no. 10458.

[84] Tardieu, *op. cit.*, pp. 61-64; Caillaux, *op. cit.*, pp. 50-52; Albin, *op. cit.*,
p. 127; Piquet, *op. cit.*, p. 201; Raymon Poincaré, *The Origins of the War*, p. 89.

[85] Tardieu, *op. cit.*, p. 62.

network of railroads. None of these materialized;[86] instead, they were killed either by English protest, by the bankruptcy of the *maghzen,* or by the friction that continued between France and Germany. The concession relative to lighthouses came nearest realization, but was crushed by the English protest that her share was too small and by her demand that the concession be submitted to open competitive bidding according to the provisions of the Act of Algeciras. England consistently refused to promise to withdraw all English bids except those included in the Society of Public Works, and this refusal blocked the program of the Society.[87] The bankrupt condition of the government had a great deal to do with preventing the actual development of any concession. The loan of 1910 was used to pay the debts of the *maghzen.* The loan of 1911 included provision for public works; but the *maghzen* was not to receive that loan in time to save the land from French exploitation.

The real cause of the breakdown of the Accord was the failure of Germany and France to agree on the practical questions which arose when specific concessions were under consideration. France wished to limit the work of the Society to construction and not include operation of the work after construction. Germany took the diametrically opposite view and interpreted the agreement so as to include operation as well as construction of each concession. France claimed such an interpretation was contrary to the Act of Algeciras.[88] Tardieu protested this interpretation because, according to his quotation, the charter of the Society clearly included construction and operation. He insisted that the French foreign office should have objected at the time of the creation of the Society if it deemed this provision contrary to the Act of Algeciras. Once having accepted the charter, France was not in a position to protest the use of this right.[89] France and Germany also differed in

[86] *Ibid.,* pp. 68-74; Caillaux, *op. cit.,* pp. 50-52.

[87] Tardieu, *op. cit.,* p. 66; Caillaux, *op. cit.,* p. 51; Feis, *op. cit.,* p. 417; Grey to Bertie, March 16, 1911, *Br. Docs.,* vol. VII, no. 195; Notes of Crowe, W. Langley, Nicolson, and Grey to note communicated by Paul Cambon, Mar. 14, 1911, *ibid.,* no. 192. Crowe stated that France knew that England had "formally refused to give any support to an international syndicate of which France holds 50%, Germany 30%, and Great Britain 5%. . . ."

[88] Tardieu, *op. cit.,* pp. 68-74; Caillaux, *op. cit.,* p. 51; Feis, *op. cit.,* pp. 415-417.

[89] *Op. cit.,* pp. 70-72.

8

their interpretation of the extent of the work of the Society. Germany wished to grant to the Society all concessions issued in Morocco; France wished to limit this grant and especially to restrict its work in the field of railroad construction. According to Feis, the real reason France failed to support the monopolistic interpretation of Germany was "probably a dislike of giving German enterprise any real foothold in Morocco through this condominium. Monopolistic support of this syndicate would have meant constant discussion with the Wilhelmstrasse and a loss of freedom which the French Government wished to retain. In certain enterprises it was judged desirable that Germany should have no participation. . . ." [90] The particular enterprises that France wished to reserve were, in the main, certain railroad concessions.

In the game of economic imperialism railroads usually occupy a position of prime importance. The fate of the Moroccan Society of Public Works hung upon its success in solving the ticklish question of railroad concessions, and upon the fate of the Society hung the fate of the Accord of 1909. It was for this reason, perhaps, that France delayed approaching the question until December, 1910. The French plan, the first evidence of which appeared in that month, involved the construction of two lines, the Casablanca-Settat and the Oudjda-Taourirt lines, both of which she designated as military roads in an effort to avoid submitting the projects either to competitive bidding, as provided by the Act of Algeciras, or to the scheme of coöperation arranged for in the Accord of 1909.[91] On December 21, 1910, the German embassy in Paris presented to the French foreign office a note stating that foreign merchants were not favorable to the Casablanca-Settat road and considered that at all events the project should be adjudicated according to the Act of Algeciras.[92] France replied that the expense of the road was not to be charged to the Moroccan treasury but to French capital, and that the road was to be built as a military road to facilitate the movement of troops in the Chaouya where she was engaged in the task of pacification. At the

---

[90] *Op. cit.,* p. 417.

[91] Pichon to Cambon, Jan. 7, 1911, *Affaires du Maroc,* 1910-1912, no. 34.

[92] Pichon to Cambon, Jan. 7, 1911, *ibid.,* no. 34, enclosure I, note sent by the German embassy in Paris Dec. 21, 1910.

same time she expected the road to aid the commerce of the area.[93] She promised, indeed, that the line "would be open without differential tariffs and without any inequality of treatment," except in so far as military needs required preferential treatment.[94]

On January 19, 1911, and again on January 23, Schoen discussed the situation with Pichon and agreed to recognize the military character of the Casablanca-Settat line, but refused to grant the same attributes to the Oudjda-Taourirt road. Pichon pointed out that France was in military occupation of both Oudjda and Taourirt, and that it would be impossible for any power other than France to construct any railroad near the Algerian frontier. He also claimed that the Franco-Moroccan agreement gave to France the right to construct such a line.[95] On February 2 Schoen again spoke of the railroad question and at that time made clearer the basis of German opposition to the eastern line. Germany, he stated, would not oppose the military construction of the Chaouya line, nor of the line from the frontier to Oudjda, but the prolongation of that line to Taourirt was too great an extension of the military idea and would have to be submitted to adjudication according to the Act of Algeciras. Otherwise a special accord was needed. Schoen favored an arrangement with the Moroccan Society of Public Works. Pichon pointed out that as the sultan was bankrupt, the roads could not be constructed as a commercial venture open to competitive bidding, but he agreed to negotiate the question with the German foreign office.[96]

Cambon's report to Pichon on February 2 expressed more clearly the German viewpoint, and exposed the deep suspicion with which Germany viewed any French proposal in Morocco. She attached great importance to the Oudjda-Taourirt line, not so much because of its integral value, but because it could easily form the beginning link in a line from the Algerian frontier by way of Oudjda, Fez, and Meknez, to Casablanca. If she were to grant to France the right to build the first segment as a military road, Germany feared a precedent would be established which France

---

[93] *Ibid.,* enclosure II, note sent to the German embassy in Paris, Dec. 25, 1910.
[94] Pichon to Cambon, Jan. 19, 1911, *ibid.,* no. 45.
[95] Pichon to Cambon, Jan. 19, 1911, *ibid.,* no. 45; Pichon to Cambon, Jan. 23, 1911, *ibid.,* no. 49.　　　　[96] Pichon to Cambon, Feb. 2, 1911, *ibid.,* no. 56.

would call into play with each extension of the line and thus avoid both the application of the Act of Algeciras and the Accord of 1909.[97] No mention had been made of such an extension of the road; but Germany foresaw that France, in control of a military road that tied the Algerian frontier to the Atlantic ocean and traversed the valuable Sebou-Moulouya Plain, would be in a position to control the political as well as the economic destiny of Morocco. Cambon recognized the difficulty in harmonizing French and German interests and did not believe that France could arrange for the construction of the road on principles laid down in the Accord of 1909, because of the "dangerous distrust of the extension that we wish to give to this diplomatic arrangement on economic matters. . . ." He also believed that "the operation and control of railroads ought to be considered as having a political character; but their construction does not seem to be able to escape the rule of adjudication such as is provided by the Act of Algeciras. . . ." He then advised Pichon to point out to Schoen that if the Moroccan Society of Public Works were to construct the Oudjda-Taourirt line, then "in case where the railroad from Taourirt would be prolonged some day, it will be provided in the same conditions and that no German society will come forth to thwart the Moroccan Society. . . ." [98] Pichon picked up this suggestion and instructed Cambon, February 26, to secure from Kiderlen consent to the proviso that if the Moroccan Society took part in the building of the first segment of the eastern line, no German company would bid on any later extension of the line.[99] On March 1 Kiderlen agreed to this proposal on the condition that France make a reciprocal agreement relative to French companies.[100]

Schoen had earlier presented to Pichon a note explaining the German attitude on the entire question. Germany wished to solve the entire problem of railroad building as one problem and not treat each small segment as a separate question. In this manner, misunderstanding could best be avoided, for the terms of any arrangement made with regard to any segment would affect the

[97] Cambon to Pichon, Feb. 3, 1911, *ibid.*, no. 57.
[98] *Ibid.*   [99] Pichon to Cambon, Feb. 26, 1911, *ibid.*, no. 71.
[100] Cambon to Pichon, Mar. 1, 1911, *ibid.*, no. 75.

decision of all sections. For instance, France could easily create a monopoly through her construction of the Oudjda-Taourirt line by the simple process of using rails and materials not produced in Germany. All such questions needed to be settled before any construction was undertaken. Moreover, Germany wanted the line from Tangier to Fez instead of the Casablanca-Fez line to be constructed first. Consequently Berlin attached great importance to a solution that dealt with the homogeneity of materials to be used, priority of the Tangier-Fez line, and "compensation to be reserved to Germany industry in return for the adhesion of the German government to the construction, without adjudication of the military lines in the Chaouya and in the region of Oudjda." [101]

In conformity with these principles, Kiderlen, on March 2, presented a detailed proposal for solving the railroad problem. The French military administration was to coöperate with the Moroccan Society of Public Works in the construction of the Oudjda-Taourirt line and was to entrust the construction of the Casablanca-Settat line to an entrepreneur who, in turn, was to promise to work with the Moroccan Society of Public Works. On both lines material such as "neither German industry nor French industry may be excluded from the possibility of making bids" was to be used. The line from Tangier to Fez was to be submitted to public adjudication as soon as possible and before any other line except the two above mentioned. The French and German governments were to use their influence non-officially to obtain railroad concessions for the Moroccan Society of Public Works. Equality of treatment was to be awarded to all nationals in the use of all roads constructed.[102]

These proposals arrived just as Pichon was replaced by Cruppi as minister of foreign affairs. To Cruppi the point by which the two governments agreed to use their influence to secure concessions for the Moroccan Society seemed unwise, for it would inevitably bring forth protest from England and Spain, as they were already dissatisfied with their percentage allotment in the Moroccan Society of Public Works.[103] Cambon explained that the clause

---

[101] Pichon to Cambon, Feb. 26, 1911, *ibid.*, no. 71, enclosure, note of Schoen, undated, p. 105.   [102] Cambon to Pichon, Mar. 2, 1911, *ibid.*, no. 77.
[103] Cruppi to Cambon, Mar. 4, 1911, *ibid.*, no. 84.

under question merely provided that Germany and France use
their influence upon their own nationals in order to avoid competition from outside French and German firms and did not affect
English or Spanish nationals. He optimistically believed that England and Spain would recognize the great advantage to commerce
which would result from the construction of railroads and of the
Tangier-Fez line in particular, and consequently he did not expect
a protest from either nation. He stated that the object of the
Moroccan Society was to rid France of German competition by
granting her a limited satisfaction, and that the entire North
African program of France was tied to this question of the
Tangier-Fez line; for if Germany did not receive satisfaction on
this question, she would block the entire railroad program that
France was anxious to carry out.[104]

Conferences on March 5, 6, and 7 resulted in a revised project
which varied slightly from Kiderlen's original proposal. The proposal relative to the Oudjda-Taourirt line was not changed, but
that relative to the Casablanca-Settat line was altered so as to
obligate the entrepreneur who secured the concession to commission the Moroccan Society to execute the work. The conditions
attached to the use of materials, the priority of the Tangier-Fez
line, and the proviso for equality of treatment in the use of all
lines remained unchanged. The chief change dealt with the question of future concessions. The clause incorporated as Article 5
was Cambon's formula and read, "The French government and
the Imperial government will employ semi-officially their influence
in order that, in public adjudications which will take place conformable to the Act of Algeciras for the construction of railroads
and in which the Moroccan Society will probably take part, this
Society obtain the concession. . . ." [105] Cruppi hesitated to accept
such a far-reaching proposal and urged Cambon to come to Paris
to discuss the question, as it was difficult to reach an understanding by telegraph.[106] Cambon, however, insisted that it would be

---

[104] Cambon to Cruppi, Mar. 4, 1911, *ibid.*, no. 85.

[105] Cruppi to Cambon, Mar. 5, 1911, *ibid.*, no. 88; Cambon to Cruppi, Mar. 6,
1911, *ibid.*, no. 89; Cambon to Cruppi, Mar. 7, 1911, *ibid.*, no. 91.

[106] Cruppi to Cambon, Mar. 7, 1911, *ibid.*, no. 92.

impossible for him to leave Berlin before March 22.[107] Cruppi, while still urging the ambassador to come to Paris, asked him if the agreement treated only of the construction of lines and would leave France free to operate the roads as she pleased.[108] Cambon replied that "neither in the instructions which I have received from Paris, nor in my conversations with the Wilhelmstrasse, has it up to now been a question of operation. . . . The operation does not constitute an opening for German industry, but the placing in action of a public service. . . ." Again Cambon urged upon Cruppi the need for securing an agreement of a general nature. "I fear," he said, "that if we do not conclude a general entente with Germany which assures our future liberty of action in matters of railroads in Morocco, we may be obliged by special negotiations in proportion to the construction of each line . . ." to grant concessions to Germany who would be able on each occasion to draw into the discussion "considerations foreign to the Moroccan question." [109]

At this stage in the negotiations, England entered the arena. On March 14 Paul Cambon gave to Grey and Nicolson a résumé of the Franco-German railroad negotiations and discussed the entire question with them. Nicolson recognized the value to France to be rid of German competition in the zone of Morocco reserved to her, but he believed that the railroad concessions would have to be open to public bidding in which all could take part. If France wanted to restrict her own nationals, that was her affair; but he advised France to consult Spain before reaching an agreement on the Tangier line.[110] Grey at this time reserved decision, but on March 16 officially informed France through Sir Francis Bertie that British firms must have a chance and protested the grant of a monopoly to the Moroccan Society. To Cambon's suggestion that the best solution was to increase British share in the Moroccan Society, Grey replied that even if that were

[107] Cambon to Cruppi, Mar. 8, 1911, *ibid.*, no. 95.
[108] Cruppi to Cambon, Mar. 9, 1911, *ibid.*, no. 96.
[109] Cambon to Cruppi, Mar. 9, 1911, *ibid.*, no. 97.
[110] Paul Cambon to Cruppi, Mar. 14, 1911, *ibid.*, no. 109; Note of Nicolson to note presented by Paul Cambon, Mar. 14, 1911, *Br. Docs.*, vol. VII, no. 192.

done, independent British firms would ask to participate in open
bidding according to the Act of Algeciras and that he would be
compelled to support their claims.[111] English protest called forth
the suggestion from Cambon that Article 5 be clarified by stating
clearly that French and German restraining influence was to be
exercised on their own nationals only and not upon the nationals
of other powers. To this suggestion Kiderlen agreed,[112] but soon
further complications entered the discussion.

On March 28 Schoen presented to Cruppi a note withholding
German consent to the proposed Franco-Moroccan loan until the
railroad question was settled,[113] and thus linked two questions
that Tardieu claimed, "had nothing in common." [114] In the light of
the financial status of the sultan, Tardieu's claim is scarcely justified; for securities demanded by the loan mortgaged the sultan's
resources to such an extent as to make railroad construction at
Moroccan expense impossible. Any railroad built would have to
be financed by the concessionaire nation, a fact which would certainly give to such concession a definite political tint.

Despite this check, negotiations continued; and, on April 8,
Cambon proposed that France and Germany use their influence
for a period of ten years to secure concessions for a new company
to be formed in which Germany would have a 25 per cent share.
Kiderlen at this conference injected the question of the operation
of the roads and insisted that in the recruiting of personnel, there
be reserved to Germans a part proportional to their participation
in the capital.[115] On April 12 Kiderlen also asked that the time
limit be extended from ten to twenty years, and that "as in the
Moroccan Society where the Germans have 30 per cent (the Aus-
trians being sub-concessionaires of 5 per cent) the German capital
ought to be represented in the proportion of 30 per cent and not
25 per cent." He then returned to the question of operation, and
stated that his chief fear was that, in spite of guarantees of eco-

---

[111] Grey to Bertie, Mar. 16, 1911, *Br. Docs.*, vol. VII, no. 195; Grey to Bertie,
Mar. 22, 1911, *ibid.*, no. 196.

[112] Cambon to Cruppi, Mar. 19, 1911, *Affaires du Maroc*, 1910-1912, no. 128.

[113] Cruppi to Berckheim, Mar. 29, 1911, *ibid.*, no. 139.

[114] *Op. cit.*, p. 81.

[115] Cambon to Cruppi, Apr. 9, 1911, *Affaires du Maroc*, 1910-1912, no. 165;
Caillaux, *op. cit.*, pp. 257-259.

nomic equality, if the personnel did not include some Germans it would result in discrimination at least through negligence if not in a more overt manner.[116]

The question of personnel was tied to the explicative letters exchanged between Schoen and Cambon on February 9, 1909, which stated that the February Accord implied the non-candidature of German subjects "to functions of directors or of technical counselors of Moroccan public services having or susceptible of having a political character or of instructors in these services." Since the offices of directors, technical counselors, and instructors were specifically listed as not open to German subjects, were other positions tacitly admitted as being open to them?[117] Cruppi opposed this interpretation, as he did all the German suggestions, and considered that Kiderlen was merely trying to drag out the negotiations so as to exact "disturbing and onerous concessions." He urged Cambon to limit the negotiations to the two military roads.[118]

Cambon, obviously more anxious than Cruppi to secure an agreement, urged him to give Kiderlen some satisfaction, as the Pan-Germans, discontented with the Accord of 1909, were active in their efforts to force their government back upon the Act of Algeciras. Cambon again advised him to reach an agreement solving the entire railroad question, because any restricted agreement would mean continued bickering between the two foreign offices.[119] In the meantime, France had entered on negotiations with Spain relative to the distribution of capital in the Tangier-Fez line; and, on June 10, Zimmermann, undersecretary of foreign affairs, with whom Cambon had discussed the question, raised no objection to a Franco-Spanish entente on the subject of the line from Tangier to El Ksar, the section which would fall in the Spanish sphere; but he preferred to wait on an expression of opinion from his chief, who, as it happened, was then at Kissingen.[120]

Cambon's conversation with Kiderlen at Kissingen a few days

---

[116] Cambon to Cruppi, Apr. 12, 1911, *Affaires du Maroc,* 1910-1912, no. 173.
[117] Tardieu, *op. cit.,* p. 81.
[118] Cruppi to Cambon, Apr. 17, 1911, *Affaires du Maroc,* 1910-1912, no. 188.
[119] Cambon to Cruppi, Apr. 21, 1911, *ibid.,* no. 207.
[120] Cambon to Cruppi, June 10, 1911, *ibid.,* no. 361.

later was no mere conference on railroads but dealt with the entire
scope of Franco-German relations; and although as late as July
12[121] a new railroad project was formulated, the question was by
then entangled with the greater problem of the general Franco-
German relations. Plans to make operative the Accord of 1909 in
the field of railroad development were as yet in this nebulous stage
of proposal and counter-proposal when the crisis of 1911 reopened
the entire Moroccan question. Mutual distrust and suspicion had
rendered fruitless the long, tedious negotiations.[122] In other fields
of venture the Accord of 1909 met no more success than in that
of railroads, not even when by a far stretch of interpretation, it
was brought into operation in the development of the Congo.

In 1898 France had granted a monopolistic concession of a
large section of the French Congo to a society of colonization,
the N'Goko Sangha company. From 1898 to 1908 Germans from
the Cameruns came into this territory, lived there in factories,
and without paying any taxes took from the territory quantities
of ivory and rubber.[123] Tardieu, a powerful defender of the company, estimated that the territory thus occupied reached an extent
of approximately 150,000 acres. These Germans, it is true, recognized this land as nominally French; but as France had made
no effort to establish her authority over the district, they ignored
the fact of French jurisdiction and acted as though they themselves were sovereign.[124] However, it is doubtful that the N'Goko
Sangha firm was suffering any considerable financial or economic
loss;[125] but it was not long before the company, aided by its press
and political supporters, began to complain to the French government against the infractions of its rights. Caillaux asserted
that the company was not justified in its complaints. He claimed
that it had been founded by Mestayer, who, "after having rapidly
dissipated a large patrimonial fortune, had the happy chance to

---

[121] Selves to Cambon, July 12, 1911, *ibid.*, no. 448.

[122] Tardieu, *op. cit.*, pp. 74-85; Caillaux, *op. cit.*, pp. 51-54; Feis, *op. cit.*, p. 418.
Bernadotte Schmitt stated that with the failure of the railroad projects "the
ill humour of the Wilhelmstrasse became more apparent from day to day. The
Panther, as it were, began to load its guns. . . ."—*England and Germany*, p. 310.

[123] Tardieu, *op. cit.*, pp. 163-204; Caillaux, *op. cit.*, pp. 54-71.

[124] *Op. cit.*, p. 172.

[125] Wolfgang Hallgarten, *Vorkriegs Imperialismus*, p. 234.

receive, thanks to very high relations, a concession in the Congo."
The company was organized by Belgian capitalists and industrialists of northern France, and Mestayer was made director,
whose idea, Caillaux claimed, was to make as much money with as
little work as possible. Caillaux charged that the company did
nothing to develop its concession, not even to the extent of fur-
nishing the natives with supplies. German traders came in, supplied this deficiency, and received ivory and rubber in exchange.[126]

At all events, negotiations between the company and the French
government in 1905 resulted in an agreement for an indemnity to
be paid the company in the nature of an extension of the conceded
territory and the government's renunciation of royalty on the new
concession for a period of ten years.[127] This did not solve the problem; for what was needed was an effective policing of the frontier
by the French government.[128] Negotiations to adjust the difficulties on the frontier were under discussion when the first Moroccan
crisis and the conference of Algeciras shoved them aside. Efforts
to revive the question failed, and the concessionaire company decided to bring suit in a German court at Hamburg for compensation against damages done by German nationals.[129] Caillaux considered the suit was merely a move to force the French government to take action and not a serious effort on the part of the
company to receive any material compensation from the German
court.[130] The French minister of foreign affairs and the French
minister of colonies advised against the suit, and the minister of
colonies refused to turn over to the company the dossier necessary
to prove its contentions. The right of France to issue such a
monopolistic concession came into the question and, as the court
sought to interpret the Act of Berlin[131] as applied to French
Congo, the foreign offices were forced to take cognizance of the
suit. In other words, the suit of the N'Goko Sangha company

---

[126] *Op. cit.,* pp. 57-59.   [127] Tardieu, *op. cit.,* p. 187; Caillaux, *op. cit.,* p. 55.

[128] See the report of Captain Cottes in Tardieu, *op. cit.,* pp. 187-190, 335-338.

[129] Tardieu, *op. cit.,* pp. 196-199; Caillaux, *op. cit.,* p. 60.

[130] *Op. cit.,* p. 61.

[131] In 1885 in a conference at Berlin, the major powers agreed to equality of
commerce within certain defined limits in the Congo basin.—General Act of the
Conference of Berlin, G. Fr. de Martens, *Nouveau Recueil général de traités,*
2 series, vol. X, pp. 414-427.

against the offending German nationals could not remain a private affair. Upon the insistence of the foreign office, the N'Goko Sangha company dropped legal action but turned to the French government for adjustment of its claims by diplomatic means.[132]

A commission was at that time delimiting the frontier between the French Congo and the Cameruns and the question was allowed to rest until this task was finally finished.[133] By December, 1908, the commission reported its work complete, and the complaints of the company again appeared before the foreign office; but as both France and Germany were then anxious to complete the Franco-German Accord of 1909 and did not wish to introduce any discordant element into the situation, the French foreign office refused to press the matter.[134] Instead, the complaints of the company were tossed back and forth between the minister of colonies and the minister of foreign affairs.[135] The company, determined to settle the matter, threw the question into parliament by claiming from the government an indemnity of 2,500,000 francs.[136] On December 16, 1908, the commission of foreign affairs of the chamber of deputies recognized the right of the company to compensation and instructed the minister of foreign affairs to seek an arrangement which would conciliate both parties to the question.[137] Pichon, after an interview with Lancken, May, 1909, reached the conclusion that nothing could be won by diplomatic means.[138] He then sought to solve the problem by placing in operation the Accord of 1909. To do this he must first settle the question of English aggression into the same territory.

At the time of the organization of the N'Goko Sangha company, English firms were installed and carrying on a lucrative trade in the French Congo.[139] These English houses, one of which was the firm of John Holt, Hatton, and Cookson, disputed the rights of the French company to monopoly control of the Congo

---

[132] Tardieu, *op. cit.,* pp. 196-198; Caillaux, *op. cit.,* p. 60. Millies-Lacroix was minister of colonies and Pichon minister of foreign affairs.

[133] Tardieu, *op. cit.,* pp. 194-195.   [134] *Ibid.,* p. 195.

[135] *Ibid.,* p. 199; Paul Deschanel before the chamber of deputies, April 5, 1911, *Annales de la chambre des députés,* session ordinaire de 1911, vol. I, pp. 2224-2225.   [136] Tardieu, *op. cit.,* pp. 200-201; Caillaux, *op. cit.,* p. 59.

[137] Tardieu, *op. cit.,* pp. 200-201.   [138] *Ibid.,* p. 388; Caillaux, *op. cit.,* p. 61.

[139] This account of the English claims is taken from Tardieu, *op. cit.,* pp. 209-288.

on the basis of equality of commerce established by the Act of
Berlin. For five years, French courts by their judgments and the
French government by its communications to the British government affirmed the right of France to establish such a régime within
her own colony. According to Tardieu, the campaign in the press
and in parliament against the exploitation of the natives in the
Congo was the work of the British firms who, to break down French
resistance to their demands, organized a campaign of public opinion led by leagues of humanitarian tendencies and by chambers
of commerce. They hoped thus to force diplomatic action to secure
either the suppression of the régime of concessions or the payment
to the Liverpool firms of a heavy indemnity. Tardieu attributed
materialistic aims to the philanthropic work of Edmund Morel
and his associates. The activity of the anti-concessionaires spread
to France where Jaurès was an enthusiastic leader. After four
years' resistance the French government capitulated, and in May,
1906, awarded to the English firms an indemnity of 1,500,000
francs and approximately 70,000 acres of land. Yet even after
this, English houses continued to extend their factories into the
territory. The N'Goko Sangha company refused to participate
in the settlement made in May, 1906, and in November of the same
year sued Holt, Hatton, and Cookson for damages. The tribunal
of the Seine authorized the company to attach the indemnity to
be paid to the English firms to the amount of 603,000 francs. The
press campaign became active again in an effort to force the
French government to pass over the decision of the court. The
minister of foreign affairs was interested exclusively in satisfying
the British government and avoiding a diplomatic conflict. As the
N'Goko Sangha company held claims against both British and
German firms, Pichon thought he could solve the Franco-German
and the Franco-English difficulties in the Congo on the same basis as
the Accord of 1909, by forming a Franco-German consortium to
operate along the Congo-Camerun frontier. To do this it was necessary to clear the claims of the N'Goko Sangha company.

Pichon discussed the question of a Congo consortium with
Lancken in a tentative fashion on May 15, 1909,[140] and on June

---

[140] Tardieu, *op. cit.*, p. 288; Caillaux, *op. cit.*, p. 62. Lancken states that the
idea of the consortium was Tardieu's.—Oscar von der Lancken Wakenitz,
Meine Dreissig Dienstjahre, 1888-1918, pp. 90-91.

5, 1909, consulted Millies-Lacroix, minister of colonies. Millies-Lacroix was replaced by Trouillot before the former had completed his study of the project.[141] Pichon in July, 1909, approached the N'Goko Sangha company with his plans. The company expressed its willingness to coöperate and to turn over a part of its territory to the consortium on the condition that some adjustment be made relative to the indemnity due for German aggression and to the attachment against the English firm.[142] It was evidently conscious of the fact that such an arrangement might make a refusal of its claims a cause for international embarrassment and thereby augment its position before the French government.[143] Pichon, at all events, recognized that "if not in right at least in equity," the French government owed to the society "a pecuniary compensation for the troubles which it has undergone in the exercise of its concessions";[144] and by February, 1910, both Pichon and Trouillot were agreed that the payment to the company of the indemnity and of the attachment against the English firm was preliminary to the company's acceptance of the consortium.[145] Negotiations were then instituted between the National Liberal vice-president of the Reichstag, M. Semler, a leader of the German groups,[146] and the N'Goko Sangha company for the details of the convention. Apparently the two were working toward an agreement[147] when the question was called before a sub-committee in the ministry of colonies. This commission began investigation of the agreement and also interrogated the opponents of the concession, such as the League of Protection of the Natives. The long investigation provoked delays irritating to the German companies who wished to begin operation.[148] The proposal was further delayed by the action of the budget commission, which was forced to consider the question because of the indemnity involved.[149]

Opposition to payment of the indemnity was strong in the budget commission and from there spread to the general public. Some,

---

[141] Tardieu, *op. cit.*, p. 289; Caillaux, *op. cit.*, p. 62.

[142] Tardieu, *op. cit.*, pp. 298-302; Caillaux, *op. cit.*, p. 63.

[143] Hallgarten, *op. cit.*, p. 235.   [144] Tardieu, *op. cit.*, pp. 299-300.

[145] *Ibid.*, p. 300.   [146] Hallgarten, *op. cit.*, p. 235.

[147] Tardieu, *op. cit.*, pp. 300-312; Lancken, *op. cit.*, p. 92.

[148] Tardieu, *op. cit.*, pp. 312-322.   [149] *Ibid.*, p. 324; Caillaux, *op. cit.*, p. 67.

such as Edmund Morel, opposed the proposal on the grounds of opposition to the payment of an indemnity to a concessionaire company, who, they considered, had used its grant solely to exploit the natives. Tardieu stated that the reason for such popular opposition was the fact that the aims for the solution adopted were never published. Instead the only fact the public had was that the government proposed to give an indemnity of more than 2,000,000 francs to a financial society.[150] Others opposed the arrangement on the grounds that an extension of the Accord of 1909 to apply to the Congo was both unwarranted and inadvisable. If the Accord were not limited to Morocco, Germany would be asking for participation in French enterprise everywhere.[151] Even in the face of this opposition, Pichon, in November and again in December, 1910, wrote encouraging letters to German representatives which clearly showed that he expected the plan to succeed.[152] The budget commission, however, accepted the principle that the award would not be made without parliamentary approval.[153] To offset part of the objection, which by this time was rampant in the press, Pichon, January 27, suggested the formation of a reciprocal company operating on German soil, for example, in the Cameruns.[154] This proposal was, of course, dependent upon the completion of the first project. Until his overthrow, Pichon maintained the view that the organization of a Franco-German consortium in the Congo would do much to relieve the strain between the two countries and would further the success of the Moroccan Accord; but before he could accomplish his purpose, the Briand ministry was overthrown March 2 and the Monis cabinet took control, with Cruppi as minister of foreign affairs.

Early in March, 1911, the Monis cabinet took up the question of the N'Goko Sangha consortium.[155] At the conference, Berteaux, minister of war, M. Messimy, minister of colonies, and Caillaux, minister of finance, were opposed to the project.[156] M. Conti, under-director of political affairs in the foreign office, attached

---

[150] Tardieu, *op. cit.*, pp. 324-332.   [151] Caillaux, *op. cit.*, p. 67.

[152] *Ibid.*, p. 68; Tardieu, *op. cit.*, pp. 318-320.

[153] Caillaux, *op. cit.*, p. 69; Tardieu, *op. cit.*, p. 339.

[154] Caillaux, *op. cit.*, p. 70; Tardieu, *op. cit.*, p. 343.

[155] Caillaux, *op. cit.*, p. 74; Tardieu, *op. cit.*, p. 345.

[156] Caillaux, *op. cit.*, p. 74.

great importance to the agreement and in a long note urged the cabinet to accept the program of its predecessor. He concluded by warning the cabinet that the failure of this consortium would risk provoking Germany to "disagreeable manifestations to which Germany is accustomed. . . ." [157] According to Caillaux, the cabinet then consulted Cambon, who reported that he did not believe that the affair was of great importance, as Kiderlen in a conversation a few days earlier had expressed regret that the consortium seemed not likely to succeed, but had not stressed the matter. To Cambon's statement that in France they were not able to understand why all the land involved was to be French territory, Kiderlen replied that he understood the objection, but made no suggestion for a counter consortium to operate on German soil. Cambon also stated that all negotiations on the subject had been carried on by business men and was not the work of his office.[158]

On March 29 M. Messimy declared in the budget commission that the indemnity would not be paid and that the consortium would not be formed, and the same day informed the N'Goko Sangha company of the fact.[159] On April 4, the question arose in the chamber of deputies and M. Caillaux announced that the Franco-German consortium would not be formed and the indemnity would not be paid.[160] Caillaux later stated that he fought the consortium "with all my power because it appeared to me harmful to my country." [161] In rejecting the consortium, the Monis cabinet had treated the question as a strictly colonial one and had apparently ignored the international complications involved. Both Tardieu[162] and Pichon considered the cabinet culpable for thus treating as a private matter a question that had occupied the attention

[157] *Ibid.*, p. 75; Tardieu, *op. cit.*, p. 345.

[158] Caillaux, *op. cit.*, pp. 74-76. Cambon was at that time urgently trying to conclude the Moroccan railroad agreement.

[159] *Ibid.*, p. 75; Tardieu, *op. cit.*, p. 346.

[160] Tardieu, *op. cit.*, p. 346; Caillaux, *op. cit.*, p. 76; Caillaux before the chamber of deputies, April 5, 1911, *Annales de la chambre des députés,* session ordinaire de 1911, vol. I, pp. 2222-2223. The N'Goko Sangha affair was debated in the chamber, April 4, 5, and 6. See especially the report of Viollette and the speeches of Messimy, minister of colonies, Jean Morel, Jacques Piou, Caillaux, and Jaurès.—*Ibid.*, pp. 2134-2274.

[161] Caillaux's answer to Crowe's charges, *Br. Docs.,* vol. VIII, addendum, p. 796.

[162] Tardieu, *op. cit.*, p. 347.

of the foreign offices of the two countries for some twenty months. Pichon could not understand Cambon's statement that the matter was a private affair when the project "had been negotiated at Berlin under the auspices of the embassy of France, at Paris under the auspices of the embassy of Germany." [163] But the consortium was dead; [164] the railroad negotiations were dragging out their tedious course; Fez was threatened; and the French were seriously considering a relief expedition. It was not a time to irritate Germany with further failures. The Congo consortium was thus able to prolong itself into the Congo-Camerun railroad project.

Early in April, Schoen came to see Cruppi and asked some compensation for the failure of the N'Goko Sangha consortium to satisfy the German nationals, especially Semler and his group. [165] Schoen claimed this compensation as a right and based his claim upon the letter that Pichon had written to him on December 15, 1910. Pichon's letter read in part: "Your compatriot, M. Semler, left Paris today after being assured of the good disposition of the French government in that which concerns the project of the Franco-German consortium for the exploitation of a region situated in French Congo on the Camerun frontier. . . ."

Pichon then stated that M. Semler and the French company had reached an agreement on the questions submitted by the commission of colonial concessions, with a few reservations dealing with the territory affected, the number of enterprises, and the question of control and operation. He concluded by stating that "The French government approves, in principle, these dispositions, but it considers that the constitution of the consortium would be realized only after solution of the question according to parliamentary view. . . ." [166] Schoen concluded his interview with the comment that it was necessary for France to show that she did not wish to exclude all coöperation between German and

---

[163] Pichon before the senate, Feb. 8, 1912, *Annales du senat,* session ordinaire de 1912, vol. I, p. 231.

[164] Tardieu, *op. cit.,* p. 348; Caillaux, *op. cit.,* p. 71; Albin, *op. cit.,* p. 237.

[165] Tardieu, *op. cit.,* p. 352; Caillaux, *op. cit.,* p. 76; Albin, *op. cit.,* p. 160.

[166] Pichon before the senate, Feb. 8, 1912, *Annales du senat,* session ordinaire de 1912, vol. I, p. 231.

9

French nationals.[167] Cruppi, who had not known of the letter,[168] reported this interview to Messimy and Caillaux and the three recognized the need of avoiding trouble at this time when the question of the relief expedition to Fez was pressing.[169]

Towards the last of April, the subject was revived when Lancken came to see Caillaux[170] and, in the course of the conversation, criticized the Fez expedition, and spoke of the need for compensating German nationals for the failure of the N'Goko Sangha project, and asked if the failure of the consortium indicated that France did not wish to work with the Germans at all. Caillaux replied that the refusal in one instance did not mean refusal in all. Lancken then introduced the proposal for a Congo-Camerun railroad project with French and German coöperation.[171] Caillaux, ostensibly in favor of the proposal,[172] promised to discuss the matter with Cruppi, and on May 3 Cruppi, Messimy, and he agreed to investigate the matter.[173] Caillaux stated that Cruppi asked him to inquire into the project and, in order to avoid involving the government, he asked Fondère, director of river navigation in the Congo, to go to Berlin and negotiate with M. Semler. Before Fondère's departure, Caillaux stressed to him that the negotiations were of a private nature.[174] Tardieu pointed out that this was exactly the procedure instigated by the Accord

---

[167] Tardieu, *op. cit.*, p. 352; Caillaux, *op. cit.*, p. 76.

[168] Caillaux stated that neither Cruppi nor Cambon knew anything of this letter before Schoen presented it to Cruppi.—*Ibid.*, p. 76. Caillaux considered that by this letter Pichon had given *"without reserve"* the consent of the government to a Franco-German society and that as a consequence the government was compelled to take into consideration Schoen's demands.—*Ibid.*, p. 69.

[169] *Ibid.*, p. 77.

[170] *Ibid.*, pp. 77-78; Tardieu, *op. cit.*, p. 353; Albin, *op. cit.*, p. 160; Caillaux's answer to Crowe's charges, *Br. Docs.*, vol. VIII, addendum, p. 795.

[171] Lancken asserts that the idea was Semler's.—*Op. cit.*, p. 94. Hallgarten states that this proposal was nothing more than the Tardieu-Semler project in another form.—*Op. cit.*, p. 236.

[172] Lancken, *op. cit.*, p. 94.   [173] Caillaux, *op. cit.*, p. 78.

[174] *Ibid.*, p. 78; Tardieu, *op. cit.*, p. 353; Albin, *op. cit.*, p. 163; Zimmermann to Kiderlen, June 15, 1911, *G. P.*, vol. XXIX, no. 10574; Lancken, *op. cit.*, p. 95. Reference to this private mission of Fondère occurred in practically every speech made in the senate during the debate on the November 4, 1911 treaty. See for example, Jenouvrier, Feb. 5, 1912, Villaine, Feb. 6, 1912, Pichon, Feb. 8, 1912, *Annales du senat*, session ordinaire de 1912, vol. I, pp. 156-167, 176-180, 228-239.

of 1909, according to which the two governments were to seek to associate their nationals in common enterprises. In this matter, as in the N'Goko Sangha, the first moves had been those of the government.[175] Fondère was in Berlin from May 11 to May 14, and on May 17 he reported to Caillaux, who, as minister of finance, referred him to the minister of foreign affairs within whose jurisdiction the affair lay.

On May 24 Semler came to Paris and in Lancken's presence drew up a contract to be submitted to the two governments.[176] Caillaux, when the contract was presented to him, professed surprise at its completeness, since he had expected only a general outline.[177] The contract provided for a railroad serving Camerun and French Congo and terminating at a point on the frontier near Oubanghi. The two governments were to guarantee to the company interest on the line, each government taking to its charge the expense of the guarantee on the portion of the line that traversed its territory.[178] On May 25 Fondère submitted the contract to M. Messimy[179] and on June 7 the affair was reported to the cabinet.[180] Caillaux now opposed the project because he considered that under its terms France would be duped. The railroad planned with its terminus at Oubanghi would draw the trade of the region to Camerun ports and place that section of French Congo under economic bondage to German ports. Caillaux was convinced that Germany in the Congolese affairs wished to secure "gratuitously, under the mask of private interests, an economic participation analogous to that which she had acquired in Morocco by the Accord of 1909 . . ." and that, having gained all she wanted in the Congo, would refuse to give way in Morocco.[181]

The French cabinet refused the project, but agreed to study suggestions for some such plan of a more general nature.[182] On June 10, Schoen was informed of the decision of the cabinet.[183] He reported to his foreign office that Cruppi, in discussing the Camerun-Congo railroad project, had said that the French gov-

---

[175] Tardieu, *op. cit.*, p. 354.   [176] *Ibid.*, pp. 354-355; Caillaux, *op. cit.*, p. 79.
[177] *Ibid.*, p. 80.   [178] *Ibid.*, p. 80; Tardieu, *op. cit.*, p. 354.
[179] *Ibid.*, p. 355.   [180] *Ibid.*, Caillaux, *op. cit.*, p. 84.   [181] *Ibid.*, pp. 84-86.
[182] *Ibid.*, p. 84; Tardieu, *op. cit.*, pp. 356-359. Monis was not present at this meeting of the cabinet.   [183] Tardieu, *op. cit.*, p. 358.

ernment would be glad in this connection to discuss the entire North African question. Cruppi then talked with Lancken and stated clearly to him that "France could not bind herself to such a fruitful undertaking without being sure that Germany is ready for a friendly agreement also in other North African questions. Lancken affected lack of understanding. I answered on my side . . . that the Semler project springs solely out of private initiative and is not to be connected with the Moroccan question. . . ." [184] Lancken did not trust the sincerity of French offers, and Kiderlen thought that a "negotiation on a far-reaching basis only could be begun when the French government through a vigorous procedure . . . was made pliable. . . ." [185] The collapse of the Congo-Camerun railroad project added one more failure to the list of futile defeats to which the economic clauses of the Franco-German Accord of 1909 had been subjected. In still another field, perhaps a field most important of all, was the Accord to meet failure. This failure resulted from the conflicting mining interests. The story is that of the Mannesmann brothers.

---

[184] Schoen to F. O., June 15, 1911, *G. P.,* vol. XXIX, no. 10573.

[185] Editor's footnote to the despatch, Schoen to F. O., June 15, 1911, *ibid.,* no. 10573.

Chapter VI

THE MANNESMANN BROTHERS

European captains of industry were attracted by the fabulous accounts of iron, gold, copper, antimony, silver, lead, and sulphur that presumably lay hidden in the subsoil of Morocco, and saw therein a rich field from which the deficiency in minerals in their respective countries could be repaired. The alluring prospect of iron in abundance tantalized the insatiable appetites of the iron-masters of Europe. Phosphates, needed by Germany and exploited by France with great profit since 1912, were apparently ignored by the rival mining claimants. Only incidental notice was taken of the potential oil wealth of the Meknez district in the briefs presented by the parties actively engaged in disputing their rights to Moroccan mineral wealth. Not the Chaouya and Sebou plains with their phosphates and oil, but the Riff, the Atlas, and the Sous with their elusive but glamorous offers of iron and gold were the coveted regions. To the concessionaire who might secure the right to work these districts would come fame and fortune for himself, and for his country a treasure that could not be over-valued. John Bakeless stated the situation in this manner: "The Moroccan question, which repeatedly led Europe to the verge of war, was partly a result of the Franco-German conflict over iron. Moroccan exports are mainly agricultural; but the German iron-masters, facing a probable shortage of ore in the very near future and casting about the world for deposits from which to make up their lack, coveted the mines, as yet unworked, known to exist in that country. . . ." [1] The French, English, and Spanish iron-masters were no less anxious to secure concessions, but the Germans attracted more attention due to the aggressive action of the Mannesmann brothers, of whom there were many, "all pushing." [2]

[1] *The Economic Causes of Modern War*, p. 154.

[2] Theodore Wolff, *The Eve of 1914*, p. 34. There were six of these brothers according to Eugene Staley, *op. cit.*, p. 55. *Der Grosse Brockhaus* names only five, Reinhard, Otto, Max, Alfred, and Karl. Reinhard was evidently

In 1906 Reinhard Mannesmann on a wedding trip visited the coast of Morocco, where the natives showed him specimens of iron ore.[3] He then went to Tangier and urged Rosen to give him aid in securing a mining concession from the sultan, Abdul Aziz.[4] The support of the German government was necessarily slow; for the conference of Algeciras, early in that year, had determined that the sultan should issue a mining law in conformity with European practice,[5] and although the Act of Algeciras did not definitely state the fact, it was generally understood that no concession was to be granted until the mining law had been promulgated. Formulation of the mining law was delayed owing to the generally disturbed conditions in Morocco; and in the summer and fall of 1906 when the Mannesmanns first became interested in the field, the law was as yet in a nebulous state. The German government was willing to support the Mannesmanns' activities and recommended to Rosen to call the attention of the sultan to their wishes, as a concession might give them a priority claim when the law was issued.[6] Rosen, always more aggressive in his demands for German rights in Morocco than was his foreign office, seemed to have given them active support. In fact, partisans of the firm said that he urged them on.[7]

In the fall of 1906, the Mannesmanns, during the absence of Rosen, apparently secured from Abdul Aziz a concession that amounted to a monopoly grant.[8] Approximately a year later,

---

the head of the house. The brothers first founded a seamless tube factory in their home town, Remscheid, then expanded to Düsseldorff where the central office was established. While active in the Moroccan question they founded the Marokko-Mannesmann Compagnie in Hamburg with fourteen establishments in Morocco. In 1932, next to the United Steel Company, the Mannesmann company was the most important metallurgical industry in Germany. The company had subsidiaries in Komotau, Czechoslovakia, in Paris with factories in Saarbrücken, and in London with factories in London and Newport. In the British Mannesmann Tube Company, the German share in 1928 was 93 per cent. —*Der Grosse Brockhaus*, edition 15, vol. XII, p. 87.

[3] Staley, *op. cit.*, p. 55.

[4] *Ibid; Weissbuch: Denkschrift und Aktenstücke über deutsche Bergwerkseninteressen in Marokko*, p. 5.   [5] *Affaires du Maroc*, 1906, no. 37.

[6] Tschirschky to Rosen, Nov. 6, 1906, *Weissbuch*, no. 4.

[7] Staley, *op. cit.*, p. 55.

[8] Tschirschky to Rosen, Nov. 6, 1906, *Weissbuch*, no. 4; Ben Sliman to Rosen, Nov. 23, 1908, *ibid.*, no. 5; Feis, *op. cit.*, p. 414.

October 23, 1907, Rosen reported to the Berlin office that the sultan had agreed to the concessions in Tangier and Larache and had "recognized the priority right of Messrs. Mannesmanns to the mines investigated and reported in writing by them, and had in mind concession after the mining law was formulated. . . . The list drawn up by the Mannesmanns include gold, silver, copper, petroleum, but mainly iron in the Riff and in all accessible parts of Morocco. In case the mining law corresponds to our wish and Prussian mining laws . . . very great objects are assured our mining industry. . . ." But he added, "in this case the Mannesmanns have pledged themselves later to enter into the Moroccan syndicate. . . ." [9]

In 1907 an international syndicate known as the Union of Mines had been formed by a group of industrialists in order to develop the mineral resources of Morocco. According to the charter of the company French industrialists were to hold 50 per cent of the capital; German, 20 per cent; English, 10 per cent; Spanish, 6 per cent; Italian, 4 per cent; and Portuguese, 2 per cent. The president and eight directors were to be French; the vice-president and two directors were to be German. Spain was to have two directors, and England, Italy, and Portugal were to have one each. [10]

Among French industrialists interested in the international syndicate were Schneider-Creusot, Compagnie Marocaine, and Hoskier; while among the German firms were numbered Krupp, Gelsenkirchen, and Thyssen. [11] The Union of Mines undertook to prospect for mines, but they were handicapped by the fact that they awaited the promulgation of the mining law and also by the fact that at every turn they faced the opposition of the Mannesmanns. The mining struggle narrowed itself to a conflict between the Union of Mines and the Mannesmann Brothers, only to broaden again in such manner as to draw into its vortex the foreign offices of France and Germany and to enlist in opposite ranks the public opinion of both countries.

---

[9] Rosen to F. O., Oct. 23, 1907, *G. P.*, vol. XXI, part II, no. 7286.

[10] Tardieu, *op. cit.*, p. 45.

[11] Wolff, *op. cit.*, p. 33; Feis, *op. cit.*, p. 414; Staley, *op. cit.*, p. 60; Morel, *op. cit.*, p. 129, footnote 2.

In June, 1908, the Moroccan minister of foreign affairs informed the dean of the diplomatic corps at Tangier that, as many commercial concerns were anxious to exploit the mines, the sultan had decided to instruct "the engineer who is in charge of public works to form, conjointly with his adjutants, a law including all the conditions necessary and all the measures which would guarantee the conservation of the rights of the Sherifian government. This law will then be submitted to the *magzhen* who will examine it and approve or modify it. . . ." [12] The fact that the engineer in charge of public works was a Frenchman seemed to have excited the Germans. When the question was submitted to the diplomatic corps, the German minister, apparently upon the request of German interests in Morocco (including the Mannesmanns), insisted that the law must first be submitted to the diplomatic corps for approval.[13] Accordingly, on August 20, 1908, the diplomatic corps agreed that "conforming to Article 112 of the Act of Algeciras, this law can not be promulgated before having been submitted to the diplomatic corps in order to permit it to assure itself if the law is according to foreign legislation on the matter. . . ." [14] Further progress in the development of the mining law was forced to await the outcome of the struggle for the throne being waged between Mulay Hafid and Abdul Aziz; but the scramble for mining concessions refused to wait.

Mulay Hafid started his struggle in the south, and to the south went an agent of the Mannesmanns interested in guarding the rights of the firm and securing from the pretender extensive grants. Mulay Hafid was badly in need of funds to further his cause, and he was willing to grant concessions in return for cash. One authority states that the reason that the Mannesmanns were the most favored of all the concessionaires flocking around the rebel leader was that they had cash in hand.[15] The extent to which the Mannesmanns financed the revolt of Mulay Hafid while he was

---

[12] El Boukili to Count Koziebrodzki, minister of Austria-Hungary, dean of the diplomatic corps, June 23, 1908, *Affaires du Maroc,* 1908-1910, no. 22, Annex II.   [13] Rosen to F. O., Aug. 11, 1908, *Weissbuch,* no. 14.

[14] Koziebrodzki to Boukili, Aug. 20, 1908, *Affaires du Maroc,* 1908-1910, no. 22, Annex III; Wangenheim to F. O., Aug. 20, 1908, *Weissbuch,* no. 15. The note of the diplomatic corps to El Boukili, Aug. 20, 1908, is also given in *Weissbuch,* no. 16.   [15] Staley, *op. cit.,* p. 59.

still in the south is not determined, but that they were in direct negotiations with him before his recognition is not doubted. On October 7, 1908, Mulay Hafid, who was not officially recognized by the powers until December, signed a mining law proposed by the Mannesmann brothers and issued to them an extensive concession which included practically all the mineral resources of Morocco.[16] The new sultan was not inclined to show favoritism, however, and issued similar extensive grants to English agents.[17] The difference lay in the fact that the British government refused to acknowledge the grant and English industrialists refused to take up the concession,[18] while the Mannesmanns were more than eager to do so. Although the proposed mining law and the concession to the German firm were not published but only registered in the German consulate accompanied by Vassel's reservations as to their validity,[19] news of the situation reached the French minister, Regnault, who, on October 26, telegraphed Paris that he had heard that "two Germans have formed with Mulay Hafid a mining law." [20]

By the end of the year 1908 German official support of the Mannesmanns began to weaken. Rosen advised the agents of the firm that by playing Mulay Hafid's game they would lose a great deal of money, and he recommended to them that they come to an agreement with the Union of Mines.[21] On January 15, 1909, Rosen told Harris, the London *Times* correspondent in Tangier, that two German agents of the Mannesmanns had gone to Fez to secure mining concessions, but that their action would not prejudice the prospects of the international syndicate. He acknowledged that he had recommended to his government that the claims of the firm be

---

[16] Vassel to Rosen, Oct. 10, 1908, *Weissbuch,* no. 21; Mannesmann to Bülow, Dec. 29, 1908, *ibid.,* no. 24.

[17] Stemrich to Rosen, Sept. 9, 1908, *ibid.,* no. 26; Wangenheim to F. O., Oct. 14, 1908, *ibid.,* no. 27; Ashmead-Bartlett, *op. cit.,* Appendix I, pp. 525-529.

[18] *Ibid.,* pp. 346-349; Rosen to F. O., Nov. 10, 1908, *Weissbuch,* no. 28.

[19] Vassel to Rosen, Oct. 10, 1908, *ibid.,* no. 41; note on negotiations in the consulate of Fez, Oct. 8, 1908, *ibid.,* no. 22.

[20] Regnault to Pichon, Oct. 26, 1908, *Affaires du Maroc,* 1908-1910, no. 22.

[21] Staley, *op. cit.,* p. 60; Staley in a footnote quotes Vassel as saying "that Mulay Hafid had been toying with the Mannesmanns" and that "the Sultan seems to have grasped the idea that it is his divine right to squeeze the Mannesmanns. . . ." He cites as his source a *Confidential Preliminary Whitebook.*

fully considered by the German group in the international syndicate, but that the proportion of participation of the various nationalities be not changed.[22] The Mannesmanns' claims to the extensive concession issued by Mulay Hafid in October were not supported by the German foreign office. Instead, Schoen informed them that the government could not support their claims and advised them to come to an agreement with the Union of Mines.[23] The Krupp firm offered to the Mannesmanns one-fourth of the German share in the international syndicate, but the brothers refused the offer.[24] Despite these facts, their concession of October was confirmed by Mulay Hafid in March, 1909, with the explicit knowledge of the German foreign office which asserted that this action was merely to keep the claim alive and was not the establishment of a definitive concession.[25] As the Mannesmanns began to lose official backing they began to develop an extensive and well-organized publicity campaign to advance their cause. In 1909 they so spread the idea that the German government was supporting their claims, that Schoen felt it necessary to send a denial to Paris and Tangier and to inform Max Mannesmann of his action.[26]

The changed viewpoint of the German government rested partially upon the Accord of 1909. According to that well-known instrument, the two nations were "to seek to associate their nationals in the enterprises in which they obtained the concessions." The Union of Mines was already created and formed an effective medium for the coöperation of German and French nationals in a very lucrative field, if only the discordant element, the Mannesmann brothers, could be induced to join the international syndicate. Coöperation between French and German industrialists in the profitable sphere of minerals could not be effected if a German firm contested all concessions granted the Union on the basis of a prior title to identical concessions. Consequently, the first necessary step for making operative the Accord of 1909 in the mining ventures was to clear the field of the Mannesmanns.

[22] Lister to Grey, Jan. 15, 1909, *Br. Docs.*, vol. VII, no. 147.

[23] Note to Schoen, Jan. 6, 1909, *Weissbuch*, no. 37.

[24] Staley, *op. cit.*, p. 61.

[25] London *Times*, Jan. 25, 1910; *L'Afrique française*, 1910, pp. 89, 91.

[26] Schoen to Max Mannesmann, March 24, 1909, *Weissbuch*, no. 36.

The Guiot Mission, which undertook to place in operation the Accord of 1909, dealt extensively with the Mannesmann question. Langwerth's note dealing with the conference stated that the German officials made clear to Guiot the position of the German government in the question, and asked him, in turn, to make it clear in Paris in order to avoid "under all circumstances . . . the suspicion that we [Germany] play in this business a double game, in which we officially support the syndicate and underhand the Mannesmann firm." Langwerth asserted that Germany could not deny support to the Mannesmanns "up to a certain degree," and concluded that "the best solution of the existing difficulties relative to this . . ." problem would be, if possible, "through a geographic limitation of interest spheres, to bring about an agreement between the different interests. . . ." [27] Schoen stated that France was willing to come to an agreement on the basis of the Accord of 1909, and that the German foreign office persuaded the Mannesmanns to adopt this course and even helped the negotiations "with all the means at our disposal. . . ." [28]

As a result of the attitude of the two foreign offices, a conference between the Union of Mines and the Mannesmanns took place in Paris from April 6 to April 25, 1909.[29] Max and Otto Mannesmann represented the brothers, and Lancken the German foreign office. It was possible to adjust the situation by a fusion of the two companies or by a territorial partition of the mineral deposits. The Mannesmanns refused to fuse unless they were given 50 per cent of all the shares in the Union of Mines,[30] and they at first also demanded that they receive 50 per cent of all the beds in which they might be in competition with the Union of Mines and a participation in the railroads associated with these mines.[31] At the same time, they refused to provide a list of the beds that they claimed by right.[32] Tardieu stated that this fact aroused in "the

[27] Stemrich to Rosen, May 17, 1909, *G. P.*, vol. XXIX, no. 10458. Editor's footnote gives Langwerth's report.

[28] W. E. Schoen, *Memoirs of an Ambassador*, p. 116.

[29] *Weissbuch*, nos. 46-61, gives a report of this meeting; Tardieu, *op. cit.*, p. 46; Staley, *op. cit.*, pp. 62-63.

[30] Radolin to F. O., April 14, 1909, *Weissbuch*, no. 51; Staley, *op. cit.*, p. 63.

[31] Radolin to F. O., April 22, 1909, *Weissbuch*, no. 54.

[32] Tardieu, *op. cit.*, p. 46.

Union of Mines and even in the German embassy some skepticism of the validity of these mysterious rights." [33] After long negotiations, a compromise on the basis of division of the fields seemed to have been reached "when the Mannesmann brothers suddenly decided that they could sign nothing without the approval of their brother, Reinhard, who was in Tangier. He refused to come to Paris or to deal by telegraph. Negotiations were thus broken off, though the German government strongly advised the Mannesmanns to accept the Union offer. . . ." [34]

Although this first effort to secure harmony between the two groups had apparently failed, Peyerimhoff, as a representative of the Union, soon went to Tangier to negotiate with the perverse Reinhard and, if possible, to effect a settlement. [35] The Union proposed a territorial partition that would leave the Union and the Mannesmanns free in their own zones and offered to the Mannesmanns the Riff.[36] Pichon on May 16 informed Saint-Aulaire that Lancken had told him that he feared the conference in Tangier would gain nothing, but added that "The German government carrying absolutely equal interest in the two parties had charged Rosen to do all possible in order that they arrive at an agreement. . . ." Pichon, in turn, urged Saint-Aulaire to do his utmost to effect a settlement.[37] Although both governments worked assiduously to settle the difficulties between the two parties, the conference failed; and on May 21, 1909, Saint-Aulaire telegraphed to Pichon that the pourparlers were again broken off. Rosen expressed his regrets and acknowledged the spirit of conciliation with which the representative of the Union of Mines had worked.[38]

[33] *Ibid.*

[34] Staley, *op. cit.,* p. 63. See also Rotenhan to F. O., April 24, 1909, *Weissbuch,* no. 57.

[35] Schoen to Krupp, May 3, 1909, *ibid.,* no. 63; Rosen to F. O., May 10, 1910, *ibid.,* no. 64; Staley, *op. cit.,* p. 64.   [36] Tardieu, *op. cit.,* p. 47.

[37] Pichon to Saint-Aulaire, May 16, 1909, *Affaires du Maroc,* 1908-1910, no. 192; Stemrich to Radolin, May 14, 1909, *Weissbuch,* no. 66; Radolin to F. O., May 15, 1909, *ibid.,* no. 67.

[38] Saint-Aulaire to Pichon, May 21, 1909, *Affaires du Maroc,* 1908-1910, no. 198; Rosen to F. O., May 21, 1909, *Weissbuch,* no. 68. In the note treating of a conversation with representatives of the Mannesmanns in the foreign office, May 11, 1909, occurs the statement that Radolin was convinced the Mannes-

Again the obstinacy of the Mannesmanns had defeated a settlement, and the foreign offices turned back to the question of the promulgation of the mining law.

In June, 1909, Lancken submitted to the French foreign office a note stating that Germany wished to facilitate the work of the Union of Mines and had sought without success to secure an agreement between it and the Mannesmanns. This company, to give their firm an international character, had sold stock to non-Germans among whom were several French industrialists. Lancken assumed that the French group besieged its foreign office with the same persistence with which its German co-workers plagued his office. He, therefore, proposed that the powers present to the sultan a mining law which would solve the problem. "This law ought to sanction in a general fashion the principle of priority; it ought to take account, in the limits of equity, of the claimed rights of interest dating from times anterior to the publication of the law. It ought to foresee the creation of a competent organ, impartial and neutral, which, in the quality of a judge or arbiter, is to examine the claims of the different interests and decide the following questions. . . ." The questions listed were: the value to attach to claims made prior to the promulgation of the law; adjustment of the rights of different claimants to the same territory; and distribution of the mining zones after promulgation of the law.[39] To this note France replied that she was willing to discuss the question of the mines, but, as was known, she opposed any concession that savored of a monopoly. She agreed that a mining law must be formed soon and assumed that "rights legitimately acquired ought to be examined with a benevolent equity according to the principles of the Act of Algeciras. . . ." [40] In July Germany proposed that an impartial committee composed of specialists from France, England, Germany, and Spain, as the interested countries, form a

manns would agree to nothing.—Aktennotiz betreffend eine Unterredung mit Vertretern der Herrn Mannesmann im Auswärtigen Amt am 11 Mai 1909, *ibid.,* no. 65.

[39] Pichon to Saint-Aulaire, June 17, 1909, *Affaires du Maroc,* 1908-1910, no. 206, enclosure I, note sent to F. O. by Lancken, June 6, 1909.

[40] *Ibid.,* enclosure II, note sent by the French F. O. to the German embassy in Paris, June 16, 1909.

mining law which they would then submit to the sultan.[41] The interested governments accepted the proposal and selected Paris as the meeting place.[42] France chose M. Aguillon, inspector general of mines, as her representative on the committee.[43]

The committee started its work in November, 1909[44] but did not complete it until June of 1910.[45] The long delay was due in part to the technical difficulties in drafting the law, but in the main to the interest of the Mannesmanns in the personnel of the arbitration court that was to be created and empowered to adjust conflicting claims.[46] Pichon, in March of 1910, wrote to Cambon that France was anxious to solve the Mannesmann difficulty, but that he did not wish to confuse it with the question of the promulgation of the mining law. The proposed arbitration court was "absolutely independent of the Mannesmann question" and "it would have the same reason for being if the conflict between the Mannesmann and the Union of Mines did not exist. . . ." Pichon described the plan of the court as "the most liberal which it is possible to institute," as it submitted to arbitral decision all claims and in this manner offered "all guarantees of impartiality." [47] But the pourparlers continued to drag, and on May 18, 1910, Schoen wrote that the negotiations in Paris over the mining law had reached unexpected difficulties, and that Germany must take more time to consider the various points.[48] Radolin on the same day warned his government of the danger involved in a failure of the mining law negotiations, which he considered would result in the destruction of all the advantages won by the creation of the Accord of 1909. Failure of the conference would result in a hostile reaction in diplomatic circles and might force Germany to a defense of the Mannesmanns, perhaps in a more than diplomatic manner. The Mannesmanns, he

[41] Pichon to French representatives in London, Berlin, Madrid, July 16, 1909, *Affaires du Maroc*, 1908-1910, no. 227.

[42] Berckheim to Pichon, July 21, 1909, *ibid.*, no. 229; Pichon to Saint-Aulaire, July 29, 1909, *ibid.*, no. 239.

[43] Pichon to French representatives in London, Berlin, and Madrid, July 16, 1909, *ibid.*, no. 227.

[44] Schoen to Radolin, Oct. 30, 1909, *Weissbuch*, no. 70.

[45] Tardieu, *op. cit.*, p. 58; Pichon to Regnault, June 8, 1910, *Affaires du Maroc*, 1908-1910, no. 468.   [46] Tardieu, *op. cit.*, p. 58.

[47] Pichon to Cambon, March 9, 1910, *Affaires du Maroc*, 1908-1910, no. 430.

[48] Note of Schoen, May 18, 1910, *G. P.*, vol. XXIX, no. 10508.

stated, "probably wish the negotiations to fail because they hope from anarchic conditions to draw more profit."[49] William II and Pichon were in London at the time[50] and upon Bethmann Hollweg's request, William II talked to Pichon about the mining law.[51] Pichon regretted the delay, stated that the point of friction was the court of arbitration, and reported that it would probably be some months before the difficulties could be overcome.[52] Contrary to his expectations, the conference completed its work on June 8, 1910; and Pichon reported to Regnault that the law was to be issued by the *maghzen* and then submitted to the diplomatic corps for approval, at which time any nation not represented on the committee might submit its views.[53] According to Tardieu, the mining law was never promulgated because of the objections which the Netherlands raised to some of the technical details.[54] Before these objections could be smoothed out, the French protectorate was established and thereby the nature of all concessions was changed.

Throughout the years 1910 and 1911 the Mannesmanns were struggling with all their skill and available resources to secure a mining law favorable to their interests and to gain from their alleged concessions a profitable return. To carry out their purpose they secured lawyers to prove the legality of their claims and summoned to their aid all conceivable agencies that might through effective propaganda create a public sentiment supporting their cause.[55] So intense and so widespread was their activity that they successfully changed their private interests into a matter of national concern. They argued that they had undertaken the task of exploiting the mines of Morocco in order to save their nation

---

[49] Radolin's statements are included in a footnote to note of Schoen, May 18, 1910, *ibid.*

[50] Pichon and William II were in London to attend the funeral of Edward VII.

[51] Bethmann Hollweg to William II, May 18, 1910, *G. P.*, vol. XXIX, no. 10509; Tardieu, *op. cit.*, p. 48; Staley, *op. cit.*, p. 68.

[52] Editor's footnote to Bethmann Hollweg to William II, May 18, 1910, *G. P.*, vol. XXIX, no. 10509.

[53] Pichon to Regnault, June 8, 1910, *Affaires du Maroc*, 1908-1910, no. 468.

[54] *Op. cit.*, p. 58.

[55] Accounts of the propaganda activities of the Mannesmanns are given in Schoen, *op. cit.*, p. 115; Staley, *op. cit.*, pp. 65-68; *L'Afrique française*, 1910, pp. 89-91, 44-45; Wolff, *op. cit.*, p. 34; Gauvain, *op. cit.*, vol. II, p. 412; and the Reichstag debates cited below.

from a disastrous shortage in iron, and that they refused to agree
to the offers of the Union of Mines solely from patriotic motives,
that is, for the sake of their country's future. They also argued
that they had been urged forward by the German government and,
after expending much time and money, had been dropped as soon
as "their activities no longer suited the purpose of the Foreign
Office." [56] They so presented their case as to leave the impression
that they were better guardians of the future of the German nation than the conservative and bureaucratic Wilhelmstrasse.[57]
Large sums of money were spent in inspired newspaper articles
and in the purchase of newspapers for the purpose of spreading
their propaganda. The Mannesmanns had at their service the facilities of the Pan-German League, which supported them to the
fullest extent.[58] Pamphlets issued by Dr. Class, president of the
League, presented a formidable array of arguments that had as
their purpose the acquisition of sections of Morocco, preferably
the Sous.[59] The success of their propaganda was so marked that
newspapers in general, other than the Socialists and officially inspired papers, took up the cry.[60] In fact, this propaganda, used
in the first instance to convert public opinion, soon translated
itself into vigorous pressure upon the government. Otto Hammann, director of the press bureau in the foreign office, stated that
the "Germans besieged the Foreign Office in Berlin with complaints
and grievances about unjust treatment in the award of public
commissions and concessions. . . ." [61] Schoen, as foreign minister,
found himself "in 'the mud line' and . . . not only pelted with mud
and stones, but also shot at with poisoned arrows, to an extent,
indeed, which far exceeded the accepted limits of the extreme can-
dour customary in political warfare." Indeed, the "excitement
caused by the Mannesmann affair was so great and so widespread
that it led to an avalanche of the most violent attacks on the

---

[56] Staley, op. cit., p. 66.   [57] Wolff, op. cit., p. 34.

[58] Staley, op. cit., p. 69; Heinrich Class, Wider den Storm, pp. 150-152.

[59] Marokko Verloren (1904) and Westmarokko Deutsch (1911) are typical of
the pamphlets issued by the Pan-German League.—Mildred Wertheimer, "The
Pan-German League, 1890-1914," in Studies in History, Economics, and Public
Law, vol. XCII. See also Class, op. cit., pp. 105-107.

[60] Staley, op. cit., p. 65.

[61] Otto Hammann, The World Policy of Germany, 1890-1912, p. 220.

Foreign Office and its responsible head personally." [62] Still hoping to force the government to support their claims, the Mannesmanns carried their activities into the Reichstag, where in December, 1909, and again in March, 1910, the question was debated at length.

On December 9, 1909, Bassermann, a National Liberal and a Pan-German, attacked Schoen for his policy relative to the mining situation and defended the claims of the Mannesmanns.[63] On December 10 Schoen answered these charges and presented the view of the German government. He argued that the Mannesmann claims did not correspond to the "spirit of the Algeciras Act and especially to Article 112," that "the so-called mining law of October 6, 1908, could not be the mining law perceived in the Algeciras Act and is not recognized by the Algeciras powers as such . . . ," because it was kept secret and known only to the Mannesmanns and thus permitted them to secure a monopoly concession. Schoen pointed out that the claims of the brothers were opposed not only by foreign powers but also by various private interests in Germany. The conflict was in no way a Franco-German conflict but a question of two groups, each composed of mixed nationalities.[64]

Schoen's defense failed to satisfy his opponents, who, on December 11, returned to the charge and heaped upon him violent criticism for his action. He was accused of weakness, of being pro-French, and of general neglect of German interests. Typical of the speeches directed against him was that of Liebermann von Sonnenberg, another Pan-German, who, after criticizing the weakness of the foreign secretary, proclaimed that "we would greet with joy in the interest of the German Reich the news" of a Mannesmann's monopoly. He argued that Germany "could use very

---

[62] Schoen, op. cit., p. 118. Stemrich wrote to Kiderlen, December 23, 1909, "Here in Berlin it is rather disagreeable. You see the Mannesmann excitement in the papers. Actually it is unfounded. . . . The state secretary Schoen is perhaps not wrong in considering that the affair has a personal point against him. . . ."—Jäckh, op. cit., vol. II, p. 40. The London Times congratulated Schoen and Bethmann Hollweg on their "upright and sensible" views and recognized their inheritance would force them to give some recognition to the Mannesmanns and their Pan-German defenders.—London Times, Jan. 19, 1910.

[63] Stenographische Berichte des Reichstags, vol. 258, pp. 182-193; Wertheimer, op. cit., p. 134.

[64] Stenographiche Berichte des Reichstags, vol. 258, pp. 205-209.

well the ore treasures there," and that the secretary of state for foreign affairs should "do everything and pledge our government's power that the Mannesmann brothers be supported . . ."; but instead he had heard that Schoen had warned the Mannesmanns that they "should not give further great sums of money and loans to the sultan . . ."; yet it was in this manner that they had won valuable concessions for German interests. Furthermore, he accused Schoen of being too inclined to accept the arguments of the French group. To Schoen's statement that the conflict was one between two groups of mixed nationalities and not a Franco-German conflict, Liebermann replied that although there were French in the Mannesmann group and Germans in the Union of Mines, the Mannesmann firm was controlled by the German majority and the Union of Mines by the French majority. He concluded with the statement, "The Mannesmann interests are at the same time German interests and therefore should be represented by the German government. . . ." [65] Schrader, on December 13, criticized the procedure employed for the promulgation of a mining law and reminded the powers that, according to the Algeciras Act, "the sultan was to make a mining law and on the basis of this law to issue concessions. . . ." Now the powers seemed to say that they were to make the law.[66] The attacks in the Reichstag rendered difficult the work of the mining law commission in session in Paris.

Again on March 14, 15, and 16, 1910, the Mannesmann partisans carried the fight to the floor of the Reichstag. Haussmann defended the policy of the government in upholding its international treaties and again tried to convert the issue into one between two private firms instead of a question of national interests, a Franco-German conflict.[67] The Pan-German Gustave Stresemann,[68] prompted by vigorous cheers from the National Liberals, delivered an eulogistic speech in defense of the Mannesmanns.

---

[65] *Ibid.*, pp. 235-238. Liebermann von Sonnenberg was a member of the Deutsche Soziale and Reform Party and a member of the Pan-German League. —Wertheimer, *op. cit.*, p. 135.

[66] *Stenographische Berichte des Reichstags,* vol. 258, pp. 271-276.

[67] *Ibid.*, vol. 260, pp. 2101-2105.

[68] Stresemann was a member of the National Liberal party and of the Pan-German League.—Wertheimer, *op. cit.*, p. 135.

Stresemann rejoiced that Germany still produced such men, for he believed that all their efforts had been spent with only German interests in view. Their interest was German interest. He doubted whether France would be as world-minded as the German foreign office if the case were that of a French firm.[69] Scheidemann defended the foreign office and criticized especially the monopoly character of the Mannesmann concession, which violated German customary policy of supporting equality of commerce in Morocco. The issue, to Scheidemann, was not just one between France and Germany but between the Mannesmanns and "all the civilized world."[70]

The volley of censure that thus descended upon the government compelled Bethmann Hollweg to rise to its defense. In his speech on March 16 he stated, among other points, that "If Germany . . . should recognize as valid this mining law, on which the Mannesmanns' claims rest, then it must place itself in direct opposition to the resolution of the diplomatic corps of August 20, 1908. . . . No real, no just, no political reason gives us the right to draw back from this Accord of August 20, 1908. . . ." Any breach of this agreement of the diplomatic corps "would mean nothing else than a breach of the Treaty of Algeciras. . . ." The value of the Mannesmanns' concessions was not worth Germany's violation of the treaty. "So far as it is possible within the boundaries which are drawn for us by international treaties and agreements to further the economic interests of the Messrs. Mannesmanns, we have done and will do in the future. . . ." He complained of the Mannesmann publicity campaign and announced that the *White Book* had been published in answer to their charges.[71]

The debates in the Reichstag naturally attracted the attention of other nations. The London *Times* praised "the earnestness and sincerity" of Bethmann Hollweg's speech and denounced the Mannesmann pretensions as "indefensible for all but the extreme Chauvinists. . . ."[72] The *Journal des Débats* called the attention of its readers to the situation and especially the asperity with

---

[69] *Stenographische Berichte des Reichstags,* vol. 260, pp. 2133-3140.

[70] *Ibid.,* pp. 2143-2150.   [71] *Ibid.,* pp. 2162-2164.

[72] London *Times,* March 10, 1910 (Berlin correspondent), March 17, 1910 (Editorial).

which the brothers had defended their interests, and paid tribute
to their skill in making "the patriotic cord vibrate with such vir-
tuosity in the Pan-German press that they have succeeded in transforming an affair of mines into an affair of state. . . ." This paper
also praised the German government for its perfectly loyal attitude and acknowledged that "It is Germany who has taken the
initiative in defending the liberty of economic competition in
Morocco. . . ." [73] Schoen later described the policy of the German
government thus:

> Much as it would have been in Germany's interest that the so-
> called Mannesmann rights should be recognized, and the deposits
> of ore in Morocco exploited, we could not urge them with the force
> we were asked to exert, because this would have brought us into
> conflict with the Moroccan political law formulated by all the
> Powers, partly indeed on our initiative. In attempting to insist
> on the view taken by Mannesmann Bros. we should not only have
> been repudiating our own signature, but we should have had to
> enter on a struggle with an overwhelming majority of the Powers—
> not with France alone, as was purposely asserted—which would
> certainly have ended in a diplomatic defeat. The only practicable
> way out of the difficulty was for the different groups of interests
> to come to an agreement amongst themselves under the benevolent
> guidance of the Government concerned. [74]

Schoen, anxious to eliminate this problem that consistently
plagued his office, had, in January, 1910, proposed two conferences operating simultaneously, one at Berlin between a delegate
of the German participants in the Union of Mines and one of the
Mannesmanns; the other at Paris, between a French delegate of
the Union and one of the brothers. [75] Cambon, in reporting this
proposal to Pichon, stated that Krupp, as a German director in
the Union, was willing to accept the suggestion. [76] Pichon accordingly submitted the proposal to the Union of Mines, and received
from its president a reply to the effect that the Mannesmanns had
been the ones who had broken off the preceding negotiations and
that new offers should come from them, but that if the German

[73] Gauvain, *op. cit.*, vol. II, p. 412.   [74] Schoen, *op. cit.*, p. 115.
[75] Tardieu, *op. cit.*, p. 47.
[76] Cambon to Pichon, Jan. 11, 1910, *Affaires du Maroc*, 1908-1910, no. 368.

members in the Union wished to negotiate, he would submit their suggestions to the Union.[77] The Union decided, however, that such conferences as Schoen suggested would destroy its autonomy as an international organization, and refused to accept the Schoen proposal.[78]

Further suggestions for a renewal of negotiations were blocked by the Mannesmanns' desire to await the results of the Reichstag debates of March 14, 15, and 16. On March 3, 1910, Stemrich reported to Cambon that the Mannesmanns would not accept a Union of Mines proposal to negotiate until the Reichstag, or at least the budget commission, had deliberated on their claims. In regard to this statement, Cambon remarked that "The Brothers Mannesmanns raised themselves up not against France alone but against all Europe and against the Act of Algeciras . . ." and added that "it would not appertain to the Reichstag to settle difficulties of interpretation in matters of international conventions. . . ." [79] When news of this conversation reached the Union of Mines, it denied having made any proposals to the Mannesmanns since the past June. Pichon reported this denial to Cambon but repeated the desire of the French government to secure an agreement between the two groups.[80]

The Reichstag debates had not proven satisfactory to the Mannesmanns; for although their partisans had been untiring in their efforts to force the foreign office to a support of their claims, the government mustered sufficient strength to justify continuing its policy. Consequently, the Mannesmanns became for the moment more conciliatory and chose Walter Rathenau, a sagacious German industrialist, as their representative to go to Paris and effect a settlement.[81] Rathenau agreed to accept the commission if the German government approved, although he claimed to know "little of the people and none of the affair." [82] Schoen stated that he readily gave consent.[83] During a conversation with Pichon in London, May 18, 1910, William II informed him that Rathenau

[77] Pichon to Cambon, Jan. 14, 1910, *ibid.,* no. 370.   [78] Tardieu, *op. cit.,* p. 47.

[79] Cambon to Pichon, March 3, 1910, *Affaires du Maroc,* 1908-1910, no. 425.

[80] Pichon to Cambon, March 5, 1910, *ibid.,* no. 428.

[81] Staley, *op. cit.,* p. 68; Tardieu, *op. cit.,* p. 48.

[82] Tardieu, *op. cit.,* p. 48.   [83] Schoen, *op. cit.,* p. 117.

was coming to Paris to settle the Mannesmann affair. Eight days later, Radolin duly introduced Rathenau to Pichon, who in turn introduced him to the Union of Mines representatives.[84] Rathenau informed the Union that he had the support of Schoen, Pichon, and Briand, and stated that "It is necessary that there be in the Accord neither vanquished nor vanquisher." The Union agreed.[85] He then proposed a partition of Morocco into mining zones. But the Union refused, as the arrangement proposed would form a monopoly and would give Germany control of half of Morocco. The Union proposed not a territorial but a mineral partition according to which the Mannesmanns would receive all the iron and the Union the rest of the minerals. Each would turn over twenty per cent of its net profits to the other. All this, however, Rathenau refused. Then the Union accepted the principle of territorial division but on the condition that the partition affect only the mines already prospected and leave the future prospects free, and that the south and the west of Morocco, where the Union had been prospecting, be left to it. Rathenau agreed and a project was drawn up on May 28. On May 31 one of the Mannesmanns arrived. From that time on, every new day brought forth a new proposal from the Mannesmanns. On June 8 Rathenau in disgust resigned his commission.[86] Again the obstinacy and the uncertain attitude of the brothers wrecked a conference.

With the change of ministers, Kiderlen replaced Schoen and in July the German foreign office complained that the Mannesmann brothers had threatened to appeal directly to its new head to defend their interests. Zimmermann advised Kiderlen that if such a situation arose, he would do well to reply that only two possibilities remained. The Mannesmanns should either "accept as generally as possible the treaty agreed upon by your fully commissioned Dr. Rathenau and to seek through his mediation to secure even now the consent of the Union to this, in which case, you can be certain of the support of the foreign office; or you present your claims, without previously having concluded a treaty with the Union, before the court of judicature established by arbitration

---

[84] Tardieu, *op. cit.*, p. 48.   [85] *Ibid.*, p. 49; Staley, *op. cit.*, p. 68.
[86] Tardieu, *op. cit.*, pp. 49-51; Staley, *op. cit.*, p. 69.

according to the mining law. . . ." [87] The temper of the foreign office was evidently no more favorable to the Mannesmanns, although a change of ministry had taken place, than before; but neither had the temper of the brothers changed. The problem continued to annoy the new officials as it had the old.

A suggestion for solving the difficulties through the creation of a new international syndicate with the largest shares falling to the Union of Mines and the Mannesmanns was presented in late 1910.[88] Schoen, now German ambassador in Paris, appeared sympathetic. The Union feared that the new proposal would mean the absorption of French industrial interests by international finance. To clarify the situation, the German embassy specified that shares in the new society be distributed with the Union of Mines holding 50 per cent, the Mannesmanns 40 per cent, and the Anglo-German group 10 per cent; and that furthermore the management be invested in a directory of six, three named by the Union and three by the Mannesmanns. The Mannesmanns asked for a reimbursement of their advances to the sultan from the first returns and the "assurance, in order to give satisfaction to the Pan-German press, that forty per cent of the iron that these groups would exploit, would be offered to German factories at market price. . . ." The Union refused because the capital furnished by the industry and finance of Germany, when the percentage allotment of the Germans in the Union of Mines and in the Anglo-German group was added to the per cent allotted to the Mannesmanns, would far surpass that granted to French industrialists and financiers.[89] The uncertain conditions that resulted from the French expedition to Fez interrupted the negotiations, and the Union of Mines decided to let the matter rest until the question could be thrown into the arbitral court planned for by the mining law.[90]

Economic penetration of Morocco was far from quiescent while the negotiations were in progress, as both the Union of Mines and the Mannesmanns continued their activities in an effort to discover paying beds of minerals. July 12, 1909, Dr. Muehlon,

[87] Zimmermann to Kiderlen, July 13, 1910, in Jäckh, *op. cit.,* vol. II, p. 120.
[88] Tardieu, *op. cit.,* p. 51; Staley, *op. cit.,* p. 69.
[89] Tardieu, *op. cit.,* p. 51; Staley, *op. cit.,* p. 69.   [90] Tardieu, *op. cit.,* p. 51.

who had been sent by Krupp as a representative of the Union of
Mines to investigate conditions in Morocco, reported that the
Union had decided to go ahead with prospecting in three terri-
tories, Tangier and the Riff, from Mogador to Sous, and in the
High Atlas. In Tangier and Mogador permanent bureaus were to
be established, the one at Tangier to be controlled by a German,
Langenheim, the one at Mogador by a French engineer. Expedi-
tions into the High Atlas were to be of an itinerant nature.[91]

But the Mannesmanns pressed forward with greater vigor than
did the Union. In 1909 Alfred Mannesmann, in an attempt to
enter the Sous, had been arrested by Moroccan officials, but with
the aid of the French legation had been released. The next year,
he tried again but with little success.[92] In 1911 the Mannesmanns
redoubled their efforts to secure advantageous concessions, especially in the south, although on March 5 Lister, in notifying Grey
that a German warship was to visit Casablanca in a few days,
stated he saw no objections to the visit of the vessel and interpreted it as a kind of "moral assistance to German commercial and
agricultural enterprise in the Shawia, which is particularly active
just now under the lead of the Mannesmanns. . . ." [93] But the Sous
district was much more attractive to the Mannesmanns. Johnstone, the British vice-consul in Mogador, reported on January
21, 1911, that he understood that the Germans were buying land
in great quantities around Funti and that he had been informed
that the Mannesmanns had the idea of securing interests which
would enable them to open a port south of Agadir.[94] May 5, 1911,
Goschen informed Grey that news was current in Berlin that "a
party of German engineers and traders had landed at Mogador
and are purchasing land at high prices. I hear that Press Bureau
have informed an inquiring journalist that the Government have
no knowledge as to the truth of the report but that the Mannesmann firm were very active people and that there was no knowing

[91] Lancken to Erkert, July 12, 1909, *G. P.*, vol. XXIX, no. 10460.
[92] *L'Afrique française,* July, 1911, p. 265; *Questions diplomatiques et coloniales* (1911), July 16, 1911, p. 113.
[93] Lister to Grey, March 5, 1911, *Br. Docs.*, vol. VII, no. 191.
[94] Lister to Grey, Jan. 30, 1911, *ibid.*, no. 188, enclosure, Johnstone to Lister, Jan. 21, 1911.

what they might be doing. . . ." [95] On May 9 Billy reported similar charges made by Marc, French consul at Mogador, in which Marc charged the Germans of purchasing land in Agadir at an exorbitant price, since the visit of the French ship to that port.[96] A few days later agents of the Mannesmanns arrived at Arksis, south of Agadir, and opened up communications with the natives. In his report to Cruppi on May 19 Billy stated that the agents had sold sugar, tea, and cotton goods to the natives;[97] but in his report of June 8 he stated that the consul at Mogador had sent detailed confirmation of the fact that "the agents of M. Mannesmann have remained ten days at Arksis and have distributed gratuitously to the Sbouis natives some sacks of rice, sugar, barley, and tea, and two guns and 2,000 cartridges, after which they left, announcing an early return with a new cargo. . . ." [98] On June 14 he reported that the agents had returned to Arksis but found their reception so doubtful that they sailed away.[99] The Mannesmanns penetrated even farther inland.

Beginning in January, 1911, M. and Mme. de Lacharrière, agents of the *Comité du Maroc,* made an extensive trip through the southern section of Morocco and went overland from Marrakech to Taroudant. On June 6 Billy reported that Lacharrière had returned to Marrakech and that he found Germans active in the Sous section in distributing money and presents to all the chiefs or notables in an effort to secure a monopoly of commerce in that valley. Lacharrière claimed that these Germans were trying to buy property in Taroudant and in the neighborhood of the city, and were persuading the natives that the port of Agadir was to be opened and reserved to German commerce.[100] In his account of his trip, published in 1912, he gave a more detailed account of the activities of the Germans he found in the Sous section. He reported that there were present three agents of the Mannesmanns who were trying to persuade the natives that the

[95] Goschen to Grey, May 5, 1911, *ibid.,* no. 251.

[96] Billy to Cruppi, May 9, 1911, *Affaires du Maroc,* 1910-1912, no. 272.

[97] Billy to Cruppi, May 19, 1911, *ibid.,* no. 302.

[98] Billy to Cruppi, June 8, 1911, *ibid.,* no. 349.

[99] Billy to Cruppi, June 14, 1911, *ibid.,* no. 378.

[100] Billy to Cruppi, June 6, 1911, *ibid.,* no. 344.

Germans were strong and the French were weak, and that, therefore, they should grant to the Germans what they wanted. He
also reported that a chief expressed astonishment that he should
ask about agriculture, since all the Germans ever asked about
were mines. He repeated his charges that the Germans were
buying land rights from chieftains and added that they were
paying for them by issuing protégé certificates.[101] Obviously, any
such purchase of land or mining rights was in violation of international agreements. Activities of the Mannesmanns in encouraging the caids of the Sous to expect German protection were known
to the German foreign office. Zimmermann commented that these
activities were contrary to the Madrid convention[102] and the
Algeciras Act.[103] Nevertheless, claims of the Mannesmanns in the
Sous district formed a convenient excuse for the German foreign
office in July, 1911. German diplomats could answer the embarrassing question as to what German interests lay in the Sous
valley by the statement that "Messrs. Mannesmann certainly had
large interests in those regions." [104]

Frequent complaints about underhanded activities were flung
back and forth between the two groups. France accused the Mannesmanns of supporting Mulay Hafid in his revolt against Abdul
Aziz and of encouraging him to resist the demands of France in
her arrangement of the loan of 1910, of purchasing land in violation of regulations laid down in international agreements, and of
securing in an underhand fashion monopoly grants of mineral
concessions.[105] The Mannesmanns, on their side, issued counter

---

[101] Lacharrière, *op. cit.*, pp. 155-173.   [102] See pp. 20-21, *supra*.

[103] Note of Zimmermann, June 12, 1911, *G. P.*, vol. XXIX, no. 10572.

[104] Corbett to Grey, July 6, 1911, *Br. Docs.*, vol. VII, no. 362. Corbett credited
Count Podewils with this statement.

[105] Lancken to F. O., Feb. 17, 1910, *G. P.*, vol. XXIX, no. 10499. Lancken
reported a conversation with Pichon in which Pichon asked for German assistance in the loan of 1910, especially as the policy of the sultan's was to stir up
distrust between France and Germany, and in which "The Mannesmanns might
have also their hand in the game. . . ." Schoen in a marginal note to this despatch
commented that German public opinion was constantly on the alert for incidents
which could be interpreted as a violation of the Act of Algeciras due to the
interest in the Mannesmann case.

Charges that the Mannesmanns, through their protégés, tried to prevent the
establishment of the French protectorate even after the Treaty of 1911, frequently crop out. See, for example, Maurice, *op. cit.*, pp. 173, 180.

charges against the French. They accused the French authorities of permitting exploitation of mines along the frontier before the mining law was issued.[106] To this charge, Lyautey replied that since French occupation of the frontier section, prospectors from many nations had flocked into the territory, and that it was impossible to keep them from prospecting, but that no exploitation of mines had been permitted.[107] When a French ship entered the port of Agadir performing its duty in guarding against contraband trade, Mannesmann partisans became nervous and asked the German government to give the Reichstag an explanation of the move, since "that is the key to the most valuable territory, to the mining treasure in the most valuable part of Morocco . . . , also a territory in which the Mannesmann brothers' concessions have been granted by the sultan of Morocco. . . ." [108] Kiderlen explained the situation and calmed their fears.[109] Among the several factors that contributed to the failure of the Accord of 1909 as applied to mining interests was this mutual suspicion which translated every move of the opposing party into an act of chicanery or trickery; and this in the eyes of the victim justified acts of reprisal. Such an atmosphere was not conducive to coöperation in economic concessions as provided for in the February Accord.

The Franco-German Accord of 1909 failed to operate in the mining field because the German government was not able to present a clear title to German coöperation. The mortgage of the Mannesmann claims too greatly encumbered their actions. Tardieu stated that Germany was accustomed to regulate the activities of her industrial concerns but that she was unable to exercise control over the powerful Mannesmann firm. He accredited the success of the firm in defying the government to the tremendous influence which it exercised over public opinion.[110] Theodor Wolff, former editor of the *Berliner Tageblatt*, conferred upon the Mannesmanns the title of "the first German Captains of industry who succeeded

---

[106] Pichon to Regnault, Jan. 23, 1910, *Affaires du Maroc*, 1908-1910, no. 372; Cambon to Pichon, March 7, 1910, *ibid.*, no. 429.

[107] Regnault to Pichon, Jan. 31, 1910, *ibid.*, no. 374.

[108] Bassermann before the Reichstag, Dec. 10, 1910, *Stenographische Berichte des Reichstags*, vol. 262, pp. 3557-3558.

[109] Kiderlen-Waechter before the Reichstag, *ibid.*, p. 3591.

[110] *Op. cit.*, pp. 53, 16, and footnote p. 17.

in turning their business into a matter of national concern," and likewise hailed them "pioneers of the new technique." He defined this new technique as the method used by a private enterprise in transforming itself into a political power by using all the resources of agitation and expending large sums of money "to bend the foreign policy of the German Empire to its will." Wolff's "Captains of industry" believed that "the very reason for the existence of the German Empire and the proper aim of its policy was to stand forth in shining armour in the advocacy of individual business interests and to throw its sword into the scale, . . . on behalf of every 'go-getter' captain of industry, and of every influential industrial group. . . ." [111]

The objectives that motivated the opposition of the Mannesmann brothers to the plans of their government have been variously described. Their partisans claimed that they were moved solely by patriotic motives; to secure iron to supply their country's deficiency.[112] Hammann stated that the Mannesmanns wanted to force the foreign office to secure a protectorate over the Sous region, but did not specify whether their interests were of a private or patriotic nature.[113] Extreme opponents of the firm believed that the Mannesmanns were not interested in actual economic development of the mineral resources of Morocco, but were a financial concern interested in making as much profit as possible with as little expenditure as possible. They secured concessions of doubtful legality and with these as weapons expected to force the German government to furnish them with sufficient support to transmute these concessions into large profits. Since they were in a position to block the work of the Union of Mines, they expected to force the Union to pay handsomely for their coöperation either in the form of legal recognition of their mining concessions in large sections of Morocco, or in the form of a large percentage of the shares in the Union of Mines. Tardieu believed that the latter was their plan; for they would then benefit from the collaboration of the "most reputable metallurgists of Europe" and from the credit facilities of the Union, which would aid them in financing

---

[111] *Op. cit.,* pp. 33-35.

[112] See, for example, the various debates in the Reichstag.

[113] Hammann, *op. cit.,* p. 220.

any future prospecting for mines.[114] Not being able to secure their objective, the Mannesmanns refused to accept any plan proposed until after the Franco-German Treaty of November 4, 1911 had been published.[115] The vigorous imperialism of the Pan-Germans, adroitly marshalled by the Mannesmanns in their own service, had routed the Accord of 1909 and inflicted upon its protagonists an ignominious defeat. The economic clauses of that instrument operated no more successfully in the field of mines than it had in railroads or other public works.

The unvaried defeat which met all efforts to make the economic clauses of the Accord of 1909 operative had by 1911 disillusioned all but the incurably optimistic. The vision of a future of peaceful and profitable Franco-German coöperation had been rudely dispelled. An analysis of the forces involved necessitates the decision that the vision was only a dream. The Accord of 1909 was not a masterpiece of diplomacy but an agreement couched in such vague terms[116] that each party was at liberty to interpret the Accord to its own advantage. The mere interpretation of terms would inevitably lead to friction. Schoen had foreseen this difficulty and had commented, before the agreement was signed, that "a formula which would give a political program so precise that misunder-

---

[114] *Op. cit.,* p. 46.

[115] This treaty convinced them of the futility of their opposition, and they agreed to a settlement according to which they received 40 per cent of the shares in a new society, the Union of Mines 40 per cent, and French industrialists the remaining 20 per cent.—Staley, *op. cit.,* p. 70; Foreign Office to Board of Trade, Nov. 27, 1911, *Br. Docs.,* vol. VII, no. 719. Grey considered the per cent allotted to England too small, but as English industrialists had never taken up the full quota of their allotment in the Union of Mines, he felt a protest was inopportune.—*Ibid.* Cambon, in reporting the settlement, commented, "The Mannesmann affair is finally settled. Ouf!—It has not been very easy. . . ."—Cambon to Kiderlen, Nov. 14, 1911, *G. P.,* vol. XXIX, no. 10784. A law of the French protectorate provided for settlement of mining claims by a court of arbitration. Operating under this law, a court of arbitration composed of one German, one Frenchman, and an appointee of the King of Norway, awarded the Mannesmanns 30,000 gold francs in recognition of twelve of their two hundred claims. The question was thus removed from the international field; but the Mannesmanns sought additional compensation from the German government and secured some awards, though many of the cases were still pending when Hitler came to power.—Staley, *op. cit.,* pp. 71-72.

[116] Stuart, *French Foreign Policy,* p. 283; Maurice, *op. cit.,* p. 136; Tardieu, *op. cit.,* pp. 85-87; Schmitt, *op. cit.,* pp. 306-308; Caillaux, *op. cit.,* p. 37.

standing in meaning would be excluded, would be very difficult to find. . . ." [117] The framers of the Accord dodged the issue by avoiding precision in terms, and left such details for the future.

The basis upon which the entire Accord rested was a clear distinction between economic and political interests,[118] but this complex modern order does not permit such distinction. Instead, political and economic interests shade imperceptibly into each other and defy the skill of the most expert political economist who attempts to disentangle and classify their elements. Special political interests were recognized as appertaining to France, and the right to economic coöperation was conceded to Germany. When efforts were made to place into practical operation these rights assumed by the Accord as lying in two distinct fields, the problem stood forth in bold relief; but the solution was not carved in like boldness. In the question of the railroad negotiations, for example, the major issue was the problem of determining when a railroad project ceased being an economic investment and became a political venture. If Germany granted to France the right to build a military road from Oudjda to Taourirt, French political interests would be served but at the expense of German economic interests. On the other hand, if France yielded to German economic contentions, French political interests might be endangered. The bankruptcy of the sultan aggravated the situation. The sultan had no funds with which to further the economic development of his country and could finance public works constructions only through loans from foreign powers to whom he would gradually be compelled to mortgage most of his resources. But obviously a sultan whose economic resources are mortgaged to a foreign power cannot be politically independent of that power. France must, therefore, hold within her own hands all financial contracts with the *maghzen* in order to safeguard her own political interests. But similarly, Germany must safeguard her economic interests, which could easily be strangled by French financial pressure upon the bankrupt ruler; and consequently, she tied the question of railroads to the loan of **1911**, while France wished to keep the two

---

[117] Note of Schoen, Jan. 9, 1909, *G. P.,* vol. XXIV, no. 8479.

[118] Stuart, *French Foreign Policy,* p. 283; Tardieu, *op. cit.,* pp. 85-87; Maurice, *op. cit.,* p. 144.

separated. France might try to stretch the political clauses to the utmost, and Germany might try to expand the economic clauses to their greatest breadth; but the essential fact remained that France could not concede full economic coöperation to Germany without endangering her political interests; and Germany could not risk the establishment of French political preponderance without endangering her economic interests. The interests of France and Germany in Morocco did not lie in two separate and distinct spheres, one economic and the other political, but formed one imperialistic prize the politics and economics of which were inextricably mingled.

Every aspect of the Accord of 1909 is characterized by its vagueness. Even if the French and German foreign offices had agreed upon a definite delimitation of the political and economic spheres, misunderstanding due to variation in interpretation of the economic clauses would inevitably have arisen. Germany interpreted the economic clauses of the Accord as a pledge made by the two governments to form Franco-German syndicates who were to be issued whatever desirable concessions Morocco had to offer. France did not, however, consider herself bound to create such syndicates but only pledged to encourage the activities of business men in that direction.[119] In other words, Germany would place the blame for the failure of economic coöperation upon the French government, while France would place it upon the financiers and industrialists of both countries. France claimed that her form of government prevented the interference of the government in the economic field, but that the close alliance between government and business in Germany made such interference on the part of the German government possible. Yet it was Germany who signally failed to force one of her industrialists to yield to the common interest. The Mannesmann brothers were as intractable as the N'Goko Sangha company.

The two nations also differed in their interpretation of the extent to which economic coöperation was to be carried.[120] Germany

---

[119] Tardieu, *op. cit.*, pp. 17, 85.

[120] Davis, *op. cit.*, pp. 413-414; Tardieu, *op. cit.*, p. 85; Schmitt, *op. cit.*, pp. 307-308. Schmitt considered the entire Accord as a trap for France. He stated: "In other words, France and Germany would establish an *economic condomi-*

had in mind a Franco-German condominium. France, conscious of her obligation to England and Spain, if not of her obligations under the Act of Algeciras, wished to recognize the rights of the nationals of other powers and especially the rights of the English and Spanish nationals. Germany, owing nothing to England or Spain, would leave to France the task of satisfying these nations from her own quota. If France divided her share with England and Spain, Germany would be left in a predominant position in every economic concession; and France, in her political position, would be left in a very precarious situation. The French foreign office, however, failed to state the situation clearly and firmly, but through the use of indefinite, vague phrases alternately encouraged Germany to hope for great economic concessions and discouraged her by needless delays or by renunciation of the proposed project.[121] Germany, in June, 1911, had given up hopes of securing any economic concessions under the terms of the Accord of 1909.

The Act of Algeciras had recognized the independence and territorial integrity of the Sherifian empire, had internationalized some of the administrative functions, and had guaranteed the open door and economic equality to all nations. The Accord of 1909 recognized the political preëminence of France in Morocco, and created an economic order in which France and Germany were to receive a privileged, if not a monopolistic, position. The two cannot be harmonized. The cry that the Act of Algeciras had been

---

nium and secure a virtual monopoly, in spite of the open door supposedly guaranteed by Article CVII of the Act of Algeciras! Germany was now suggesting the very procedure, the possible application of which by France alone had been one of her bases of action in 1905-6. If one remembers also that in German eyes commerce and politics were inseparable, one may well ask whether the political ascendancy of France, theoretically recognized by Germany, would not have been found illusory and meaningless. Not until the Morocco question was finally solved by the agreements of November, 1911, was it realized that Germany had set a trap into which France walked most unsuspectingly. . . . The commercial and industrial conquest of Morocco by Germany would nullify the political influence of France, to secure which had been the object of the *entente cordiale:* if the German economic designs were not successful, the Wilhelmstrasse could then reopen the whole question, on the ground that the convention of 1909 had remained a dead letter. . . ."

[121] Schoen, *op. cit.,* p. 144; Stuart, *French Foreign Policy,* p. 291; Tardieu, *op. cit.,* pp. 85-87.

violated should have been raised in 1909 and not left quiescent until 1911. The effort to make the two treaties operative at the same time could only result in failure. England demanded that concessions of public works be open to public bidding as guaranteed by the Act of Algeciras. Under this system of adjudication, France and Germany could not guarantee that any specific concession would fall to any particular syndicate. A system of private contract must supersede the system of adjudication if the Accord of 1909 were to function. In case that should happen, the rights of nationals of other powers would depend upon the good will of France and Germany and not upon the Act of Algeciras. France, in her effort to hold to both agreements, failed to make either effective.

An analysis of the causes for the failure of the Accord of 1909 cannot ignore the internal conditions within France and Germany. The foreign offices were in no sense free agents but were subject to the coercive power of public opinion. This was more true in France than in Germany, but even in Germany the propaganda of the Mannesmanns had prevented the foreign office from solving the mining problem. According to Halévy, the Accord of 1909 broke down in France "because of the fierce resistance of the French nationalists who thought it too international, and of the French Socialists who thought it too capitalistic. . . ." [122] French Socialists had defeated the payment of the indemnity to the N'Goko Sangha company, a necessary preliminary to the success of that particular project. French nationalists had fought the idea of a Franco-German railroad project. Another significant French element destructive of the Accord was the frequent ministerial changes. Projects for Franco-German coöperation started under Pichon were renounced by the Monis cabinet and treated as though they were simple colonial matters with no international complications. Cruppi, foreign minister in the Monis cabinet, with no diplomatic experience, had apparently no concept of the complexities involved in the various issues with which he had to deal; Caillaux, interested in securing a workable arrangement with Germany, instituted non-official negotiations, which resulted only

---

[122] Elie Halévy, *The World Crisis of 1914-1918: An Interpretation*, p. 24.

in heaping upon him the recriminations of Socialists and Nationalists alike and giving to Germany further cause to doubt the sincerity of the French government. The element of uncertainty that
hung over the actions of the French foreign office prevented a
successful solution of any of the problems involved in economic co-
operation between French and German nationals.

The essentials necessary to a successful operation of any treaty,
mutual faith between the contracting parties and sincere desire
of each to make effective the agreements reached, were lacking
where France and Germany were the interested parties. France
feared that Germany would extend her economic participation to
infringe upon the political rights assured to France. Germany
feared that France would translate her political rights into a
virtual protectorate and monopolize economic concessions by
virtue of those rights. This mutual distrust found expression
among the nationals of each country in a more virulent form than
in the respective foreign offices. Forced to breathe this atmosphere
of suspicion, the Franco-German Accord of 1909, framed in
general and indefinite terms, broke down in its economic aspects.
Its political aspects found no better success.

Chapter VII

FRANCE AND DECADENT MOROCCO

French prestige, French ambition, French colonial policy demanded that France be recognized as the heir apparent to the Sherifian throne. Delcassé had secured from Spain, England, and Italy the recognition of this French right of inheritance; but the Act of Algeciras, created at Germany's instigation, had prolonged the demise and withheld the legacy so long as the tottering empire could maintain a semblance of sovereignty. By this Act, Germany had foiled French plans but had secured no advantages for herself. Discontented with the existing arrangement, the two nations formed the Franco-German Accord of 1909, whose vague economic and political clauses were contrary to the Act of Algeciras; for France agreed to a system bordering close upon a Franco-German economic condominium, in exchange for which Germany, "pursuing only economic interests in Morocco, recognized that . . . the special political interests of France are there closely tied to the consolidation of internal peace and order, and decide[d] not to interfere in these interests. . . ." The Act of Algeciras only prolonged the life of the Sherifian empire without restoring to it any semblance of vitality. Consequently, Mulay Hafid in 1911, unable to subdue the revolt of his subjects and to free the Europeans from the besieged city of Fez, was forced to call upon France for aid. Could France rely upon her own interpretation of the Accord of 1909 and answer his call? Would France and Germany agree any more closely in their interpretation of the political clauses of the Accord than they had of its economic clauses? France by her march to Fez forced an answer to these questions.

The French expedition to Fez, however, can be understood only in the light of the position attained by France prior to 1911. Her program in North Africa necessitated international recognition of her political preponderance in Morocco—a recognition she bid fair to attain when in 1905 Germany forced upon her the Conference of Algeciras. Although the resultant Act internationalized various functions in the administration of the Sherifian empire, it recognized the unique position of France and Spain and accorded to them a preponderant share in the relative percentage distribution of functions.[1]

The major percentage of the capital in the State Bank was French; France was always represented on the customs commission; and the police force of Morocco was under the supervision of France and Spain, as was the regulation of contraband. According to the Act of Algeciras, the sultan was to develop a police force recruited from the Moroccan musulmen, commanded by Moroccan caids, and apportioned among the eight ports open to commerce. This police force was to be instructed by Spanish and French officers.[2] When in 1907 France, with the reluctant aid of Spain, occupied Casablanca, she invoked, as justification for her action, her obligations involved in the police clauses of the Treaty of Algeciras plus the right of a nation always to protect its nationals. She justified her extension of this right to include the Chaouya district on the grounds that the city of Casablanca could not be made safe so long as the outlying district was in a state of chaos.[3] French occupation of the Oudjda district was based on treaties signed in 1901 and 1902 between France and Morocco, by which France was to coöperate with the Sherifian empire in maintaining peace on the frontier between Algeria and Morocco.[4] As the Act of Algeciras did not specifically annul these treaties, France considered them still in operation.

The Act of Algeciras gave to France the exclusive right to enforce the regulations dealing with contraband trade on the Algerian frontier, to Spain the same right in the Riff country, and to the two powers conjointly the right to supervise contraband in general. By agreement with the powers, which was renewed each year, France and Spain secured from the sultan the right to enforce the regulations relative to contraband trade thus laid down in the Act of Algeciras.[5] In the renewal for 1910, recognition

---

[1] See pp. 45-46, supra. [2] See p. 45, supra.
[3] See pp. 48-53, supra. [4] See pp. 29-30, supra.
[5] Negotiations dealing with renewal of the right to regulate contraband may be found in Affaires du Maroc for any specific year. For example, see Affaires du Maroc, 1908-1910, for negotiations relative to the renewal for 1910.

of the right of France and Spain to extend supervision of contraband to non-open ports was specifically recognized.[6] In the execution of that mandate, France aroused the suspicion of the German
public, if not of the German government, as to the purity of
French motives. In November, 1910, the French cruiser, *Du
Chayla,* while carrying out its function of supervising contraband
trade, stopped at Agadir and the commander Sénès went ashore.[7]
This incident made the headlines of German newspapers and provoked questions in the German Reichstag:[8] What right had a
French cruiser in a closed port of Morocco? Kiderlen presented the
case to the French government and received the reply that the
French "warship had done nothing except exercise surveillance
of contraband of arms," [9] a traffic which prospered in and around
Agadir. Sénès' visit on land, Pichon stated, was only a courteous
call on local authorities.[10] Kiderlen thereupon made this explanation to the Reichstag, and the case was officially closed. French
defenders made much ado over this incident in the summer of 1911;
for in retrospect they saw the German protest in December, 1910,
as a precursor of the German *coup* of July, 1911.[11] The incident
may be taken as evidence of German interest in southern Morocco
but not as proof of an embryo German plan maturing some six
months later. Interest in the possibilities of Agadir as a commercial port was widespread in Germany, it is true, but was not
limited to that nation alone. That France was interested was shown
in Billy's report of Sénès' visit, especially when he emphasized
that "the natural port of Agadir is the best that they encountered
on all the littoral of Morocco," [12] and in Cambon's comment on
this report, "that which struck me particularly is the information

---

[6] Regnault to Pichon, March 24, 1910, *Affaires du Maroc,* 1908-1910, no. 443.

[7] Billy to Pichon, Nov. 20, 1910, *ibid.,* 1910-1912, no. 22.

[8] Zimmermann to Schoen, Dec. 16, 1910, *G. P.,* vol. XXIX, no. 10517; Pichon
before the chamber of deputies, Jan. 12, 1911, *Annales de la chambre des
députés,* session ordinaire de 1911, vol. I, pp. 20-21.

[9] Cambon to Pichon, Dec. 10, 1910, *Affaires du Maroc,* 1910-1912, no. 26.

[10] Pichon to Cambon, Dec. 15, 1910, *ibid.,* no. 28.

[11] Cambon to Cruppi, April 9, 1911, *ibid.,* no. 166; Henry W. Steed, *Through
Thirty Years,* p. 341; Metternich to Bethmann Hollweg, July 21, 1911, *G. P.,*
vol. XXIX, no. 10617.

[12] Billy to Pichon, Nov. 20, 1910, *Affaires du Maroc,* 1910-1912, no. 22.

relative to the anchorage of Agadir." [13] The question of making Agadir an open port was freely discussed by the chancelleries and the press of Europe, and all recognized the unique value of Agadir as a port.[14]

The interplay of suspicion and mistrust that marked the course of Moroccan affairs was evident in this discussion. Billy suspected Germany of making an agreement with Spain relative to Ifni, and consequently expected Germany to oppose the opening of Agadir as an act "which might upset their game, whatever it was." To this comment, Lister added that Billy might be right, and that this might explain why "the mere mention of Agadir acts upon the Germans like a red rag to a bull." [15] Germany evidently believed that France planned to secure an advantageous position in Agadir and then persuade the sultan to open the port.[16] Marc, French consul at Mogador, presented a similar charge against the Germans, whom he accused of hastening soon after Sénès' visit to purchase land in Agadir with little attention to legality of procedure.[17] If the port were to be opened, they wished to be in on the ground floor. The official German view expressed approval of opening the port, on condition that the sultan "inform simultaneously the signatory powers and take measures in order that the interests of all the nations are treated in an equal manner." [18] Her official position was on sound legal grounds. England and France investigated the advisability of opening the port of Agadir but hesitated because of the self-evident fact that Agadir, the best natural port on the coast, would kill Mogador, a poor artificial port.[19] A multiplicity of causes thus kept Agadir a closed port until 1912.

---

[13] Cambon to Pichon, Dec. 17, 1910, *ibid.,* no. 29.

[14] Cambon to Pichon, Jan. 3, 1911, *ibid.,* no. 33.

[15] Lister to Grey, Feb. 5, 1911, *Br. Docs.,* vol. VII, no. 189.

[16] Cambon to Pichon, Jan. 3, 1911, *Affaires du Maroc,* 1910-1912, no. 33; Billy to Pichon, Jan. 31, 1911, *ibid.,* no. 53, enclosure, Seckendorff to Rappard, dean of the diplomatic corps at Tangier, Jan. 23, 1911.

[17] Billy to Pichon, Jan. 31, 1911, *ibid.,* no. 272, enclosure, Marc to Billy, Apr. 24, 1911.

[18] Billy to Pichon, Jan. 31, 1911, *ibid.,* no. 53, enclosure, Seckendorff to Rappard, Jan. 23, 1911.

[19] Billy to Cruppi, May 9, 1911, *ibid.,* no. 272; Cruppi to Billy, Apr. 4, 1911, *ibid.,* no. 148.

As France extended her political activities during the years 1910 and 1911, her experience with contraband was repeated. Her political interest was closely tied to the maintenance of peace and order, whose twin requisites, money and an army, Mulay Hafid did not have. French efforts to supply this deficiency changed German suspicion to hostility and open protest. In 1877 France had signed an agreement with Sultan Mulay Hassan which created the French military mission.[20] French officers were to instruct and direct certain functions of the Moroccan army. These functions carried with them certain disadvantages that were bound to react upon the prestige of France either in the eyes of the natives or in those of European countries. For example, the sultan's idea of the proper punishment to inflict upon a rebellious subject or tribe did not always conform to the ideas of civilized nations. In the fall of 1909 Mulay Hafid was guilty of barbarous cruelties perpetrated upon prisoners. Such acts were revolting to Europeans and even to the natives of the capital and reacted in such a fashion as to injure the prestige of the French officers who were directing the *mehallas* that made the arrests; and this, in turn, hurt the prestige of the French nation.[21] France, in an effort to offset such reactions and also sincerely desirous to prevent a repetition of similar cruelties, proposed to the diplomatic corps at Tangier that the powers send Mulay Hafid a collective note of protest.[22] Meanwhile, Gaillard, in the name of his country, protested to the sultan against such cruelties. Mulay Hafid agreed that these acts would not recur, but he added that, in as barbarous a country as Morocco, methods must be used which would not, in truth, be recognized in civilized countries.[23] Regnault, indeed, still considered that the collective note was necessary;[24] and, after agreement with the other members of the corps, the note was presented. The sultan promised to avoid such punishments in the future.[25] Yet, despite his promise, he was soon guilty of using

---

[20] See p. 17, *supra.*

[21] Saint-Aulaire to Pichon, Aug. 18, 1909, *Affaires du Maroc,* 1908-1910, no. 252.

[22] Regnault to Pichon, Aug. 28, 1909, *ibid.,* no. 264; Pichon to Regnault, Aug. 25, 1909, *ibid.,* no. 259; Regnault to Pichon, Aug. 23, 1909, *ibid.,* no. 257.

[23] Regnault to Pichon, Sept. 2, 1909, *ibid.,* no. 274.

[24] *Ibid.*   [25] Regnault to Pichon, Sept. 13, 1909, *ibid.,* no. 284.

uncivilized humor in murdering a leader of a rebellious tribe.[26] Regnault advised his government to refuse to the sultan the services of French instructors as long as he practiced such barbarities,[27] but promises of better conduct kept the French officers in the sultan's service.

More disturbing to France was the danger attached to service with the *mehallas*[28] in the field. The major portion of the sultan's army was recruited from the tribes for a specific campaign and was demobilized as soon as that expedition was accomplished. Training under such conditions was a difficult task, and the usual condition was that the men were only half trained when they went into a campaign. This feeble training rendered any active service with the *mehallas* dangerous. The chief danger, however, lay in the uncertain nature of the loyalty of the men. Pay, ammunition, and provisions for the troops were always slow and uncertain. At any moment the native troops were likely to become irritated at the lack of pay or the lack of provisions, and turn against the French officers who were accompanying them; for they were inclined to lay the blame for all their inconveniences upon the foreigner. The jealousy of the native chiefs, who resented the position accorded the French instructors, naturally increased the danger.[29] Complications that might have far-reaching results could easily arise from the death of a French military instructor while on duty with a *mehalla* in the field.

France seemed to be conscious of the situation, not only as it affected the individuals involved, but as it affected the entire Moroccan situation; but her ministers did not seem to be able to solve the difficulty. Pichon, April 23, 1909, instructed General Mangin, in command of the French military mission, to obtain from the sultan measures necessary to the security of the instructors and to the effective operation of the French military

---

[26] Regnault to Pichon, Sept. 17, 1909, *ibid.,* no. 290.

[27] Regnault to Pichon, Sept. 25, 1909, *ibid.,* no. 300.

[28] A *mehalla* was a division of the sultan's army recruited from the tribes but officered by French instructors. The *mehalla* was distinct from the feudal army led by the tribal chieftains. See p. 17, *supra.*

[29] Saint-Aulaire to Pichon, April 16, 1909, *Affaires du Maroc,* 1908-1910, no. 172; Tardieu, *op. cit.,* pp. 130-135.

mission, but he did not specify what this would involve.[30] The
sultan would not consider a military mission effective that did
not carry its work into the active field of campaign against rebellious tribes; yet he was not in a position to guarantee payment to
his troops as a necessary condition to the safety of the foreign
instructors. Pichon, on June 21, 1909, sent instructions to the
French mission that he did not think it possible "to oppose in
principle and in an absolute manner a refusal to the demands of
the sultan on this subject . . . ," as it would cause the new
ruler to consider that France had deserted him and would injure
French influence, which had been carefully built up by Commander
Mangin. He added instructions to Mangin to examine each request
of the sultan's with minute care, in order to determine if he had
taken the necessary precautions for the safety of the foreign instructors; and, in case he considered that these precautions had
not been taken, Mangin was to "suspend sending instructors with
the *mehallas* or to order their return to Fez." Pichon was assured
that "Commander Mangin will take these dispositions only if
the gravity of circumstances appear to impose it upon him. . . ." [31]
Continued reports of the danger involved in such service[32] caused
Pichon to authorize the French commander not to let any French
officer or sub-officer go with the *mehallas* and to recall all to Fez.[33]

As the sultan was at that time faced with a rather serious revolt, he turned to Turkey and secured the services of a Turkish
major and ten sub-officers, but at the same time he continued to
urge the service of the French mission.[34] On December 6, 1909,
Pichon modified his instructions so as to permit the French officers
to accompany the *mehallas* under the following conditions: the
plan of operation should be made with the agreement of the chief
of the mission; regular pay, supplies, and munitions must be

---

[30] Pichon to Saint-Aulaire, April 23, 1909, *Affaires du Maroc*, 1908-1910,
no. 178.

[31] Pichon to Saint-Aulaire, June 21, 1909, *ibid.*, no. 211.

[32] Pichon to Regnault, Aug. 19, 1909, *ibid.*, no. 253; Regnault to Pichon, Sept.
27, 1909, *ibid.*, no. 303.

[33] Tardieu, *op. cit.*, p. 134.

[34] Saint-Aulaire to Pichon, Nov. 9, 1909, *Affaires du Maroc*, 1908-1910, no.
335; Tardieu, *op. cit.*, p. 136.

guaranteed the soldiers; discipline was to be rigidly maintained among the troops, who were to refrain from pillage and to respect all wounded and prisoners.[35] Such conditions were impossible of fulfilment, owing to two factors: the sultan did not have the funds necessary to guarantee either the payment of his troops or their equipment; and, as a result of leaving poorly trained natives without pay, it was impossible to prevent pillage. While he was still trying to persuade the French to continue their services, the sultan was faced with a serious revolt among the Hayiana tribes. In an effort to suppress the rebellion, he sent against them three *mehallas* under Turkish instructors. The expedition was a disastrous failure; and, although they were not in charge of this particular campaign, the French officers were considered responsible, for the Moroccans believed all *mehallas* were under French control. The effect of the entire situation was to lower French prestige in the eyes of the natives.[36] France considered it necessary to regain her position by closer supervision of the sultan's army.

The question of the military mission became entangled in the negotiations that led to the loan of 1910, and as a result France secured the dismissal of the Turkish instructors and the promise that none other than French subjects should be employed in such service.[37] Mangin now secured the consent of the sultan to a reform of the entire military system, which would require an increase in the number of French officers in the mission.[38] These reforms were already planned by the sultan in November of 1910 when he addressed his army and explained to his troops that the reason for his action was to make them a more efficient fighting force and assured them that the reforms did not include anything contrary to the rules of the Koran. He agreed to adopt European discipline in the army, to turn over the management of the pay of the troops to Mangin, and to exile from Fez all those in the army who refused to serve in the newly organized divisions.[39]

Apparently Mangin had in mind the creation of a standing

[35] Pichon to Saint-Aulaire, Dec. 6, 1909, *Affaires du Maroc,* 1908-1910, no. 348.

[36] Billy to Pichon, Nov. 15, 1910, *ibid.,* 1910-1912, no. 17, enclosure, Mangin to Billy, Nov. 9, 1910; Tardieu, *op. cit.,* p. 137.   [37] See pp. 92-95, *supra.*

[38] Billy to Pichon, Nov. 9, 1910, *Affaires du Maroc,* 1910-1912, no. 14.

[39] Billy to Pichon, Nov. 15, 1910, *ibid.,* no. 17, enclosure, Mangin to Billy, Nov. 9, 1910.

army efficiently trained and equipped, and to effect this object he needed additional French officers to aid him. Accordingly, on November 9, 1910, he requested that the military mission be increased by the addition of a military doctor, a military interpreter, two infantry officers, a cavalry officer, and an artillery or an engineering officer. Billy urged Pichon to grant this request immediately, as the military reforms would permit the sultan to raise imposts in the regions which he had not as yet been able to reach and would inspire respect for the sultan among the discontented tribes.[40] In December Mangin repeated his request and asked for ten officers and twenty under-officers, stating that the military reforms, if carried out, would establish "definitively our military influence in this country and avoid all possible competition. . . ." [41] On December 30 Billy informed Pichon that the sultan wished to go to the south and that the thirty new instructors should be sent as soon as possible and certainly before the sultan left Fez.[42] The sultan was offering to the French government an effective method of establishing her political influence in the country and France failed to take advantage of her opportunity. Instead, departmental jealousy and red tape tied up Mangin's plans.

Pichon reported the General's requirements to the minister of war.[43] In answer to Mangin's first request, Brun sent four instructors;[44] but in response to the second request he asked for detailed information, which the commander then sent.[45] In February, 1911, Pichon reported that ten instructors had been named and urged upon Brun that the other instructors be named at once.[46] A conflict arose between the minister of war and the foreign office as to their respective jurisdictions;[47] and not until March 21, after a change of ministry, were any additional instructors named,[48] and then the one named was on duty at Casablanca and could not be released until October.[49]

---

[40] Billy to Pichon, Nov. 9, 1910, *ibid.*, no. 14.

[41] Billy to Pichon, Dec. 12, 1910, *ibid.*, no. 27.

[42] Billy to Pichon, Dec. 30, 1910, *ibid.*, no. 32.

[43] Tardieu, *op. cit.*, p. 143.   [44] *Ibid.*, p. 144.   [45] *Ibid.*

[46] Pichon to Billy, Feb. 16, 1911, *Affaires du Maroc*, 1910-1912, no. 66.

[47] Tardieu, *op. cit.*, p. 149.

[48] Cruppi to Billy, Mar. 21, 1911, *Affaires du Maroc*, 1910-1912, no. 130.

[49] Tardieu, *op. cit.*, p. 150.

In the meantime other complications arose. Spain presented her protest to any increase in the French mission, and asked for the right to send Spanish military instructors to work with the French.[50] Spain feared that with the increased number of *mehallas* under the control of French instructors, the sultan would collect taxes in the Spanish zone, using these French-officered *mehallas* for the work. This, to Spain, would seem a definite infringement of her rights.[51] France replied that the troops would be mainly used in the center of the country, and that as France had the exclusive right to operate the military mission, she could not permit the admission of Spanish officers, and that she had no intention of strengthening the Moroccan army in order to serve French interests.[52] If Spain joined France in the military mission, suspicion would inevitably arise that the two nations planned aggressive action.[53] Spain then asked for negotiations which would lead to a new arrangement between herself and France;[54] but France refused on the plea that any new arrangement with her would necessitate a new one also with England and thus reopen the entire Moroccan question.[55]

Military reforms were intimately tied to the financial situation and, as was to be expected, were non-effective so long as the sultan remained bankrupt. Consequently, one phase of the negotiations that El Mokri was busily engaged upon in 1911 and that Spain followed with a watchful eye dealt with the question of financing the military reforms. The long delay involved in negotiating the loan of 1911 prevented the sultan from obtaining the necessary funds to effect his purpose.[56] His futile efforts to increase taxes upon the tribes in order to finance his army merely resulted in increased discontent, and his military changes in turn intensified native hostility. In the meantime, Mangin, with insufficient person-

---

[50] Pichon to Geoffray, Jan. 24, 1911, *Affaires du Maroc,* 1910-1912, no. 50; Pichon to Geoffray, Feb. 4, 1911, *ibid.,* no. 59, enclosure I, note sent by Perez Caballero to F. O., Jan. 26, 1911.

[51] Pichon to Geoffray, Jan. 24, 1911, *ibid.,* no. 50.

[52] Pichon to Geoffray, Feb. 4, 1911, *ibid.,* no. 59, enclosure II, note sent to the embassy of Spain, Feb. 4, 1911; Pichon to Geoffray, Feb. 9, 1911, *ibid.,* no. 62.

[53] Pichon to Geoffray, Feb. 9, 1911, *ibid.,* no. 62. [54] *Ibid.*

[55] *Ibid.;* Pichon to Goeffray, Feb. 5, 1911, *Affaires du Maroc,* 1910-1912, no. 60.

[56] Billy to Pichon, Jan. 14, 1911, *ibid.,* no. 39.

nel, could not organize an efficient fighting force. His introduction of European methods into the army increased the feeling against the foreigner, especially as the disgruntled natives dismissed from Fez spread the idea that this system was contrary to the Koran. Her half-way measures in dealing with the military problem left France in a position more ticklish than ever before. She failed to improve matters in her handling of the financial situation.

The Franco-Moroccan loan of 1910 had been arranged to settle the debts of the sultan, but had made no provision for future obligations. By December, 1910, the *maghzen* was bankrupt.[57] The powers opposed the levying of taxes on their protégés. Any increased taxes on the tribes provoked discontent if not actual rebellion, usually tinctured with religious opposition. Tax receipts fell to the vanishing point.[58] Consequently, El Mokri returned to Paris to secure additional loans for his government.[59] The earlier loan of 1910 had so mortgaged Moroccan resources that there was little left as security for a new loan. From an economic or financial standpoint a new loan was not to be considered, but from the political standpoint France could not ignore the situation. Pichon realized this and appointed Regnault and Guiot to work with Klotz, minister of finance, to solve the question. The purpose of the loan was expressed as threefold: to pay the remainder of the debts of the *maghzen* not liquidated by the earlier loan; to organize a military force sufficient to assure collection of internal taxes; and to provide for the construction of the ports of Tangier and Casablanca and other public works of prime urgency.[60] On January 18, 1911, Pichon stated that France was ready to lend Morocco

[57] Pichon to Klotz, Dec. 3, 1910, *ibid.*, no. 25.

[58] *Ibid.*; Feis, *op. cit.*, pp. 411-412; Jaurès before the chamber of deputies, Mar. 24, 1911, *Annales de la chambre des députés*, session ordinaire de 1911, vol. I, pp. 1801-1805. The utter bankruptcy of the sultan's government was revealed in his inability to visit Meknez, Rabat, Tangier, and Marrakech because of lack of sufficient funds to finance the trip. The trip to Rabat, Meknez, and Marrakech was the customary migration to the southern capital, but the proposed visit to Tangier was unusual and excited much comment.—London *Times*, Nov. 28, 1910, Feb. 28, 1911 (Tangier correspondent); Belgian report, Apr. 15, 1911, *Belg. Doks.*, vol. IV, no. 109; El Mokri to Pichon, Feb. 6, 1911, *Affaires du Maroc*, 1910-1912, no. 61.

[59] Pichon to Klotz, Dec. 3, 1910, *Affaires du Maroc*, 1910-1912, no. 25.

[60] *Ibid.*

30,000,000 francs to be used to reimburse the 13,000,000 francs of debts contracted by the sultan before June 30, 1909, to care for the expense of the police of ports up to 2,500,000 francs, and to furnish the sultan with money to develop the *mehalla*. For security, France was willing to abandon her special claim for 2,740,000 francs annuity until the customs could cover both.[61] El Mokri urged haste in completing the loan, as every delay injured the monarch's position in the eyes of his people and rendered still more difficult the restoration of order. Naturally enough, too, delay in the political negotiation accentuated the uneasiness of the financiers in the situation and made more difficult the marketing of the bonds even if the loan were perfected.[62]

On February 18, 1911, Pichon transmitted the text of the loan project to Billy.[63] According to this text, the State Bank was to advance 2,350,000 francs for the payment of the police for the ensuing year and 5,000,000 francs a year for three years for the organization of the Moroccan army. Of this 5,000,000 francs, 1,500,000 francs could be deducted the first year to pay the pressing general needs of the government. To reimburse itself, the State Bank was authorized to reserve 50 per cent of the excess of the revenue after the service charges on the loans of 1904 and 1910 had been paid, and the 5 per cent of the customs reserved to the sultan, and 100,000 francs of the funds reserved for the French annuity. In addition, the *tertib*[64] from the tribes other than those in the Chaouya was to be used for security for this advance. If the *tertib* were not paid, the *maghzen* was to pay an equal share from the old customary taxes. The remaining points were settled through loans of longer maturity. The loan for public works was divided into three sections: 15,000,000 francs for the port of Tangier; 18,000,000 francs for the port of Casablanca; and 10,000,000 francs for the railroad from Tangier to El Ksar. The security for these loans was 50 per cent of the excess of the revenue after the service charges for the loans of 1904 and 1910 and the ad-

[61] Pichon to Geoffray, Jan. 18, 1911, *Affaires du Maroc*, 1910-1912, no. 43.
[62] El Mokri to Pichon, undated, *ibid.*, no. 61.
[63] Pichon to Billy, Feb. 18, 1911, *ibid.*, no. 67.
[64] The *tertib* was a tax imposed upon arable land, fruit trees, and cattle in place of the old Koranic taxes. See p. 18, *supra*.

vances to the State Bank were paid, the product of farming or administration of the railroads, and the taxes of the lighthouses, and other taxes in the Chaouya to the extent of 700,000 francs annually, and 5 per cent of the customs not yet reserved. Various technicalities delayed the completion of the loan until March 14, 1911, when Mokri signed the agreement.[65] Difficulties now arose with foreign powers.

In January, 1911, Pichon had informed Spain that France was willing to lend Morocco 30,000,000 francs.[66] Spain, through her ambassador, Perez Caballero, stated her objections to the loan as well as to the increase in the personnel of the French military mission. She feared that the new French loan would endanger the security that formed the basis of the Spanish loan of 1910 and therefore wished to have incorporated into an arrangement with France the provision that Spanish agents should supervise their share of the customs and the rents from the mines and that Spanish officers would be attached to the military mission. France opposed these measures as she insisted that control of the customs was arranged by international agreement and that any change in the nature of securities of the former loans would affect all bondholders and thus could not be disturbed.[67]

When Spain was notified of the completion of the loan, she objected on the grounds that the new loan plus the new military mission increased French power in Morocco without a corresponding increase in Spanish power. Caballero claimed that, according to the agreement of 1904, Spain was to be given a chance to express her opinion before any Franco-Moroccan treaty was made. This France had ignored in making the new treaty, as she claimed that the provision only meant that France was to notify Spain that negotiations were in progress and this she had conscientiously done. Spain also objected to the military arrangement and to the guarantees underlying the loan, especially the *tertib* and the ancient imposts, which could be collected only with great difficulty. If the sultan used French-officered troops to collect these taxes,

[65] Mokri to Cruppi, Mar. 13, 1911, *Affaires du Maroc*, 1910-1912, no. 105; Cruppi to Paul Cambon, Mar. 16, 1911, *ibid.*, no. 122.

[66] Pichon to Geoffray, Jan. 18, 1911, *ibid.*, no. 43.

[67] Pichon to Caballero, Feb. 13, 1911, *ibid.*, no. 63.

the power of France would be greatly enhanced and would infringe upon Spanish rights in the Spanish zone. If the *tertib* in the French sphere and the receipts of the ports of Casablanca, Mogador, Mazagan, Saffi, and Rabat were sufficient to guarantee the French loan, then Spain would not object; but this was clearly not the case. Moreover, the proposed Tangier-El Ksar railroad lay in the Spanish zone, and Spain considered that she should have been consulted on this point, if on no other. France insisted that Spain should not dispute Morocco's right to build such a road and that it would be built according to the provisions of the Act of Algeciras.[68] The London *Times*, staunch in its support of France, defined the attitude of Spain as entirely unjustified and selfish.[69]

On April 18, 1911, Caballero again presented to Cruppi a long note stating Spanish objection to the loan, the provisions of which, he claimed, operated as a detriment to Spain in her sphere. He objected to the *tertib* in the Spanish sphere being mortgaged to the French loan for the reorganization of the military forces. France had answered his former objection to the use of French-officered troops collecting the *tertib* in the Spanish zone by the statement that they would not be used in the extreme north or extreme south of Morocco. Caballero now came forth with the argument that if that were true, there was less reason for confiscating the *tertib* in the Spanish region to pay for the organization of troops which were to be used exclusively in the French sphere. He again made extensive objections to the arrangement relative to the Tangier-El Ksar line and proposed that a new project be worked out between France and Spain.[70] Nothing came of this proposal, for the course of events swept it aside. Spanish consent to the loan was never secured.

Germany also presented her protest against the loan. Cambon reported, March 19, 1911, that when Kiderlen was informed of the agreement he had appeared satisfied that the matter was solved;[71] but on March 28 Schoen presented a note to the French

---

[68] Geoffray to Cruppi, Mar. 17, 1911, *ibid.*, no. 123; Caballero to Cruppi, Mar. 18, 1911, *ibid.*, no. 124; Cruppi to Geoffray, Mar. 30, 1911, *ibid.*, no. 140.
[69] London *Times*, Mar. 25, 1911.
[70] Caballero to Cruppi, Apr. 18, 1911, *Affaires du Maroc*, 1910-1912, no. 189.
[71] Cambon to Cruppi, Mar. 19, 1911, *ibid.*, no. 127.

foreign office which, as has been noted, linked together the question of the Moroccan loan and the negotiations on Moroccan railroads in progress between Germany and France. Germany was of the opinion, so read the note, that the agreement "which burdened the Moroccan finances with considerable new charges could not be separated from the question actually pending of railroads to be constructed in Morocco. . . ." Although she reserved the right to make further statements, Germany for the time remarked that the financial basis of the new arrangement should be approached with caution, as the securities considered seemed to be either too vaguely defined or likely to involve difficulties.[72] Germany and Spain opposed the new loan agreement, because it seemed to them that the treaty offered to France an opportunity to increase her power in Morocco without offering to either of them any type of compensation. Not even the arrangement relative to public works seemed to offset the advantages given to France. France was not able to overcome their objections, and Morocco was delayed in receiving the funds she desperately needed to reorganize her army and to meet the expenses of her government. Mulay Hafid, unaided, was not able to quell the growing revolt, and France was drawn into action.

Chronic disorders characterized the reign of Mulay Hafid as they had that of his predecessor. The reports of French agents in Morocco were filled with accounts of local disturbances provoked by banditry, jealousy of tribal chieftains, lack of pay or provisions for the troops, pillaging, and manifestations of religious fanaticism. With these accounts were coupled complaints against the treatment meted out to French protégés by agents of the sultan. Reports that the sultan had ordered taxes collected from European subjects and protégés from which they had been exempt by treaty and that agents of the sultan had arrested French protégés without cause and confiscated their property, their land and herds of cattle, sheep, horses, or mules were frequently received. Protest to the sultan after long delay usually resulted in dismissal of the offensive caid and adjustment of the specific incident but did not prevent recurrence of similar inci-

---

[72] Cruppi to Berckheim, Mar. 29, 1911, *ibid.*, no. 139, enclosure, note sent by the embassy of Germany at Paris, Mar. 28, 1911.

dents.[73] As the sultan suffered more and more from financial strangulation, these incidents occurred more frequently. Mulay Hafid had to face the same situation as had Abdul Aziz. Financial pressure forced him to levy new taxes that the natives resented as being contrary to the Koran and the enactment of which they laid to the door of the hated foreigner. Naturally the native would resent paying increased taxes when his neighbor, a foreign protégé, was exempt. Efforts to collect such taxes by using French-officered-and-instructed *mehallas* aggravated the situation. Mulay Hafid, instead of freeing them from foreign domination, had apparently fastened the yoke even more firmly. Sporadic revolts in the year 1910 had shown the necessity for a reorganization of the Sherifian army and an adjustment of finances, but nothing was accomplished in either respect before 1911. The year 1911 opened under none too favorable auspices for Mulay Hafid. Discontent and rebellion faced him at every turn. Chaotic conditions too easily produce incidents that lead to foreign invasion in defense of nationals. France, who was the nation chiefly interested in the maintenance of peace and order within the realm, was already in the Chaouya and Oudjda districts. The year 1911 saw her move farther inland.

---

[73] *Affaires du Maroc,* 1908-1910 and 1910-1912, give many accounts of such incidents.

Chapter VIII

THE MARCH TO FEZ

In the hotbed prepared by the chronic disorders, the financial bankruptcy, and the military weakness of the Sherifian empire matured the seeds of French imperialism, long carefully nursed by watchful diplomats, shrewd business men, and colonial enthusiasts. The solicitous care with which the plant had been guarded brought about the reward in 1911, for in that year France won her objective—a protectorate over Morocco. Before she achieved success, force of circumstances more than conscious effort on the part of her government had led her to Fez, an expedition fraught with many perils since the international terrain was not as yet ready to receive the full flowering of French policy. Her anxiety over the international situation, however, did not prevent her from assuming what she interpreted as her responsibility for the maintenance of order within the Sherifian empire when the siege of Fez, coupled with the rebellion of the Zaers, laid bare the utter debility of the Moroccan government.

The rebellion of the Zaers was from its beginning a revolt against the French. January 17, 1911, Billy telegraphed to Pichon that General Moinier had reported an attack made by a group of Zaers upon a division of the French army led by Lieutenant Marchand. The lieutenant and four of his companions had been killed.[1] The incident was reported to the sultan and redress demanded, but the sultan was in no position to take any action on the western tribe, and continued disturbances were reported from the Zaer territory.[2] On March 8 the vice consul at Larache reported that six of the western tribes living in the Gharb, among whom were the Zaer, had formed an alliance to prevent Mulay Hafid's passing through their territory. Conditions in the Gharb, according to his report, were daily growing more threatening.[3] General

---

[1] Billy to Pichon, Jan. 17, 1911, *Affaires du Maroc,* 1910-1912, no. 42.

[2] Billy to Pichon, Jan. 23, 1911, *ibid.,* no. 48; Billy to Pichon, Feb. 15, 1911, *ibid.,* no. 64. [3] Billy to Cruppi, Mar. 8, 1911, *ibid.,* no. 94.

Moinier described the situation as critical and asked for reinforcements.[4]

Although no action was taken under Pichon,[5] Cruppi, his successor, decided the circumstances warranted France taking some measures to assure peace. News of the proposed move appeared in the papers[6] and caused Kiderlen to ask Cambon about French plans.[7] Kiderlen said that he did not question French rights to punish the aggressors, but that German public opinion was stirred up by the newspaper reports, and that Germany feared France "by successive small military operations" would be "progressively drawn into a sort of occupation always more extended which would end by annulling the Act of Algeciras. . . ." He, therefore, thought that the government of France should express its purpose.[8] On March 14, 1911, Cruppi notified the courts of Europe that the purpose of the French government was to "assure, in the limits of the Chaouya, the execution of measures of order and of police which are necessary to the protection of French posts, to safeguard the tribes of the Chaouya, as well as security of commercial relations . . . ," and that France did not have in mind any extension of its zone of occupation. To attain her purpose France had ordered two battalions and two artillery divisions to Casablanca.[9] France also asked Mulay Hafid to arrest and

[4] Billy to Pichon, Jan. 23, 1911, *ibid.*, no. 48.

[5] Schoen to Bethmann Hollweg, Feb. 23, 1911, *G. P.*, vol. XXIX, no. 10523.

[6] For example, the *Journal des Débats*, Mar. 11, stated that the council of ministers had not taken a decision but met that day to discuss the situation. "It is doubtful that one meeting will suffice for its members, novices for the most part in this delicate matter, in order to form a definitive opinion. But it is probable that all are agreed without other consultation to demand legitimate reparations as a result of the ambuscade of Merchouch. . . ." Opinions differed as to means. This paper objected to sending troops in but recommended blocking the outlets of the Zaer and forcing them to surrender. "In all cases, in treating the affairs of Morocco, the government ought never to lose sight of general conditions of foreign policy. It is to that that all the rest ought to be subordinated. . . ."—Gauvain, *op. cit.*, vol. II, pp. 421-424. The London *Times* reported that "the persistent announcements that the French government did not intend to interfere have certainly succeeded in eliciting a considerable demonstration of public opinion in favour of a policy of action. . . ."—Mar. 11, 1911.

[7] Cambon to Cruppi, Mar. 11, 1911, *Affaires du Maroc*, 1910-1912, no. 101.

[8] Cambon to Cruppi, Mar. 13, 1911, *ibid.*, no. 102.

[9] Cruppi to French representatives at Berlin, Madrid, Lisbon, Rome, Brussels,

punish the culprits upon his arrival at Rabat and in the meantime to instruct the governors at Rabat and Salé and the khalif at Casablanca to close the markets of the villages to the natives of the tribe of Zaer until those associated with the death of Marchand had been arrested and the necessary reparation had been made.[10] The sultan expressed his willingness to arrest the culprits, but he feared that the sending of additional French troops into the Chaouya would stir up the fanatics and complicate the situation.[11] At all events he could not carry out his promise, and France decided that she would need to occupy Rabat, where the Zaers secured supplies.[12] On April 5, 1911 Cambon discussed this measure with Kiderlen, who raised no special objection at that time but commented that he feared the effect such a move would have upon German public opinion.[13] On the same day Cambon wrote a lengthy explanation of French action to Kiderlen, in which he stated that the occupation of Rabat would place France in a position to punish the Zaer and also would place her in a position to aid the Europeans at Fez if the need arose.[14] To this note Kiderlen replied that occupation of Rabat, "a second important port at the side of that of Casablanca, would be considered as a step toward the elimination of the Algeciras Convention since everything is calm, at the present, at Rabat. . . ." Kiderlen repeated his fears that this occupation would stir up the popular passions and make all arrangements between France and Germany more difficult. He, therefore, urged France to take military action only under the pressure of extreme necessity.[15]

French occupation of Rabat might be justified under the police

---

London, Saint Petersburg, Vienna, The Hague, Washington, and Stockholm, Mar. 14, 1911, *ibid.,* no. 110; Bertie to Grey, Mar. 14, 1911, *Br. Docs.,* vol. VII, no. 194.

[10] Cruppi to Billy, Mar. 16, 1911, *Affaires du Maroc,* 1910-1912, no. 116.

[11] Billy to Cruppi, Mar. 25, 1911, *ibid.,* no. 134.

[12] Cruppi to French representatives at Rome, Vienna, Brussels, The Hague, Washington, Lisbon, Stockholm, Apr. 6, 1911, *ibid.,* no. 156; Cruppi to French representatives at London, Madrid, St. Petersburg, Apr. 4, 1911, *ibid.,* no. 149.

[13] Cambon to Cruppi, Apr. 5, 1911, *ibid.,* no. 154.

[14] Cambon to Kiderlen, Apr. 5, 1911, *G. P.,* vol. XXIX, no. 10526; Cambon to Cruppi, Apr. 9, 1911, *Affaires du Maroc,* 1910-1912, no. 166, enclosure I, Cambon to Kiderlen, Apr. 5, 1911.

[15] Kiderlen to Cambon, Apr. 7, 1911, *G. P.,* vol. XXIX, no. 10527.

power granted by the Act of Algeciras, if such action were necessary to quell disorders; but the use of Rabat as a base from which to carry on operations in the interior would require a broad construction of the Act—a decision based on "implied powers." Recognizing the fact that a broad construction of a fundamental law defies limitations, Germany saw France gradually spreading over all Morocco. First Oudjda, then Casablanca, now Rabat had fallen into her hands; and perhaps only too soon Fez would follow. The German leaders had not as yet, however, worked out their plans; and they waited for France to become more deeply involved before they acted.

The question of the punishment of the Zaers and the consequent occupation of Rabat were from their origin tied to the question of rescuing the Europeans at Fez, a problem pregnant with serious international complication; for Fez, the capital of Morocco, lay deep within the interior. France would be hard pressed to justify legally her occupation of a city far from the coast; but if she assumed the responsibility of safeguarding Europeans in the interior, she necessarily would find repeated need for military action. The police power granted France and Spain by the Act of Algeciras could not be stretched sufficiently to reach from the eight listed ports to the capital city. The Franco-German Accord of 1909 might prove more flexible, for Germany had recognized that "the special political interests of France" were there "closely tied to the consolidation of internal peace and order" and had agreed "not to interfere in these interests." France was simply faced with the problem of interpreting her mandate. Since her political interests would preclude any other nation's rescuing endangered Europeans, was French responsibility such as to require her to assume the task? To this question the French government replied in the affirmative. As a natural corollary, France must judge when the chronic state of disorder in Morocco reached the acute stage of danger to Europeans necessitating French military action. Had the revolt around Fez in the spring of 1911 reached that stage? The French reply was again an affirmative, but the German was an emphatic "Nein." The two contradictory accounts describe the situation.

The causes for the insurrection that broke out around Fez were many. Discontent began to smoulder early in January, 1911, when Mulay Hafid unwisely tried to force upon four tribes acceptance of caids who belonged to different tribes.[16] More far-reaching in its effect was the policy of ever-increasing demands for revenue, which resulted not only in increased levies but in the enactment of new taxes. Now new taxes were always subject to the criticism that they were objectionable to Koranic law and were always capable of turning economic discontent into religious war. El Glaoui, the grand vizier for Mulay Hafid, was blamed for the outbreak because of his extortion and the brutality of his agents and also because of his intrigues against the sultan.[17] Gaillard accused him of paying all his personal expenses by exactions from the tribes in the territory.[18] Although this charge was probably true, the demands necessary to meet the financial obligations of the sultan would have been oppressive enough, in any case, to produce an outbreak. At any rate, these exactions irritated the influential rich, who then stirred up the masses by appealing to their religious prejudices.[19] The effort of the sultan to organize a regular army met opposition, partially because the semi-independent tribes resented any agent's enhancing the power of the sultan and partially because of religious objections to the new discipline instituted by Mangin.[20] Seckendorff, German consul in Tangier, stated that the main cause was the new military rule dictated to the sultan by Mangin, "as a result of which two Moroccan soldiers were publicly executed for desertion. The death sentence for desertion was against the religion of the entire Moroccan people and all who knew Moroccan affairs were not surprised at the outbreak. . . ." [21] The London *Times* substantiated Seckendorff's view and remarked that "The public execution at Fez of two Moorish soldiers for theft and desertion from the army

[16] Billy to Pichon, Jan. 10, 1911, *Affaires du Maroc,* 1910-1912, no. 37.

[17] Billy to Cruppi, Mar. 4, 1911, *ibid.,* no. 83; Billy to Selves, Aug. 7, 1911, *ibid.,* no. 493, enclosure, report of Gaillard.

[18] Billy to Cruppi, Mar. 2, 1911, *ibid.,* no. 78, enclosure, Gaillard to Billy, Feb. 27, 1911.   [19] Billy to Selves, Aug. 7, 1911, *ibid.,* no. 493.

[20] Schoen to Bethmann Hollweg, Apr. 28, 1911, *G. P.,* vol. XXIX, no. 10546, quoted Botkin, Russian represntative at Tangier, as giving the army situation as the cause for the outbreak.

[21] Seckendorff to Bethmann Hollweg, Mar. 6, 1911, *ibid.,* no. 10524.

caused much adverse comment" in Tangier.[22] On the other hand, the French charged El Glaoui with duplicity in his dealings with the French mission and laid to his door the rumor that the two soldiers had been executed at the command of Mangin, when actually the sultan had issued the order upon the insistence of the grand vizier himself.[23] As stated above, efforts to improve the military status of the sultan had progressed only far enough to excite the animosity of the natives and not far enough to be effective.

On February 26, as the growing restlessness of the tribes became menacing, the sultan decided to send troops against the Cherarda, who, with the Beni M'Tir, were active in stirring up trouble, and asked for French instructors to accompany the *mehallas*.[24] Mangin, after consultation with Gaillard, consented, as he hoped to check an extension of the movement by immediate action.[25] A revolt of the Cherarda and their neighboring tribes could prove serious, because their territory lay on the route to Tangier and an extension of the movement might block all access to the coast. But the news that the sultan was sending troops to punish the Cherarda called into action practically all the tribes west and northwest of Fez, united in their opposition to the sultan.[26] Mangin advised the grand vizier to suppress the rebellion among the tribes who started the trouble and under no condition to exact a heavy indemnity. Such treatment would have a quieting effect upon the entire group; but if a heavy indemnity were exacted, all would unite against him.[27]

---

[22] London *Times,* Feb. 6, 1911.

[23] Billy to Cruppi, Mar. 4, 1911, *Affaires du Maroc,* 1910-1912, no. 83. The reports of the French agents were full of complaints of the exactions, the disloyalty, and the unscrupulousness of the grand vizier.

[24] Billy to Cruppi, Mar. 2, 1911, *ibid.,* no. 78, enclosure, Gaillard to Billy, Feb. 26, 1911.

[25] Billy to Cruppi, Mar. 2, 1911, *ibid.,* no. 78, enclosures, Gaillard to Billy, Feb. 26 and Feb. 27, 1911. Seckendorff stated that "Mangin opposed the expedition at first but the intervention of the consul at Fez brought him around. . . ."— Seckendorff to Bethmann Hollweg, Mar. 6, 1911, *G. P.,* vol. XXIX, no. 10524.

[26] Billy to Selves, Aug. 7, 1911, *Affaires du Maroc,* 1910-1912, no. 493; Billy to Cruppi, Mar. 4, 1911, *ibid.,* no. 86, enclosure, Gaillard to Billy, Feb. 28, 1911; Seckendorff to Bethmann Hollweg, Mar. 6, 1911, *G. P.,* vol. XXIX, no. 10524.

[27] Billy to Cruppi, Mar. 4, 1911, *Affaires du Maroc,* 1910-1912, no. 86, enclosure, Gaillard to Billy, Feb. 28, 1911.

On February 28 the troops left Fez to march against the Cherarda and their allies. Mangin accompanied the *mehalla* when it first left the city, but he soon returned, and Bremond took over the command of the division. The departure of these troops left only about two hundred men in Fez.[28] Dr. Vassel at first thought that this would be sufficient for the maintenance of order; but as the revolt spread, he reported continual disturbances of public order, such as unexpected attacks on caravans and plundering of farms and villages. On March 1 Vassel reported that the road to Meknez and the usual caravan road to Rabat were unsafe but that the road to El Ksar was open. He explained the revolt as one against the sultan and El Glaoui and not against Christian and Moorish traders. "The only Christian they opposed was Major Mangin whom they held responsible," but as the *maghzen* was "no more master in its own house," the restoration of order would be difficult.[29] Reports of Gaillard and Vassel confirmed the information that the couriers were robbed and that it was almost impossible to get their despatches to Tangier. On March 2 Vassel reported that "Fez is quiet, but the population stands with its heart on the side of the revolt. . . ." The danger to the Germans in Fez was not great at the time, but he feared that a defeat of the *mehalla* "would lead to a bad situation." [30] Gaillard reported, March 3, that the sultan had sent to the south for additional troops, as there was not a sufficient number to garrison Fez and Meknez and at the same time dispatch troops against the rebellious tribes.[31] On March 7 he reported that the southern troops would not be able to reach Fez because the Beni Ashen, allies of the Cherarda, had agreed to prevent their passage from Rabat to Fez.[32] Practically every report of the French representatives in Morocco added a new tribe to the rebellious group.

By the middle of the month the situation seemed to clear slightly, and more promising reports came from Fez.[33] Gaillard

[28] Billy to Selves, Aug. 7, 1911, *ibid.,* no. 493; Billy to Cruppi, Mar. 4, 1911, *ibid.,* no. 86, enclosure, Gaillard to Billy, Feb. 28, 1911; Seckendorff to Bethmann Hollweg, Mar. 6, 1911, *G. P.,* vol. XXIX, no. 10524.

[29] Seckendorff to Bethmann Hollweg, Mar. 6, 1911, *G. P.,* vol. XXIX, no. 10524.
[30] *Ibid.*
[31] Billy to Cruppi, Mar. 3, 1911, *Affaires du Maroc,* 1910-1912, no. 79.
[32] Billy to Cruppi, Mar. 7, 1911, *ibid.,* no. 93.
[33] Billy to Cruppi, Mar. 13, 1911, *ibid.,* no. 103; Billy to Cruppi, Mar. 14, 1911,

urged the sultan to conciliate the rebels; but he refused and at the same time complained that the failure of France to send him funds had made it impossible for him to restore order and that, without aid, he would have to accept the condition of the Berbers and adopt an anti-European policy.[34] The sultan did enter into negotiations with the rebels, but, although Beni M'Tir chiefs were allegedly the leaders, the other tribes refused to accept any arrangements that the Beni M'Tir made.[35] The failure to secure any practical results from these negotiations convinced the natives of the weakness of the sultan and hence aggravated the revolt.[36] El Glaoui offered to resign in an effort to relieve the situation, but Mulay Hafid refused to grasp at this expedient since he feared that El Glaoui would simply use his opportunity to go to the south and foment trouble there.[37]

On March 27 Mangin reported that the troops in Fez were demoralized, inasmuch as their chiefs were all opposed to the sultan; that the personnel of the mission on duty with the *mehallas* was not in danger as long as they were able to pay the troops, but "in eight days there will be no more money for the *mehallas*." [38] On the same day Gaillard reported that all the tribes in the north of Morocco were hostile to the sultan and only awaited an opportunity to revolt. The sultan had urged the recall of the troops to Fez; but Mangin and Gaillard had advised against it, as the *mehalla* was all that kept open communications to Tangier and its recall would mean a siege. "We would find ourselves here with a force that would be sufficient to defend the city but a great deal too weak to put down the revolt, and famine would lead us rapidly to capitulate. . . ." [39] Billy reported this information to Cruppi and urged that measures be taken to protect the French

ibid., no. 108, enclosures, Gaillard to Billy, Mar. 7, 1911, and Mangin to minister of war, Mar. 5, 1911; London *Times*, Mar. 13, 1911 (Tangier correspondent).

[34] Billy to Cruppi, Mar. 20, 1911, *Affaires du Maroc*, 1910-1912, no. 129.

[35] Billy to Cruppi, Mar. 25, 1911, *ibid.*, no. 133; Billy to Cruppi, Mar. 27, 1911, *ibid.*, no. 137; Billy to Selves, Aug. 7, 1911, *ibid.*, no. 493.

[36] Billy to Cruppi, Mar. 31, 1911, *ibid.*, no. 141; Billy to Selves, Aug. 7, 1911, *ibid.*, no. 493.

[37] Billy to Cruppi, Mar. 27, 1911, *ibid.*, no. 137.

[38] Billy to Cruppi, Apr. 2, 1911, *ibid.*, no. 143.

[39] Billy to Cruppi, Apr. 2, 1911, *ibid.*, no. 144, enclosure, Gaillard to Billy, Mar. 27, 1911; Lister to Grey, Apr. 3, 1911, *Br. Docs.*, vol. VII, no. 199.

instructors and that aid be sent to the Gharb to prevent an upris-
ing there.[40] Reports of British agents carried similar stories of
the seriousness of the situation. A Moor in the confidence of the
British viewed the situation with alarm. He agreed that if Fez
were surrounded, the inhabitants would insist upon capitulating;
but he did not believe "that the tribes will enter the town, or that
any of the excesses concomitant with such a victorious entry will
take place. The awe inspired by Moulay Idris, the patron saint
of Fez, is very great, and the whole town, or at any rate the old
part of it, is looked upon as 'his sanctuary.' . . ."[41] Vassel's
report for March 24 refused to recognize the danger, and Seckendorff informed Berlin that the "alarming news about the increasingly dangerous situation in Fez, spread by the journalists of
this country, appear unfounded."[42] Vassel was correct in reporting the situation improved around March 24, but his report was
dispatched before the breakdown of the official negotiations between the sultan and his rebellious subjects, immediately after
which conditions grew worse. In view of the facts that food prices
in Fez were rising to exorbitant heights, that the rebels were constantly receiving reinforcements, that the Berbers had looted the
practically deserted palace of the sultan situated a mile outside
the walls of the capital, and that the disorders in the environs of
Fez were such as to prevent the sultan from holding the customary
ceremony of the Feast of Mulud—a ceremony which had not been
omitted since 1822—the London *Times* Tangier correspondent
refused to accept the Teutonic optimism and stressed the seriousness of the situation.[43]

The danger that a revolt against an unpopular sovereign would
be transformed into a Holy War against Christians lurked constantly in this barbarous Mohammedan country. Even if this
danger were avoided, the fear still existed that enraged and undis-
ciplined natives, indifferent to international complications, would
fail to make any distinction between Europeans and natives as
they wreaked their vengeance upon all who crossed their path. The

---

[40] Billy to Cruppi, Apr. 2, 1911, *Affaires du Maroc*, 1910-1912, no. 143.
[41] Lister to Grey, Apr. 3, 1911, *Br. Docs.*, vol. VII, no. 199.
[42] Seckendorff to F. O., Mar. 30, 1911, *G. P.*, vol. XXIX, no. 10523.
[43] London *Times*, Mar. 9, 17, 18, 29, and Apr. 5, 1911.

Europeans in Fez were formed into small groups by their consuls so as not to excite the public; but if the city were taken, there was no guarantee against a massacre.[44] France was convinced of the seriousness of the situation; and on April 4 Cruppi warned St. Petersburg, London, and Madrid that if the tension were not relieved, he would be compelled to "take certain military measures in order to assure the security" of the colony at Fez.[45] In notifying the remaining powers of Europe on April 5 and 6, he explained that France found herself obliged to quell the disturbances among the Zaers, and that this would probably force her to occupy Rabat and, in case the necessity arose, to send a division to Fez in order to relieve the foreign colony there. "We hope that this necessity will not arise. If we find ourselves forced to act, our intervention will maintain the sovereignty of the sultan and will exercise itself only in conformity with the principles of the Act of Algeciras. . . ."[46] Cruppi took care to state to Russia that France counted on her friendly support and to inform England that he was in communication with Spain.[47] Nicolson inferred from the statement of Paul Cambon that France had also as one of her objects that of assisting the sultan to retain his throne—a fact which, if true, would mean that she "would never be able to leave the country and in fact that what was intended merely as a temporary measure to meet an urgent need might develop into a more permanent and far-reaching proceeding. . . ."[48]

---

[44] Billy to Selves, Aug. 7, 1911, *Affaires du Maroc,* 1910-1912, no. 493, enclosure, Gaillard's report.

[45] Cruppi to French ambassadors at St. Petersburg, London, and Madrid, Apr. 4, 1911, *ibid.,* no. 149.

[46] Cruppi to French representatives at Rome, Vienna, Brussels, The Hague, Washington, Lisbon, Stockholm, Apr. 6, 1911, *ibid.,* no. 156.

[47] Cruppi to French ambassadors at St. Petersburg, London, and Madrid, Apr. 4, 1911, *ibid.,* no. 149.

[48] Nicolson to Bertie, Apr. 6, 1911, *Br. Docs.,* vol. VII, no. 202. Paul Cambon's report of this conversation is not given in the French *Yellow Book,* and it is impossible to determine whether Nicolson's inference was justified. The published account of Cruppi's instructions did not authorize such a statement. Perhaps Cambon did here attempt to sound the British government in order to discover the degree to which France could depend on its support. Nicolson, however, had consistently viewed the situation with alarm and may have drawn an unwarranted conclusion. Maintenance of a sultan on his throne was a program of more far-reaching consequences and a more direct violation of the

Turning to Spain, Cruppi gave her assurances that France would keep her informed of every move. Despite his precaution, the Spanish government remained nervous over the situation and gave him to understand that "an occupation, even temporary, of Taza or of Fez by French forces would denote a great change in the equilibrium of influences in Morocco" and that Spain would then occupy her zone according to the agreement reached in 1904.[49] The Spanish minister of foreign affairs, Prieto, urged that France and Spain keep each other constantly in touch with their plans; but Geoffray, French minister to Madrid, pointed out that a too-close coöperation would arouse suspicion of the other powers, who would then call a conference which would result in the further internationalization of Morocco. Certainly Spain did not want that.[50] Cruppi agreed with Isvolski, Russian ambassador in Paris, that it was important to keep Spain satisfied in order not to throw her "into the arms of Germany and the Triple Alliance," [51] but he could not avoid "losing patience with the Spanish government. They were acting in an underhand manner. . . ." He was convinced that "the German government were advising them in regard to Morocco in the hope of bringing about a misunderstanding between the Spanish and French governments. . . ." [52] Each member of the Triple Entente was anxious over the Spanish situation, not as a unit in itself, but because of the suspicion of German intrigues. Isvolski[53] and Crowe[54] both expressed the fear that Germany would profit from Spanish discontent and urged Cruppi to recognize the situation and avoid

Act of Algeciras than a program merely designed to rescue endangered Europeans. France could not guarantee a sultan his throne without great extension of her own power in the land, and in this contingency she would very likely require strong support from Great Britain, whose pledges obligated her to aid the French program. It was this fact that apparently disturbed Nicolson.

[49] Cruppi to Geoffray, Apr. 8, 1911, *Affaires du Maroc*, 1910-1912, no. 159, enclosure, note presented by the Spanish embassy, Apr. 6, 1911; Grey to Bunsen, Apr. 15, 1911, *Br. Docs.*, vol. VII, no. 209.

[50] Geoffray to Cruppi, Apr. 7, 1911, *Affaires du Maroc*, 1910-1912, no. 157.

[51] Isvolski to F. O., Mar. 15, 1911, Isvolski, *Der Diplomatische Schriftwechsel*, vol. I, no. 43.

[52] Bertie to Grey, Apr. 13, 1911, *Br. Docs.*, vol. VII, no. 207.

[53] Isvolski to F. O., Apr. 13, 1911, Isvolski, *op. cit.*, vol. I, no. 53.

[54] Note of Sir E. Crowe, Apr. 15, attached to despatch Bertie to Grey, Apr. 13, 1911, *Br. Docs.*, vol. VII, no. 207.

any overt act that might give her an excuse for acting. Grey expressed his conviction that Spain was determined to make difficulties for France, "whether at Germany's instigation or not we do not know, but we may at any rate be sure that if Germany does not take advantage of the cir[cumstance]s to make further trouble she will exact a price for not doing so. . . ." [55]

Cruppi, although suspicious of German intrigues in Spain, naïvely stated on April 13 that he expected no trouble from the German Emperor or the Imperial government, but at the same time he acknowledged that he "was anxious in regard to the tone adopted by the German Mercantile world and a portion of the German press. . . ." [56] To Isvolski's question as to "what position the governments, which had underwritten the Algeciras Act, and especially Germany, had taken in face of this communication," he answered that "she has met no kind of opposition, and at present in Berlin a full friendly exchange of ideas about the affair is taking place between the French Ambassador and Kiderlen-Waechter. The affirmation of certain papers that the German government uses this opportunity in order to secure from France concession and compensation in other questions, for example, in the question of the Bagdad railroad, is completely false. . . ." [57] On April 5 Jules Cambon had communicated the French program to Kiderlen, first orally and then in writing. A survey of the interviews which then took place between the two reveals disturbing elements to which Cruppi seemed blind.

According to Cambon, Kiderlen's first response was not unfavorable,[58] but on the next day he refused to agree to the views which Cambon had expressed in his written letter. Cambon attributed this change of attitude "to outside influences which were exercised upon him, or perhaps, even to certain imprudences of our press. . . ." [59] In his letter of April 5 Cambon had explained that because of the situation threatening the safety of Europeans at Fez, of the danger that any effort to bring them to the coast

---

[55] Note of Grey attached to despatch Bertie to Grey, Apr. 13, 1911, *Br. Docs.*, vol. VII, no. 207.   [56] Bertie to Grey, Apr. 13, 1911, *ibid.*, no. 207.

[57] Isvolski to F. O., Apr. 13, 1911, Isvolski, *op. cit.*, vol. I, no. 53.

[58] Cambon to Cruppi, Apr. 5, 1911, *Affaires du Maroc*, 1910-1912, no. 154.

[59] Cambon to Cruppi, Apr. 9, 1911, *ibid.*, no. 166.

would encounter, and of the inability of the *maghzen* to punish the Zaer, France feared it might be necessary for her to occupy Rabat so as to be in a position to go to the aid of the Europeans in Fez if the need arose. He urgently endeavored to convince Kiderlen that France had "no other care than to assure the security of the Europeans and of avoiding a catastrophe which could have most grave consequences," and that she would act only "under the pressure of most extreme necessity, and her action conservative of the sovereignty of the sultan will be exercised in the spirit of the Act of Algeciras. . . ." [60] His efforts were futile; for Kiderlen, in his conversation with Cambon on April 6, announced that the state of public opinion and the attitude of the French press were such that he could not accede to the views of the French government on the occupation of Rabat, as it would be contrary to the Act of Algeciras. Cambon insisted that only temporary occupation was considered and that that was not a violation of the Algeciras Act. "They will not believe you in Germany," Kiderlen replied, "if you speak of temporary occupation. When has one seen an occupation of this nature end? Was it so in Egypt? . . ." He then expressed his view that the Act of Algeciras rested on the "false basis that Morocco is an organized state," and threw forth the cue that "if the sovereignty of the sultan disappears, Germany will leave you free to do what you wish with Morocco provided you give her a share. In the meantime, it is necessary to maintain the state of things as they are. . . ." Cambon did not consider that he was authorized to discuss the point raised and merely repeated that the occupation would be temporary.

Kiderlen took the opportunity to complain of the lack of good will on the part of France in the execution of the Accord of 1909 and mentioned especially the failure of the N'Goko Sangha affair and the delay in the railroad negotiations. [61] Early in the conversation he had countered Cambon's argument that Germany had acknowledged to France political preëminence in Morocco by recalling that that recognition had been based on maintenance of

---

[60] Cambon to Kiderlen, Apr. 5, 1911, *G. P.*, vol. XXIX, no. 10526.

[61] Cambon to Cruppi, Apr. 9, 1911, *Affaires du Maroc*, 1910-1912, no. 166, enclosure II, conversation with Kiderlen, Apr. 6, 1911.

economic equality, which France had failed to respect. Pressed for details, he spoke specifically of the complaints of Germans in Casablanca that it was more and more difficult for the Germans to secure land, although the caids protected the purchases made by the French.[62] Cambon urged Kiderlen not to make his formal reply a refusal pure and simple, for that would "neither facilitate the conclusion of the Accord on the railroads nor the relations of the two governments. . . ." [63] Cambon, in his conversation with the British[64] and with the Russian[65] representatives in Berlin, described Kiderlen's attitude in this interview as stiff and ungracious and at first inclined to give "a categorical refusal to enter into any exchange of views respecting a French military intervention." On the seventh, the conversation was continued with only a slight modification of tone. Kiderlen spoke of his written reply, which he would make in answer to Cambon's letter of the fifth, and gave the advanced report that it would discuss both Rabat and Fez and "would conclude that, in case where an action should become necessary to Fez, the German government was disposed to an exchange of views with France in that which concerns the measures that might be taken of common accord. . . ." Cambon asked Kiderlen to explain the term "common accord." Did he mean a joint military expedition to Fez? To this question Kiderlen replied in the negative. Cambon then judged that Kiderlen meant to discuss the question of the need to go to Fez and that Kiderlen recognized that the obligation to save foreigners in Fez rested on France.[66] In the evening Kiderlen handed Cambon his written reply with the statement, "Be sincere, I pray you and play with the cards on the table! When you are at Fez you will never leave . . . ," and again he indicated that he would be willing to see a revision of the Act of Algeciras.[67]

[62] *Ibid.;* Cruppi to Cambon, Apr. 14, 1911, *ibid.,* no. 177, gives a discussion of these complaints and French denial of the charges.

[63] Cambon to Cruppi, Apr. 9, 1911, *ibid.,* no. 166, enclosure, conversation with Kiderlen, Apr. 6.

[64] Goschen to Nicolson, Apr. 7, 1911, *Br. Docs.,* vol. VII, no. 203.

[65] Schebeko to Sazonov, Apr. 13, 1911, B. de Siebert, *Entente Diplomacy and the World,* no. 670.

[66] Cambon to Cruppi, Apr. 9, 1911, *Affaires du Maroc,* 1910-1912, no. 166, enclosure, conversation with Kiderlen, Apr. 7.   [67] *Ibid.*

The formal German response to the French note of April 5, presented in this manner to the French representative in Berlin, conceded that "The Imperial government understands perfectly well the uneasiness of the government of the Republic in regard to the fate of the Europeans at Fez. Fortunately the last news on the situation in the interior of Morocco are better and there is not there, it appears, imminent danger. . . ." The occupation of Rabat or any military occupation in Morocco, the note continued, would be likely to excite public opinion in Germany and be interpreted as a violation of the Act of Algeciras. For this reason Kiderlen urged France to take no military action unless it became absolutely necessary. "If, as a result of an aggravation, not foreseen for the moment, the French government believed indispensable an action in favour of the European colonists at Fez, the Imperial government would be entirely disposed to enter with the French government into an exchange of views on the measures which France would judge necessary to take. . . ." [68] Cambon caught the significance of Kiderlen's covertly expressed implications and warned his government to proceed cautiously, for France must not abandon the sultan and "ought not furnish the pretext for a proposition that would tend to the dissolution of the Sherifian Empire." [69] He feared that Germany, using Spain for a tool, might find in the renewal of the police mandate a pretext for bringing the Moroccan question to a head and specifically warned his government against this contingency. He also expressed his conviction that although Kiderlen had not specified what he wanted, Germany would be willing to end the independence of Morocco "if we abandon to Germany a port on the Atlantic. . . ." But this condition was exactly that which France could not grant and "which England does not wish at any price." [70] Thus, as early as April 8, appeared a glimpse of the idea of com-

---

[68] Kiderlen to Cambon, Apr. 7, 1911, *G. P.*, vol. XXIX, no. 10527, also included in the report, Cambon to Cruppi, Apr. 9, 1911, *Affaires du Maroc,* 1910-1912, no. 166.

[69] Cambon to Cruppi, Apr. 9, 1911, *Affaires du Maroc,* 1910-1912, no. 166.

[70] Goschen to Nicolson, Apr. 14, 1911, *Br. Docs.,* vol. VII, no. 208; Cambon to Cruppi, Apr. 9, 1911, in Caillaux, *op. cit.,* pp. 257-259. In the letter as quoted in Caillaux, *op. cit.,* Cambon was more specific in his warning to the foreign office than in his letter quoted in *Affaires du Maroc,* 1910-1912, no. 166.

pensation. Cambon's report of his interviews with Kiderlen clearly shows that the German reply was not as favorable as Cruppi would have one believe, and that the Russian and English opinion that if Germany did consent "she would demand a high price" came nearer a true interpretation of the situation. Kiderlen had not denied to France the right to go to Fez; but his replies, stripped of their diplomatic trimmings, were in the nature of a warning that if she did go to Fez, she would be faced with European as well as Moroccan complications.

The situation in Morocco, however, pressed for solution, and the French government, harassed by warning notes from Germany and Spain, besieged by pleas for aid from Morocco, attacked by the press[71] simultaneously for its imperialistic aggression and for its weak defense of national rights, scarcely knew where to turn. Its efforts to heed all calls merely subjected it to charges of vacillation. From French and English sources came reports on April 9, 12, 13 that Bremond was in need of munitions and Fez had none to send him, that some of the caids in the *mehallas* were plotting against the French instructors, that the sultan made promises to the tribes only to break them, which caused additional complications, that the departure of supplies for Bremond was blocked by the bandit, Raissouli; in sum, the situation was not only not improved but was worse.[72] The German consul in Tangier denied that the situation was threatening to Europeans and accused the Spanish and French newspapers of deliberately leading public opinion astray; yet he was forced to report an attack on Fez on April 2. But with microscopic discrimination, he announced that the battle caused a "little panic" but "not any kind of a riot." [73] Again, on April 16, he delivered encouraging news that the situation in Fez was quiet and that order ruled at Meknez, but again he must report attacks made

---

[71] *Journal des Débats,* Apr. 10, 1911, urged the government to restrict her activities to protection of foreigners in the ports and avoid interference within the interior of Morocco—Gauvain, *op. cit.,* vol. II, p. 435. London *Times,* in an editorial, Apr. 11, argued that France must protect the Europeans in Fez.

[72] Billy to Cruppi, Apr. 9, 1911, *Affaires du Maroc,* 1910-1912, no. 164; Billy to Cruppi, Apr. 12, 1911, *ibid.,* no. 171; Billy to Cruppi, Apr. 13, 1911, *ibid.,* no. 174.

[73] Seckendorff to Bethmann Hollweg, Apr. 10, 1911, *G. P.,* vol. XXIX, no. 10530.

from the south.[74] The Belgian consul at Tangier shared the complacent attitude of his German colleague. He considered the turbulent conditions as merely the normal life of Morocco, and which if left alone would right themselves; but by painting the disturbances in dark colors, the European press was building for France that opportunity to extend her control for which she had been longing. He even feared that Germany, lulled to sleep by the Accord of 1909, would allow France to accomplish her aim with none to oppose her save Spain.[75]

But France, trusting the reports of her own representatives and fearful of another Khartum, decided to send reinforcements into the Chaouya and notified the powers of her move.[76] Cruppi also instructed Moinier, French commander in charge of the Chaouya district, to send supplies of munitions and money to Mangin and Bremond and to use for this mission Moroccan troops in the Chaouya.[77] Unfortunately, German reception of this first definite step taken by France was by no means encouraging. Zimmermann, who received Cambon's communication, replied that "according to telegraphic communication arriving today from the Imperial minister in Tangier, the situation in Fez gave no kind of cause for anxiety . . . ," and he hoped that "military measures of France in inner Morocco, which would stir up our public opinion very much, would not come into consideration. . . ." [78] Again news from Morocco forced France onward. Gaillard's despatch of April 13, which reached Cruppi on the 18th, stated, "We are blockaded at Fez," and reported that Bremond had not been able to return to Fez and that Mulay Hafid called for troops from the Chaouya. Gaillard declared that if the sultan lost, the Europeans in Fez would be in a critical situation, as any newly proclaimed sultan would find it difficult to control the Berbers.[79] Even the German despatch of the eighteenth, less optimistic, reported

[74] Seckendorff to F. O., Apr. 16, 1911, *ibid.*, no. 10531.

[75] Belgian Report from Tangier, Apr. 15, 1911, *Belg. Doks.*, vol. IV, no. 109.

[76] Cruppi to French representatives at Madrid, London, and St. Petersburg, Apr. 17, 1911, *Affaires du Maroc*, 1910-1912, no. 185.

[77] Cruppi to Billy, Apr. 17, 1911, *ibid.*, no. 184.

[78] Note of Zimmermann, Apr. 17, 1911, *G. P.*, vol. XXIX, no. 10532; Cambon to Cruppi, Apr. 17, 1911, *Affaires du Maroc*, 1910-1912, no. 187.

[79] Billy to Cruppi, Apr. 18, 1911, *Affaires du Maroc*, 1910-1912, no. 193.

that Fez was surrounded and that it was not known if the Europeans in the city were in danger, but concluded that they should have fled ere this to their consulates for protection.[80] This conclusion seems not in harmony with Seckendorff's insistence that Europeans were not threatened. German newspapers of April 19 carried charges that France and Spain were purposefully exaggerating the situation in order to justify their conquest of the country. The French paper, *Journal des Débats*, warned the government against a policy of conquest and resented the suggestion that France buy German consent by admission of German stock on the Paris bourse.[81] The French government lacked no advice of any color or strain, but the reports of the eighteenth had convinced it that further action was necessary.

On April 19 the Monis cabinet informed England, Spain, and Russia that as Fez was in danger, France, at the sultan's request, had instructed her agents in Morocco to aid in forming a Sherifian *mehalla* in the west to go to the aid of the capital. "The Government also considers the formation of a French company; we hope still that the sending of this company will not be needed, but it will serve for a demonstration destined to exercise a moral effect on the rebels and it could in case of necessity bring succor to the foreign colony." [82] This section of the note served as an advanced notice of the intended action of France. On the same day Cruppi told Schoen that "news from Fez is unfavorable, Fez is isolated, communications broken off" as a result of which the sultan had sought aid of France, who, in response, had "sent four battalions to the Chaouya in order to prevent a spread of the agitation there." France was compelled to protect the Europeans in Fez; and "on the grounds of the Franco-German February Accord," he expected that Germany would make no difficulty.[83] Schoen replied that he was not empowered to interpret how far German recognition of French special interest might apply, but that he

[80] Seckendorff to F. O., Apr. 18, 1911, *G. P.,* vol. XXIX, no. 10533.

[81] Gauvain, *op. cit.,* vol. II, p. 441.

[82] Cruppi to French representatives at London, Madrid, St. Petersburg, Apr. 19, 1911, *Affaires du Maroc,* 1910-1912, no. 196.

[83] Schoen to F. O., Apr. 19, 1911, *G. P.,* vol. XXIX, no. 10534.

was not convinced of the necessity for sending troops to Fez. Moreover, the advance of French troops or of a native contingent under French leadership would be more likely to excite the natives to a Holy War than to allay the discontent.[84] Performing a similar function for his government, Cambon brought the question to the attention of Bethmann Hollweg, who, in his turn, warned France against the danger of the advance of French troops provoking a Holy War, denied the need for such an advance, and expressed Germany's fear that if France entered Fez she would never leave. "I can only insist on the importance that the Act of Algeciras should be observed, for the difficulties will begin to start from the moment when the French troops will be at Fez. Also it is not possible for me to encourage you. All that I am able to do is to counsel prudence . . . ," was Bethmann Hollweg's admonition, which he re-emphasized by concluding the conference with these words: "I do not say no to you, because I do not wish to take the responsibility for your compatriots; but I repeat it, I do not encourage you. . . ."[85]

Schoen talked to several of the French ministers on the situation. Monis "complained . . . about the difficult inheritance, which he had taken over" and assured him "that French aims were thoroughly loyal and without ulterior motives. . . ." Cruppi was less disturbed and, in his optimistic way, thought that the situation would not prove too difficult. He also spoke of the loyalty and prudent conduct of the French government and assured Schoen that no advanced step would be undertaken without previous exchange of views with Germany. More significant was the reaction of finance minister Caillaux, who "was very candid" and who failed to see any reason for the excitement and jealousy of the German public over Morocco, since it was evident that France's position as the neighbor of the Sherifian empire was deeply affected by the state of peace and order within the country. Schoen remarked that if France would once show herself sincere about the open door in Morocco, German public opinion would

---

[84] Schoen to Bethmann Hollweg, Apr. 20, 1911, *G. P.*, vol. XXIX, no. 10537.

[85] Bethmann Hollweg to Schoen, Apr. 19, 1911, *G. P.*, vol. XXIX, no. 10535; Cambon to Cruppi, Apr. 19, 1911, *Affaires du Maroc*, 1910-1912, no. 200.

quiet itself.[86] German newspapers became increasingly unfriendly, however, and the Pan-German organs insisted that France was responsible for the situation in Morocco and that Germany must hasten to reap her opportunity and through negotiation with France gain her share of the decadent empire.[87] The *Cologne Gazette* wondered how long the French government would be able to hold out against the "Beni M'Tir of the boulevards. . . ."[88] The attitude of the German press provoked the comment from the London *Times* that it was apparent that "German interest in Morocco is infinitesimal as compared with German interest in the European possibilities of a Moroccan question."[89]

The open attacks in the German press and the oblique inferences in the official statements of the German government produced confusion, which hung as a bewildering fog over the Quai d'Orsay as its members tried to catch through the mist a glimpse of what they might expect from Berlin. Baron Greindl, Belgian chargé d'affaires at Berlin, was not disturbed over the possibility of German complications, for he did not believe that at this time there was the least desire on the part of Germany to play an active rôle in Morocco. "They ought long ago, . . . to have lost any illusion on the value of the Act of Algeciras, which France signed with the firm intention of never observing it. She has never stopped an instant in pursuing her plans of annexation. . . ." This enthusiastic supporter of German policy, even when in July German action refuted all his earlier prognostications, made an admission favorable to the French case. "In pledging itself by the Agreement of February 8, 1909, not to interfere in the political interests of France in Morocco, the Imperial government," he admitted, "doubtless knew that the French government would interpret this clause as an encouragement to continue in the same path and that they would regard the promise to respect the independence of Morocco as a dead letter. To withdraw now would be for France a cruel humiliation. . . . Germany has no reason to inflict this upon her and, moreover, after eight

---

[86] Schoen to Bethmann Hollweg, Apr. 23, 1911, *G. P.,* vol. XXIX, no. 10541.
[87] London *Times,* Apr. 25, 1911 (Berlin correspondent).
[88] *Ibid.,* Apr. 24, 1911 (Berlin correspondent).   [89] *Ibid.,* Apr. 25, 1911.

years of sufferance, it would not be possible to change this attitude without being determined to go to war. This is immeasurably more than Morocco is worth. . . ."[90]

As yet France had taken only two steps—reinforcement of French troops in the Chaouya, and organization of a Moroccan *mehalla* in the west to send to Fez. But news from the capital continued disquieting. The London *Times* informed the British public that the "situation in Fez is rapidly becoming desperate. . . . There can be no doubt that the town is in imminent danger of being taken by the rebellious tribes. . . . It is natural that the French government should be seriously considering what steps they may have to take in accordance with the responsibilities placed upon them by the Act of Algeciras and by their other agreements. . . ." The *Times* feared that complications might arise that would draw both Germany and Spain into the scene.[91] This editorial appeared April 21, the same day that Seckendorff reported to his foreign office that conditions were better.[92] Dr. Vassel's report of April 15, transmitted to Berlin by Seckendorff April 23, conceded much more than any German report since March 24. This report read: "Situation unchanged, for the Sultan serious, for the Europeans in Fez not dangerous, but for commerce bad. . . ."[93] One wonders if the responsibility for the lives of the Europeans had rested on the shoulders of the German government, whether Vassel's third phrase would have read differently.

France, with responsibility resting upon herself, was frankly worried by the reports of Billy, received April 25, that the Berber tribes had met at Meknez, had pillaged the village, and proclaimed a new sultan,[94] and by the news from the consul at Rabat that the *mehalla*, far from being ready to make a campaign, was composed of "fatigued men, poorly armed, without money, without direction or command, or any preparation for war . . ." and that the caids of this *mehalla* feared that if the

---

[90] Greindl to Davignon, Apr. 21, 1911, *Belg. Doks.*, Sup. I, no. 66.

[91] London *Times*, Apr. 21, 1911 (Editorial).

[92] Seckendorff to F. O., Apr. 21, 1911, *G. P.*, vol. XXIX, no. 10536.

[93] Seckendorff to F. O., Apr. 23, 1911, *ibid.*, no. 10540.

[94] Billy to Cruppi, Apr. 25, 1911, *Affaires du Maroc*, 1910-1912, no. 218.

troops went to Fez, the tribes of the Haouz would revolt.[95] To
this disquieting news was added the report that the Gharb was
greatly excited.[96] Disturbances in this region, especially if they
extended so as to reach the environs of Larache, would catapult
Spain squarely into the imbroglio. Already nervously afraid that
France was ambitious to "Tunisify" Morocco, Spain would view
with suspicion any effort of France to quell disturbances in the
Gharb.[97] Nevertheless, France gave orders to General Moinier to
advance the native *mehalla* of the Chaouya towards Fez and to
move the French company to the Bou-Regreg, the limits of the
Chaouya, in order to move rapidly to Fez in case of necessity.[98]
On April 25 Cruppi informed the chancelleries of Europe of this
move.[99]

The responses of the various courts were cautious. Some held
an undercurrent of warning. Caballero, Spanish ambassador at
Paris, remarked that if French troops went to Fez, the sovereignty
of the sultan would be diminished and that this would have its
repercussions upon the Spanish zone. What then was Spain to
expect in northern Morocco?[100] Austria replied that she would
adopt a waiting attitude and reserve action so long as France
observed the Act of Algeciras but "of course, a too long sojourn
of French troops in Fez would give the business a political character. . . ."[101] Zimmermann, speaking for Germany, stated that
he thought the French government was sincere, but that the
march to Fez would lead to grave issues, and that any prolonged
occupation of Fez would so impair the Act of Algeciras and the
Franco-German Accord as to make it impossible to foresee what
might happen.[102]

Cruppi revealed his uneasiness in a conversation with Schoen
at a diplomatic reception, in which he asserted that "in the face

[95] Billy to Cruppi, May 1, 1911, *ibid.*, no. 244, enclosure, Leriche, consul at
Rabat, to Billy, Apr. 25, 1911.

[96] Billy to Cruppi, Apr. 24, 1911, *ibid.*, no. 214.

[97] Cartwright to Grey, Apr. 22, 1911, *Br. Docs.*, vol. VII, no. 214.

[98] Cruppi to Billy, Apr. 24, 1911, *Affaires du Maroc*, 1910-1912, no. 215.

[99] Cruppi to French representatives at London, Berlin, St. Petersburg, Rome,
Madrid, Washington, Stockholm, The Hague, Brussels, Lisbon, Apr. 25, 1911,
ibid., no. 219.   [100] Cruppi to Geoffray, Apr. 25, 1911, *ibid.*, no. 221.

[101] Pallavicini to Szécsen, Apr. 25, 1911, *Ö. U. A.*, vol. III, no. 2519.

[102] Cambon to Cruppi, Apr. 26, 1911, *Affaires du Maroc*, 1910-1912, no. 225.

of the constant danger in which the Europeans, especially the French officers, are, the government would not be able to answer for it, if it does not take all suitable precautions. . . . We cannot let our own nationals be massacred. . . ." He assured the ambassador that France "has no kind of intention of conquest or permanent occupation and under all circumstances will hold herself to the text and the spirit of the international treaties . . . ," and since "France's special interest in the maintenance of order and peace in the Sherifian kingdom is generally recognized, her right of intervention in that prudent form in which it is now planned, is, therefore, perhaps, indisputable. . . ." Schoen thereupon turned the conversation into a discussion of the limits of the Act of Algeciras. This Act, he asserted, though recognizing the special interest of France, had as its purpose the maintenance of the sovereignty of the sultan, which sovereignty the French march to Fez would come nearer destroying than strengthening. "A sultan, who can maintain himself only with the help of French bayonets, will not only lose every respect in the eyes of Moorish muselmen, but also become an object of smouldering hate. . . ." He pointed out that French action would tend to lead to a protectorate; but he reaffirmed, "We do not wish to protest against the planned French advance, but only again give expression to the hope that so far-reaching events, as an occupation of Fez would be, may be avoided; not only on account of their effect in Morocco, but also on account of their reaction on our relations formed so satisfactorily since the Moroccan accord. . . ."[103] This was Bethmann Hollweg's reply, "I do not say no to you . . . but . . . I do not encourage you . . . ," clothed in a more elaborate dress. In the entourage of official Berlin, only the Kaiser seemed unconcerned about the affair. Notified of the situation on April 25, he declared that he did not care who was sultan so long as he maintained order and that he did not fear international complications, for "no one will undertake anything, least of all England. . . ." His attitude was that the farther France marched in Morocco, the less she would threaten the German frontier.[104] Cruppi assured

---

[103] Schoen to Bethmann Hollweg, Apr. 26, 1911, *G. P.*, vol. XXIX, no. 10544.
[104] Bethmann Hollweg to William II, Apr. 25, 1911, *ibid.*, no. 10542; Jenisch to F. O., Apr. 26, 1911, *ibid.*, no. 10543.

Bertie that the French government "had no hidden designs. The relief of Fez was a duty to humanity and to the honour of France. They were resolved to keep strictly to the terms of the Algeciras Act and within the limits of their rights and their engagements to England, Spain, and Germany. . . ." Bertie, alone of the diplomats at Paris, did Cruppi the honor of believing him.[105]

From Morocco came the news that Bremond had returned to Fez, that the blockade was worse, and that the sultan had requested the aid of French troops. That was on April 27.[106] On the thirtieth, Gaillard reported that Fez was more closely blockaded and was actually menaced, that the newly proclaimed sultan was exciting the natives to a Holy War, and that the native troops from the Chaouya would not be able to handle the situation.[107] On April 28 the French company crossed the Bou-Regreg.[108] The march to Fez had begun.

And yet Cruppi still seemed to hope that the native troops would effect the relief of the capital and that the French troops would not enter into the campaign. He again assured the interested powers that if the troops "were forced to go to Fez they would remain only for such a brief period as might be absolutely necessary to put the sultan on his legs again. The French government had no ulterior object in view in the action which they were taking. They intended strictly to conform themselves to the Act of Algeciras and their other treaty engagements and they desired to avoid raising any European question. . . ." Bertie commented that he believed these statements of the French government, "for it was to the interest of France that they should be observed. . . ." He had no fear that France would close the open door in Morocco as had Count Szécsen, the Austrian ambassador to Paris, "for such a proceeding on the part of France would alienate the sympathies of the British public and lose her the support of His Majesty's Government. . . ."[109] Nicolson hoped that the Moorish troops could relieve Fez, for it would simplify

[105] Bertie to Grey, Apr. 26, 1911, *Br. Docs.*, vol. VII, no. 220.

[106] Billy to Cruppi, May 5, 1911, *Affaires du Maroc*, 1910-1912, no. 252, enclosure, Gaillard's report of Apr. 27.

[107] Billy to Cruppi, May 5, 1911, *ibid.*, no. 253, enclosure, Gaillard's report of Apr. 30.   [108] Cruppi to Geoffray, Apr. 28, 1911, *ibid.*, no. 237.

[109] Bertie to Grey, Apr. 29, 1911, *Br. Docs.*, vol. VII, no. 236.

the situation; but, "owing to the extent to which the rebellion appears to have spread, I rather doubt if order can be re-established without the active intervention of French troops. . . ."[110] France's ally, Russia, authorized her agent to notify Germany that the Russian government "recognized the operation of France in Morocco as correct and natural" and would appreciate Germany's showing the same attitude.[111] This position was taken by Russia in spite of the fact that the Russian agent in Tangier[112] had joined the chorus of the Belgian[113] and German representatives in decrying French action as unwarranted and imperialistic aggression. For one brief report, the British minister, Lister, seemed inclined to accept their views sufficiently to advise his government that if the German report from Fez were true, "the French column should not continue its advance." [114] His report failed, however, to change the opinion of the British government that the action of France was compelled by the force of events in Morocco. Germany's ally, Austria, continued her position that so long as the Act of Algeciras was not violated, she would make no protest.[115]

It was, indeed, another power, Spain, who, with all the annoyance of a troublesome gnat, buzzed around the French and English foreign offices with her protests and her threats of action. France and England tried to pacify her, but with little success. Neither was influenced by the force of her arguments, but, rather, by the dread that the more sinister power, Germany, would change this annoying pest into something infinitely more destructive. Spain argued that French action had opened the door to the application of that second contingency in the Franco-Spanish treaty, which would give her freedom of action in the northern zone, and that she was, therefore, justified in occupying certain posts within that region.[116] France and England urged her to be

---

[110] Nicolson to Goschen, May 1, 1911, *ibid.,* no. 240.

[111] Neratov to Schebecko, May 1, 1911, Isvolski, *op. cit.,* vol. I, no. 65.

[112] Schoen to Bethmann Hollweg, Apr. 28, 1911, *G. P.,* vol. XXIX, no. 10546.

[113] Belgian report from Tangier, May 2, 1911, *Belg. Doks.,* vol. IV, no. 111; Belgian report from Tangier, May 5, 1911, *ibid.,* no. 113.

[114] Lister to Grey, May 4, 1911, *Br. Docs.,* vol. VII, no. 248.

[115] Pallavicini to Szécsen, May 4, 1911, *Ö. U. A.,* vol. III, no. 2536.

[116] Cruppi to Geoffray, Apr. 29, 1911, *Affaires du Maroc,* 1910-1912, no. 241.

patient, and not to force open the entire Moroccan question by premature action.[117] The two friends were convinced, however, that Germany was giving to Spain diametrically opposite advice. Reports of continued disturbances in the Gharb, of Spanish preparations around Larache, and of unusual Spanish activity around Ceuta increased the uneasiness in the French and English official circles.[118] Any overt act by Spain might be interpreted by Germany as giving her the right to demand a new adjustment of the Moroccan question. France and England were convinced that German agents were encouraging Spain to undertake such an overt act in order to furnish Germany with the desired opportunity.[119] Kiderlen's response to the French communication of April 28 did nothing to allay this suspicion.

On April 28 Cambon, in delivering the official communication of his government to the German secretary of state for foreign affairs, stated that a French military advance had become necessary in order to rescue the French and other Europeans living in Fez. This action, he asserted, did not violate the Algeciras Act, and, moreover, his government expressly declared that it had no intention of occupying Fez or of injuring the sovereignty of the sultan or of violating the principle of the open door. Its aim, he insisted, was solely to take measures to protect its nationals. Kiderlen expressed his confidence in the "loyal intentions of the French government," but his further remarks set the foreign offices aquiver. "Occasionally," he impassively stated, "events are stronger than one thought and finally lead to things which one has not intended. I must, therefore, now declare that, in case French troops remain in Fez, so that the sultan rules only with the help of French bayonets, we would consider him no more as the sultan established through the Algeciras Act. We would in this case consider the act as dissolved and resume completely our liberty of action. . . ." [120] The *Norddeutsche Allgemeine Zeitung*, in a

---

[117] *Ibid.*; Bunsen to Grey, May 3, 1911, *Br. Docs.*, vol. VII, no. 246; Grey to Bertie, May 3, 1911, *ibid.*, no. 245.

[118] Billy to Cruppi, May 4, 1911, *Affaires du Maroc*, 1910-1912, no. 249; Cruppi to Billy, May 4, 1911, *ibid.*, no. 250; Billy to Cruppi, May 10, 1911, *ibid.*, no. 274.

[119] Minute by Nicolson, Apr. 28, 1911, *Br. Docs.*, vol. VII, no. 230.

[120] Note of Kiderlen, Apr. 28, 1911, *G. P.*, vol. XXIX, no. 10545; Cambon to Cruppi, Apr. 28, 1911, *Affaires du Maroc*, 1910-1912, no. 239.

semi-official fashion, published on April 30 a statement of German policy of "watchful waiting," which was in substance a public announcement that if the French government were forced to go beyond its declared program, Germany would consider such action a breach of the Act of Algeciras of such importance as to "restore to all the powers their complete freedom of action. . . ." [121] The crucial question was: What use did Germany intend to make of this "liberty of action"? Cambon was convinced that, "in the event of French troops entering Fez, Germany would indicate that the Algeciras Act had been violated and must be subjected to a revision; that an entirely new situation was created rendering obsolete the Algeciras Act and the 1909 Franco-German Agreement; and that a new order of things must be set up. By that new order of things Germany must have compensations, probably Mogador on the Atlantic seaboard, and possibly also a port on the Mediterranean. . . ." [122]

France communicated this fear to England and gained assurance of support, coupled with advice to move cautiously and enter Fez only if such a move were unavoidable,[123] for the British government was afraid France might give Germany an excuse for action. Bertie, disturbed by Cambon's diagnosis of the situation, infected Isvolski[124] with some of his own anxiety, while Nicolson imparted a similar nervousness to the Russian ambassador in London, Benckendorff.[125] Before the reports from these two reached St. Petersburg, France had sought the support of their government, for "in view of the uncompromising attitude of the Berlin cabinet, a favorable solution of the Moroccan question would depend on the support which the Paris Cabinet in its present difficult position received from its friends at St. Petersburg

---

[121] Schoen to Bethmann Hollweg, May 7, 1911, *G. P.*, vol. XXIX, no. 10555, editor's footnote; London *Times*, May 1, 1911 (Berlin correspondent).

[122] Minute of Nicolson, Apr. 28, 1911, *Br. Docs.*, vol. VII, no. 230. Goschen reported that Cambon stated Kiderlen answered his argument that the Fez expedition was covered by the Accord of 1909 in this manner: "Oh, the 1909 agreement! that was a piece of Schoen's work—we needn't talk about that. . . ." Cambon reminded him that Kiderlen had helped to frame the Accord himself.— Goschen to Nicolson, Apr. 29, 1911, *ibid.*, no. 234.

[123] Minute by Nicolson, Apr. 28, 1911, *ibid.*, no. 230.

[124] Isvolski to Sazonov, May 11, 1911, Isvolski, *op. cit.*, vol. I, no. 72.

[125] Benckendorff to Neratov, May 9, 1911, Siebert, *op. cit.*, no. 672.

and London. . . ." [126] On May 1 Neratov, Russia's acting foreign minister, instructed Schebeko, Russian ambassador to Berlin, to inquire of Kiderlen what were his intentions. On May 4 Schebeko carried out these instructions and Neratov, in the light of Schebeko's report, informed Paris that Berlin had given a satisfactory answer and that Russia supported France.[127] The statements of Russian agents to English representatives in Berlin and Vienna repeated the assurance of Russian support of France.[128] Neratov's reply to Pourtalès, according to the German ambassador's report to the chancellor, was not the hearty support which France desired. Neratov recognized the correctness of the German view and remarked that the French government would not violate the Act of Algeciras.[129] This somewhat oracular pronouncement left the question of Russian attitude much in doubt.

Despite the fact that French troops were moving toward Fez, that Spain was threatening to occupy posts in the north, that Germany was speaking of "liberty of action," that Russia had adopted a lukewarm attitude, and that England was urging caution, Cruppi maintained his optimism. This optimism, Isvolski labelled "as dangerous and unjustified" and, in contrast, he designated the German position as "a very adroit and advantageous" one.[130] As late as May 3, Cruppi told Schoen that he still hoped that things would end well without French troops' going to Fez and assured Schoen that France would maintain her treaty obligations.[131] Schoen reported this conversation with the comment that the French government wished to maintain its pledges, but

[126] Schebecko to Sazonov, Apr. 28, 1911, *ibid.*, no. 671.

[127] Kiderlen to Pourtalès, May 6, 1911, *G. P.*, vol. XXIX, no. 10552. See also editors' footnote, p. 112.

[128] Goschen to Grey, May 4, 1911, *Br. Docs.*, vol. VII, no. 247; Cartwright to Grey, May 5, 1911, *ibid.*, no. 491.

[129] Pourtalès to Bethmann Hollweg, May 9, 1911, *G. P.*, vol. XXIX, no. 10557.

[130] Isvolski believed that "German diplomacy is master of the situation and not only can take its position according to the development of things; but also can suddenly bring to a head the Moroccan question in accordance with the general course of its internal or foreign policy. Herein appears to me indeed the danger . . . that Cruppi scarcely values rightly. This danger seems to me more serious as Cruppi, so far as I can judge, has no entirely clear and definite program in Morocco. . . ."—Isvolski to Sazonov, May 11, 1911, Isvolski, *op. cit.*, vol. I, no. 72. Also given in Siebert, *op. cit.*, no. 673.

[131] Schoen to F. O., May 3, 1911, *G. P.*, vol. XXIX, no. 10550.

he doubted its power to hold back the advance in the face of the activities of men interested in colonial expansion, military men, and the cry of the chauvinists.[132] Morel agreed with Schoen in his analysis of the situation and charged "the concerted clamours of the orchestra of which the *Comité du Maroc* holds the baton, and whose chief performers are to be found in the *Temps* and *Le Matin*. . . . ," with forcing the French government to advance to Fez against its will.[133] The *Journal des Débats* deplored the effort of the chauvinists to tie the honor of the French flag to the sultan's fate and pleaded with the government not to undertake a policy of conquest. The *Journal* resolutely opposed the idea of a new bargain with Germany.[134] To these critics of the French chauvinists was added the German publicist and historian, Schiemann, who attacked the influence of the *Temps* on French foreign policy and the pressure of the French financiers whose loans bound Mulay Hafid into a debt slavery from which he could not extricate himself. He gave vent to his irritation by stating that neither Monis "nor the political novice at the head of the French foreign office, Herr Cruppi, had the inclination to plunge into a Moroccan adventure. They have to give way to the suggestion which came from the *Temps* and its hintermen—to whom we perhaps are not wrong in numbering Herr Delcassé. . . . The question is, who makes the foreign policy of France, the government or the *Temps?*" [135]

Nevertheless, while diplomats argued and journalists fumed, events in Morocco rapidly moved to a climax. On May 6 Cambon informed Schoen that news from Morocco was unfavorable and that action to aid Fez "will be unavoidable." [136] On the seventh, Caillaux told Lancken that the situation in Fez necessitated a French advance but that the occupation of the city would be short.[137] On the tenth, Grey told Sir F. Cartwright that the "news from Fez was bad: the town was cut off from supplies; the people

---

[132] Schoen to Bethmann Hollweg, May 4, 1911, *ibid.*, no. 10551.

[133] *Op. cit.*, p. 120.

[134] *Journal des Débats*, Apr. 30, May 2, May 8, 1911, Gauvain, *op. cit.*, vol. II, pp. 450, 459, 447.

[135] Theodor Schiemann, *Deutschland und die Grosse Politik* (1911), pp. 114, 115, published first in the German newspaper, *Kreuzzeitung*, Apr. 26, 1911.

[136] Schoen to F. O., May 6, 1911, *G. P.*, vol. XXIX, no. 10553.

[137] Schoen to F. O., May 7, 1911, *ibid.*, no. 10554.

inside were getting short of ammunition, and food also was running short. With the revolted tribes outside and approaching starvation inside, it was obvious that the only thing for the French to do was to relieve Fez by the quickest possible route. . . ." He hoped that when the European colony had been rescued, France would restore order quickly, "but at present the first thing to do is to relieve Fez as soon as possible. . . ." Although there were not many British in Fez, it devolved upon England, so Grey acknowledged, to see that they were protected, and "if the French had not been taking measures to relieve the place, we should have had to ask them to do so. . . ." [138] The London *Times* continued to keep the British public informed of the seriousness of the situation.[139]

On May 12 Cruppi received the report which Gaillard had dispatched on the fourth, describing the situation in Fez as "more and more critical" and stating that he and Mangin considered that it was necessary "to hasten as soon as possible the march of the expeditionary column. . . ." [140] On May 14 Cruppi informed the nations of Europe that France had ordered Moinier to advance to Fez without delay but to hold the city no longer than necessary. Moreover, he took the precaution to declare again that "the aim of the action of the French forces rests always on assuring the sovereignty of the sultan, the integrity of territory, and the liberty of commercial transactions, which are closely tied to

---

[138] Grey to Cartwright, May 10, 1911, *Br. Docs.*, vol. VII, no. 260. In answer to an interpellation in Parliament, McKinnon Wood, speaking for the government, stated: "The number of British subjects residing at Fez on 27th March, 1911, apart from persons of Moorish parentage, was ten. Of these six were women and two were children. His Majesty's Government do not contemplate any active measures. They consider that the arrangements being made under French supervision will afford the necessary protection to British subjects at Fez. . . ." Dillon then asked, "Has the Government any information which would give them cause for believing that there is any danger to Europeans?" McKinnon Wood replied, "No, we have no such information."—*Parliamentary Debates,* 5th series, vol. XXIV, p. 1566, House of Commons, Apr. 25, 1911. Less than a month later, Nicolson stated that "the reports which we have received from our consul and from Dr. Verdon entirely corroborate the information which the French consul, who I know to be a very calm and cool-judging man, has sent to his Government."—Nicolson to Bertie, May 17, 1911, *Br. Docs.*, vol. VII, no. 275.   [139] London *Times,* May 8, 1911.

[140] Billy to Cruppi, May 12, 1911, *Affaires du Maroc*, 1910-1912, no. 278, enclosure, Gaillard to Billy, May 4, 1911.

the maintenance of the security and of order of Morocco. . . ." [141] Meanwhile, General Moinier, urged to do nothing to hurt the independence or diminish the prestige of the sultan and to complete the work of the expeditionary corps as rapidly as possible,[142] hastened forward to his goal and arrived before Fez May 21. His report, "All Europeans are safe, despite the gravity of the situation," [143] was greeted with unfeigned joy by some and by caustic comments from others.[144] Had not German observers consistently maintained "All Europeans are safe"? The fact that the city had resisted siege until May 21 is, however, not adequate proof that it could have resisted indefinitely or that the Europeans would have escaped unharmed if the city had fallen to the rebels.

Moinier took up a position which commanded the capital but carefully refrained from entering the city with foreign troops. He then began negotiations with the sultan and secured his agreement to reforms that would obviate a return to the abuses that had provoked the revolt.[145] The grand vizier was dismissed.[146] Some of the tribes remained hostile, and against these Moinier took military action. He found it necessary to march into the city of Meknez in order to subdue the disorders aroused by the pretender.[147] Cruppi continued to announce the intention of France to withdraw her troops as soon as possible and declared that the newspaper charges that she was on the road to establishing a protectorate were false.[148] On June 10 he told Schoen that Cambon had been authorized to inform Germany that General Moinier had been instructed to leave Fez by the route southward to the Mamora forests and to leave further work of pacification to the

---

[141] Cruppi to French representatives in London, Madrid, Berlin, St. Petersburg, Rome, Vienna, Washington, Tangier, Brussels, The Hague, Stockholm, Lisbon, May 14, 1911, *ibid.*, no. 284; note of Zimmermann, May 15, 1911, *G. P.*, vol. XXIX, no. 10559.

[142] Cruppi to Billy, May 16, 1911, *Affaires du Maroc*, 1910-1912, no. 292.

[143] Billy to Cruppi, May 23, 1911, *ibid.*, no. 307; Isvolski to Neratov, May 24, 1911, Siebert, *op. cit.*, no. 679.

[144] Schiemann, *op. cit.*, p. 156.

[145] Billy to Cruppi, May 30, 1911, *Affaires du Maroc*, 1910-1912, no. 322; Billy to Cruppi, May 31, 1911, *ibid.*, no. 328.

[146] Billy to Cruppi, May 31, 1911, *ibid.*, no. 328.

[147] Billy to Cruppi, May 31, 1911, *ibid.*, no. 329.

[148] Schoen to Bethmann Hollweg, May 30, 1911, *G. P.*, vol. XXIX, no. 10563.

Sherifian troops under French instructors.[149] On June 20 Goiran instructed Moinier to complete the submission of the tribes by negotiation and, if possible, not to employ force; and he added that "in order to show that our occupation of Fez will not be prolonged outside of a delay strictly necessary to pacification, the government invites you to consider transferring our camp to Ras El Ma, and leaving at Fez only *maghzen* troops and forces necessary in order to assure the care of the city. . . ." [150] On June 30 the London *Times* announced that General Moinier had made arrangements to station native garrisons at Meknez and Fez and that the French troops were expected back in the Chaouya by the middle of August.[151]

Although occupied during the months of May and June with the task of rescuing the Europeans at Fez and of pacifying the rebellious tribes, France labored hard to keep her diplomatic fences in repair. Austria remained aloof and instructed her diplomats to base their conduct on the principles of the Algeciras Act.[152] Russian and British diplomats were less cool. Isvolski, who had read the instructions sent to Moinier, saw "no reason to doubt the sincerity of the intention of the French government . . ." but added that "the entire question is only whether its execution will be possible and whether it will not draw France into stubborn battle against Moroccan anarchy and at last will lead to complete occupation of the entire land and thereby to international complication. . . ." [153] He consistently regretted the optimism of Cruppi that made him unaware of the complications involved in each ad-

---

[149] Schoen to F. O., June 10, 1911, *ibid.,* no. 10564.

[150] Goiran to Moinier, June 20, 1911, *Affaires du Maroc,* 1910-1912, no. 393.

[151] London *Times,* June 30, 1911. On June 9 the *Morning Post* expressed its approval of the "skill and determination" with which France had conducted the relief expedition and regretted that certain German papers were "beginning to use strong language on the subject of certain private German claims in Morocco. . . ." The *Morning Post* had confidence "in the purpose of France to respect the bona fide rights of subjects of other than French nationality in Morocco," and asserted that this would be "facilitated if such claims are not made the subject of an agitation to create anti-French feeling in Germany. . . ."—Leader from the *Morning Post,* June 9, 1911, p. 6.

[152] Aehrenthal to Austrian representatives in Rome, Paris, London, St. Petersburg, Madrid, Constantinople, Washington, Tokio, The Vatican, June 9, 1911, *Ö. U. A.,* vol. III, no. 2541.

[153] Isvolski to Neratov, June 6, 1911, Isvolski, *op. cit.,* vol. I, no. 89.

vance of the French government. In an equally depressed tone, Nicolson asserted that the French would be compelled to occupy Fez and that "a mere expedition for the protection of Europeans would not be a particularly alarming undertaking but that the experience of all European States, beginning with England, shows that it is easier to occupy a city than to withdraw again. . . ." [154] With France at Fez, and with Spain occupying strategic points, Germany, he feared, would present her demand for compensation, which "will be a pretty large one." [155] Even Grey, though consistently loyal to the French cause, was afraid that the "French have got too deeply in to get out and they will have to go through with a partition of Morocco, in which there will be some difficult and rough water to navigate, and some price to be paid. . . ." [156] He confided to Bertie that "If the Act of Algeciras does go by the board, the partition of Morocco between France and Spain will ensue. I do not suppose that it would be impossible to get Germany's consent; but it would be necessary to pay a price for the consent, though that price need not necessarily be anything in Morocco. . . ." [157]

Berlin advised Schoen, on May 9, to hold back and not show too much interest in French plans and French news from Morocco, as, for the present, "a great as possible restraint might further our interest best. . . ." [158] Upon receipt of the official news of Moinier's arrival before Fez, Zimmermann congratulated Cambon on the relative ease with which French troops had attained their objective.[159] On May 30 Cruppi reaffirmed to Schoen the intention of the French government to stay within its program and denounced all newspaper reports of the French desire for a protectorate as "phantasies." The sphinx-like attitude of Berlin was beginning to undermine the blind optimism of Cruppi and caused him to declare that if France had to advance farther than the announced program, she would discuss the situation with the pow-

[154] Benckendorff to Neratov, May 9, 1911, Siebert, *op. cit.*, no. 672.
[155] Nicolson to Bunsen, May 17, 1911, *Br. Docs.*, vol. VII, no. 276.
[156] Grey to Bertie, June 9, 1911, *ibid.*, no. 314.
[157] Grey to Bertie, June 1, 1911, *ibid.*, no. 307.
[158] Zimmermann to Schoen, May 9, 1911, *G. P.*, vol. XXIX, no. 10556.
[159] Cambon to Cruppi, May 24, 1911, *Affaires du Maroc*, 1910-1912, no. 311.

ers, but that "they seem, in Berlin, not inclined to talk. . . ." [160]
Schoen, like Isvolski, believed Cruppi was too optimistic over the
situation in Morocco and really did not know where the force of
events was leading him.[161] Schoen, in his report to Bethmann Hollweg on June 9, summarized the situation within the Sherifian empire, the advance of the French troops, the dismissal of El Glaoui,
and the activities taken to pacify the tribes, and concluded that
the sultan had become not only militarily but politically dependent on France.[162]

The German government took the position the first week of June
that it would not object to the French being at Fez "for a reasonable time for the purpose of restoring order"; but it still thought
that the force of events would be too strong for France to withdraw. England tried to discover what Germany meant by a reasonable length of time. Bethmann Hollweg dodged the question.
Zimmermann replied that, in his personal opinion, "a month or
six weeks would give them ample time to do all that they had to
do." Bethmann Hollweg remarked, June 1, that "the situation in
Morocco does not cause me the very slightest feeling of anxiety,"
and Kiderlen was reported as having said that "when France contented herself with peaceful penetration, time was on her side and
the game was in her hands. By precipitating matters she has lost
her advantage and the game now bids fair to be in our hands." [163]
All the courts of Europe were anxious to discover how Kiderlen
planned to play the game in which he now held a favored position.
Before Kiderlen played his cards, Spain threw an extra ace into
his hands.

As France moved toward Fez, Spain did not conceal her intention to occupy Tetuan or any other point she deemed advisable.
Cruppi, accordingly, sought and obtained the support of England
for his effort to keep her quiet.[164] Confident that Germany was
urging Spain on, he thought that the solution of the problem was

---

[160] Schoen to Bethmann Hollweg, May 30, 1911, *G. P.*, vol. XXIX, no. 10563.
[161] Schoen to Bethmann Hollweg, June 9, 1911, *ibid.*, no. 10566.
[162] *Ibid.*
[163] Goschen to Grey, June 1, 1911, *Br. Docs.*, vol. VII, no. 306; Goschen to
Grey, June 2, 1911, *ibid.*, no. 308.
[164] Bunsen to Grey, May 10, 1911, *ibid.*, no. 258; Nicolson to Bertie, May 17,
1911, *ibid.*, no. 275; Bertie to Grey, May 14, 1911, *ibid.*, no. 268.

to convince Germany that England was determined "to uphold
the Act of Algeciras and the Secret Agreements regarding Morocco. . . ." Then Germany would probably cease encouraging
Spain to "advance unreasonable claims and complications would
be avoided. . . ."[165] Nicolson reported that England was doing
her "best to restrain Spain from taking any precipitate action,"
but that "we must be prepared for the Spaniards moving on to
Tetuan in the event of France going either to Fez or Taza.
. . ."[166] This warning was issued May 17, four days before
Moinier appeared before Fez. In fact, Isvolski's letters were full
of the uneasiness of the Paris cabinet over the Spanish situation,
and of his constant advice to Cruppi to come to some agreement
with his neighbor in order not to push her into the arms of Germany. Spain was demanding her rights under the secret treaty of
1904, which gave her complete mastery of her sphere. France considered these demands as dangerous "because they amounted to a
real partition of Morocco and could give Germany an excuse to
announce the annulment of the Algeciras Act. . . ." Cruppi recognized the danger, but believed that Spain must be kept in check
in order to avoid the greater danger of German interference.[167]
So on May 20 France offered her a project recognizing her rights
on the Fez-El Ksar-Tangier railroad, her claims in the distribution of public works, and the exemption of her sphere from the
work of Moroccan troops officered by French.[168] Unhappily, she
was not by any means appeased. Maurice Bunsen, the British
minister to Madrid, worked with his French colleague, Geoffray,
to effect a satisfactory compromise but was forced to report that
not "much has been gained beyond keeping the Spaniards out of
Tetuan at least till France had got into Fez. . . ."[169] The Spanish argument that French action had brought into operation the
second contingency foreseen in the secret treaty of 1904 and had
given to Spain freedom of action within the sphere allotted to her

[165] Bertie to Grey, May 14, 1911, *ibid.,* no. 268.

[166] Nicolson to Bertie, May 17, 1911, *ibid.,* no. 275.

[167] Bertie to Grey, May 27, 1911, *ibid.,* no. 291; Isvolski to Neratov, May 18,
1911, Isvolski, *op. cit.,* vol. I, no. 74; Isvolski to Neratov, May 24, 1911, *ibid.,*
no. 78.

[168] Cruppi to Geoffray, May 20, 1911, *Affaires du Maroc,* 1910-1912, no. 303.

[169] Bunsen to Nicolson, May 27, 1911, *Br. Docs.,* vol. VII, no. 294.

continued to be dinned into French and British ears.[170] The threat of Spanish occupation of Tetuan hung constantly before their eyes. This threat was soon transformed into reality.

In fact, Spain was thoroughly in earnest. On May 24 she notified France that she had extended her police power in Tetuan outside the prescribed limits.[171] On June 3 Billy reported that Spanish troops had advanced in the direction of Tetuan,[172] and the same day the Spanish agent notified the French foreign office that disturbances near El Ksar had increased to a degree which required the dispatch of Spanish ships in the hope that the moral effect of their presence would contribute a quieting effect upon the district.[173] On June 8 Spanish troops were landed at Larache, ostensibly to quiet the disturbances in the Gharb, especially those near El Ksar. The troops marched from Larache to El Ksar on June 9.[174] When the news that these troops had landed on Moroccan soil reached Paris, a storm of protest rolled forth from the French press. The act was defined as a "crass violation of the Algeciras Act," as dangerous to the international situation, as a deliberate move to force the Moroccan question before Europe.[175] On June 9 France was officially informed of Spanish occupation of Larache and El Ksar.[176] Spain justified her action at Larache and El Ksar on the need to protect her nationals, since two of her protégés had been assassinated. France countered this argument by the assertion that the protégés in question were brigands whose bad conduct had caused Germany to mark them off her own list of protégés whereupon Spain had granted them protection.[177] As

---

[170] Isvolski to Neratov, June 6, 1911, Isvolski, op. cit., vol. I, no. 87; Bunsen to Grey, May 27, 1911, Br. Docs., vol. VII, no. 293.

[171] Cruppi to Geoffray, May 24, 1911, Affaires du Maroc, 1910-1912, no. 313.

[172] Billy to Cruppi, June 3, 1911, ibid., no. 337.

[173] Geoffray to Cruppi, June 3, 1911, ibid., no. 339.

[174] Billy to Cruppi, June 9, 1911, ibid., no. 352; Zimmermann to Schoen, June 10, 1911, G. P., vol. XXIX, no. 10569; Schoen to F. O., June 11, 1911, ibid., no. 10570.

[175] Journal des Débats, June 10, 1911, in Gauvain, op. cit., vol. II, p. 475; London Times, June 12, 1911 (Paris correspondent); Schoen to Bethmann Hollweg, June 10, 1911, G. P., vol. XXIX, no. 10571.

[176] Cruppi to Geoffray, June 9, 1911, Affaires du Maroc, 1910-1912, no. 353.

[177] Geoffray to Cruppi, June 9, 1911, ibid., no. 357; Billy to Cruppi, June 10, 1911, ibid., no. 362.

a matter of fact, the Spanish government took little trouble to argue the point; for its true purpose was simply to offset the advantage gained by France in the latter's march to Fez. Sir Edward Grey, who no doubt agreed with Bunsen that Spain should be quiet and rely on England to see her through,[178] showed his displeasure to the Spanish ambassador and informed him that "if Spain by tearing up the secret agreement with France forces a partition of Morocco there is no certainty that her zone will be recognized. . . ." [179] Cambon hoped "Germany would not take Spain's impulsive step too seriously . . . ," [180] but even Cruppi began to fear that perhaps things were more involved than he at first had realized.[181]

Although warned throughout the year by the challenging statements of Jaurès and the less chauvinstic press,[182] Cruppi had somehow hoped to rescue the Europeans from Fez and to return without causing international difficulties. The force of events proved too strong for the inexperienced foreign minister. Convinced that the Europeans in Fez were in danger, that the duty to rescue them lay upon her and her alone, France, protesting her allegiance to the Act of Algeciras and the special accords with England, Spain, and Germany, had advanced step by step to Fez. Whatever might be French protests, French control in Fez could not be harmonized with the internationalization of the empire or the independence of the sultan's realm. Unless France could withdraw her troops and avoid a repetition of similar expeditionary moves, the Act of Algeciras might well be buried. Spain, doubtful of French ability to withdraw and suspecting France of intention to filch from Spain her promised share of the Sherifian empire, placed no faith in French avowals and occupied Larache, El Ksar, and Tetuan. Germany, denying that the Europeans were in danger but not refusing to France the right to go to Fez, had courteously but firmly counselled "prudence," had warned against too

---

[178] Bunsen to Nicolson, May 27, 1911, *Br. Docs.*, vol. VII, no. 294.

[179] Grey to Rennie, June 15, 1911, *Br. Docs.*, vol. VII, no. 323.

[180] Goschen to Grey, June 11, 1911, *ibid.*, no. 317.

[181] Communication of Villa Urutia, June 20, 1911, *ibid.*, no. 327.

[182] For example, see Jaurès before the chamber of deputies, June 16, 1911, *Annales de la chambre des députés,* session ordinaire de 1911, vol. II, pp. 321-325; Gauvain, *op. cit.*, vol. II.

long a French sojourn in Fez, and had used such disturbing phrases as "liberty of action," "compensations," and "reasonable length of time." Kiderlen still kept his choicer cards concealed, while the diplomats of Europe nervously waited for him to play his hand. France had won the first trick. Who was to win the second?

Chapter IX

COUP D'AGADIR

The genesis of the famous "*Panther's* Spring" lies in the tangled web of economic and diplomatic projects devised to make operative the Franco-German Accord of 1909, whose early demise had left Germany irritated, discontent, and suspicious of French motives. That dramatic stroke was approached through a labyrinth of diplomatic conferences, among which stands in a position of major prominence the controversial Kissingen interview. The maneuvers immediately preceding this interview form an interesting background. Jules Cambon, the sagacious and tactful French ambassador in Berlin, thoroughly cognizant of the imperialist attitude of the German public and sensitive to the undercurrents playing around the German foreign office, had repaired to Paris in early June to consult with his home government on the difficult situation which faced him at his post. He was especially insistent that the French government give Germany satisfaction in the then-pending railroad negotiations;[1] for he feared that a failure of these plans would precipitate German action, an action that he could not forecast but that he feared might be threatening. Although he was not able to convince his government of the urgency of a settlement of the railroad situation, he returned to Berlin with instructions to find out what the German leaders "had on their chest";[2] and to approach the German officials with proposals for an adjustment of all Franco-German difficulties with the sole exception of the "Lost Provinces."[3]

On June 11 Cambon, again in Berlin, discussed with the chancellor the railroad proposals, adjourned discussion on the Spanish situation, and then, turning to the topic of Fez, reported that

---

[1] See Chapter V, *supra,* which discusses the railroad situation and Cambon's interest in a solution of the problem. See also Schmitt, *op. cit.,* p. 310.

[2] Caillaux, *op. cit.,* p. 97; Tardieu, *op. cit.,* p. 407.

[3] Caillaux, *op. cit.,* p. 97; Cambon to Cruppi, June 11, 1911, *Affaires du Maroc, 1910-1912,* no. 366; Cambon to Cruppi, June 11, 1911, *ibid.,* no. 365; Cambon to Cruppi, June 12, 1911, in Caillaux, *op. cit.,* p. 261,

General Moinier was preparing to depart and leave the city in the control of Sherifian troops. Bethmann Hollweg in reply repeated the statement that German officials had by that time made trite: first it had been "if you go to Fez you will not leave," and now it was "if you leave Fez you will be forced to return." Cambon parried with the aphorism, "One is not able to prevent the fruits from ripening, nor Morocco from falling one day under our influence." With this introduction, he broached the question of a general settlement of Franco-German difficulties by which German opinion would be given "the satisfactions that would permit it to see without disturbance the development of French political influence in Morocco. . . ." Bethmann Hollweg, inexperienced in foreign affairs and confident of the ability of his foreign secretary, contented himself with a polite remark that he would consider the proposal but advised Cambon to see Kiderlen.[4] Zimmermann, when Cambon had discussed the status of the railroad project with him, had also advised him to call upon the foreign secretary.[5] This indication that Germany might be willing to break her menacing silence was welcome news to France, and the French ambassador thereupon made his plans to interview that disciple of Bismarck and Holstein who now held the foreign office, the Swabian, Kiderlen-Waechter.

In the interim, Cambon attended the races at Grünewald and was gratified with the reception accorded him by the Emperor but was more interested in the comments made to him by the Crown Prince. The Crown Prince spoke to him of Morocco and refuted Cambon's statement that the French were leaving Fez with the blunt comment, "You tell me this, but I do not believe anything of it, for you have there a superb occasion which you are going to seize and you have . . . only to give us there our share. . . ."[6] In reporting this remark to Cruppi, Cambon explained that it was important only "in showing the view of the court and military circles in Germany. . . ." He added, however, "I am convinced that we will be obliged effectively to buy our liberty, but the importance

[4] Cambon to Cruppi, June 11, 1911, *Affaires du Maroc,* 1910-1912, no. 366; Bethmann Hollweg to Schoen, June 16, 1911, *G. P.,* vol. XXIX, no. 10575.

[5] Cambon to Cruppi, June 10, 1911, *Affaires du Maroc,* 1910-1912, no. 361.

[6] Tardieu, *op. cit.,* p. 407; Cambon to Cruppi, June 12, 1911, in Caillaux, *op. cit.,* pp. 259-262.

is that the price which we will have to pay will be neither Mogador nor any portion whatsoever of Morocco . . . ," [7] for to grant Germany any part of Morocco would be counter to all French plans since 1905 and would destroy the entente with England.[8] With this conviction firmly rooted in his mind, Cambon set forth to interview Kiderlen.

The London *Times*, June 21, published the following interesting notice received from their Berlin correspondent, June 20: "The French Ambassador in Berlin, M. Jules Cambon, arrived at Kissingen today with his wife and daughter who intend to take the waters. As the German press noted, the German Foreign Secretary, Herr von Kiderlen-Waechter is still at Kissingen, where he had spent several weeks, and assumes that the French Ambassador is also there for a 'cure.' It may be added that M. Cambon is in reality passing through Kissingen on his way to France for a few days' leave. . . ." [9] Thus was announced to the public the historic meeting between the two who as antagonists, "as terrible friends and dear enemies," [10] fought out the various issues in, and finally worked to a solution of, the crisis of 1911. Kiderlen-Waechter, brusque, cynical, tactless, often truculent, with a certain strain of brutality and coarseness in his humor, was withal a shrewd, capable, and clever opponent[11] for the suave French diplomat. Kiderlen had long experience in the diplomatic field; and, although he served most of his tenure in Bucharest, he was frequently called by Bülow for temporary service in the foreign office. Cambon and Kiderlen had worked together on the Casablanca

---

[7] Cambon to Cruppi, June 12, 1911, *ibid.*, p. 260.

[8] Tardieu, *op. cit.*, p. 408.

[9] London *Times*, June 21, 1911 (Berlin correspondent).

[10] After the conclusion of the negotiations of 1911, Cambon sent Kiderlen his photograph with the inscription, "To my dear friend and terrible enemy." Kiderlen returned the favor with the inscription reversed, "To my terrible friend and dear enemy."—Cambon to Kiderlen, Nov. 5, 1911, Jäckh, *op. cit.*, p. 140 and footnote; Friedjung, *op. cit.*, vol. III, p. 29; Genevieve Tabouis, *The Life of Jules Cambon*, pp. 194-195. Take Jonescu mentioned the photograph of Cambon on Kiderlen's desk.—*Some Personal Impressions*, p. 65.

[11] London *Times*, June 29, 1910 (Editorial); Paul H. Schwabach, *Aus Meinen Akten*, p. 195; Brandenburg, *op. cit.*, p. 360; H. F. Eckardstein, *Persönliche Erinnerungen an König Eduard*, p. 83; Wolff, *op. cit.*, pp. 20-22; Gauvain, *op. cit.*, vol. II, p. 225; W. Andreas, "Kiderlen-Waechter," in *Historische Zeitschrift*, vol. CXXXII, p. 249; B. H. M. von Bülow, *Memoirs*, vol. III, p. 464.

"deserters affair" and in forming the Accord of 1909 and were therefore familiar with the manners and technique of the other. Kiderlen's reputation as a follower of Bismarck, as a devotee of the "strong manner," as a brusque, self-willed diplomat [12] was well known to Cambon, but the intellectual force, the diplomatic experience, and the calm assurance of the man [13] were also familiar to the French ambassador. Kiderlen recognized in his opponent a capable, tactful, experienced and persistent diplomat [14] who would prove an antagonist worthy of his mettle. A certain mutual respect existed between the two which rendered them suitable agents for their respective governments in carrying on the difficult negotiations that now faced them. As they took the "cure" in the famed springs and enjoyed their rest in the beautiful valley of Kissingen, the two diplomats faced the delicate problem of Franco-German relations.

Cambon's reports of his interviews at Kissingen form the basis for any account of the conferences, for Kiderlen had surprisingly little to say about the conversations which there took place. On the first day Kiderlen's manner was "extremely reserved," and his attitude was one of indifference toward any suggestions tentatively thrown out by Cambon for a discussion of general Franco-German relations.[15] Cambon realized that the task of discovering what Germany wanted would prove difficult, but on the next day the conversation took a more lively turn. He reported that it was Kiderlen who approached the Moroccan question with an inquiry about the Spanish situation, to which he replied that as Spain had violated the Act of Algeciras, certainly Germany would take the same position as France had done on that issue; and he emphasized the fact that France had maintained her pledge and up-

---

[12] Gauvain, *op. cit.*, vol. II, p. 225, vol. III, p. 363; Brandenburg, *op. cit.*, p. 360; Tabouis, *op. cit.*, p. 195.

[13] Schwabach, *op. cit.*, pp. 194, 195; Bethmann Hollweg, *Betrachtungen zum Weltkriege*, vol. I, p. 30; Brandenburg, *op. cit.*, p. 360; Eckardstein, *op. cit.*, p. 83; Jonescu, *op. cit.*, pp. 57, 58; Jacques Dorobantz, "M. de Kiderlen-Waechter," in *Questions diplomatiques et coloniales* (1910), p. 89; Jäckh, *op. cit.*, vol. II, p. 202.

[14] Friedjung, *op. cit.*, vol. III, p. 29; Davis, *op. cit.*, p. 415.

[15] Cambon to Cruppi, June 22, 1911, *Affaires du Maroc*, 1910-1912, no. 399; also published in Caillaux, *op. cit.*, pp. 263-267. Tardieu gives a summary of the interview.—*Op. cit.*, pp. 407-417.

held her obligations under that Act. Kiderlen, in his usual mocking manner, dryly remarked, "Very well, but why should I com-
pliment you on it? Is it necessary to consider as a merit that one
holds to his promises?" The ambassador shifted the topic to the
sacrifices France had made in Morocco only to receive another
shaft of Swabian irony with the abrupt question, "Who asked you
to do it?" Cambon replied, "The Sultan, our consul, the consul of
England, all believed the danger"; but, as Kiderlen at once remarked, the consul of Germany was conspicuously omitted from
the enumeration.

After this diplomatic juggling for position and testing of opponents, the two approached more nearly the crux of the difficulty.
Kiderlen asserted that France had left behind in Fez a situation
different from that which she had found there and that a Morocco
with French forces spread throughout the country and with a
sultan devoted to France created a different situation from that
conceived by the Act of Algeciras. Cambon reminded him of the
Accord of 1909 in which Germany had conceded to France political influence. "I do not contest your influence," replied Kiderlen,
"but who says influence does not say protectorate, and it is a
veritable protectorate that you are in the process of organizing.
That is neither in the Act of Algeciras nor in the Accord of
1909. . . ." Cambon evidently did not stress the matter; but he
could have answered that the Accord of 1909 did not speak of
"influence" but in its phraseology came more nearly to the term
"protectorate," for it recognized the predominant political interest
of France in Morocco. He, in this instance, seemed to have devoted
his efforts to convincing his opponent that in a barbarous country, a delimitation of the term "influence" was, at least, very difficult.

It was in order to avoid such misunderstandings that France
was anxious to discuss and reach an agreement on all the questions that divided the two nations. Kiderlen first met the overture
with silence but at last said, "Ah, well, I share your sentiment,
but if we restrict our conversation to Morocco, we will not succeed; it is useless to replaster that which has been done on the
subject of Morocco and which seems today to be cracked. . . ."
Cambon agreed, especially as "You recall you have at other times

spoken to me of Morocco, but . . . it is desirable to say immediately that if you wish to have any part of Morocco, it would be better not to commence the conversation; the opinion in France would not accept it on this ground and, moreover, in the interest of our good relations, it would be better for us not to multiply the visits . . . *one may seek elsewhere.* . . ." The italicized clause carried with it unlimited possibilities.

Cambon, for his part, was apparently interested only in turning German attention from Morocco; for he was obsessed with the fear that Germany would demand a partition of that country. He wished to avoid the position of having to refuse such a demand, but to concede would be impossible. Each of the two opponents was trying to avoid the position of making definite proposals or demands and at the same time trying to force his antagonist into the position of demander. Cambon had inadvertently given the advantage momentarily to Kiderlen, who was quick to recognize the fact as his reply, "Yes, one may . . . but it is necessary for you to say what you wish," clearly indicated. The French ambassador then veered to safer grounds and asserted that he could not state definitely what was wished, "for these ideas are new . . ."; but he agreed to submit them to his government when he returned to Paris and asked the German secretary on his side to consider what he wished. After this interplay, the conversation turned to less important matters; but an hour afterwards, as the two separated, Kiderlen took care to say, "Bring us something from Paris." [16] Was there a covert threat of blackmail hidden in Kiderlen's words? The Imperial Government was not averse to the use of such tactics, as its attitude toward Great Britain during her trouble with the Boer republics clearly showed. Might not France prove to be an easier victim than virile Britain?

The two statements, "One may seek elsewhere" and "Bring us something from Paris," coupled with Cambon's emphatic announcement that "if you wish to have any part of Morocco, it would be better not to commence the conversation," form the significant points in these interviews. The question arises to what extent the first two of these statements involved an offer of compensation. One authority concludes that though the offer was not

---

[16] Cambon to Cruppi, June 22, 1911, *Affaires du Maroc*, 1910-1912, no. 399.

definitely made, it "was an open secret that territory in the Congo was meant." [17] It is true that newspapers had been free with the discussion of the possibility of offering Germany compensation in the Congo for a free hand in Morocco, and that tentative suggestions of compensation in some nature had been bandied back and forth in the diplomatic correspondence. Cambon was convinced that some compensation must be offered Germany, but he was not in a position at this time to make a definite offer. The advantage in negotiation would, moreover, have been lost to him if he had made such an offer. Neither Cambon nor Kiderlen bound their governments, but they had approached the issue as one that might be settled through the medium of concessions. The one definite, concrete statement that had been made was Cambon's flat refusal to consider Morocco as a subject for partition.

Cambon's report of the Kissingen interview, as printed in the French *Yellow Book*, is in substance that given above. In a letter to Poincaré, January 18, 1912, he throws further light upon the episode.[18] When the question of publication of the despatches relative to the interview had been raised, Cambon complained of the deletions that had been made in his official report. "In this account I reported that I recalled to M. de Kiderlen that he had formerly spoken to me of Mogador and that we put aside all claims of this nature . . ."; but upon the insistence of the German government, Selves had agreed that Kiderlen's statement that "he had not spoken of Mogador in the course of these negotiations" would not be refuted because of the difficult position in which he was placed by the charges made against him by the Pan-Germans. Cambon protested against this omission in his report and stated that Zimmermann told him, "It is clear that M. de Kiderlen spoke to you formerly of Mogador, but you understand the great interest which there is for him that no mention should be made of the suggestions that he made to you in this regard. . . ." To this Cambon replied that "the negotiation that ended in the Treaty of November 4, 1911, would be without cause, if it were not explained by the fact that Germany had manifested the intention of

---

[17] Friedjung, *op. cit.*, vol. III, p. 23.

[18] Cambon to Poincaré, Jan. 18, 1912, *Documents diplomatiques français*, 3rd series, vol. I, no. 485.

taking hold in Morocco and that we refused. . . ." In this document, Cambon made the definite charge that Germany wanted a foothold in southern Morocco.[19]

At the close of the Kissingen interview the situation stood thus: Cambon had left open vast possibilities in his phrase, "one may seek elsewhere," and had refused emphatically only one point in which Germany might be interested—Morocco. Kiderlen had indicated his willingness to approach the question through the medium of negotiation. His statement, "Bring us something from Paris," certainly justified Cambon in his belief that Germany would await his return from Paris before injecting any more complications into an already complicated situation.

Cambon held his last conversation with Kiderlen on June 22. On June 23 he went to Paris and that evening orally announced to Cruppi that he would present his written report the next morning. At eight-thirty on the morning of June 24, Cambon brought this report to the foreign ministry. But Cruppi was no longer foreign minister. On the evening of June 23 the Monis cabinet had been overthrown[20] and not until the evening of June 28 was the Caillaux cabinet completed.[21] June 29 was the earliest possible moment that Cambon's report could have received the serious attention of the French government.

The issues which had overthrown the Monis ministry had been domestic, and the threatening domestic situation[22] absorbed the attention of Caillaux in forming his cabinet. In the light of later revelations, however, one doubts that the new premier was as ignorant of the foreign situation as he stated.[23] Although he probably had not at that moment received the reports on the Kissingen

---

[19] Further indication of German desire for Mogador was reported to Grey by Rattigan, British attaché at Tangier. He stated, "Secretary of Austrian Legation let slip yesterday in conversation with me that Germany would like to obtain Mogador. . . ."—Rattigan to Grey, May 1, 1911, *Br. Docs.*, vol. VII, no. 239.

[20] The problems of electoral reform, workmen's pensions, and regulation of wine production had weakened the government majority and the debate on appropriations for the army, which led to a discussion of reorganization of military personnel, resulted in the defeat of a proposed vote of confidence. Thereupon the Monis ministry resigned.—*Annales de la chambre des députés*, session ordinaire de 1911, vol. II, pp. 435-447; *Annual Register*, 1911, pp. 310-312; Caillaux, *op. cit.*, p. 104.   [21] Tardieu, *op. cit.*, pp. 417, 418.

[22] Caillaux, *op. cit.*, p. 104.   [23] *Ibid.*, p. 105.

interviews, he was certainly cognizant of the reserves that the German government had made relative to the expedition to Fez, and his opponents claimed that he had opened non-official negotiations with Kiderlen prior to the Kissingen interview.[24]

However, the premier's first care seems to have been to adjust his cabinet to the difficult domestic situation. He shifted Cruppi to the position of minister of justice and first offered the portfolio of the foreign office to Léon Bourgeois, who refused.[25] He then turned to Poincaré but again met a refusal.[26] His next selection, M. de Selves, a senator and prefect of the Seine, accepted the portfolio. It was unfortunate that at this crucial moment the foreign office was entrusted to a man who had had no diplomatic experience, who knew nothing of the complicated tangle of Moroccan affairs or of its interrelationship with the larger problem of European security.[27] Selves had proven himself a capable administrator of his department, but that did not qualify him for the position of foreign minister. The *Journal des Débats*, though ignorant of the details of the Kissingen conversations, expressed the situation clearly. "M. de Selves," so stated this journal, "receives a heavy heritage. As new in the diplomatic career as was his predecessor last March, he is faced by a situation perhaps more difficult. . . . It is to M. de Selves that is reserved the task of drawing France without damage from its delicate position. In our opinion the greatest danger that he runs is that of nourishing the illusion that the maneuver is easy. In reality the maneuver is of extreme delicacy. It demands a sure eye, a profound knowledge of the smallest details of the terrain, a very firm hand. . . ."[28] None of these qualifications did Selves possess.

Caillaux, who reserved for himself the post of minister of interior, was much more prepared to take over the foreign office than the official to whom he entrusted that function; for his heritage had given him longer ministerial service. Neither his millionaire inheritance nor his youthful dandyism[29] had turned him from the footsteps of his father, a minister and politician of note in

[24] See, for example, the charges of Sir Eyre Crowe, Chapter XIII, *infra*.
[25] Caillaux, *op. cit.*, p. 105.   [26] *Ibid.*
[27] *Ibid.*, p. 106; Tardieu, *op. cit.*, pp. 441-444; Schoen, *op. cit.*, p. 147.
[28] *Journal des Débats*, June 29, 1911, in Gauvain, *op. cit.*, vol. III, p. 485.
[29] A. Fabre-Luce, *Caillaux*, pp. 38, 46.

15

his day.[30] The son, Joseph Caillaux, began his political career in the field of finance,[31] a field which later became his specialty. In 1898, at the age of thirty-five, he entered the chamber of deputies, where he soon climbed to prominence. He first served as minister of finance in the Waldeck-Rousseau cabinet,[32] and, as we have noticed, again held that office under Monis. Although primarily interested in finance, his private transactions with international bankers plus his interest in government finance forced him to keep abreast of the international situation and, as a result, his knowledge of foreign policy was broader than his official positions seemed to indicate. During the late administration, he had been consulted on various questions of foreign policy and had shown his special interest in the Moroccan question by his non-official negotiations with Lancken on the Congo-Camerun railroad project.[33] He had long been known as sponsor of a policy of rapprochement with Germany.

The cabinet member best informed on the entire Moroccan situation was, of course, Delcassé, whom Caillaux retained as minister of the navy, a position he had held under Monis. His presence in the Monis cabinet had provoked controversial comment. Some accused him of recommending aggressive action on the part of the government,[34] but he seemed to have become the least aggressive of its members and urged France to move cautiously. The Belgian ambassador in Paris, Guillaume, believed Berlin knew that Delcassé had become "the most pacific element." [35] Regardless of that fact, he had not been considered as a possibility for the foreign office, simply because French political leaders, mindful that Germany had forced his dismissal in 1905, feared the international repercussions [36] which might result from such an appointment. It

---

[30] *Ibid.*, p. 31.

[31] He held the post of inspector of finance in Algeria.—*Ibid.*, p. 16.

[32] *Ibid.*, pp. 16, 26.   [33] See Chapter V, *supra.*

[34] C. R. Beazley, "Die Verantwortlichkeit für den Weltkrieg," in *Berliner Monatshefte,* Jan. 1930, p. 49. Veit Valentin speaks of Delcassé's entrance into the cabinet as an "alarm signal."—*Deutschlands Aussenpolitik von Bismarck's Abgang bis zum Ende des Weltkrieges,* p. 98.

[35] Guillaume to the F. O., July 12, 1911, *Belg. Doks.,* vol. IV, no. 130.

[36] The story is told that Kiderlen at the time of the ministerial crisis in France told Bethmann Hollweg and the Kaiser that he would not object if Delcassé were called to the premiership, whereupon each of the two at a dinner

was, therefore, not the well-informed and competent Delcassé who took over the foreign office on June 29, 1911, but the inexperienced M. de Selves, who above everything needed time to enable his mind to pierce that diplomatic maze which shrouded his task. Time was the one thing he was not granted.

At noon, July 1,[37] Selves officially received the German ambassador, Schoen, who presented to him the following *aide mémoire:* [38]

Some German firms, established in South Morocco and especially at Agadir and in its environs, are alarmed at certain fermentations among the tribes of this region which the recent events in other parts of the country seem to have produced. These firms have addressed themselves to the Imperial Government to ask from it protection for their life and their property. On their demand, the Government decided to send to the port of Agadir a warship, in order to lend in case of need, aid and succor to its subjects and protégés as well as to considerable German interests engaged in the said region. When the state of things in Morocco will have returned to its former calm, the ship charged with its protective mission will leave the port of Agadir.

Selves, although surprised, met the news with "wonderful calm" and asked if it were a question of a planned step or a *fait accompli* and was told that it was a *fait accompli.*[39]

with Pierpont Morgan made an opportunity to say to the French naval attaché that Germany desired Delcassé at the head of the French government. The attaché naturally reported this to Paris and Paris, of course, issued a formal protest against such unwarranted meddling in French affairs. Kiderlen said he made the best of the bad business by commenting that the chancellor and Kaiser had made the remark with the best of intentions. Kiderlen was provoked at the exaggerated import placed upon his remark by his superiors.—Kiderlen to the Baroness Y, in Caillaux, *op. cit.,* p. 275; Goschen to Grey, July 12, 1911, *Br. Docs.,* vol. VII, no. 373.

[37] Selves to French representatives in London, St. Petersburg, Madrid, Berlin, Rome, Vienna, Tangier, July 1, 1911, *Affaires du Maroc,* 1910-1912, no. 418; *Temps,* July 3, 1911; *Le Matin,* July 2, 1911.

[38] Kiderlen to Schoen, June 30, 1911, *G. P.,* vol. XXIX, no. 10578. Dr. F. W. Pick, in his account of the diary written by Dr. William Charles Regendanz, stated that this noted German business man, a director in the Hamburg-Marokko-Gesellschaft, of which Messrs. Warburg of Hamburg were the principal shareholders, in consultation with Baron Langwerth of the foreign office, prepared the address that was sent to the foreign office presumably by the distressed German firms, and this was the decisive argument used to persuade the Kaiser to accept Kiderlen's program.—*Searchlight on German Africa,* pp. 8-20.

[39] Schoen to Bethmann Hollweg, July 3, 1911, *G. P.,* vol. XXIX, no. 10586.

Thus, before Cambon could possibly have fulfilled Kiderlen's request, "Bring us something from Paris," France was confronted with a *fait accompli*. Kiderlen had played his hand: the *Panther* dropped anchor at Agadir. The German foreign secretary had evidently not been idly waiting the return of the French ambassador. In fact, Kiderlen left Kissingen on June 24 and joined his Emperor at Kiel. Details about the conferences which probably took place between Kiderlen and Bethmann Hollweg and between these two and the Emperor are unknown.[40] The laconic telegram, "Ships Approved," dispatched by Kiderlen, June 26, from aboard the *Hohenzollern* embodies the essential results.[41] On June 27 instructions were sent to the *Panther* to proceed to Agadir,[42] that port in southern Morocco which had long been recognized as the best natural harbor on its Atlantic littoral and the port most strategically located for a naval base, well situated to guard the African and South American trade routes. The *Panther* was thus transformed from an insignificant little cannon boat[43] into an instrument of war dangerously threatening the peace of Europe.

The juxtaposition of events as they occurred around the French and German foreign offices during the last few days of June refutes claims that France failed to fulfil the promise held open at Kissingen. Kiderlen and Cambon had held their last conference on June 22. They each adjourned to consult their superiors, but Cambon was faced with a chaotic condition in the foreign office when he appeared to present his report. Kiderlen secured the consent of his Emperor to his program two days before the Caillaux cabinet was constituted. Orders were sent to the *Panther* June 27;

---

[40] Editor's footnote to despatch, Kiderlen to F. O., June 26, 1911, *ibid.*, no. 10576. Dr. Pick gives additional light in revealing that the "Emperor's friend, Ballin, the head of the Hamburg-Amerika-Linie," prepared the Kaiser for Kiderlen's and Bethmann Hollweg's reports.—*Op. cit.*, pp. 20, 21.

[41] Kiderlen to F. O., June 26, 1911, *ibid.*, no. 10576.

[42] Kiderlen to F. O., June 27, 1911, *ibid.*, no. 10577.

[43] The *Panther* was a small cannon boat of 62 metres length and carrying no more than 125 men. On July 4, the *Panther* was relieved by the *Berlin*, a ship of 104 metres length and carrying 273 men and 13 officers. The two ships alternated their stay at the port. A table of their movements is given in *Br. Docs.*, vol. VII, Appendix VI. The exact date of the arrival of the *Panther* is not determined. The description of the two ships is taken from Albin, *op. cit.*, p. 31; *Journal des Débats*, July 5, 1911, in Gauvain, *op. cit.*, vol. III, p. 10.

selves took over the French foreign office June 28. Kiderlen sent his instructions to Schoen on June 30; but by that time, as the German official reported, the proposal was not a planned move but a *fait accompli*. Germany had delayed sending notification to the various foreign offices until the *Panther* neared its destination.

In the light of this documentary evidence, Hammann and Brandenburg are not justified in charging Cambon with dilatoriness. Hammann stated that Kiderlen expected Cambon to make a definite offer, but "after his return from Paris, where he had gone for information, Cambon did not appear in the foreign office for days. Kiderlen now proceeded to carry out his plans. He went to Kiel, and there obtained the Kaiser's consent to sending to Agadir the small gun-boat *Panther*. . . ."[44] Brandenburg declared that "evidently Kiderlen wished to wait before taking decisive steps till he saw whether Cambon brought back any definite and formal offers with him from Paris. But when the Ambassador had been back for several days and made no move, he thought France intended to let things drag on till she had Morocco safely in her pocket, and so he decided to proceed with his original plan at once. . . ."[45] Kiderlen did not wait for several days after the ambassador's return to Berlin, but issued his orders for action before Cambon left Paris. In like measure it is difficult to accept the statement that Kiderlen "came finally to the conviction that without drastic measures France in the main would not be induced to negotiate . . ." and that the sending of the *Panther* "was nothing but the announcement . . . compelled by the . . . restraint of the Parisian cabinet, of our [German] wish to negotiate. . . ."[46]

Kiderlen was fully aware of the ministerial crisis in progress in France, but he did not give France an opportunity to present definite offers after the Kissingen interview, even if she had been inclined to do so. Yet he knew that the new premier, Caillaux, was notoriously friendly to conciliation and to compensation.[47] The one thing Cambon had refused Kiderlen was a part of Morocco; all

---

[44] *Op. cit.*, p. 221.   [45] *Op. cit.*, p. 374.

[46] Bethmann Hollweg, *op. cit.*, vol. I, p. 30.

[47] Hammann, *op. cit.*, p. 221; Schoen, *op. cit.*, p. 147; Schoen to F. O., May 7, 1911, *G. P.*, vol. XXIX, no. 10554; Schoen to Bethmann Hollweg, May 7, 1911, *ibid.*, no. 10555.

else was left in the realm of possibility. Why then the haste on the part of the German pilot to secure a "clenched pledge" before negotiations began? Did he hope for more than Cambon had left open? Although his movements from Kissingen to Agadir indicate haste, his action was not the result of a sudden whim, but the culmination of a well-matured plan. Wolff, then editor of the *Berliner Tageblatt*, whose mocking references to Kiderlen's "yellow waistcoat" had created a feeling of animosity between the two,[48] cynically remarked, "It has to be admitted that our people made long preparations for their mistakes and went about their frivolous moves without any precipitation. . . ." [49] Kiderlen's preparations for his eventual move went back to the early spring.

It should be recalled that by the first of May conditions in Morocco were rapidly approaching a crisis; France had notified the powers that she would probably be compelled to rescue the endangered Europeans, though as yet General Moinier had not been ordered to advance to Fez. On May 3 Kiderlen drew up a lengthy memorandum[50] on the Moroccan situation and outlined the course of action Germany was to follow. In this memorandum he first summarized the chaotic condition which existed in the Sherifian empire and concluded that Morocco must prove itself capable of development, which seemed doubtful, or she must sooner or later be absorbed by her more powerful neighbor, France. He acknowledged that the Act of Algeciras did not give him grounds to dispute French right to protect her nationals—which France repeatedly asserted was her sole purpose in going to Fez. According to his analysis of the situation, however, if France went to Fez, rescued the Europeans, and retreated to the coast, French public opinion would object; the tribes would consider it an act of weakness; and new disturbances, calling for new intervention, would arise. Events would sooner or later make of the Act of Algeciras a mere fiction. Germany must consider what change in her policy would be necessitated by this changed circumstance. Kiderlen's decision was that, since France had declared she had no intention of remaining permanently in Fez, Germany, as soon as

[48] Dorobantz, *op. cit.*, p. 89; Wolff, *op. cit.*, p. 23.
[49] Wolff, *op. cit.*, p. 43.
[50] Note of Kiderlen, May 3, 1911, *G. P.*, vol. XXIX, no. 10549.

French troops entered Fez and began to organize themselves there, should "ask in a friendly manner in Paris how long the French government consider a sojourn of their troops in Fez requisite. France would scarcely be able to do otherwise than name to us a space of time. Naturally, after its lapse, under any kind of pretext the retreat will be prolonged further. Then the moment would come for us to declare to the signatory powers that . . . the Act is thereby through the force of events broken up and full freedom of action given back to the collective signatory powers. . . ." At this point, he argued, it would be necessary for Germany to decide what use to make of this freedom.

The occupation of Fez, he insisted, would be preliminary to French absorption of Morocco. "We would attain nothing through protest and would suffer thereby a moral defeat hard to endure. We must, therefore, assure ourselves an object for the negotiations then following, that would make the French inclined to compensation. . . ." He then advanced to the significant question of what object should Germany seize. In developing this point, he argued that if France were justified in protecting her nationals, Germany would also be justified in protecting hers. "We have great German firms in Mogador and Agadir; German ships could betake themselves into these harbors and for the protection of these firms. They could be stationed there entirely friendly—only to prevent the anticipatory arrival of another power in these important harbors of southern Morocco. . . ." [51] "In possession of such a clenched pledge," he concluded, Germany "would be able to look quietly on the further development of things in Morocco and to wait to see whether perhaps France will offer us suitable compensation in her colonial possessions, in return for which we could then leave the two ports. . . ." He explained his selection of these two harbors on the grounds that they were at a distance from England

---

[51] Although later Kiderlen justified his *coup* on the grounds that southern Morocco was unprotected, he here seemed to fear that France might extend her military activities to this region and deprive him of his excuse for action. Perhaps he thought that the first move in this region must be Germany's if she wished to establish any claim to the territory; for if France were in possession of the land, even a "clenched pledge" would be difficult to secure. At all events, he considered it essential to his program that a German vessel must be the first to anchor in a southern port.

and would lessen her opposition.[52] Wolff remarked that this argument "is surprising, and [that] one wonders whether Kiderlen and his staff were quite serious when they said this. Perhaps it was no more than a pleasant little burst of South German humour. . . ."[53] But this was not the only reason for the choice of these two harbors. Kiderlen inserted two additional ones, "the extremely fruitful hinterland" especially the mining resources, and the fact that Agadir "is said to be the best harbor of the land on its Atlantic coast. . . ."[54] Kiderlen had already, April 28, given expression to his idea that French occupation of Fez would grant freedom of action to the remaining signatory powers,[55] and on May 3 he had determined the procedure he would follow in meeting other eventualities.

Although the memorandum of May 3 presumably lay concealed in the files of the foreign office, a clue to German action leaked into the press. On May 8 the *Press Central*, a German news agency, published the statement that Germany was preparing to send three cruisers to Morocco, to moor off Casablanca, Rabat, and Mogador.[56] The *Norddeutsche Allgemeine Zeitung*, as the government organ, published an immediate denial and denominated such news mere sensationalism.[57] The *Journal des Débats* made the comment that such tactics pursued by the chauvinistic newspapers simply emphasized the uneasy tension which pervaded the European courts and made difficult any peaceful negotiations, yet it seemed to accept without question the official denial of the German government.[58]

There has been much conjecture as to how this particular news item reached the German press. Some have sought to interpret it as a clever move on the part of Kiderlen to test the terrain, to gain an insight into the possible diplomatic reception such an action

[52] Note of Kiderlen, May 3, 1911, *G. P.*, vol. XXIX, no. 10549.

[53] *Op. cit.*, p. 45.

[54] Note of Kiderlen, May 3, 1911, *G. P.*, vol. XXIX, no. 10549.

[55] See Chapter VIII, *supra*.

[56] Cambon to Cruppi, May 8, 1911, *Affaires du Maroc*, 1910-1912, no. 263; editor's footnote to Kiderlen's note of May 3, 1911, *G. P.*, vol. XXIX, no. 10549.

[57] Editor's footnote to Kiderlen's note of May 3, 1911, *G. P.*, vol. XXIX, no. 10549; Cambon to Cruppi, May 8, 1911, *Affaires du Maroc*, 1910-1912, no. 264.

[58] *Journal des Débats*, May 11, 1911, in Gauvain, *op. cit.*, vol. II, p. 462.

might obtain from the great powers.[59] Eckardstein, at one time an official in the German foreign office but at that time a private citizen, presented a different view of the situation.[60] In his *Persönliche Erinnerungen an König Eduard,* he stated that during the evening of May 3 he had dinner with Matthias Erzberger, a Reichstag deputy of the Center Party. Erzberger told him that he had spent the preceding night "at grips with his Swabian countryman, Kiderlen-Waechter. The conversation with Kiderlen had been highly interesting, for he had made to him very important disclosures about his planned Moroccan policy and asked him to prepare a favorable sentiment for it within the Center Party." Erzberger then related that Kiderlen planned to make a clean sweep of the Moroccan question and, if need be, go to the extreme to secure that objective. "Probably in the shortest possible time, three to four warships of the present German squadron will be sent to the west coast of Morocco and will be stationed in Agadir and Mogador, perhaps also in Rabat. . . ." Eckardstein stated that this information frightened him; for he knew that if Germany tried to force concession from France against her will, it would certainly mean war with the Triple Entente strongly united against Germany. "England would stand on the side of France with her entire power on sea and land." According to his statement, he was determined to prevent Kiderlen's carrying out his program and to do this he "came to the conclusion that the only possibility lay in a far-reaching publicity in the press." Since he was no longer in the state service, he considered that he was free to do whatever he wished with the information. Consequently, "after mature reflection," he gave "the news about the imminent sending of a German squadron to the west coast of Morocco through a friendly journalist to the press. . . ." As this caused a stir, Kiderlen was forced to give his denial to the planned program.

Eckardstein indeed took upon himself the credit for forcing Kiderlen to modify his program from one of sending a squadron to the west coast of Morocco to a demonstration involving only

---

[59] Tardieu, *op. cit.,* p. 389; Fritz Hartung, "Die Marokkokrise des Jahres 1911" in *Archiv für Politik und Geschichte,* 1926, Part II, p. 67.

[60] *Op. cit.,* pp. 85-91.

one cannon boat.[61] England would have been much more excited by the first move than she was by the second, and Eckardstein's anxiety seemed to be centered around her action. It is true that Kiderlen's note of May 3 did not indicate that he had in mind the sending of a large naval force to Morocco. He did use the term "German ships," but he was speaking of two harbors, Mogador and Agadir; he could easily have meant one for each port; and he specifically stated that the ships were to be stationed in the harbors only as a demonstration, in other words, as a "clenched pledge." Movement of an entire squadron would almost certainly have meant war. But Eckardstein's explanation of the premature publicity given Kiderlen's plan seems more plausible than that it was a move of the foreign secretary's. The official denial appeared too quickly for a thorough testing of the international situation. Public acceptance of Kiderlen's denial was rather general, but the publication left its mark in the fears expressed by the various diplomats who were at that time trying to fathom Kiderlen's designs.

While inopportune publicity might prove irritating to the chief of the foreign office, his much more difficult task was that of convincing the Kaiser that his program was both necessary and expedient. William did not wish to become involved in the Moroccan difficulty, and he feared that his advisers would press him to some action similar to the Tangier move. He wished, therefore, to guard against such pressure. On April 22 we find him writing his chancellor that France would probably have to undertake greater military action in Morocco, but "I am of the opinion that it is not to our interest to prevent it. . . . Probably the wish will get abroad among us . . . to send warships. With warships we could . . . accomplish nothing. I pray you, therefore, to meet the eventual clamour for warships in advance. . . ."[62] Bethmann

---

[61] Kiderlen's note was dated May 3, and Eckardstein stated that his interview with Erzberger took place on the evening of that day. Although the note was not read to the Kaiser until May 5, there is nothing to indicate that the plan had been revised during the interval. Even the premature publicity does not seem to have greatly influenced the foreign secretary, for the actual course of events followed rather closely the note of May 3. It is true ships were sent only to Agadir where the original plan called for vessels at both Agadir and Mogador.

[62] William II to Bethmann Hollweg, Apr. 22, 1911, *G. P.*, vol. XXIX, no. 10538.

Hollweg assured his master, "The wish for sending warships has up to now not been current with us. Corresponding to Your Most Gracious Majesty's instruction I will meet, in advance, the eventual wish relative to this. . . ." [63] The Kaiser's uneasiness was for the time being allayed. Nevertheless, on May 3 Kiderlen prepared his memorandum involving action directly counter to the opinion expressed by his imperial master.

The editors of *Die Grosse Politik* stated that the purpose of the memorandum of May 3 was to convert the Kaiser to the program to which the foreign office was already committed. The letter was read to William II on May 5 and "found the consent of the monarch." The same day, Bethmann Hollweg telegraphed, "Personal changes, Morocco, England, leave granted unchanged." The editors interpreted this jumbled telegram as one which, among other things, gave consent to the Moroccan program.[64] On May 11, Kiderlen wrote, "The Kaiser has approved my Morocco program (also with ships for Agadir)." [65] William II, annoyed at Kiderlen's diplomatic technique, later confessed that "at the beginning of May in Karlsruhe the chancellor had developed with me the entire program of our negotiations relative to Morocco. I declared myself agreed and now at the beginning of July we are exactly on the same spot!" [66] Nevertheless, Kiderlen found it necessary to hasten to Kiel the last few days of June to secure the imperial consent to the dispatch of ships to Agadir. Either the Kaiser was not thoroughly converted in May or Kiderlen found him a vacillating master whose consent once obtained must be re-secured two months later.[67]

Some insight into the attitude of the Emperor may be gained through the comments he was reputed to have made during his visit to England. Eulenburg reported him as saying that "he was tired

[63] Bethmann Hollweg to William II, Apr. 22, 1911, *ibid.*, no. 10539.

[64] Editor's footnote to Kiderlen's note of May 3, 1911, *ibid.*, no. 10549, p. 101.

[65] Jäckh, *op. cit.*, vol. II, p. 122; also published in editor's footnote to Kiderlen's note of May 3, 1911, *G. P.*, vol. XXIX, no. 10549.

[66] Bethmann Hollweg to William II, July 10, 1911, *G. P.*, vol. XXIX, no. 10600, marginal note of William II.

[67] Dr. Pick in his review of the Regendanz diary stresses the point that the Kaiser was kept in ignorance of the plan until the trap was ready to be sprung and was only informed of the details on June 25.—"New Light on Agadir," in *Contemporary Review*, Sept. 1937, p. 328.

of being molested constantly by Kiderlen and Bethmann Hollweg with Morocco . . . he had really had enough and did not wish to hear [even] the word Morocco again. . . ." [68] The question was brought up in a subsequent conversation between British and German monarchs in which George V asked the Kaiser what Germany intended to do with her "freedom of action" in case the Act of Algeciras was destroyed. William replied that Germany "would never wage war for Morocco," but he pointed to compensation which might come into the question "on the frontier of our African colonial possessions. . . ." To this statement, Bethmann Hollweg noted, "The King hereupon remarked nothing." [69] William later reported that he had told George of the planned Agadir action and that the latter had not objected. The English King, however, denied this interpretation of the conversation, although his denial was not as convincing as was the earlier comment made by Bethmann Hollweg. George V stated to Mensdorff, the Austrian minister in London, "I will not deny that he perhaps could have said something of a ship, although I do not remember it. If he did, I thought of Mogador; in any case he did not name Agadir . . . and I absolutely did not express to him my own or my government's consent to any such action. . . ." [70] Much more significant in the development of events was the fact that William II rejoiced over the favorable reception accorded him in England and interpreted this reception as indicative of British desire for friendly relations with Germany. He was, therefore, more easily convinced that Kiderlen's program would not lead to war, a contingency against which he consistently fought.

On May 3 Kiderlen had determined the procedure he would follow in meeting every eventuality except the possibility that French troops might be successfully withdrawn and that France might be induced to negotiate without pressure. Both official and non-official indications of French willingness to negotiate appeared early in May.

---

[68] Eckardstein, *op. cit.*, p. 92.

[69] Note of Bethmann Hollweg, May 23, 1911, *G. P.,* vol. XXIX, no. 10562.

[70] Mensdorff to F. O., Sept. 29, 1911, *Ö. U. A.*, vol. III, no. 2669. See also H. W. Wilson, *The War Guilt*, p. 131.

Schoen reported on May 7 that, with the exception of Berteaux, minister of war, and Delcassé, the greater part of the government had been drawn into drastic action like the march to Fez by pressure from the chauvinists. The French government was in a situation from which it was difficult to extricate itself, but various proposals appeared in the press suggestive of possible solutions. They all amounted to this: Germany to guarantee France freedom of action in Morocco and in exchange receive compensation of a colonial or economic nature. Among other possible objects that might prove satisfactory as compensation had been mentioned the cession of French Congo for which Germany was to renounce Togo. Schoen then commented, "The exchange idea . . . seems to be not only an idle journalistic combination. . . ." It was true that the French foreign minister, Cruppi, confident that events in Morocco would not reach a crisis, had not mentioned the question to him, but Cambon had indicated that perhaps a "new Moroccan accord with Germany" might be necessary. The real basis for Schoen's belief that the idea of compensation was rooted in official approbation lay in a conversation which he had with "a financier of this country [France] standing in close relations to Caillaux, the finance minister, who in the cabinet plays a leading rôle. . . ." From the financier's report Schoen gained the idea that Caillaux wished to make a treaty with Germany, and appeared to see "in French colonial possessions, valuable exchange objects for us. . . ." More damaging in evidence against Caillaux was the further comment of the unnamed financier that the finance minister considered "the opposition of Germany to an active French Moroccan policy would immediately be given up, if they renounce to her a naval base important for her maritime position relative to England, in a Moroccan harbor on the Atlantic ocean. . . ." Such an arrangement might be reached as "England not having a strong government at the present could not offer serious opposition. . . ." [71] There is no proof that Caillaux was willing to grant as much as the reported statement of the unnamed financier indicated; but Schoen, in a shorter despatch of May 7, reported that he (Caillaux) had stated to Lancken that for freedom of

[71] Schoen to Bethmann Hollweg, May 7, 1911, *G. P.,* vol. XXIX, no. 10555.

action in Morocco France was willing to make concession to Germany in another quarter.[72]

A rather exaggerated statement of French willingness to make concessions was given in a marginal note of the Kaiser's, dated May 25. "Dr. Leo Delbrück . . . who had just returned from Paris, told me it was declared to him by various important persons that we could demand from them in colonial cessions whatever we wished, we would immediately receive it. Yes, even they would gladly pay us a milliard if we would only not disturb them in Morocco. Let us therefore make a regular offer. . . ."[73] Neither Schoen's report nor the Kaiser's comment moved the Wilhelmstrasse to any action; instead, Kiderlen-Waechter awaited the course of events to mature his plans. Yet it is significant to note that early in May German officials believed that Caillaux was willing to offer large concessions for freedom in Morocco.

At all events, the German plan ripened as events developed. On June 8 Spain, to offset General Moinier's activities around Fez, occupied Larache and on the ninth, El Ksar. On the tenth, Germany was informed that General Moinier had been instructed to leave Fez. On the twelfth, Zimmermann, undersecretary of state, drew up the completed plan.[74] In many respects this memorandum repeated the opinions expressed by Kiderlen on May 3, but reemphasized certain points in the light of events which had developed since that date. Zimmermann noted that there were certain Frenchmen, among whom might be numbered Caillaux, who desired to form an agreement with Germany over the Moroccan question. Nevertheless, he believed that France would gradually become master in northern Morocco and that German commerce and industry would suffer, although it would be impossible to point to any one specific case that might be labeled as a violation of the Act of Algeciras. Continuous friction would thus result.

On the question of compensation Zimmermann stated, "One must realize that France will not spontaneously offer Germany something of value. . . ." The press would turn upon Germany "as soon as we present a serious demand. . . ." As France and England

---

[72] Schoen to F. O., May 7, 1911, *ibid.*, no. 10554.

[73] Editor's footnote to despatch, Kiderlen to F. O., June 26, 1911, *ibid.*, no. 10576.   [74] Note of Zimmermann, June 12, 1911, *ibid.*, no. 10572.

were in accord on the Moroccan question, the English press would join the French press in turning the public opinion of Europe against any German demand. As a result France would secure Morocco without granting to Germany adequate compensation. Consequently, he asserted, only one way offered itself by which Germany could be sure that France would grant her adequate compensation or "we assure ourselves at least first in southern Morocco a stretch of territory whose natural wealth and apparent mineral wealth, compensate us in an acceptable manner for French mastery in the remainder of Morocco. . . ." He then reëmphasized the value which southern Morocco, especially the Sous, had for Germany since the Warburg and Mannesmann firms had been active in the region. In this section of his report, the undersecretary toyed with the idea of making southern Morocco German, although he mentioned first the general term "adequate compensation."

Zimmermann continued his analysis with a statement of procedure. The Spanish situation had rendered the time opportune, and Germany should now announce that the Act of Algeciras was violated and that Germany had regained her freedom of action. "As soon as these declarations are communicated to the Parisian cabinet and the remaining signatory powers, four cruisers, with as much speed as feasible, should be dispatched to Mogador and Agadir (two in each port), but communication of this is to be made to the Quai d'Orsay and in Madrid, as well as the remaining cabinets, only when we may suppose the cruisers will reach their destination twenty-four hours later. . . ." In this manner Zimmermann hoped to avoid a counter-move on the part of France, who might place her own cruisers in the designated ports before the German ships could reach them.

The under-secretary planned to use the German press to develop a sentiment in favor of the German move and to meet the furor which he knew would arise in the French press. He believed France would then present serious compensation offers; but if she failed to do so, he suggested that she be informed that Germany knew of the secret treaty made with the sultan in early April. According to this treaty, as published in *Die Grosse Politik*, the sultan asked that French troops be sent from the Chaouya to Fez to reëstablish order, and in return agreed to respect the "advice given by the

French government" and guaranteed "to the French government entire freedom to act in the interest of the pacification of the disturbed regions. . . ." [75] Why he considered that this might prove an effective threat if the more drastic action of the dispatch of ships failed is not clear. Perhaps he hoped to frighten the French with English defection, since he stated that England would not cause trouble if Germany only let them understand that she herself would talk with England "when France shall have offered us suitable compensation objects in French Congo. . . ." [76] Zimmermann apparently realized that England would need some assurances if she were to remain quiet. Both the note of May 3 and that of June 12 recognized that England herself was an interested party.

Zimmerman sent his *promemoria* to his chief, who, as we know, was enjoying a rest at Kissingen. Kiderlen in reply, June 16, proclaimed his complete agreement with the memorandum and asserted that he did not believe that without "an independent intervention in Morocco" Germany would be able to receive "from the French a really acceptable concession. . . ." As he was then expecting Cambon, he expressed his willingness to await an expression from the French ambassador. However, he intended to indicate to him that as Morocco was such a valuable prize, "a compensation morsel would cost the French a terrific piece of flesh from their body." "We must, however, under all circumstances assure to ourselves our position for negotiation through independent action, and this question must be decided before His Majesty depart for the northland trip." [77] On June 16 Kiderlen was convinced that he must secure his "clenched pledge" before negotiations with France were opened. Ten days later he was of the same opinion. The Kissingen interview had apparently no effect upon his plans. He did not expect, and had no intention of awaiting, the fulfilment of the commission, "Bring us something from Paris," which he had issued to Cambon. On the contrary, he hastened to

---

[75] Seckendorff to F. O., July 29, 1911, *ibid.*, no. 10567; verbal translations of treaties between France and the *maghzen, ibid.*, appendix, pp. 133-136. There is no indication of such a treaty given in the French documents, although Gaillard was pressing the sultan for reform in connection with the loan of 1911 and the military service rendered by French officers.

[76] Note of Zimmermann, June 12, 1911, *ibid.*, no. 10572.

[77] Editor's footnote to Zimmermann's note of June 12, 1911, *ibid.*, p. 142.

Kiel to secure the consent of the Kaiser before he could proceed on his northland trip. The outcome of that visit, as we have related, was the dispatch of the *Panther* to Agadir.

The official notes presented by the German diplomats to the respective chancelleries of Europe,[78] as well as the semi-official publication which appeared in the *Norddeutsche Allgemeine Zeitung*,[79] stated that the *Panther* had been moved to Agadir to protect German nationals endangered in that region. Such an excuse was obviously fatuous. Agadir was a closed port; no German subjects had a legal right to have interests in that village. Within the entire Sous valley there were only three German nationals, agents of the Mannesmann brothers; and within the port itself there was none.[80] If Germany had expected to stand upon the strength of this argument, the logical harbor for her to have selected would have been Mogador, the port in which the greatest per cent of German trade was centered.[81] Both ports had been mentioned by Kiderlen and by Zimmermann, and there is no clear indication why, in the final analysis, Agadir was the port selected. The fact that the Pan-Germans had for a decade clamored for German acquisition of southern Morocco, especially for the best port on the Atlantic, Agadir, lent color to the charge that Germany was casting covetous glances toward that region. Germany may have chosen Agadir more effectively to stress her claim that the Act of Algeciras was dead, that international obligations as they related to the Sherifian empire were absolved. She may have been influenced by the fact that in an open port she would be faced with the complications of Franco-Spanish police power:

[78] Kiderlen to Schoen, June 30, 1911, *ibid.*, no. 10578; Kiderlen to Metternich, June 30, 1911, *ibid.*, no. 10579.

[79] Editor's footnote to Kiderlen to Schoen, June 30, 1911, *ibid.*, no. 10578, p. 154; Count de Salis to Grey, July 2, 1911, *Br. Docs.*, vol. VII, no. 342.

[80] Poincaré, *op. cit.*, p. 77; Tardieu, *op. cit.*, pp. 425-427; *L'Afrique française*, July, 1911, p. 264; Dr. Frank before the Reichstag, Nov. 11, 1911, *Stenographische Berichte des Reichstags*, vol. 268, pp. 7778-7781. Regendaz, on June 28, ordered Wilberg, a geologist employed by the "Hamburg-Marokko-Gesellschaft," to leave Mogador and hasten to Agadir; but because of delays, the "Endangered German" arrived four days after the *Panther* anchored outside Agadir.—Pick, *Searchlight on German Africa*, pp. 21-22.

[81] Billy to Selves, Sept. 13, 1911, *Affaires du Maroc*, 1910-1912, no. 546; Leclerc, *Situation économique du Maroc, 1908-1909*, Second Part, "Statistiques du mouvement commercial & maritime du Maroc."

16

in Agadir no such complications would arise. A port policed by French- or Spanish-officered *mehallas* would, moreover, have weakened the argument that Germans in the district were without protection. Sheer expediency as related to the movement of the ships may have dictated the choice. The French argument that if protection were requisite, the task devolved upon France, not Germany, is unanswerable if the Accord of 1909 meant anything; yet German apologists must concede that the dispatch of a gunboat was a political, not an economic, act. Whatever was the determining factor, "protection of German nationals" was merely a covering phrase and was so interpreted by the press and the official courts of Europe. Schoen's comments to Selves when he presented the famous *aide mémoire* of July 1 gave a clearer expression of German purpose.

Schoen, for his part, in executing the orders sent him from Berlin, ignored the Accord of 1909 and fell back upon the Act of Algeciras. He stated that the Act had already been violated so many times that one could not quote it with authority, and a return to the *status quo ante* was hardly possible, yet "the German government was ready to enter into an amicable exchange of views on a solution of the Moroccan question satisfying to all the powers and eliminating it once for all from international politics." Selves replied that he was convinced of the usefulness of a conversation between France and Germany on the Moroccan question, but that the sending of a German warship modified in a serious manner the tenor of such a conversation.[82] Selves, if he had been more familiar with the intricacies of the Moroccan problem and of the earlier maneuvers of the foreign office, could have replied that France had already expressed a willingness to negotiate. Germany had then expressed her willingness to open conversation with France, but before doing so she had grabbed a crown jewel for which the heir apparent must pay a ransom. Be that ransom large or small, it remained in the eyes of the populace a ransom. Any negotiation begun in such a fashion would of necessity be

[82] Selves to French representatives in London, St. Petersburg, Madrid, Berlin, Rome, Vienna, Tangier, July 1, 1911, *Affaires du Maroc,* 1910-1912, no. 418; Selves to the same, July 2, 1911, *ibid.,* no. 421.

handicapped by the strident chorus of the chauvinists and imperialists on both sides. Truly enough, Kiderlen had made his first move, but his objective remained concealed. Newspapers and diplomats alike tried to penetrate his motives; and in their various guesses, some of them fantastic in the extreme, lay a nervous apprehension of imminent danger. Popular excitement and bitterness would inevitably render a calm, peaceful solution of the difficulties impossible. The immediate reception accorded the German announcement of her *fait accompli* was not, after all, indicative of the intense feeling that later found expression.

A general tendency toward restraint marked the editorial comment of all French papers except those of the extreme nationalists.[83] "Surprise" was the term most frequently used. They all seemed to recognize that Germany's move was really indicative of her desire to negotiate; and, although they might not approve of her over-emphatic method of expressing her wish, they were agreed that negotiations were essential. The consensus of French opinion, which only the day before rejoiced over reports of the Kissingen interview, expressed bewilderment that German officials considered vigorous action requisite in order to persuade France to parley. All blame, however, was not reserved for Germany. *Le Journal des Débats* was quick to criticize the French government for the aggressive imperialistic policy that had led France into a veritable *cul-de-sac*,[84] while the *Temps* was equally quick to attack the government for its slowness in action, especially in not meeting the Spanish move with open opposition.[85] *Le Matin*, not to thwart the action of the government, urged calmness, but added a note of warning to the German government: "The Wilhelmstrasse will commit a great error if it allows itself to be encouraged by the absence of emotion among the French public to proceed to other acts in Morocco; the calm of the French hides a very strong indignation which will manifest itself very clearly if the German provocation continues. . . ."[86] French opinion expressed irritation

---

[83] *L'Afrique française*, July, 1911, p. 264; *Temps*, July 3, 1911; *Le Matin*, July 2 and 3, 1911; *Berliner Tageblatt*, July 3, 1911; Carroll, *op. cit.*, p. 241.

[84] *Journal des Débats*, July 2, 1911, in Gauvain, *op. cit.*, vol. III, p. 5.

[85] *Temps*, July 3, 1911.   [86] *Le Matin*, July 3, 1911.

that Germany took advantage of a ministerial crisis to effect her *coup,* an advantage which was further accentuated by the fact that President Fallières and the foreign minister had planned a trip to Holland. *Le Matin* went so far as to accuse the Imperial government, "which is believed to exercise great influence in Holland," of looking "unfavorably on the fact that for the first time in history, a French president pays an official visit to the court of Holland. . . ." [87] If Berlin expected, as a by-product of its action, to interfere with the proposed trip, it was to be disappointed. The French officials realized that any modification in their plans would tend to increase the gravity of the situation by giving authoritative acknowledgment of the existence of a crisis. The slightest inadvertent act might change the element of surprise into alarm or panic and unloose an excited public opinion which would in turn aggravate the situation. Consequently, the papers greeted with pleasure the announcement that the proposed trip would be carried out as planned, regretting, at the same time, that these two officials would be absent during the first critical days in which French policy must be determined.

Although they received the news with calm surprise, French papers of all political faiths emphasized the seriousness of the situation by speaking of the *coup d'Agadir* as a European affair.[88] Appeals to the Act of Algeciras and to the Accord of 1909 played a prominent part in the case against Germany as presented by the French press. Frequent mention was made of the cry recently raised by Germany when a French cruiser chanced to anchor off Agadir. The editorials of July 2 and 3 were largely groping for an explanation which might relieve the general feeling of stunned surprise. Their repressed tone did not hide the fact that the Agadir crisis, its causes and, much more important, its probable consequences, formed the universal topic of conversation in all French circles, whether it were the garden party of the Elysée where were gathered the foreign diplomats[89] or the gather-

---

[87] *Ibid.*

[88] *Le Matin,* July 2, 1911; *Temps,* July 3, 1911; *Journal des Débats,* July 2 and 3, 1911, in Gauvain, *op. cit.,* vol. III, pp. 1-10.

[89] *Le Matin,* July 3, 1911.

ings of men on the streets who hastily bought the extras which first brought the news to the populace.[90] The early restraint of the French press soon broke down, but while it lasted, it received the approval of the foreign press.

German public opinion was almost as surprised as French by Kiderlen's sudden move and was as uncertain of his ultimate objective. German editors were equally aware that protection of nationals formed only a diplomatic curtain behind which lay the true motive. It was the *Berliner Tageblatt* (whose editor, Wolff, had little respect for a mailed-fist diplomacy) that pointed out that Germany in her official notification of her action reversed her former position and came nearer the French and Spanish viewpoint, "as in the official communication published, Germany recognized the existence of anarchistic conditions in Morocco which made it appear that the protection of nationals in the south could not be guaranteed other than through the sending of a armed force. . . ." This journal interpreted the sending of the *Panther* as "a sign of an unfavorable turn in the negotiations between Berlin and Paris. . . ." The same editorial called attention to the fact that Agadir was the port frequently mentioned as an object of compensation to Germany for her renunciation of the remainder of Morocco; but, as the official circles had wrapped themselves in silence as to their purpose, it made no attempt to fathom that silence, only demanding of the foreign office that it make known its designs, as "the German people had a right to know what was going on, where its serious interest came into question. . . ."[91]

The statement issued by the foreign office was accepted without question by the official papers but was ignored completely by the Pan-Germans. To the Pan-German press, represented by such papers as the Krupp-owned *Post* and the *Rheinisch-Westfälische Zeitung*, the energetic action of their countryman proved conclusively that his Bismarckian title was justified. They greeted Kiderlen's *coup* as a prelude to that objective for which they had long been working, German occupation of southwest Morocco; and they saw no other motive behind his action.[92] Schiemann reported

[90] *Berliner Tageblatt*, July 3, 1911.   [91] *Ibid.*, July 2, 1911.
[92] *Ibid.*, July 3, 1911; Felix Rachfahl, *Kaiser und Reich, 1888-1913*, p. 333.

that German newspapers and people gave almost unanimous approval of Kiderlen's move.[93] Although this statement may be true, the manner of approval varied. The official papers applauded quietly, the Pan-Germans jubilantly, and the liberals critically.[94] Wolff awaited further developments before giving the government wholehearted approbation. In all cases, the early relatively calm acceptance of the news by the German public was, just as in France, to give way to a storm of public excitement.

Outside Germany and France the *Panther's* Spring attracted surprisingly little public attention. The London *Times* carried editorials on the subject on July 3 and July 4 in which it criticized the "dramatic strokes in which the diplomacy of Berlin would seem to take a curious pleasure," [95] praised the French press for its "matter-of-fact temper," denied the need for protection of German nationals in the region, and accepted the general interpretation that "no exaggerated significance need be attached to the incident" as it was the German "manner of stimulating conversations. . . ." [96] The *Daily Mail, Daily Chronicle,* and the *Morning Leader* urged calmness and refused to recognize the situation as tragic.[97] With the exception of the *Daily Graphic* and the *Daily News,* who were reported as less favorable to the French case,[98] the English papers gave an unqualified support to France.

Germany did not gain from the Austrian press a support commensurate to English support of France. In fact, the Austrian press ranged from indifference to hostility in its attitude. Its viewpoint was one of resentment that Germany acted without preliminary notification to its ally and of determination not to be drawn into a political whirlpool that promised to carry no gains at all for Vienna except the dubious honor of playing a "brilliant second" to Berlin. The Viennese press announced that the affair was simply a German problem in which Austria was not interested but which she at least expected would be solved without any consequences liable to engulf the Triple Alliance.[99]

---

[93] *Kreuzzeitung,* July 5, 1911, in Schiemann, *op. cit.,* p. 208.

[94] Carroll, *Germany and the Great Powers, 1866-1914,* pp. 656-659.

[95] London *Times,* July 3, 1911 (Editorial).   [96] *Ibid.,* July 4, 1911.

[97] Quoted in *Temps,* July 3, 1911.   [98] *Ibid.*

[99] Quoted in *Le Matin,* July 3, 1911. See also Carroll, *Germany and the Great Powers,* p. 651.

Not the ally, Austria, but Spain really exulted over German action. "We rejoice to see Germany take hold in Morocco," wrote the *Liberal*, and considered the spot well chosen.[100] The conservative papers in general praised the diplomacy of Germany because its action had strengthened the Spanish position. France must now discuss the situation with both Spain and Germany, and Spain expected German support in her claims. The republican papers were more restrained in their joy than the conservatives and urged a peaceful solution of all difficulties.[101] The Spanish press, along with the German, French, Austrian, and English, agreed that the Moroccan question had now entered a new phase which placed a heavy responsibility upon the diplomats of Europe but which need not result in disaster. The press of Europe withheld judgment until the diplomats could act. All eyes focused upon the Quai d'Orsay, from which must emanate a counter-move.

---

[100] Quoted in *Berliner Tageblatt*, July 3, 1911.

[101] *Temps*, July 3, 1911; *Berliner Tageblatt*, July 3, 1911.

Chapter X

THE GERMAN ENIGMA

The imperialistic game as played in Morocco had been a series of moves and counter-moves with the score shifting first in favor of France and then of Germany. When the march to Fez bid fair to turn the decision to his rival, Kiderlen played his trump card: the *Panther* moved to Agadir. The apprehension with which France had watched for some move from Berlin was now changed to consternation, but the new cabinet was conscious of the gravity of the situation and determined to formulate a program that would again place the game in French hands. Even the inexperienced foreign minister remained cool, wisely received Schoen's first communication with calm, and reserved decision until he had consulted his colleagues. As soon as the German ambassador departed, he discussed the affair with Jules Cambon and then adjourned to inform the premier of the situation.[1] Caillaux's immediate reaction to the news was that Germany had deliberately taken advantage of the ministerial crisis and of the proposed trip to Holland with the hope that the new ministry might commit some indiscretion that would furnish Germany herself with a pretext for further action. For that reason he was delighted with Selves's reasonable and prudent reply to the German ambassador.[2]

Premier and foreign minister faced the task of substituting for this evasive temporary response an official answer. To Caillaux's question as to which measure he favored, Selves suggested sending a French ship either to Agadir or to Mogador after first consulting England on the question. The premier gasped at such a suggestion but agreed first to consult the minister of marine. Delcassé, then immediately called into the conference, strongly opposed the idea, stressing the fact that "to send a ship to Mogador was a gesture of weakness—it would appear that they dared not go to

---

[1] Reports of the activities of the ministers on July 1 and July 2 were carefully reported by such papers as *Le Matin* and *Temps*. See also Caillaux, *op. cit.*, p. 106.   [2] *Ibid.*, pp. 107, 108.

Agadir—that to send one to Agadir would mean war. . . ." [3]
Tardieu and Caillaux have since stated that in this conference
among the three, Caillaux, Selves, and Delcassé, it was decided
to delay all action other than a note of inquiry to the chancellor
and to consult England and Russia before pushing any move. The
plan for sending ships to the Moroccan coast was to await further
developments.[4]

Under date of July 1, Selves notified the French representatives
at the various courts of Europe of Schoen's visit and requested
those in London and St. Petersburg to ask of the respective governments their opinion of the situation. To London he added, "It
might be possible that we shall be led to send a warship to Mogador.
Would the English government be disposed to take, in such an eventuality, an analogous measure?" [5] Here the conflict between Selves
and Caillaux appeared in the first moments of the crisis, for this addition was not in harmony with the decision reached in conference
between these two and Delcassé. Caillaux insisted that if Selves
had not agreed with the decision taken at this conference, he should
have made himself clear upon that point, whereupon the premier
would have called a meeting of the cabinet, presented the case, and
abided by the decision there taken.[6] As it was, Selves, out of harmony with his chief, instructed the French ambassador in London
to sound out the British government on the possibility of dispatching warships to a Moroccan port after the French officials had
decided against such a measure. Since the Caillaux ministry had
no intention of following such a program, Selves's persistence
only served to reveal to the British government the lack of harmony and unity in the French cabinet—a situation that frequently
caused Grey to complain that he knew not what France wanted.[7]
Apparently through leaks in government circles, the press heard
of the proposed move; for discreet statements that the French
government had discussed the possibility of "opposing ship to

[3] *Ibid.*, pp. 108-109; Tardieu, *op. cit.*, pp. 433-435.

[4] Caillaux, *op. cit.*, pp. 108-109; Tardieu, *op. cit.*, pp. 433-435.

[5] Selves to French representatives in London, St. Petersburg, Madrid, Berlin,
Rome, Vienna, Tangier, *Affaires du Maroc*, 1910-1912, no. 418.

[6] Caillaux, *op. cit.*, pp. 111-113.

[7] See, for example, Grey to Bertie, July 19, 1911, *Br. Docs.*, vol. VII, no. 397.

ship" appeared in French papers and in general met disapproval. Caillaux learned of the maneuver on July 4.

While they awaited the response from St. Petersburg and London, French officials were busy with the problem. In the afternoon of July 1, Caillaux informed the French president of the situation and in the evening of the same day conferred at length with Jules Cambon and the Spanish ambassador, Perez Caballero.[8] The decision was issued that the proposed trip to Holland was not to be altered in any of its points. At all events, on the evening of July 3, President Fallières, accompanied by Selves, left Paris. Before their departure they had attended the garden party at the Elysée where were gathered together the various government officials and diplomats in Paris. Schoen here gleaned some insight into the attitude of the French officials. Herbette, war minister, regretted the difficulties which Germany had raised but offered the suggestion that the entire trouble might be solved if "the appearance of the *Panther* before Agadir should restrict itself to a court visit. . . ."[9] Selves was inclined to protest the *fait accompli*, and Schoen found it necessary to persuade him that Germany had no intention of causing war.[10] Caillaux, more conciliatory, expressed French willingness to negotiate; but he warned Schoen that if German troops were landed at Agadir or further ships were sent, public opinion would become aroused and the French government would find negotiation difficult. Schoen hastened to inform him that troops were not to be landed and that, so far as he knew, no further ships were to be sent.[11] The departure of Selves from Paris and the temporary substitution of Caillaux himself in the foreign office was not, it seems, unwelcome news at Berlin.

Selves left the city on the evening of July 3 and Caillaux immediately took over his duties. His first interest was to discover what support he could really expect from Russia and England. Germany, it appears, had notified all the powers signatory to the Act of Algeciras of her action at the same time that she had notified

[8] *Le Matin*, July 3, 1911.

[9] Schoen to F. O., July 2, 1911, *G. P.*, vol. XXIX, no. 10585; Schoen to Bethmann Hollweg, July 3, 1911, *ibid.*, no. 10586.

[10] Schoen to Bethmann Hollweg, July 3, 1911, *ibid.*, no. 10586.

[11] *Ibid.*

France; and when Paul Cambon, the dignified, capable, and eminently cultured French ambassador in London, was in receipt of Selves's instructions, he approached the British government on the issue.[12] Now, as Sir Edward Grey was absent from the city, no official reply could at that time be forthcoming;[13] but returning two days later on July 3, he informed Cambon that evening that England also considered the situation serious, though he refrained from any comment until the cabinet meeting scheduled for the next day. Grey reported in regard to this conference that Cambon had "expressed strongly his personal view that we should send a ship to Agadir. . . ."[14]

Apparently as a result of this interview, the French ambassador telegraphed his home government for further instructions in case England refused to join France in the naval demonstration.[15] This message, presented to Caillaux on July 4, threw him into a minor panic. It was his first information of Selves's action. He formed an answering telegram, which he submitted to Delcassé for confirmation before dispatching.[16] This telegram instructed the ambassador to avoid giving England the idea that France was considering the dispatch of a warship to either Agadir or Mogador but to inform the British government that since the German government had expressed a desire to discuss the situation, France was in a position to ask first what the Imperial government wanted and "according to the reply which it will make and after this reply, it will be time to decide if we ought to make in the waters of southern Morocco any naval demonstration whatsoever. . . ."[17] This message crossed one from London in which Cambon reported that the British cabinet had ruled against the advisability of sending a ship to Agadir. Grey said that if England sent a ship "it

[12] Paul Cambon to Sir Edward Grey, July 1, 1911, *Br. Docs.*, vol. VII, no. 340. See Un Diplomate, *Paul Cambon, Ambassadeur de France*, pp. 4-8, for an excellent characterization of Paul Cambon.

[13] Tardieu, *op. cit.*, p. 433.

[14] Grey to Bertie, July 3, 1911, *Br. Docs.*, vol. VII, no. 351. Paul Cambon was kept constantly informed by his brother, Jules, of all the details of his actions.— Un Diplomate, *op. cit.*, p. 252. See p. 242, *infra*, for Jules' reaction to this proposal.   [15] Caillaux, *op. cit.*, p. 110; Tardieu, *op. cit.*, p. 434.

[16] Caillaux, *op. cit.*, p. 110.

[17] Caillaux to Paul Cambon, July 4, 1911, *Affaires du Maroc*, 1910-1912, no. 427.

must be with instructions to remain as long as the Germans remained; we could not send a ship and then remove it before the German ship went. . . ."[18] This opinion was slightly at variance with that expressed by Nicolson, who believed that the two governments should send ships, "if only to ascertain what the Germans are doing there. The vessel need only stay a short time and then proceed to the nearest port whence she could communicate by telegraph. . . ."[19]

The French and British governments were moved by a desire not to furnish Germany with a pretext for taking further action, for example, landing troops in Agadir. Since the situation was so tense that the slightest incident could precipitate serious trouble, they strove to avoid that strain which the presence of French and English ships in the same harbor as the German would inevitably bring. Selves, highly irritated by the countermanding of his orders, telegraphed Bapst, director of political affairs in the foreign office, that "the telegram which was sent to London yesterday causes me distress." Furthermore, he continued, it was expedient to let the British "cabinet decide without sending it new and contradictory information, except if it were expedient to determine with it . . . the port where the ships ought to enter and the moment of their departure. . . ." He asked Bapst to present this message to Caillaux and to urge him not to prevent Paul Cambon from executing the earlier orders.[20] Albin states that Jules Cambon first approved of Selves's plan of procedure but that Caillaux convinced him later of the unwisdom of such a plan.[21] Indeed, Cambon's irritation at Kiderlen's trickery must have upset his usually sound judgment. Albin is also of the opinion that the French premier decided to countermand the orders to Paul Cambon after a conversation with Gwinner, president of Deutsche Bank, then in Paris, with whom he was on friendly terms due to his financial investments. There is no evidence to indicate that Caillaux at any time

---

[18] Grey to Bertie, July 4, 1911, *Br. Docs.*, vol. VII, no. 255. Demidov to Neratov, July 5, 1911, Isvolski, *op. cit.*, vol. I, no. 96, gives an account of the English response.

[19] Nicolson to Grey, July 4, 1911, *Br. Docs.*, vol. VII, no. 354.

[20] Selves to Bapst, July 5, 1911, *Affaires du Maroc*, 1910-1912, no. 429.

[21] Albin, *op. cit.*, pp. 28-39. Wolff also stated that Cambon supported Selves at first.—*Op. cit.*, p. 45.

favored the dispatch of warships and consequently no reason for deducing that his conversation with the German banker in the morning of July 4 changed his opinion.[22] His conduct was throughout much too conciliatory to charge him with approval of Selves's project. Later developments probably explain the fact that German sources frequently state that the proposal to face the German warship with French and English vessels was of English origin.[23] The proposal was originated and sponsored by the inexperienced Selves who, piqued by the defeat of his plan, laid the responsibility for its failure upon his premier as much as upon the British.

From a consideration of Selves's project, the French and British governments turned to an examination of other proposed plans. Sir Edward Grey, in the same conversation in which he informed Cambon that his government did not approve of sending warships, although he assured him that England intended to maintain her treaty obligations, advised him that the discussions must be "between France, Germany, Spain, and ourselves [England] and not à trois without us. . . ." He, thereupon, asked France to inform England what she "would consider a reasonable and practicable solution from the point of view of French interests. . . ."[24] Grey feared that France, Germany, and Spain would partition Morocco and leave England aside. In response to Benckendorff's question whether a conference of the Algeciras powers was advisable, he replied that he believed "for the moment direct negotiations between Germany, France, Spain, and England would be

[22] Albin, op. cit., p. 39. Tardieu states that Gwinner had had business with Caillaux while he was minister of finance and that two days before the Agadir coup Gwinner had asked him for an audience. According to Tardieu, Gwinner introduced the subjects of the Lombard railroads, the Ottoman debt, and the Bagdad railroad; but Caillaux refused to discuss any of them because they were political as well as economic and could not be discussed without considering all Franco-German relations. Gwinner replied that he was ready to discuss all. "Yes," said M. Caillaux smiling, "only I am president of the council of ministers of France and you are not chancellor of the German Empire. . . ." Gwinner then withdrew and nothing resulted.—Op. cit., p. 437.

[23] Schoen, op. cit., p. 148. Schoen's memory seemed to have failed him at this point; for his account of events during the month of July is badly jumbled, especially as to the sequence of events. His own official reports in G. P. refute his Memoirs. E. A. Stowell errs in stating that "both England and France sent ships to Agadir."—Diplomacy of the War of 1914, p. 23.

[24] Grey to Bertie, July 4, 1911, Br. Docs., vol. VII, no. 355.

preferable and that a conference should be called only in case of necessity . . ." and as "France was the power most directly interested, he would leave the initiative to her. . . ."[25] Even in the event of a conference, he thought "it would be desirable that the four Powers most interested: France, Spain, Germany, and ourselves should come to an understanding before any Conference met. . . ."[26]

Nicolson believed that if Germany were permitted to have a share in Morocco, England should lay down certain conditions that must be fulfilled before her consent would be forthcoming. Among these were the internationalization of Tangier and its neighborhood, a pledge that no ports on the Moroccan coast were to be fortified, "that Germany should not endeavor to acquire a port on the Mediterranean coast," and the maintenance of the open door.[27]

The English proposal of conversation *à quatre* did not meet the approval of the French government. Caillaux, except to announce that compensations in Morocco were impossible and that it devolved upon Germany to make the first offers, answered Paul Cambon's inquiry by postponing the issue;[28] but on the preceding day he had telegraphed Jules Cambon that if the German idea was for a general conversation "tending to remove between Germany and us the greatest number possible of the difficulties which divide us at present in diverse points of the globe . . . the accession of Spain to our pourparlers would . . . have to be refused. On the contrary we would not demand, on our side, that England and Russia would be admitted. . . . We would only reserve to ourselves the privilege, according to our expediency, of advising our friends or allies of the progress of negotiations. . . ."[29] The British government took no action upon either suggestion, that for

---

[25] Benckendorff to Neratov, July 5, 1911, Siebert, *op. cit.*, no. 686.

[26] Grey to Buchanan, July 5, 1911, *Br. Docs.*, vol. VII, no. 357.

[27] Nicolson to Lord Hardinge, July 5, 1911, *ibid.*, no. 359.

[28] Caillaux to Paul Cambon, July 5, 1911, *Affaires du Maroc*, 1910-1912, no. 430. The Belgian ambassador reported July 8 that Caillaux regretted the insistence of the British, as there would be less chance of an understanding if England were a party to the negotiations.—Editor's note to despatch, Metternich to F. O., July 4, 1911, *G. P.*, vol. XXIX, no. 10592.

[29] Caillaux to Jules Cambon, July 4, 1911, *Affaires du Maroc*, 1910-1912, no. 425.

a conversation of four interested powers, or that of a conference of the Algeciras powers, but awaited the decision of Paris.

France consulted not only England but her ally, Russia. Selves, in his telegram of July 1, had instructed George Louis, French ambassador to the court of St. Petersburg, to ascertain the Russian attitude.[30] Germany was also interested in the Russian reply, since the Potsdam Agreement[31] gave her some encouragement in the belief that Russia might be induced to weaken her support of France. Pourtalès, the German ambassador, reported that Neratov, the acting minister of foreign affairs, met the news of the German move with the remark that "France would withdraw from Morocco when the land was pacified. . . ." To the question, what would be Russian attitude toward the withdrawal of the Moroccan question from international politics, Neratov replied that he was in hearty agreement with anything that would accomplish that.[32] This report gave no intelligible indication of Russian attitude. Louis reported that Neratov expressed to him the hope that Germany would withdraw her ship if France would give renewed assurances as to her actions, but he did not believe that the question should as yet be placed before the powers.[33] The report of this conversation as given to Benckendorff did not tally with that of Louis. Neratov reported that "the French ambassador has expressed himself in favor of international negotiations in which I agree with him and not direct negotiations between France and Germany. . . . The French Ambassador adopts a negative attitude towards the idea of a Conference. . . ."[34] Either Louis did not report the entire conversation to his superiors or the two participants misunderstood each other's remarks, for Louis did not state in his report that he had expressed opposition to direct negotiations.

The reports reaching France were not reassuring, and Selves pressed for more concrete action. On July 2 he requested the Rus-

---

[30] Selves to French representatives in London, St. Petersburg, Madrid, Berlin, Rome, Vienna, Tangier, July 1, 1911, *ibid.*, no. 418.

[31] Russia had adjusted all her differences with Germany in what is known as the Potsdam Agreement.

[32] Pourtalès to F. O., July 1, 1911, *G. P.*, vol. XXIX, no. 10584.

[33] George Louis to Selves, July 2, 1911, *Affaires du Maroc*, 1910-1912, no. 422.

[34] Neratov to Benckendorff, July 2, 1911, Siebert, *op. cit.*, no. 680.

sian chargé d'affaires in Paris, Demidov, to ask his government to have its ambassador in Berlin express "its surprise and its astonishment at the measure which the Imperial government had thought it ought to take. . . ."[35] Selves reported that Demidov also promised to ask his government "to inform itself exactly of the causes that have motivated the action of the German government and . . . on the aim which is in reality pursued. . . ."[36] The next day Selves wired Louis to request the Russian government to instruct its ambassador to Berlin to interview the German government on the subject of the Agadir affair.[37] Louis promptly executed his orders and wired that Neratov agreed "without delay to telegraph to the Russian ambassador to Berlin to hold with the Imperial Office of foreign affairs a conversation in the sense which we desire. . . ."[38]

But the démarche made in Berlin was a tame affair compared to that actually requested by Selves. A firm statement of Russian "surprise and astonishment" at this stage of the game might have weakened Kiderlen's obstinacy, but Russia's meek behaviour was better designed to encourage than to restrain the Berlin government. The absence of the foreign minister, Sazonov, who was recuperating from a serious illness, had left conduct of foreign affairs in the hands of an incompetent assistant, Neratov.[39] As acting minister, Neratov might have felt that he lacked the necessary authority for an aggressive act; but a bit later he did not seem hesitant in seizing the reins and heedlessly pushing Russian interests in Persia.[40] In any case, Sazonov himself was inclined to be sympathetic with a pro-German group at the court of the Tsar,[41] and he might not have given France any stronger sup-

---

[35] Selves to Cambon, July 2, 1911, *Affaires du Maroc,* 1910-1912, no. 420; Demidov to F. O., July 2, 1911, Isvolski, *op. cit.,* vol. I, no. 95.

[36] Selves to Cambon, July 2, 1911, *Affaires du Maroc,* 1910-1912, no. 420.

[37] Selves to Louis, July 3, 1911, *ibid.,* no. 423.

[38] Louis to Selves, July 3, 1911, *ibid.,* no. 424.

[39] William L. Langer, "Russia, the Straits Question, and the Origins of the Balkan League, 1908-1912," in *Political Science Quarterly,* vol. XLIII, p. 336.

[40] See W. Morgan Shuster, *The Strangling of Persia;* Ward and Gooch, *op. cit.,* vol. III, pp. 419-424; Grey before the House of Commons, *Parl. Deb.,* 5th series, vol. XXXII, pp. 2598-2611.

[41] Fay, *op. cit.,* vol. I, pp. 266-270. Pro-German sympathies at the court of the Tsar were frequently mentioned in Sir G. Buchanan's reports to his

port than did Neratov. The influential premier, Stolypin, was also pro-German in sympathy.[42] In fact, since the Bosnian crisis had left Russia disgruntled at the weak support given her by France and irritated at British opposition to her Straits policy, this pro-German feeling had grown until it reaped its reward in the Potsdam Agreement.[43] From this accord developed a new Russo-German friendship that now won for Kiderlen a respite, and the one sensible proposal of the usually inept Selves died still-born.

In the meantime, on July 4, Count Metternich, German ambassador to London, gave his foreign office some indication of the Russian attitude. He reported that Benckendorff had asserted to Kühlmann, a member of the German embassy, that "according to his view, there was no cause for an excited conception of the Moroccan affair. . . . If the purposes of Germany be directed to a partition and to the annexation of a naval base in Agadir, then it may be met with vigorous opposition . . . but if it aimed at compensation, then serious difficulties are scarcely to be feared. . . ." [44] The German foreign office was in possession of this report before Count Osten-Sacken, Russian ambassador to Berlin, carried out the commission of his government and interviewed Kiderlen-Waechter on the subject of the Moroccan affair.[45] This interview took place July 5. Osten-Sacken asked Kiderlen "in an entirely friendly and confidential manner . . . about the meaning and purpose of our advance in Agadir. . . ." The Russian ambassador acknowledged that Russia was interested in Morocco only "as it could become an object of strife through which Russia could be drawn into joint suffering by virtue of the treaties of alliance. . . ." Kiderlen's reply first took the form of recriminations against French gradual expansion and insistence upon the need for protection of German nationals in Morocco, and then moved to an outline of future procedure. He stated that France and Germany were agreed that negotiations were necessary but differed only on the point of "who is to make the first proposals." He acknowl-

superiors. See, for example, Buchanan to Grey, Sept. 6, 1911, *Br. Docs.*, vol. VII, no. 502. [42] Fay, *op. cit.*, vol. I, p. 266.
[43] Georges Michon, *The Franco-Russian Alliance*, p. 190.
[44] Metternich to F. O., July 4, 1911, *G. P.*, vol. XXIX, no. 10591.
[45] Note of Kiderlen, July 5, 1911, *ibid.*, no. 10593.

17

edged that England and Spain had interests in Morocco; but he deemed it best, "if at first Germany and France, whose relations indeed recently have been thoroughly friendly, talk to each other. They could then next draw into confidence England and Spain, and only then the less interested powers enter. . . ." England's distrust of a Franco-German negotiation was not to be feared because of "her close relation to France . . . , however, she could be kept informed about the negotiations. . . ." At this stage of developments, Kiderlen was not opposed to the idea that England should be kept informed. He further stated that in this conversation the Russian agent had expressed his willingness for France and Germany to settle the difficulty in direct negotiation. Osten-Sacken asked and received permission to report this conversation to Paris and did so through the French chargé d'affaires in Berlin.[46]

The next day, July 6, Caillaux, in conversation with Demidov, mentioned the possibility of Russian participation in the negotiations, but he inquired of Louis, "Do you not think that the better solution would be that the cabinet of St. Petersburg, without taking part officially in the negotiations, lend us at Berlin its semi-official assistance. . . ."[47] Louis replied that "it would appear difficult for Russia to participate on the same conditions as England in eventual negotiations of France with Germany on the subject of Morocco. . . ." England had peculiarly British interests in Morocco while Russia was concerned only as an "ally of France and as a signatory of the Act of Algeciras. . . . It would therefore not be possible to insist that Russia be a party to an arrangement to intervene. Nothing, on the other hand, militates against the Russian government's continuing to give us coöperation in the same conditions as the present. . . ."[48] By July 11 Neratov had assured France of Russian support in Berlin,[49] and France had reason to hope that the rapprochement between Germany and Russia as marked in the Potsdam Agreement had not

---

[46] Berckheim to Caillaux, July 5, 1911, *Affaires du Maroc,* 1910-1912, no. 431.

[47] Caillaux to Louis, July 6, 1911, *ibid.,* no. 433.

[48] Louis to Selves, July 7, 1911, *ibid.,* no. 436.

[49] Louis to Selves, July 10, 1911, *ibid.,* no. 443; Selves to Louis, July 11, 1911, *ibid.,* no. 447.

undermined Russian sense of obligation to her ally. In point of fact, however, Russia's support had hardly gone beyond the strict letter of her treaty pledges, and her attitude throughout the crisis was decidedly lukewarm.

Yet Germany, more than France, had cause to complain of indifferent support from her ally. Zimmermann reported the Agadir move to Szögyény, Austrian ambassador in Berlin,[50] at the same time that Tschirschky, the German ambassador in Vienna, reported the situation to Aehrenthal.[51] Szögyény stated that Zimmermann requested Austria to lend to Germany her "valuable moral support." [52] Aehrenthal replied to Tschirschky that Austria-Hungary was interested only in the preservation of the open door in Morocco and that he had long thought that France would take Morocco as quickly as possible before the Triple Entente broke up. He considered that the German position was good and promised to examine any proposals for a Franco-German accord in "the spirit of the close relations existing between us. . . ." [53] In a memorandum dated July 4, he gave a more detailed explanation of Austrian position.[54] He interpreted the *Panther's* Spring as solely a question of prestige and accepted the German viewpoint with sympathy. But he pointed out that Austria was interested only in the open door in Morocco and was not in a position to promise unqualified support without first knowing what the German demands might be. "We ourselves have in the question a very secondary interest and will therefore remain in second line and keep our powder dry. . . ." He could not resist commenting that Germany had been reticent in her support of Austrian Balkan policy. He informed the French ambassador that Germany had given him "no previous warning of the dispatch of the German

---

[50] Szögyény to F. O., July 1, 1911, *Ö. U. A.*, vol. III, no. 2550. Szögyény stated that in his opinion the French had marched to Fez in order to break the rapprochement between Russia and Germany as represented in the Potsdam Agreement and that the entire solution depended upon the attitude of Russia and England.—Szögyény to F. O., July 6, 1911, *ibid.*, no. 2556.

[51] Tschirschky to F. O., July 1, 1911, *G. P.*, vol. XXIX, no. 10583; Aehrenthal to Szögyény, July 3, 1911, *Ö. U. A.*, vol. III, no. 2553.

[52] Szögyény to F. O., July 1, 1911, *Ö. U. A.*, vol. III, no. 2550.

[53] Tschirschky to F. O., July 1, 1911, *G. P.*, vol. XXIX, no. 10583.

[54] Note of Aehrenthal, July 4, 1911, *Ö. U. A.*, vol. III, no. 2554.

ship to Morocco. . . ." [55] This fact in itself piqued Aehrenthal, who was inclined to resent any action that might savor of dictation from Berlin.

The chief complaints from the German foreign office came from the fact that Aehrenthal failed to restrain the Austrian press in its derogatory comments and that he permitted the Hungarian premier, Khuen Héderváry, to issue a statement to the Hungarian parliament that the Triple Alliance did not bind Austria in Morocco.[56] Aehrenthal answered Kiderlen's complaints by the sage advice not to place so much value on press assertions and by explaining that the Hungarian's comment was given only to quiet the public.[57] Throughout the early days of July, Aehrenthal insisted that his interest was to prevent serious friction between the two interested powers. Consequently, Austria maintained a reserved attitude and only promised to examine any concrete proposals presented to her from the standpoint of her own interest.[58] Austria's official reserve plus the openly hostile attitude of her press called forth an official expression of appreciation from the French government.[59] Germany, for her part, was not only given no encouragement from Austria but met a sharp rebuff from her other ally, Italy, who, in reply to an official inquiry from the German minister, stated that the accord between Italy and France bound her not to oppose the action of France in Morocco.[60] Not unjustly, the Kaiser complained that Kiderlen's ruthless tactics had placed an undue strain upon the Triple Alliance.[61]

Spain was more in sympathy with the German case than any of the other powers. The Spanish ambassador justified the German action to Grey on the ground that the German government was convinced that it could not trust French action.[62] "If that were so," Grey replied, "then the action of the German Government

[55] Russell to Grey, July 3, 1911, *Br. Docs.,* vol. VII, no. 348.

[56] Szögyény to F. O., July 11, 1911, *ö. U. A.,* vol. III, no. 2560; Aehrenthal to Khuen Héderváry, July 12, 1911, *ibid.,* no. 2562.

[57] Aehrenthal to Szögyény, July 14, 1911, *ibid.,* no. 2565.

[58] Aehrenthal to Szécsen, July 13, 1911, *ibid.,* no. 2564.

[59] Szécsen to F. O., July 16, 1911, *ibid.,* no. 2566.

[60] Jagow to F. O., July 1, 1911, *G. P.,* vol. XXIX, no. 10582.

[61] Wilson, *op. cit.,* p. 135.

[62] Grey to Rennie, July 5, 1911, *Br. Docs.,* vol. VII, no. 358.

had been anything but straightforward. . . ." Germany, he reminded the Spaniard, had not protested the French march to Fez and had given assurances that if France should withdraw, no complaints would then be issued. "The moment when the French were carrying out the withdrawal even more rapidly than had been anticipated was not the time to accuse them of want of straightforwardness. . . ." [63] The Spanish ambassador insisted that all Germany wanted was a settlement of the Moroccan question and that this might lead to a partition.[64] Meanwhile, Spain, in reply to the German official notification of her action, stated that "the Spanish government is convinced of the necessity of a new solution of the question. After the last advance of France, an independent sultan no more exists in Fez . . ."; but as Spain was bound by her treaties with England and France, she for the present restricted herself to urging both nations to accept the idea of "a conversation among the powers for the purpose of settling the Moroccan problem. . . ." [65]

This survey of the position officially taken by the various powers during the first days of July, discloses an international vista the dominant tone of which was "watchful waiting." England, although she had refused the suggestion of aggressive action in the form of dispatch of warships to the disputed area, had lined up solidly behind France. Russia and Austria had announced their lack of primary interest in the affair, but had expressed a desire to avoid complications that might force them to fulfil their obligations to their allies, and had adopted a policy of reserve. Spain, expecting to be admitted to the negotiations and hoping to play the two rivals against each other to her own profit, stated her intentions to uphold her treaty obligations and at the same time expressed her sympathy with Germany. The alignment of powers became more distinct as a plan of procedure gradually took shape in Paris and Berlin.

The Quai d'Orsay and the Wilhelmstrasse adopted the tactics pursued by Kiderlen and Cambon at Kissingen, that of enticing one's opponent into the position of making the first bid without revealing one's own hand. According to the French viewpoint,

[63] *Ibid.*   [64] *Ibid.*
[65] Prince Ratibor to F. O., July 6, 1911, *G. P.*, vol. XXIX, no. 10594.

Germany, by her own confession the aggrieved party, must state her grievance, express her wishes; and only then need France answer either with acceptance of the German demands or with a counter-proposal. France was ready to negotiate but not before a sphinx.[66] Germany, according to the planned program drawn up by Kiderlen, held her "clenched pledge" and waited for France to make concrete offers. It was generally conceded that negotiations were to be instituted; but relative to the "impending conversations, negotiations, or conferences on Morocco" only one thing stood out clearly, and that was that France and Great Britain were determined "that the cession or promise of any Moroccan territory or any Moroccan port to Germany is entirely out of the question. . . ."[67] It also became clear that unless all other means failed, an international conference was not to be called. Neither France nor Germany wanted such a conference; for they feared that the result would be further internationalization of Morocco, an eventuality unsatisfactory to the ambitions of Teuton as well as of Gaul.[68] Nevertheless, Germany was not as yet ready to express what that ambition might be; nor was France ready to make definite offers.

This playing for position was the major but not the sole reason for the delay in forming a plan of procedure. The Caillaux cabinet was anxious to hear from England and Russia before taking any irrevocable step. Szécsen, the Austrian ambassador in Paris, explained the delay in a rather unusual fashion. According to his opinion, Selves and Fallières' visit to Holland formed an opportune subterfuge for the foreign office. France might hesitate to announce boldly that she intended to delay action until she had investigated the international situation, but she need not hesitate to delay final decision until the return of her president and foreign minister. In the meantime she was in a position to take every opportunity to secure British and Russian coöperation. He also advanced as an additional reason for delay the multiplicity of

---

[66] *Journal des Débats*, July 6, 1911, in Gauvain, *op. cit.*, vol. III, p. 15; Commandant de Thomasson, "La Crise marocaine," in *Questions diplomatiques et coloniales* (1911), Part 2, pp. 65-73.

[67] London *Times*, July 8, 1911 (Paris correspondent).

[68] Thomasson, *op. cit.*, pp. 65-73; Albin, *op. cit.*, p. 145.

treaties about Morocco with which Selves must acquaint himself, especially as "these treaties do not always square with each other and do not stand in harmony with the Algeciras Act. . . ." He acknowledged that the delay was in part due to the fact that France wished to discover what the real intentions of Germany were before she plánned her own action.[69] French delay was due in part to the absence of her two officials, in part to the desire to reach an agreement with England, but in the main to the determination to outmaneuver her opponent.

Approximately a week after the *coup d'Agadir*, France and Germany re-established contact. On July 6 Jules Cambon expressed to Schoen his dismay and fear that renewal of conversations would be difficult. Schoen quieted him somewhat, stating that "the question was too important and the situation too serious, to give room for irritability . . . ," and urged him to "return to Berlin, not merely with questions after our demands, but with positive proposals and empowerment. . . ." Cambon "showed anxiety" that Germany had in mind to take possession of part of the territory of Morocco. Schoen's reply was not one to quiet that anxiety, for he answered that German decision "would depend on what guarantee for economic activity as well as what compensation were offered. . . ." [70] That same evening Selves left Holland and the next morning again took over the foreign office. Cambon received official instructions and left for Berlin the same day, July 7.[71]

Immediately upon his return, Selves received Schoen[72] and told him that France was ready to enter into conversation as Germany had suggested; but "in order to put an end to the tension that the incident of Agadir had created, it was . . . necessary that Germany make known . . . that which she had in mind. . . ." The German ambassador stressed the conciliatory intentions of his government but insisted that the conversations take place in

[69] Szécsen to F. O., July 8, 1911, *Ö. U. A.*, vol. III, no. 2559.

[70] Schoen to F. O., July 6, 1911, *G. P.*, vol. XXIX, no. 10595.

[71] Albin, *op. cit.*, p. 47; Tardieu, *op. cit.*, p. 435.

[72] Selves to French representatives in London, Berlin, St. Petersburg, Rome, Madrid, July 7, 1911, *Affaires du Maroc*, 1910-1912, no. 437; Schoen to F. O., July 7, 1911, *G. P.*, vol. XXIX, no. 10596.

Berlin rather than in Paris. Selves objected strenuously to such a concession and argued that Schoen's action in presenting to him the German official notification relative to Agadir had the effect of opening the negotiations. He, therefore, concluded that they, Schoen and Selves, were the logical ones to conduct the negotiations; but he conceded that analogous pourparlers might be in progress at Berlin.[73] The ambassador rested upon the fact that he was without instructions but reported to his home office that Selves placed "great value" upon negotiations proceeding simultaneously at Berlin and Paris.[74] On July 8 he repeated his request that negotiations be conducted in Berlin, but again the French minister refused.[75] Kiderlen also rejected Selves's proposal when it was presented to him by Cambon in their first interview after the French ambassador's return to Berlin.[76]

Sir Francis Bertie, British ambassador in Paris, in reporting this development to Grey, asserted that "M. de Selves stated to M. de Schoen that he had no objection to conversations between the French Ambassador and the German Secretary for Foreign Affairs regarding any matter which the German Government might desire to bring before the French Government but that he (M. de Selves) was not going to give up the reins to anyone else and he must reserve to himself the right to discuss any such question with the German Ambassador who should seek instructions from his Government for the purpose. . . ."[77] In making this request, Selves displayed both diplomatic inexperience and personal pique. During the entire course of his ministry, he seemed to be sensitive to and resentful of the fact that the threads of foreign policy were being woven by hands other than his own. Diplomatic experience would have taught him that his proposal for pourparlers to be conducted simultaneously at Berlin and Paris was not feasible. The *Journal des Débats* expressed the general view when it stated, "We have refused to believe that any one has seriously thought of this combination. On the French side, it is certainly

---

[73] Selves to French representatives in London, Berlin, St. Petersburg, Rome, and Madrid, July 7, 1911, *Affaires du Maroc,* 1910-1912, no. 437.

[74] Schoen to F. O., July 7, 1911, *G. P.,* vol. XXIX, no. 10596.

[75] Schoen to Bethmann Hollweg, July 8, 1911, *ibid.,* no. 10602.

[76] Note of Kiderlen, July 9, 1911, *ibid.,* no. 10598.

[77] Bertie to Grey, July 9, 1911, *Br. Docs.,* vol. VII, no. 366.

M. Jules Cambon, signatory of the Accord of February 8, 1909, who knows most about the question. On the German side, it is M. de Kiderlen-Waechter, minister of foreign affairs of the empire, who possesses the same authority. It is, therefore, natural that these are the two diplomats to conduct the new conversations. . . ." [78] Selves lost the first round: the conversations were to be à deux with Kiderlen and Cambon as the principals; the place, Berlin.

The significant point in the conversation between Schoen and Selves on July 8 was not the dispute over the place of negotiations but the use of the term "Congo." The two reports differ in the essential question as to who first used the term. Selves wrote that he asked Schoen what were the objectives "which led the German government to make the demonstration at Agadir and at the same time to invite us to talk with it. . . ." Schoen, speaking non-officially and as a private person, replied that according to his view, "his government did not nourish pretentions of a territorial order in Morocco, but that the Congo appeared to offer a ground for negotiations. . . ." Upon this basis, Selves asked Cambon to "verify if the Congo is, in fact, the country on the subject of which the German government is desirous to talk with us. . . ." [79] Schoen reported that he urged upon the foreign minister that Cambon should not return empty-handed to Berlin, whereupon Selves introduced the idea of compensation possibilities in the Congo.[80] Regardless of which of the two introduced the topic, the Congo, on July 8, moved from the borderland of newspaper rumors and diplomatic guesses into the council room of official negotiations. In the same disputed fashion, on July 9, it entered the conversation of the two chief negotiators.

The first of the long series of conversations through which Kiderlen and Cambon fought to a solution of the Moroccan problem took place on July 9. The barometric pressure presaged a storm. Cambon's remark, "I at first found the secretary of state reserved and on his guard," [81] and Kiderlen's statement that the

---

[78] *Journal des Débats,* July 12, 1911, in Gauvain, *op. cit.,* vol. III, p. 22.

[79] Selves to Cambon, July 8, 1911, *Affaires du Maroc,* 1910-1912, no. 439.

[80] Schoen to F. O., July 8, 1911, *G. P.,* vol. XXIX, no. 10597.

[81] Cambon to Selves, July 10, 1911, *Affaires du Maroc,* 1910-1912, no. 444.

French ambassador "came with a true grave-digger air and answered my question about his health with only a light groan . . ." [82] expressed their respective reactions to the electric currents pervading the atmosphere. Silence broken only by monosyllabic questions and responses marked the first few minutes of the interview. The silence was finally dispelled by reference to the Kissingen interview and was turned into mutual recriminations of duplicity. Cambon's facial expression and gestures emphasized his skepticism as Kiderlen justified German action on the basis of need for protection for her nationals. Kiderlen was full of complaints of French failure to fulfil her obligations under the Accord of 1909. Economic equality had not been respected; German coöperation had not been granted; and, as final proof of French insincerity, the railroad projects had broken down. Such fuming was not conducive to harmonious action. Kiderlen recognized the fact and cleared the air somewhat by the comment that "pourparlers on the future" were more profitable than "recrimi-

---

[82] Note of Kiderlen, July 9, 1911, *G. P.*, vol. XXIX, no. 10598. This note of Kiderlen's appeared in Caillaux, *op. cit.*, published in 1919, pp. 278-283. A number of Kiderlen's letters appear in the second part of Caillaux's book. He received these documents through Kiderlen's friend, whom Caillaux calls the Baroness Y, and whom the editors of *G. P.* speak of as Frau von Jonina, a Russian diplomat. The editors of *G. P.* believe that Kiderlen knew the ultimate destination of his letters and that he consciously inserted cynical comments when speaking of German officials in order to impress the French with their genuineness and that his real purpose in the letters was to convince the French of his determination to achieve his aims.—Editor's footnote to note of Kiderlen, July 9, 1911, *G. P.*, vol. XXIX, no. 10598, p. 174. In these letters, Kiderlen usually addressed the Kaiser as "la fourrure," Bethmann Hollweg, as the "worm" or "eel," and the various German diplomats with equally mocking titles. Wolff attributes this trait to Kiderlen's somewhat coarse strain of humor, a type of "shirtsleeve humor," but he gives credence to the spontaneity of their use and does not accept the explanation of the *G. P.* editors.—*Op. cit.*, pp. 21, 22. Andreas accepted the correspondence as genuine but stated that it was important only in showing the tactless nature, the "coarse-grained humor" of the foreign minister.—*Op. cit.*, p. 249. Kiderlen, who complained at length of French violation of the secrecy pact, seemed not to consider that his pledge extended to his lady friend. Some of the letters to Frau von Jonina are included in Jäckh, *op. cit.*, vol. II, but none of Kiderlen's ironical comments on officials appear in any there published. The letters do not reveal any additional facts relative to the Agadir crisis but do emphasize Kiderlen's determination to attain his objectives and display rather unattractive characteristics in the man.

THE GERMAN ENIGMA   257

nations about the past." Cambon took advantage of this opening
to enter into the heart of the discussion.[83]

The Kissingen interview gave to the French ambassador an
avenue of approach. He summarized his interpretation of that
interview and asked his opponent if the gist of the conversation
had not been the idea of an understanding based on compensation
to Germany outside Morocco. At this point the German and
French accounts of the July 9 conversation vary radically. Kiderlen reported that Cambon followed his summary of the Kissingen
interview with offers of compensation in the Orient, in railroads in
Turkey, and in a heavy share in the Ottoman public debt, and
pictured the great advantage of French support to German industry and commerce everywhere. To the first proposal, Kiderlen
"dryly" remarked that Germany "had in the Orient what she
wished." To the next two suggestions, his answer that they were
"no concessions but a common economic business" was equally
dry. Only one thing, Morocco, did Cambon insist was outside the
realm of a possible compensation object. Kiderlen replied that
"nothing indicated an usurpation in Morocco" on the part of
Germany, but that "France slowly but consistently had established herself there." Gradually he brought into the conversation
his private opinion that any renovation of the Accord of 1909
would never remove the friction. He therefore "wished to present
the case—purely hypothetical, since [he] was not empowered to
do it—we [Germany] give France in Morocco *carte blanche*, but
would for that demand of France not moral but real compensation
of a colonial territory. . . ." Cambon interrupted with the words:
"They have spoken of the coast of Congo. . . ." Kiderlen replied
that he did not consider "that excluded, but we must then make
important claims; perhaps we could make the affair easier for
France by proposing an exchange of territory in which, however,
we must have the lion's share. . . ." Upon Cambon's eager request
for more details, Kiderlen withdrew again into his attitude of reti-
cency and stated that as he knew so little of colonial matters, he
must first consult his colonial secretary, Lindequist, but perhaps

---

[83] Cambon to Selves, July 10, 1911, *Affaires du Maroc,* 1910-1912, no. 444;
note of Kiderlen, July 9, 1911, *G. P.,* vol. XXIX, no. 10598.

"a frontier adjustment of Togo may be possible. . . ." Consultation with Lindequist was merely diplomatic maneuvering and was so recognized by Cambon. Kiderlen had advanced as far as he intended for the present. He was not the one to be hurried, although Cambon stressed the necessity of settling the matter quickly in order "to calm public opinion." [84]

In his report of the interview, Kiderlen stated that Cambon had made several offers of compensation outside the colonial field, each of which he had renounced, and that Cambon first mentioned the Congo. The French ambassador in his preliminary report to Selves telegraphed, "I took care not to take the initiative of any proposition. The German government will accept renunciation of all territorial pretentions in Morocco and seek with the French government colonial satisfactions in the Congo. . . ." [85] In his detailed report dispatched the following day, Cambon placed the initiative for every suggestion upon the German secretary. According to Cambon's account, the term "Congo" was introduced into the conversation in the following manner. He had summarized the Kissingen interview and described the need to take into consideration public opinion. To this Kiderlen replied, "You wish that we give up Morocco as lost entirely; ah well, for my part, I would consent to it, but . . . it is necessary to give satisfactions of a colonial nature, in the Congo, for example. . . ." [86]

The two reports varied on other points. It was agreed that no third power should be admitted to the negotiations. Kiderlen dismissed the point with the statement that the responsibility for explaining any agreement that might be reached belonged to France. Cambon replied that "England would make no difficulty" and as to Spain, France would respect her obligations, and if differences had arisen it was only that France "wished to watch her in order that she should not surpass the limits of our reciprocal engagements. . . ." [87] The French report read: "I replied to him that we would do nothing contrary to our accords with Spain and

---

[84] Note of Kiderlen, July 9, 1911, *G. P.*, vol. XXIX, no. 10598.
[85] Cambon to Selves, July 9, 1911, *Affaires du Maroc*, 1910-1912, no. 441; also published in Caillaux, *op. cit.*, p. 284.
[86] Cambon to Selves, July 10, 1911, *Affaires du Maroc*, 1910-1912, no. 444.
[87] Note of Kiderlen, July 9, 1911, *G. P.*, vol. XXIX, no. 10598.

with England . . ." and "ended by saying that we would keep
our allies, our friends, and our associates constantly advised of
our negotiations. . . ." [88] France maintained that throughout the
course of the negotiations she had insisted upon the right to keep
her allies and friends informed of all developments.

In another and rather personal point the two reports differed.
The conversation turned to a discussion of the new French ministry, and Kiderlen remarked that a strong government would be
necessary in order to carry through any satisfactory adjustment
of the present difficulty. According to Kiderlen's report, it was
Cambon who, "through a long discourse . . . sought to prove to
him that M. Caillaux is the man of the hour . . .";[89] according
to Cambon's account, it was Kiderlen who made the statement.[90]
The significance of personal references becomes evident with the
examination of the private letter sent by Cambon, not to his immediate chief, Selves, but to the premier, Caillaux. Cambon wrote
that "with a little good will and largeness of spirit" France would
be able to make a satisfactory adjustment, "but it is important to
bring to this task more of finesse than they have the custom of
showing in the bureaus at Paris. . . ." M. de Kiderlen, he continued, "is a man who likes himself to conduct the affairs and who
intends to conduct them well; he is exasperated easily when they
drag out and I have often made it known at Paris how our hesita-
tions seemed to him incomprehensible. . . ." The German foreign
secretary was "anxious to guard the susceptibilities of M. de Selves,
but he asked me if M. de Schoen would be able to go to see you.
I told him that he could when he wished, but it would perhaps be
better to wait until you had him called. I believe, therefore, that
you would do well to have him come at the moment you judge
opportune. In the main, it is M. de Kiderlen who will conduct the
negotiations from the German point of view, but it is well that he
should feel that from the French point of view you have a hand
in it. . . ." [91] Diplomats on both sides of the Rhine shoved Selves
aside, went over his head or behind his back to conduct the nego-

[88] Cambon to Selves, July 9, 1911, *Affaires du Maroc*, 1910-1912, no. 441.
[89] Note of Kiderlen, July 9, 1911, *G. P.*, vol. XXIX, no. 10598.
[90] Cambon to Caillaux, July 10, 1911, in Caillaux, *op. cit.*, p. 285.
[91] *Ibid.*

tiations without him. Official reports were transmitted to him, but important decisions were made outside the foreign office.

The French and German accounts of the first conversations differed largely on the question of initiative but agreed on the question of elements entering into the conversation. The Congo, Togo, railroads, the attitude of England and Spain, and the personalities of the French premier and the foreign minister were discussed. Germany had officially offered France a free hand in Morocco in return for compensation elsewhere, perhaps the Congo. The conversation consisted in the main of general suggestions; details awaited later development. The two negotiators parted in a friendly manner to spin the thread farther by contact with their superiors.

Selves replied to Cambon's report with instructions for him, as soon as possible, to press upon Kiderlen the need to specify what Germany wished in the Congo and to inform the German official that France was willing to reopen the railroad negotiations.[92] In the interim, Schoen, informed of the situation by his own foreign office,[93] approached Selves, who freely expressed his approval of the developments and especially of the fact that Germany had directed her attention to the Congo rather than to Morocco, because "France would not have been able to form an agreement in her own interest and with respect to England" if Morocco were the object of German ambitions.[94] Kiderlen, for his part, had urged Cambon to persuade both his government and the French press to cease threatening Germany with the mention of England and Russia;[95] but insinuations of British pressure continued to slip into diplomatic despatches and open appeals to British interests continued to appear in the press. The weapon was too valuable from the French standpoint to be lightly thrown aside.

While Cambon was receiving official approbation of his management of the first interview, Kiderlen was facing an irate master. Bethmann Hollweg's despatch reporting the interview was perforated through and through with imperial ejaculations in the

[92] Selves to Cambon, July 11, 1911, *Affaires du Maroc*, 1910-1912, no. 446.
[93] Kiderlen to Schoen, July 10, 1911, *G. P.,* vol. XXIX, no. 10599.
[94] Schoen to F. O., July 12, 1911, *ibid.,* no. 10605.
[95] Note of Kiderlen, July 9, 1911, *ibid.,* no. 10598.

form of marginal notes and an extensive epilogue.[96] The dilatory procedure followed by the two diplomats was the chief point of irritation, and the Emperor's annotations were repetitions of the phrase "after four weeks." To Bethmann Hollweg's statement that requisite authorization was lacking, he commented, "After four weeks! Why?" He expressed at length his astonishment over the report in the light of the fact that early in June he had discussed the question of compensation with the chancellor. "The chancellor at that time begged my authorization to designate the Congo. . . . It was approved by me and the foreign office understood it. . . . I would like to know what is necessary for authorization? Mine was obtained and given four weeks ago. . . ." At Kiel, the matter was discussed again, June 26, and "my consent sought, which I immediately gave. . . . They discuss and discuss and nothing comes out of it! If we lose thus our costly time, the Briton and Russian will strengthen the back of the frightened Gaul and dictate to them what they most graciously should guarantee us! . . . This kind of diplomacy is too fine and too high for my brains!" Despite his irritation, the Emperor authorized his foreign secretary to proceed, warned him of the danger of delay because of the possible interference of a third power, and laid great emphasis on the Congo.[97]

This epilogue of the Kaiser's seems to render futile all argument as to whether Cambon or Kiderlen, Selves or Schoen, first used the term "Congo." Before either of these conversations had taken place, German officials had agreed upon the Congo as the object of compensation. This note also revealed the fact that the Kaiser expected a more rapid solution of the difficulty than did his officials. In order to secure the imperial consent to their program, his advisers probably did not give him a clear picture of possible complications arising from the dispatch of a gunboat to the Moroccan coast. One authority stated that Kiderlen seemed to have expected France hastily to offer compensation, but, "to his chagrin," France delayed.[98] This description fits better the attitude of the Kaiser, who had the impression that the dispatch of the

[96] Bethmann Hollweg to William II, July 10, 1911, *ibid.*, no. 10600.

[97] Treutler to F. O., July 11, 1911, *ibid.*, no. 10601.

[98] P. T. Moon, *Imperialism and World Politics*, p. 212.

Panther would gain for Germany that which she wanted without serious complications or delays developing. On more than one occasion he repeated his complaints of the needless and dangerous delay. He could not follow the finesse and devious strategy of his foreign secretary, and fear of British interference plagued him into a state of nervous irritability.

On July 13 conversations took place in Berlin and Paris in which the French representatives pressed upon the German agents that the imperial government specify what it wanted.[99] The Berlin conversation included discussion of a rectification of the Congo-Camerun frontier and of the guarantees Germany was willing to give France in Morocco. Kiderlen stated that Germany had no intention of establishing herself in Morocco and that she realized that the sultan, being unable alone to maintain order in his kingdom, had accorded to France the right to exercise the necessary authority to guarantee the country against anarchy. Cambon considered this guarantee entirely too general to be of any value, especially as Kiderlen asked for special recognition of the rights of German mining interests in the Sous. No progress toward a solution of the crisis was made in the conversations of July 13.[100] As the Kaiser would say, they discussed and discussed and gained nothing. It was the interview of July 15 which unloosed the storm.

The conversation of July 15[101] opened with a discussion of the German renunciation of Morocco, French guarantees of the open door, and consideration of German interests in the Sous. Although no definite agreement was reached on these points, discussion proceeded calmly. The calm was rudely shattered when the topic shifted to the question of compensation. Cambon had calmly asked what were German demands. Kiderlen's response left him stunned.[102] Deliberately the German secretary had a map brought before them and coolly pointed to the Congo from the ocean to the

---

[99] Cambon to Selves, July 13, 1911, *Affaires du Maroc,* 1910-1912, no. 452; Selves to Cambon, July 13, 1911, *ibid.,* no. 451.

[100] Cambon to Selves, July 13, 1911, *ibid.,* no. 452; Bertie to Grey, July 14, 1911, *Br. Docs.,* vol. VII, no. 381.

[101] Cambon to Selves, July 16, 1911, *Affaires du Maroc,* 1910-1912, no. 455; Bethmann Hollweg to William II, July 15, 1911, *G. P.,* vol. XXIX, no. 10607.

[102] Bethmann Hollweg to William II, July 15, 1911, *G. P.,* vol. XXIX, no. 10607.

Sangha.[103] By that act, Germany laid "claims to the French Congo and indeed to all of it. . . ." [104] Cambon recovered slightly his composure and declared that "this demand would undoubtedly cause the negotiations to fail; for French opinion might consent to large compensation but not to the loss of an entire colony. . . ." [105] He then asked if Germany did not offer France something in exchange for such a large cession of territory. Kiderlen replied that northern Camerun and even the Togo might be offered, dependent upon the French grant.[106] A concrete proposal had crystallized. Germany would grant France *carte blanche* in Morocco in exchange for the entire French Congo for which she might offer Togo or northern Camerun. The ransom price had been stated. Would France pay the demanded sum? Her ambassador had refused, and his refusal was confirmed, July 17, by the foreign minister.[107] What now did Kiderlen intend to do? In fact, what lay behind this play? Did he expect to win all the Congo, or by asking for all did he hope to gain a part? Were his eyes still fastened on the Sous and his move a clever ruse planned to weaken his opponent's resistance on this vital issue? To what extent was this merely a game of bluff? If France remained obdurate, what action would Germany take? European peace was riding on a tanker of high explosives. The Kaiser, more than any of the other German officials, seemed conscious of this fact.

Bethmann Hollweg, upon receipt of Kiderlen's report of the demands presented to France, transmitted the information to his imperial master. One phrase in that report frightened the Kaiser into ejaculating, "I must immediately go home. . . ." [108] Kiderlen had pictured to his chancellor the fact that France might be stubborn in her refusal, in which case Germany, in order to secure a favorable adjustment, must proceed "forcibly." The Kaiser be-

---

[103] Cambon to Selves, July 16, 1911, *Affaires du Maroc,* 1910-1912, no. 455.

[104] Bethmann Hollweg to William II, July 15, 1911, *G. P.,* vol. XXIX, no. 10607.

[105] Cambon to Selves, July 16, 1911, *Affaires du Maroc,* 1910-1912, no. 455.

[106] *Ibid.;* Bethmann Hollweg to William II, July 15, 1911, *G. P.,* vol. XXIX, no. 10607.

[107] Selves to Cambon, July 17, 1911, *Affaires du Maroc,* 1910-1912, no. 456.

[108] For the Kaiser's reaction, see his annotations to the despatch Bethmann Hollweg to William II, July 15, 1911, *G. P.,* vol. XXIX, no. 10607.

18

lieved that Kiderlen meant to go to war if that were requisite to attain his end; for this marginal note read: "I must immediately go home. I cannot permit my government to advance in this manner without being on the spot in order to supervise entirely and to have a hand in the consequences. That would be unpardonable and too parliamentary! The King amuses himself! and meanwhile we move to mobilization. Without me that cannot happen. . . ." He also stated that his ally must be informed immediately and repeated his earlier argument that loss of time had given France opportunity to secure the assistance of England and Russia. The foreign office agent accompanying the Kaiser sought to convince him that nothing unexpected had happened, that Kiderlen's terms did not mean that a threat had been issued.[109] He was compelled, however, to wire the foreign office that, although he had somewhat quieted William II, it was clear that His Majesty would not consent to steps that might lead to war.[110]

Since the beginning of his exile in Bucharest, Kiderlen and his Imperial Master had had little respect or sympathy for each other. His appointment to the foreign office had indicated more the strength of Bethmann Hollweg's standing in the royal favor than any lessening of the monarch's antipathy to Kiderlen-Waechter.[111] Now Bülow's apt description of the new foreign secretary as one "who is liable to take the bit between his teeth, and not altogether safe unless held in tightly . . ." seemed on the point of fulfilment.[112] This Swabian was as determined to win his end before his superiors, for whom he had scant respect, as before his French antagonist. Consequently, when he received notification of the imperial displeasure, he presented his resignation.

In a lengthy memorandum[113] Kiderlen reviewed the state of the negotiation and emphasized the point that France would not concede acceptable compensation unless she understood that Germany was "determined on the most extreme measures. . . ." He then

---

[109] Treutler to Bethmann Hollweg, July 17, 1911, *ibid.*, no. 10608; Treutler to Bethmann Hollweg, July 17, 1911, *ibid.*, no. 10609.

[110] Treutler to Bethmann Hollweg, July 17, 1911, *ibid.*, no. 10609.

[111] Schwabach, *op. cit.*, p. 194.

[112] Wolff, *op. cit.*, p. 19; Bülow, *op. cit.*, vol. III, p. 464.

[113] First resignation petition of Kiderlen, July 17, 1911, in Jäckh, *op. cit.*, vol. II, pp. 128-130.

painted a picture of a great German African empire for which
Germany "must have the entire French Congo—it is the last opportunity without fighting to receive something useful in Africa.
. . . " He wanted to secure the French Congo to its junction with
the Belgian Congo, and upon the partition (often mooted) of the
Belgian Congo, Germany should see that she got the stretch that
would unite the new acquisition and German East Africa. According to his conviction, a satisfactory settlement of the existing
crisis could not be attained unless Germany convinced her opponent that she was ready indeed to take the ultimate step. "Who in
advance declares that he will not fight, can attain nothing in politics . . . !" He concluded his petition by the statement that his
phrases "proceed very forcibly" did not mean war but only a determination to break French obstinacy. Since the Emperor did
not support his procedure, he presented his resignation. On the
same day he wrote a private letter to Bethmann Hollweg in which
he stated that the negotiations would probably drag along much
longer; but the only feasible plan to secure their aim seemed to be
to wear down French opposition by "obstinate conversation," for
that was the only solution that would not provoke foreign interference.

Bethmann Hollweg refused to forward the resignation to the
Kaiser, stated that he would resign if Kiderlen did so, and asked
him to come to Berlin to discuss the matter.[114] In the meantime,
he informed the "All-Highest" that there was no need for his hasty
return; and, in order to assuage his justified concern, he assured
him that no threat had been issued to France and none was proposed, but that the negotiations would take a long time.[115] He was
more successful in cooling the irritated sensibilities of his master
than those of his subordinate.

Kiderlen, not satisfied with Bethmann Hollweg's telegram of
July 18, expressed his resentment in a new resignation petition on
July 19.[116] He pointed out that the entire plan of procedure had

[114] Bethmann Hollweg's answer to Kiderlen's first resignation petition, July
18, 1911, in Jäckh, op. cit., vol. II, p. 131.

[115] Bethmann Hollweg to William II, July 18, 1911, G. P., vol. XXIX,
no. 10611.

[116] Second resignation petition of Kiderlen, July 19, 1911, in Jäckh, op. cit.,
vol. II, pp. 132-134.

been determined before the first step was taken and that the Kaiser had given his consent to the entire program. In the preliminary discussions it was agreed that German tactics were to employ a technique that would lead the French to make the first offers of compensation. He insisted that "France must first slowly become accustomed to compensation ideas. . . ." Again he explained that the phrase which had provoked the imperial ire did not mean a direct threat to France, but "always in the course of negotiations . . . this kind of tension can enter . . . that we must declare positively to France that we are determined on the most extreme step. And if this is to have effect we must also be inwardly determined to it. . . ." As the Emperor apparently did not trust his management of affairs, he insisted upon offering his resignation. The plain truth of the matter is that Kiderlen deliberately used this threat of resignation to force his superiors to approve his program.

The chancellor was thus forced to assume the task of trying to secure imperial approval of Kiderlen's strategy. He accordingly presented to the Kaiser a lengthy review of the incidents that led to the Agadir action and appealed to the sensitive point of national prestige to press home his argument. If Germany were to let France create "a new, great, and valuable colonial territory . . . , our credit in the world, not only for the moment, but also for all future international actions, suffers an intolerable blow. . . . " If Germany were to accept only frontier rectifications, her adversary would become "so haughty that we must, sooner or later, take her to task. . . ." For these reasons, Kiderlen named the entire French Congo. If France remained obdurate, Germany had only one alternative: that was to fall back upon the Algeciras Act and demand French evacuation of Morocco, even of Casablanca. Such a demand could not be enforced without international complications and consequently should be avoided. If Germany granted France a free hand in Morocco, including southern Morocco, and thus helped her to complete her great North African empire, she (France) should be willing to pay an adequate price. "If we press with these negotiations to immediate conclusion, the French will grant us only a concession, which is not acceptable for us and compel us to return to the standpoint of the Algeciras Act, which we could maintain with propriety only under the danger of serious conflict. . . ." [117] Bethmann Hollweg with these arguments tried to persuade William II that the only way in which Germany could avoid a diplomatic defeat and at the same time avoid war, was with full confidence to empower Kiderlen to conduct the negotiations in the manner he deemed best. William was convinced, and on July 21 issued the necessary authorization. [118]

Did Kiderlen mean war? His advocates would have us believe that he was the most peaceable of men. [119] He insisted that he did not believe war would be necessary to force France to consent to his demands, but his statements from July 15 through July 20 indicated that he considered the possibility and did not quail before it. He apparently believed that France would not grant the entire French Congo unless she believed that Germany would fight if need be to secure the coveted territory, but that when convinced of that contingency, she would yield. Nobody, as a matter of fact, wanted war because of Morocco, neither Kiderlen, nor the Kaiser, nor France, nor any of the other chancelleries of Europe; but Kiderlen was playing with explosive materials. [120] National prestige, national pride, imperialistic ambitions have a way of exploding about the heads of those who play with such dangerous toys. Had Kiderlen, before he presented his demands, examined the consequences of French refusal? Brandenburg thinks not. He states that Kiderlen relied upon the reports from Paris that Caillaux favored compensations and that he seemed to have expected "with extraordinary simplicity that a threatening gesture would straightway bring forth offers of compensation from Paris . . . ," asking himself only after the deed was done what action he should take if the compensations were refused. [121] According to Hammann, "Folk psychology was not his strong point," [122] and that accounted for many of the errors in judgment made by the German foreign secretary. Too often Kiderlen failed to estimate accu-

---

[117] Bethmann Hollweg to William II, July 20, 1911, *G. P.*, vol. XXIX, no. 10613.   [118] Bethmann Hollweg to F. O., July 21, 1911, *ibid.*, no. 10614.

[119] Jonescu, *op. cit.*, p. 69; Schwabach, *op. cit.*, p. 260; Jäckh, *op. cit.*, vol. II, pp. 224-230.

[120] Eckardstein, *op. cit.*, p. 85; Wilson, *op. cit.*, p. 132; Brandenburg, *op. cit.*, pp. 376, 377; Wolff, *op. cit.*, pp. 50-52.

[121] *Op. cit.*, pp. 371, 372.   [122] *Bilder aus der letzten Kaiserzeit*, p. 84.

rately the national peculiarities of the people with whom he dealt. Wolff, consistently critical of Kiderlen's methods, stated that "to cover up diplomatic incapacity . . . ," the foreign secretary "took up a historical pose; he was not really serious about his determination to go to extreme lengths. But his pose was uncommonly dangerous. . . ." [123] If Wolff's judgment was sound, Kiderlen, in such a rôle, was a consummate actor; for he gave his gestures almost too realistic a turn and invested his threats of "extreme lengths" with distinctly ominous tones. At all events, the danger involved in such a pose stands out in bold relief when the tension in Germany is matched with that in France.

On July 17 Selves wired Cambon that France could not accept the demands presented on July 15.[124] On July 19, the same day that Kiderlen presented his second resignation petition, Cambon informed his chief that the initiative for reopening the conversation must fall upon Kiderlen; but in the meantime he considered it necessary to secure instructions from his home office in the event that the negotiations were definitely broken.[125] The Quai d'Orsay then bestirred itself to defeat the German program. Selves stated to Cambon, evidently to be retailed to the Wilhelmstrasse, that France was in constant touch with England and Russia.[126] Grey wired Bertie that if France could not concede the German demands, "the obvious course seems to be for France to make counterproposals, stating what she can concede in French Congo. . . ." [127] Isvolski reported that Selves handled affairs "with great calmness" but with determination not to renounce the Congo, and expressed the view that Germany had made these demands in the full knowledge of French refusal with the hope of securing thereby an excuse to stay in Agadir.[128] Schoen sought to relieve the tension by insisting upon the serious desire of Germany to reach an agreement but stated that Germany thought France should be willing to make a sacrifice for such a valuable prize as Morocco.[129]

---

[123] *Op. cit.,* pp. 51, 52.

[124] Selves to Cambon, July 17, 1911, *Affaires du Maroc,* 1910-1912, no. 456.

[125] Cambon to Selves, July 19, 1911, *ibid.,* no. 461.

[126] Selves to Cambon, July 20, 1911, *ibid.,* no. 463.

[127] Grey to Bertie, July 19, 1911, *Br. Docs.,* vol. VII, no. 396.

[128] Isvolski to Neratov, July 19, 1911, Isvolski, *op. cit.,* vol. I, no. 100.

[129] Schoen to F. O., July 19, 1911, *G. P.,* vol. XXIX, no. 10612.

Selves also consulted Caillaux and the minister of the colonies, Lebrun, before he notified Cambon to continue the negotiations.[130] He instructed the ambassador to refuse Kiderlen's demands but to present a counter-proposal, in which French rights in Morocco were more definitely stated and in return for which France offered to Germany certain rectifications of the Congo-Camerun frontier and a greater section through the middle Congo. He advised Cambon not to mention the economic questions in Morocco but to leave that initiative to Kiderlen. "You may," he concluded, "let M. de Kiderlen understand that this rupture would risk transforming the particular question that is treated between only our two countries into an international question. In that respect, the perspective of an international conference causes us no apprehension. . . . "[131] Selves was again threatening Kiderlen with the plain fact that France had some friends.

Before this letter could reach Berlin, an acrimonious conversation took place between Kiderlen and Cambon, on July 20.[132] Kiderlen began by complaining of the indiscretions in the French press. Secrecy, so far as it related to the press, had been agreed upon by the two negotiators; but leaks occurred and journalists announced sufficiently accurate information to inflame the public mind.[133] With the news that Germany had demanded the entire French Congo, the French press threw aside all calmness and discretion and denounced in unequivocal terms the rapacity of their Teuton neighbor. The cry that German purpose involved not only colonial acquisition but the disruption of the Triple Entente was trumpeted as stridently by the usually non-aggressive *Journal des Débats*[134] as by the more militantly nationalistic papers.[135] Kiderlen complained especially of the report that Selves had called the

---

[130] Selves to Cambon, July 20, 1911, *Affaires du Maroc*, 1910-1912, no. 463.

[131] *Ibid.*

[132] Cambon to Selves, July 20, 1911, *Affaires du Maroc*, 1910-1912, no. 464.

[133] *Journal des Débats*, July 19, 1911, in Gauvain, *op. cit.*, vol. III, p. 35; *Kreuzzeitung*, July 19, 1911, in Schiemann, *op. cit.*, p. 226. The first publication of the German demands stated only that Germany had asked for the entire French Congo and omitted any mention of Togo as an exchange object. Schwabach believes this was done purposefully to stir up public opinion.—*Op. cit.*, p. 202.

[134] *Journal des Débats*, July 19, 1911, in Gauvain, *op. cit.*, vol. III, p. 35.

[135] Carroll, *French Public Opinion and Foreign Affairs*, p. 243.

first German overtures a "ballon d'essai" which could not be taken seriously. He impressed it upon Cambon that in negotiations of such serious import, he spoke "only serious words. . . ." If the negotiations were to progress, he added, they must do so in an atmosphere of mutual respect. If the conversations were rendered impossible, Germany would take her freedom of action, demand the integral application of the Act of Algeciras, and to secure its enforcement, "will go if need be to . . . extreme lengths. . . ." Cambon explained that the offensive French phrase merely meant "first tentatives" and carried no meaning of ill will, but answered "the menace which was contained in his last phrase" with the assertion that France would go as far as Germany.[136] Imperial approval of Kiderlen's program had not been issued until July 21, but Kiderlen did not hesitate to present his threat of "extreme lengths" to the French ambassador on July 20. He still held the bit in his teeth.

One month had passed since the Kissingen interview; three weeks had passed since the *Panther's* Spring. The time had been a period of tension but also a period of hopeful waiting. The tension heightened July 15 and stood at the breaking point on July 21, when the Kaiser's fear was fulfilled. England entered the arena and placed in the balance a counterpoise which weighed very heavily on the side of France.

---

[136] Cambon to Selves, July 20, 1911, *Affaires du Maroc*, 1910-1912, no. 464.

Chapter XI

THE MANSION HOUSE SPEECH

"The news of the *Panther's* Spring was received with even greater indignation and surprise in Downing Street than at the Quai d'Orsay. . . ." [1] Downing Street probably had more reason for surprise, as all the details of Franco-German relations were not known there; but the major facts were as familiar to the British as to the French foreign office. London was surprised, not by the fact that Germany took action, but by the nature of her action. From its inception, the French march to Fez had excited uneasiness in London because the foreign office at once recognized its potential danger. It feared that international complications might arise which would force England to take a definite stand in defense of peculiarly British interests or in recognition of her obligations under the Entente Cordiale, and she naturally wished to avoid such a contingency. For this reason it had issued bits of advice to the Quai d'Orsay to proceed cautiously, though at no time had it questioned French right or need to advance to the aid of Fez. [2] But this selfsame march to Fez had provoked the *Panther's* Spring, which, in turn, had pulled the fibres of the European structure into that state of tense equilibrium where a single fresh jolt might snap the flimsy cords that held it together, thus making an end of an all-too-fragile peace. Naturally enough, Grey and his associates were irritated that the issue had been forced into a critical phase which necessitated a definition of their policy.

The lodestar of Britain's policy in 1911, as in 1905 and 1906, was her loyalty to the Entente Cordiale. Conduct of foreign affairs was in the hands of Sir Edward Grey, whose sense of loyalty and sincere devotion to his obligations had won for him the reputation of being blindly pro-French and bitterly anti-German. [3] His intense devotion to the soil of England had kept him close at home

---

[1] Ward and Gooch, *op. cit.*, vol. III, p. 440.
[2] See Chapter VIII, *supra.*
[3] Hermann Lutz, *Lord Grey and the World War*, p. 62.

and had deprived him of the enlightening influences of foreign travel. Handicapped by his lack of personal contact with foreign countries and by his meagre knowledge of foreign languages, his decisions, despite his inherent honesty and his sense of impartiality,[4] often failed to meet the exigencies of the occasion. These same defects made him susceptible to the influence of advisers upon whom he depended for information and who colored his judgment with their own prejudices.[5] Yet he consistently strove to harmonize his sense of justice with his devotion to British interest and with his loyalty to France—an impossible task! His efforts resulted only in producing a hesitant, uncertain policy, punctuated occasionally with vigorous pronouncements, which befogged rather than clarified the international atmosphere. His Moroccan program had all the elements of uncertainty that generally characterized his régime.

Loyalty to the Entente was the motif of British action, and as early as May 22, Grey, following its guidance, informed Metternich that "England in any case and under all circumstances, would fulfil her obligations to France . . . ," and answered Metternich's question as to what the consequences would be if the Moroccan government came under French influence and the Algeciras Act were violated with the clear announcement that "in the event of entanglements, all English obligations would become 'operative'. . . ."[6] Kiderlen claimed that, as early as his Bucharest days, he realized that "so long as the Morocco question was open England would side with France all over the world and on all questions at issue between us. . . ."[7] Germany, in both the notes of May 3 and of June 12, recognized that in the Moroccan question England was an interested party.[8] The ultimate success of Kiderlen's plan depended to a large degree upon the skilful use of tactics designed to hold England aloof; for if she were to enter the fray, the balance would be tilted in favor of France. From the purely selfish standpoint of a desire to see his plan succeed, Kiderlen needed to guard every avenue by which England might enter the arena and to take every

[4] Algernon Cecil, *British Foreign Secretaries, 1807-1916*, pp. 318-320, 332.

[5] Lutz, *op. cit.,* pp. 67, 71.

[6] Metternich to Bethmann Hollweg, May 22, 1911, *G. P.,* vol. XXIX, no. 10561; Benckendorff to Neratov, May 23, 1911 in Siebert, *op. cit.,* no. 674.

[7] Jonescu, *op. cit.,* p. 62; Jäckh, *op. cit.,* vol. II, p. 221.

[8] See Chapter IX, *supra.*

precaution to assure her that her entrance was unnecessary. It was to his advantage to err on the side of undue courting of British favor, but his secretive yet arrogant manner was ill-suited to the delicate task of wooing John Bull from his French mistress. He ignored the gracious courtesies that win favors and did nothing to check the development of a hostile England. The contacts between the German and British governments during the first weeks of the crisis were too few and too evasive to stimulate friendship.

On July 1 Count Metternich, the reticent German ambassador in London, delivered the official German notice of the dispatch of a gunboat to the Moroccan harbor to Sir Arthur Nicolson, who was acting in the absence of Grey.[9] Nicolson, who "believed profoundly in the German menace," [10] had frequently expressed his uneasiness over the situation created by the French march to Fez and his fear of some action by Germany that would complicate the issues. His response to Metternich, although non-official in form, expressed his opposition to the move and his distrust of the stated German motive; for he was unaware that German firms were in the closed port of Agadir or in its environs.[11] His confidential report to his chief showed that he interpreted Count Metternich's remark that "a return to the *status quo ante* was out of the question . . ." [12] as reopening the entire Moroccan problem.

When Grey returned to London on July 3, he was faced with the problem of an answer to France and to Germany. He conferred with both Paul Cambon[13] and Count Metternich and indicated the British attitude, but he reserved official answer to the German note until the cabinet meeting of July 4. To Metternich, of whom he had commented that he could always trust him to report his remarks accurately,[14] Grey stated that "the sending of a German warship to Agadir has created a new highly important and delicate situation . . ." and "that British commercial interests were . . . considerably larger than German in Morocco, and [that the] reasons

[9] Metternich to F. O., July 1, 1911, *G. P.,* vol. XXIX, no. 10581.

[10] Nicolson, *op. cit.,* p. 240.

[11] Minute by Sir Arthur Nicolson, July 1, 1911, *Br. Docs.,* vol. VII, no. 339.

[12] Minute by Sir Arthur Nicolson, July 1, 1911, in Edward Grey, *Twenty-Five Years, 1892-1916,* vol. I, p. 222. The postscript printed here does not appear in the *British Documents.*

[13] See Chapter X, *supra.*   [14] Grey, *op. cit.,* vol. I, p. 245.

given for German action would apply at least as strongly to us [England]. We could not remain passive spectators of a new settlement made between Germany, France, and Spain to take the place of the Act of Algeciras. We must take part in such a discussion. . . ." Metternich commented that England had stood aside while France and Spain had taken parts of Morocco and that Germany expected her to remain a "benevolent spectator," Grey retorted that up to forty-eight hours ago Germany had also been a spectator and that her change of position compelled a change in the British rôle. Metternich, in reporting this conversation to his government, concluded with the statement, "I have the impression that he [Grey] fears a Franco-Spanish-German partition of Morocco by which England is to come out empty-handed. . . ." [15] Grey's statements of July 3 announced Britain's intention of safeguarding her right to enter into the discussion; and the official reply, made on July 4, reëmphasized this intention.

After the cabinet meeting on the morning of July 4, Grey gave his answer to Metternich.[16] This statement was a verbal and not a written communication, although Metternich requested and received permission to make a written note of the interview in the presence of the British foreign secretary. The British reply as reported by Metternich to his foreign office reads: "British attitude cannot be a disinterested one with regard to Morocco; we must have regard for treaty obligations with France and to British interests. We consider a new situation has been created by the dispatch of a German ship to Agadir; that future developments may affect British interests more directly than have hitherto been the case; that we cannot therefore recognize any new arrangement which is made without us." [17]

This reply was the communication that the cabinet had authorized Grey to make.[18] By it England had asserted her interest in the situation in an official manner. Her response contained no definite statement of any action that she proposed to take nor did it con-

---

[15] Metternich to F. O., July 3, 1911, *G. P.*, vol. XXIX, no. 10588; Grey to Count de Salis, July 3, 1911, *Br. Docs.*, vol. VII, no. 347.

[16] Metternich to F. O., July 4, 1911, *G. P.*, vol. XXIX, no. 10592; Grey to Count de Salis, July 4, 1911, *Br. Docs.*, vol. VII, no. 356.

[17] Metternich to F. O., July 4, 1911, *G. P.*, vol. XXIX, no. 10592.

[18] Grey, *op. cit.*, vol. I, p. 223.

tain any definite request for a reply from Berlin. German reception of this message is significant.

Metternich had received telegraphic instruction from Berlin on July 4 to guide him in his conference with the foreign secretary. In case England really threatened active measures, he was to assert to Grey that "the sending of a ship to Agadir was . . . a preventative measure . . . ," that events had forced Germany to recognize the need for a new solution of the Moroccan problem, and that she must guard German interests in the same manner as England must guard her own interests. He was also cautioned to "avoid carefully . . . leaving the impression that we [Germany] wished to encourage England to an active interference. . . ." [19]

Metternich reported that, as the British did not suggest taking active measures, he withheld the statements authorized in the telegram of instructions. Instead he replied that "a new situation arose far more through the military advance of France and Spain than through the sending of a German warship . . . ," and also asserted as his personal opinion that Germany had no desire "to exclude England from an eventual new formation of things. . . ." [20] The telegraphic instructions sent to Metternich were not sufficiently clear in an announcement of German purpose to have been of value in clarifying the atmosphere in London but did at least have the advantage of an authorized statement, while Metternich's vague and unauthorized replies were more in the nature of those indefinite statements made by diplomats while awaiting definitive instructions from their superiors.

Grey's reply to the official German notification of her *coup* was not the only indication of the British attitude. The London *Times* insisted that the government must "act up to the letter and to the spirit of our treaty obligations with France in the full sense which our own honour and our friendship with that country require. We must at the same time take care to protect our interests in Morocco—interests, both economic and political, which immensely outweigh any that Germany possesses there. . . ." [21] The British public had been sufficiently excited by the news as to provoke cer-

[19] Bethmann Hollweg to Metternich, July 4, 1911, *G. P.*, vol. XXIX, no. 10590.
[20] Metternich to F. O., July 4, 1911, *ibid.*, no. 10592.
[21] London *Times*, July 6, 1911 (Editorial).

tain questions in the House of Commons, to which the prime minister, Asquith, gave a response on July 6. He asserted that he actually knew little of the negotiations then under way between France and Germany, but that he wished "it clearly to be understood that a new situation has arisen in Morocco in which it is possible that future developments may affect British interests more directly than has hitherto been the case. I am confident that diplomatic discussion will find a solution, and in the part that we shall take in it we shall have due regard to the protection of those interests and to the fulfillment of our treaty obligations to France. . . ." [22] In commenting on this speech, the London *Times* stated that "After the plain language held by the Prime Minister it will be impossible for any one to ignore the fact that we have interests in Morocco, and that we are resolved to maintain them. . . ." [23]

There was general appreciation of Asquith's speech as a declaration of British interests in Morocco "separate from those entailed on her by her engagements to France. . . ." [24] Foreign courts and press soon learned of the British reply and recognized it as an announcement of British intention to be consulted on the points at issue. The *Journal des Débats* acclaimed the speech as a public notice that "Great Britain had reappeared on the scene." [25] Aehrenthal told Cartwright, British ambassador at Vienna, that Asquith's speech might leave the impression that England no longer stood by the Act of Algeciras. Cartwright assured him that such was not the case, but that England did recognize that compensation might be awarded Germany elsewhere.[26] The Austrian ambassador to London, Mensdorff, commented that the feeling in London was general that the "German demonstration in the only good Atlantic port was directed against England and the détente between

[22] *Parliamentary Debates,* 5th series, House of Commons, vol. XXVII, p. 1341.

[23] London *Times,* July 7, 1911 (Editorial).

[24] W. S. Blunt, *My Diaries, 1898-1914,* vol. II, p. 366. Blunt quoted Belloc as saying that France and Germany were too much afraid of each other to fight and that France would not join England in a war to keep Germany out of Agadir. "We shall have therefore to make up our minds either to submit to the German seizure of Agadir or to go to war with Germany alone or find her compensation elsewhere."

[25] *Journal des Débats,* July 7, 1911, in Gauvain, *op. cit.,* vol. III, p. 17.

[26] Aehrenthal to Szögyény, July 12, 1911, *Ö. U. A.,* vol. III, no. 2561.

here [London] and Berlin could again be placed in question. . . ." [27]

The British official reply to Metternich's communication of July 1, Asquith's speech, and the general public comment had emphasized not only the fact that the British government intended to safeguard British interests and to fulfil its obligations to France but also the right of England to be consulted in any settlement that might be made. Grey was at that time urging adjustment through conversations *à quatre;* that is, between England, France, Germany, and Spain. France did not favor such a solution; and upon Caillaux's refusal to adopt it, Grey dropped his plan, although he insisted that he would not agree to a settlement being made by France, Germany, and Spain without England. He was worried for fear that a partition would take place that would ignore British interests.[28] As a matter of fact, when Spain asked both Paris and Berlin to admit her to the conferences, she met with a refusal at each place.[29] Sir Eyre Crowe accounted for these German and French rebuffs "on the hypothesis that these two Powers are in fact agreed to settle the Morocco question between them in a sense entirely satisfactory to France. Otherwise, Germany would not be so foolish as to throw away the chance of worrying France by encouraging Spain. . . ." He feared that Germany's game was to separate France and England and secure for herself a basis for a friendly coöperation with France against England. He went even further than Grey in his suspicions. "There is," he stated, "a grave risk of British economic interests in Morocco being bartered away surreptitiously by France to Germany before we are told of what is going on. . . ." He did not trust France to keep her British friend fully informed of the negotiations, and he believed Cambon should be given a hint of British distrust.[30]

Although susceptible to Crowe's influence, Grey considered it unnecessary to warn France at that time but trusted her to keep him fully informed.[31] Nevertheless, Goschen, British ambassador

[27] Mensdorff to F. O., *ibid.,* no. 2555.   [28] See Chapter X, *supra.*

[29] Bethmann Hollweg to William II, July 12, 1911, *G. P.,* vol. XXIX, no. 10604; Goschen to Grey, July 14, 1911, *Br. Docs.,* vol. VII, no. 383.

[30] Goschen to Grey, July 14, 1911, *Br. Docs.,* vol. VII, no. 383, minute of Sir Eyre Crowe, July 15.

[31] Goschen to Grey, July 14, 1911, *ibid.,* minute of Sir Edward Grey, undated.

to Berlin, had called upon Kiderlen on July 12 and presented the British protest to any negotiations between Germany, France, and Spain that excluded England.[32] Kiderlen informed the British ambassador that "such an intention did not exist at any time at least not on our side. . . ." [33] England agreed to the negotiations being conducted à deux and ceased insisting upon direct participation after she was assured that Spain was not to be included. It was not partition of Morocco but partition which ignored British interests that Grey opposed. He therefore decided that "a reserved attitude on our part is the best position to assume" until the situation was more fully developed. He did not renounce British right to interference if her interests became involved but only reserved action.[34]

Metternich had had his conversation with Grey on July 4. His next appearance at the foreign office occurred on July 12, at which time he talked with Nicolson.[35] Though his visit was ostensibly on some trivial matter, Metternich soon broached the question of Morocco. He conscientiously defended his government's alleged reason for its coup (defense of German nationals and German interests), while Nicolson countered with the accepted British view that there was no danger whatsoever in the Sous, nor was it even known that there were Germans in that region. This Metternich himself now admitted, but he stated that there were German interests there and added that the British government "must not think that Germany ever intended to exclude England from any discussion in which the future of Morocco was concerned. . . ." To this comment, Nicolson replied that the British government "would maintain a reserved attitude until they knew what Germany's aims and desires were: at present they were completely ignorant of both. . . ." [36] To

---

[32] Goschen to Grey, July 12, 1911, ibid., no. 373. This despatch gives an account of the Kissingen interview as Cambon reported it to Goschen. With reference to this report, Crowe remarked, "I confess to being, for the moment, altogether nonplussed, and can find no answer to the question: What is Germany really driving at? Herr von Kiderlen's behaviour seems almost inexplicable. . . ." —Goschen to Grey, July 12, 1911, ibid., minute of Crowe, July 17, 1911.

[33] Note of Kiderlen, July 12, 1911, G. P., vol. XXIX, no. 10603.

[34] Goschen to Grey, July 14, 1911, Br. Docs., vol. VII, no. 383.

[35] Grey to Goschen, July 17, 1911, ibid., no. 388; Nicolson to Goschen, July 18, 1911, ibid., no. 395; Benckendorff to Neratov, July 19, 1911, Siebert, op. cit., no. 688.

[36] Grey to Goschen, July 17, 1911, Br. Docs., vol. VII, no. 388.

Nicolson's surprise, Metternich then launched into a lengthy peroration, a pæan to the glorious history of Germany, which ended in a denunciation of the imperialism of France, the vanquished one, and of England—an imperialism which had built for each a great colonial empire, while Germany, the victorious, had acquired nothing of value. Germany, he declared, was justified in demanding a great deal, and none should dispute her claims. Such a disquisition was so contrary to the character of the usually taciturn ambassador that Nicolson was greatly worried, and he reported the interview to Cambon with the warning that Germany would evidently not be content with a mere rectification of the Congo frontier. From this interview, which he dubbed a "curious conversation," Nicolson gained no definite information of German purpose or objectives but only an increased nervousness as to what that unknown quantity, Kiderlen, might produce.[37] Benckendorff reported that after this interview Nicolson "looked at everything rather darkly."[38] Metternich, on his side, was quite as mystified as any of the various chancelleries and was in no position to make definite statements as to the intentions of his chief. The conference of July 12 was in no sense a response to the British reply of July 4.

Nicolson and some of his associates were almost as nervous over possible French action as they were over German. Especially did they fear that France might presently cede a Moroccan port to Germany. Grey, however, did not share this uneasiness but viewed the situation optimistically.[39] On July 10 Paul Cambon informed him that the Franco-German negotiations were to proceed on the basis of the Congo and that France wished to know if England had any objections. Grey stated that he assumed that the French Congo was what was meant and that he did not see any objections from the British viewpoint. When Cambon informed him that "under no circumstances could the French allow Germany to establish herself in Morocco . . . ," he replied that "though public opinion here would expect guarantees from Germany and some compensation for her being established in Morocco, we [England] did not mind an open port on the west coast of Morocco. We thought that

---

[37] Nicolson to Goschen, July 18, 1911, *ibid.*, no. 395.

[38] Benckendorff to Neratov, July 19, 1911, Siebert, *op. cit.*, no. 688.

[39] Grey to Bertie, July 6, 1911, *Br. Docs.*, vol. VII, no. 363.

it would be physically very difficult for Germany to turn it into a naval base, and that if she attempted to do so, so long as we had the stronger Fleet, we could prevent its being done. . . ." He added, however, that if France regarded such a concession as impossible, she would have to revert to the *status quo* of the Algeciras Act or give Germany compensation elsewhere.[40] The disinterested view which Grey evidently took relative to the Congo and his attitude toward Germany's possible acquisition of a port on the west coast of Morocco did not meet with the approval of his subordinates. In fact, the British ambassador in Paris refused to accept his lenient opinion as final and at once set forth to change it.

Sir Francis Bertie with his strong pro-French sympathies had long and efficiently served England as ambassador to Paris.[41] On July 11 he reported to Grey that he had discussed the Kiderlen-Cambon conversation of July 9 with Selves and that he had told the French foreign minister that the "Congo being of great extent, it was impossible, until German desires were made known, to judge how British interests might be affected by their being granted. . . . With respect to . . . the establishment of Germany on the Atlantic Coast of Morocco, even if there were a French Government prepared to acquiesce in such an arrangement, British Government would never consent to it for it would be contrary to vital interests of England. . . ." [42] Sir Eyre Crowe and Sir Arthur Nicolson, both apprehensive of German aggression, agreed with Bertie that it was "at least premature" for Great Britain to "disinterest herself" formally in any question of compensation on the Congo. Crowe feared that Kiderlen had no intention of accepting a frontier rectification and warned his government to "be on their guard" so long as the Germans stayed at Agadir.[43] In a despatch of July 12, Bertie urged upon his chief the necessity of preventing German

---

[40] Grey to Bertie, July 10, 1911, *ibid.*, no. 368.

[41] Steed, *op. cit.*, p. 343; E. Reventlow, *Politische Vorgeschichte des Grossen Krieges*, p. 238. Schoen complained of Bertie's pro-French sympathies. He stated that the "inciting activity against us here has gradually become so notorious that it even arouses . . . head shaking on the part of the French. . . ." He added that Bertie was the same type as Cartwright but that no one took him seriously.—Schoen to Bethmann Hollweg, Sept. 28, 1911, *G. P.*, vol. XXIX, no. 10651.   [42] Bertie to Grey, July 11, 1911, *Br. Docs.*, vol. VII, no. 369.

[43] Bertie to Grey, July 11, 1911, *ibid.*, minute by Crowe, July 12.

acquisition of a port on the Moroccan littoral.[44] Grey replied that
he had discussed the question with the admiralty, whose opinion
was that England "need not and cannot be irreconcilable about the
West Coast of Morocco. . . ." His chief concern was to prevent
France from placing the "whole burden of keeping Germany out
of Morocco" upon England.[45] Again he wrote that "we should
think anything that gave Germany a footing on the Mediterranean
absolutely irreconcilable with British interests. A footing on West
Coast regarded solely from [the] British point of view is not vital
so long as no port is fortified. We should require binding engage-
ment to that effect and could rely upon our own sea power to prevent fortifications. . . . ." Although he did not stand irrevocably
opposed to German acquisition of a Moroccan port, in the light
of the excitable nature of public opinion he considered such a solution the least desirable.[46]

This reply excited and worried Bertie as much as it did the
French foreign minister, and he turned to Nicolson in an effort to
convert the foreign office to his views. He stated that Selves was
"very much taken back by the change of attitude which Cambon
found or thought he noticed" in the British attitude. He argued at
length that Germany could not be trusted to remain faithful to any
treaty-pledge not to fortify a port in Morocco. In support of his
view he declared that Germany might decide to fortify at a time
when Great Britain was so occupied elsewhere that her protest
could easily be ignored. Under the present circumstances, England
had the support of France in her opposition to such a cession; but
there was no assurance that French support would be effective at
a later time if England found it necessary to protest German for-
tification of the port. Furthermore, he feared that if Germany
gained the impression that England was not "unalterably" opposed to "their having a commercial port," she would use the opportunity to "squeeze the French." [47]

Before the officials in the British foreign office had ceased argu-
ing over German possession of a Moroccan port, they received the

---

[44] Bertie to Grey, July 12, 1911, *ibid.,* no. 372.
[45] Grey to Bertie, July 12, 1911, *ibid.,* no. 375.
[46] Grey to Bertie, July 13, 1911, *ibid.,* no. 377.
[47] Bertie to Nicolson, July 16, 1911, *ibid.,* no. 386.

news of the Kiderlen-Cambon conversation of July 15.[48] In a private letter of July 17 Bertie pressed the foreign secretary for an expression of England's position on the vital question of German demands. Again he emphasized the danger to British interests of German acquisition of an Atlantic port or of such points as Libreville or Brazzaville.[49] His private letter to Grey was sent before he had fully discussed the situation with the French officials, and after a conference with Selves and Paul Cambon on July 18, he dispatched a "Very Urgent" telegram in which he gave to the foreign office a full report of the French account of the July 15 conversation.[50]

The French officials, interested in holding British support, naturally impressed upon Bertie the injury that the German demands would inflict upon British interests as they related to German possession of an Atlantic port on the African littoral. Paul Cambon "enlarged on the injury to British interests which if acceded to they [the German demands] would involve. Germany would have in . . . Libreville a port on the Atlantic which would detract from British interests. She would soon add to what she had taken of the French Congo the Spanish settlement between it and the Cameroons and also absorb the Portuguese possessions. . . ." Yet both Cambon and Selves believed that the real purpose underlying German action was the acquisition of a port on the Moroccan coast and that the unacceptable demands were merely a ruse employed to force the issue back upon a partition of Morocco.[51]

France had asserted that she intended to keep her friends and allies informed of the course of the negotiations. This she did, but only in so far as such action aided her. On July 18 she informed England of the German demands but carefully selected and edited her news with a view of holding British support. French officials failed to mention that Germany had offered Togo as an object of exchange. As Grey had indicated that he was not unalterably opposed to German possession of a port on the Atlantic and as he had stated that the question of the French Congo related only to France, it was to her interest to develop the idea that Germany

[48] See Chapter X, *supra*.
[49] Bertie to Grey, July 17, 1911, *Br. Docs.*, vol. VII, no. 391.
[50] Bertie to Grey, July 18, 1911, *ibid.*, no. 392.   [51] *Ibid.*

had presented unacceptable demands. For this reason, perhaps, she failed to mention the one ameliorating point in the discussion of July 15, and in all fairness she should have reported the entire negotiation. As a matter of fact, the British government gained its first news of the proposed exchange from the German side. Kiderlen gave Goschen the information on July 21, though the foreign office did not receive the despatch reporting the interview in full until July 24.[52] At all events, on July 21 the British foreign office did not know of the Togo proposal. Both England and Germany had a grievance in this connection, for France could not be trusted to transmit a reasonably unbiased report of the state of affairs. Germany complained that France took an unfair advantage and prejudiced British views in order to tighten the bonds of the Entente,[53] while England, for her part, grumbled over the difficulties of reaching a decision when only partial truths were served her.[54]

British distrust of Germany, however, was greater than distrust of France, and the conference between Selves, Paul Cambon, and Bertie had the desired effect. Sir Eyre Crowe commented, "We begin to see the light. Germany is playing for the highest stakes. If her demands are acceded to either on the Congo or in Morocco, . . . it will mean definitely the subjection of France. . . . This is a trial of strength, if anything. Concession means not loss of interests or loss of prestige. It means defeat. . . . The defeat of France is a matter vital to this country. . . ." [55] Nicolson was frankly worried and described the situation as serious. "France naturally cannot make the cession demanded of her. Germany may modify her Congo demands, but in that case she will remain at Agadir—and this would be equally unacceptable to France. . . ." [56] He urged that France and England present a united front in the crisis; for only in that manner could they hope that "Germany will moderate her demands or keep them within reasonable limits, for were she to

[52] Goschen to Grey, July 21, 1911, *Br. Docs.*, vol. VII, no. 410.

[53] Schwabach to Alfred Rothschild, July 28, 1911, in Schwabach, *op. cit.*, pp. 201-204.

[54] Memorandum by Sir Eyre Crowe respecting Franco-German negotiations, *Br. Docs.*, vol. VII, App. III, pp. 821-826.

[55] Bertie to Grey, July 18, 1911, *ibid.*, no. 392, minute of Crowe, July 18.

[56] Bertie to Grey, July 18, 1911, *ibid.*, no. 392, minute of A. Nicolson.

detect the slightest wavering or indifference on our side, she would no doubt press France with extreme rigour and the latter would either have to fight or surrender. . . ." He stressed the danger that might arise if the British government were "beguiled into admitting the harmlessness of the establishment of a large German settlement on the Atlantic Coast, for whatever engagements the Germans may give as to the innocuous character of such a settlement and of its purely commercial and peaceful intentions, there is no doubt that whenever they thought it desirable, they would convert a commercial port into a naval base. . . ." [57]

Nicolson and Crowe viewed the situation in the light of British interests and viewed it darkly.[58] Grey, harrassed by fear of German aggression, by uneasiness over possible French infidelity, and by the importunities of his subordinates, ceased to consider the cession of a Moroccan port as feasible and recommended that France offer counter-proposals since the German demands seemed unacceptable.[59] In case the negotiations failed, he suggested that the British government might well propose a conference of the Algeciras Powers and intimated that, in event of refusal, England would take whatever action might be necessary to protect her interests. He repeated his statement that his government did not consider "it vital to their interests to exclude Germany from getting any foothold in Morocco provided satisfactory conditions are obtained from her . . ." and added the further comment that the British government "cannot . . . make any admission of Germany into Morocco a *casus belli* unconditionally. . . ." Nevertheless, he insisted that such admission would be acceptable only under conditions satisfactory to France.[60] Bertie submitted the views of his chief to the French foreign office and requested that the French government should deliver to him its program in order that Grey might know what procedure it would accept before he presented the situation to the cabinet on the morning of July 21.[61] Selves replied that the pourparlers between France and Germany were not broken but

[57] Nicolson to Goschen, July 18, 1911, *ibid.*, no. 395.

[58] Benckendorff to Neratov, July 19, 1911, Siebert, *op. cit.*, no. 688.

[59] Grey to Bertie, July 19, 1911, *Br. Docs.*, vol. VII, no. 396.

[60] Grey to Bertie, July 19, 1911, *ibid.*, no. 397.

[61] Bertie to Grey, July 20, 1911, *ibid.*, no. 401.

would probably last a long time. In case the negotiations did break down, France would acknowledge British right to propose a conference; and as England would be taking the initiative, the formation of the program would belong to her. The major portion of the Selves memorandum was devoted to a denunciation of any German acquisition in Morocco on the ground that such an award would violate the Entente Cordiale and the Franco-German Accord of 1909. Consequently, France refused to admit into the conference as a subject for discussion the question of a concession "by any title whatsoever to the German government of a portion, be it ever so small, of Moroccan territory. . . ." [62]

Nicolson, concerned more over the fate of the Entente than over any other issue, advised Grey not to reply to Bertie's communication at this juncture, since "the moment may arrive when we shall have to deal with the situation on far broader grounds and from a higher standpoint than are offered by the wording of existing agreements or by the relative values of ports or districts on the western coast of Africa. . . ." He thought it wiser to await developments, but he urged his government to be careful not to give France any grounds for suspecting that the "Triple Entente is in any way weakening. Were she to come to distrust us, she would probably try to make terms with Germany irrespective of us, while Germany who would soon detect our hesitation would be inclined to impose far harder terms than may be the case at present. . . ." If France gained the idea that England had failed her, the Triple Entente would be broken and England would be faced with a hostile and triumphant Germany.[63] Nicolson, even more than Grey, was convinced that the future of British policy was inextricably bound to the maintenance of the Entente and that consequently the government must not take any action that might endanger its friendship with France.

Grey's sense of impartiality struggled with his loyalty to the Entente and caused him to write his representative in Paris a private letter, the general tenor of which was more sympathetic to German than to French views. "The French have drifted into difficulties without knowing which way they really want to go . . . ," he

---

[62] Bertie to Grey, July 20, 1911, *ibid.*, no. 403.

[63] Minute by Nicolson, *ibid.*, no. 409.

began. "We are bound and prepared to give them diplomatic support, but we cannot go to war in order to set aside the Algeciras Act and put France in virtual possession of Morocco. . . ." He added that England would not oppose French acquisition of the Sherifian empire if she could attain it peacefully, but "if we go to war it must be in defense of British interests. . . ." He then uttered a word of reprimand for France, Spain, and Germany, all of whom had violated the Algeciras Act, though "France perhaps is less wrong technically because she went to Fez at the request of the Sultan, but in effect she has turned Morocco into a French protectorate. . . ." He conceded that in justice to German ambitions, France and England must recognize that German imperialism had not received rewards commensurate to those received by the British and French, and that if either were to gain additional territory, Germany must be granted compensations. "Of course," he said, "I see that Germany is asking more than France can give in the French Congo and that these negotiations may come to nothing. If so there is only one way of getting Germany out of Agadir and that is a Conference demanding a strict return to the *status quo* of the Algeciras Act." Grey had, however, an additional proposal: partition of Morocco between France, Spain, and Germany, in which "France would get the lion's share and we [England] should want some compensation from Germany which we should look to ourselves to obtain. . . ." If partition failed, only a return to the *status quo* of Algeciras seemed possible.[64] Threat of a return to the *status quo* was a weapon Kiderlen used against France and not one to be expected in the hands of the British friend.

Grey also telegraphed Bertie his views on the question of the preëmptive rights to the Belgian Congo and expressed his opinion that "the admission of Germany to a share in French preëmption rights of the Belgian Congo might be a possible element of bargain, if Germany would withdraw her excessive demand about French Congo. . . ." He took the precaution to state that this must be "without prejudice to the rights of Belgium . . ." and that the British government must reserve the right to purchase such parts of Belgian Congo as it deemed expedient.[65]

[64] Grey to Bertie, July 20, 1911, *ibid.*, no. 405.
[65] Grey to Bertie, July 20, 1911, *ibid.*, no. 402.

Bertie, more in sympathy with Nicolson's views than with Grey's, received the latter's communications with some degree of alarm. As he "thought it advisable not to frighten" Selves, he took advantage of the discretion granted him and discussed the situation without speaking of the suggested partition of Morocco. "I think," he asserted, "that if we talked now of a partition of Morocco between France, Spain, and Germany as a settlement which would be acceptable to us, we should alarm the French Government. They might feel that they were about to be deserted by us for the benefit of Germany. . . ." Consequently, he discussed only the question of preëmption rights as a possible means of securing a reduction of German demands in the French Congo. He informed Selves that he was going to London to discuss the situation with his superiors and wished to have a definite statement of France's position before he left.[66] After his interview with the foreign minister, he saw Caillaux, who complained of the British change of attitude relative to German occupation of a Moroccan port. The French premier reemphasized the points made by Selves that France "could not at any price consent to Germany establishing herself in Morocco . . ." and that if England deserted her on that point, the Entente would suffer a serious blow.[67]

Although the report of the conversations with Selves and Caillaux did not reach the foreign office until July 22, the telegraphic report of Selves's memorandum, if not the memorandum itself, was in Grey's hands on the morning of July 21, before his meeting with the cabinet. He was cognizant of the fact that France was determined to resist German acquisition of any portion of Morocco and that she expected British support in reducing German demands in the French Congo. If Germany were determined to secure her demands or to use a refusal as a cause for remaining in Agadir, a serious situation could easily develop that would menace England as a member of the Entente. This fact weighed heavily upon the foreign secretary as he pondered upon the course of British policy. IIis subordinates, Bertie, Nicolson, and Crowe, were even more disturbed by the situation; for in addition to their loyalty to the Entente, they viewed German acquisition of a port on the Atlantic

---

[66] Bertie to Grey, July 21, 1911, *ibid.,* no. 407.
[67] Bertie to Grey, July 21, 1911, *ibid.,* no. 408.

littoral of Morocco as definitely hostile to peculiarly British interests.

Those who state that Grey "was haunted by the idea of a partition of Morocco with Germany . . ." [68] need to read the series of letters and telegrams that he dispatched to Bertie on July 19 and 20, in which he proposed partition with adequate safeguards for British interests and reiterated his views that a German port on the Atlantic coast of Morocco would not be *per se* dangerous to Great Britain. He later complained of the danger of a partition that ignored British interests or involved her treaty obligations; [69] but opposition to the idea itself came not from him but from France, from other British officials, and from the public opinion of France and England. Grey's greatest fear was that the Entente with France might be broken and in that manner British interests be endangered not only in Africa but throughout the world. Fay's statement that "Grey would have been less disturbed in his mind if he had known that Germany's real objective was the Congo and not a naval base on the Atlantic coast of Morocco . . ." [70] is true; not because he was unalterably opposed to German acquisition of a port, but because he was determined to maintain the Entente. He was uneasy over the situation because he believed that France was determined to uphold her view that the German demands were exorbitant and, being unable to penetrate the German silence, he feared the multitude of consequences that continued strain could produce.

The British public caught a glimpse of the gathering storm when on July 20 the London *Times*, whose pronouncements were usually considered as semi-official in character, published an account of the German demands accompanied by an explanatory map on which was depicted the danger of such concessions to the British Empire. The acquisition of French Congo was viewed as only the first step in a grandiose scheme by which Germany planned to secure an empire expanding so as to include the Cameruns, French Congo, the Portuguese colony of Angola, German West Africa, the Belgian Congo, and German East Africa.

---

[68] Beazley, *op. cit.,* p. 50; Lutz, *op. cit.,* p. 129.

[69] *Par. Deb.,* 5th series, House of Commons, vol. XXXII, p. 51.

[70] *Op. cit.,* vol. I, p. 287.

The article pointed out that such an empire would not only block the Cape to Cairo project but actually endanger the Union of South Africa.[71] In the same issue, the *Times*, speaking editorially, announced that these demands were "so extravagant that we shall be slow to regard them as seriously made. German statesmen . . . must know perfectly well that no French Government could for a moment entertain them. They must know equally well that no British Government could consent to suffer so great a change to be made in the distribution of power in Africa, even were a French Government to be found feeble enough to sanction it. . . ." This journal then called upon Asquith "to make good his words" of July 6 to defend British interests. "We do not, and cannot, believe," it declared, "that the claims for the French Congo and for the contingent reversion of the Congo State are anything more than audacious and not very skilful or judicious 'bluff' " and advised the government to strengthen British protest by "the visit of one or two British ships to Agadir. . . ."[72]

The warlike article of the *Times* failed to stir the British public from its lethargy. There was some belief that "Germany has made terms not only with France but with Russia, in order to break up their entente" with England and was "determined on having their naval station on the Atlantic whether we choose or not," but in general, "People don't believe in war as a possible thing concerning England. . . ."[73] The public and the government were engrossed in domestic difficulties which hid from their view the grave dangers involved in the Moroccan situation. The liberal cabinet had on its hands the bitter conflict over the reorganization of the House of Lords, which attracted more attention in the home papers than did such remote problems as the French Congo.[74] In addition, the dock strike had caused such a shortage of wheat that immediate settlement was imperative, whatever foreign entanglements might develop.[75] The fate of an African country could not excite the British public while local problems were pressing. Only

[71] London *Times*, July 21, 1911; Metternich to F. O., July 20, 1911, *G. P.*, vol. XXIX, no. 10616.   [72] London *Times*, July 20, 1911.

[73] Blunt, *op. cit.*, vol. I, p. 369 (July 20).

[74] *Annual Register*, 1911, pp. 159-180; J. S. Spender, *Great Britain: Empire and Commonwealth, 1886-1935*, pp. 381-397.

[75] Blunt, *op. cit.*, vol. I, p. 366 (July 20).

when the fate of that country was tied to British honor and prestige did the man on the street become interested. Before that took place, however, other factors entered to disturb the Asquith ministry.

British and German navies used Norwegian waters for their maneuvers and were both planning cruises into that region. On July 14, Kiderlen learned that the schedule for both navies was so timed that they would meet at Molde on July 29.[76] As the Kaiser was visiting in Norway, Kiderlen, who knew the explosive temper of his Emperor, was greatly distressed for fear of what might happen. According to his own account, he consulted Goschen to see if arrangements could be made to prevent the meeting.[77] Goschen reported that Kiderlen had explained the situation in this manner: "You know the Emperor pretty well, . . . and you can imagine how excited he will be at the sight of the two Squadrons. He will certainly want to make the most of the opportunity and there is every chance that, as an Admiral in both Navies, he will amuse Himself by putting Himself at the head of the combined squadrons and going through a series of Naval Manoeuvres—ending with a great Banquet, Toasts and God knows what. . . ." Kiderlen added that as the papers were starved for news, they would take advantage of the meeting to play it before the public, either in such manner as to indicate an Anglo-German naval agreement, which would frighten France, or in such manner as to suggest a display of force on the part of each in an effort to intimidate the other. Either of the interpretations could be flaunted in such a sensational manner as to inflame the public of all three countries. Kiderlen suggested that the British squadron delay in order to arrive only on the evening of the twenty-ninth, too late for an imperial demonstration.[78] Nicolson agreed that a meeting of the fleets would be undesirable but placed the blame for the situation upon the Germans; and, consistent in his suspicions of German motives, he remarked, "It is curious how persistent the Germans are to sow discord between us and France. . . ." He then informed Goschen that he would discuss the situation with Grey at once and send

---

[76] Kiderlen related that a sailor came to see him and told him of the meeting of the fleets.—Kiderlen to Y., July 14, 1911, in Caillaux, *op. cit.*, pp. 289-291.

[77] *Ibid.*   [78] Goschen to Nicolson, July 14, 1911, *Br. Docs.* vol. VII, no. 632.

him advice;[79] but evidently nothing was done, for on July 22 Goschen again sought instructions. Kiderlen had seen him on July 21 and repeated the warning that anything could result from such a meeting. "At the end of three days," he said, "they might either fraternise too much and exchange compliments to such an extent as to disturb the minds of other Powers; or they might on the contrary be shaking their fists in each other's faces with an equally disturbing result. . . ."[80] Nicolson had also received a disquieting private note from Admiral Bethell, which began, "We are rather anxious here about the German High Sea Fleet which is cruising in Norwegian Waters where the Atlantic Fleet is also to cruise. It is desirable that the two fleets should not meet. . . ." The admiralty asked the foreign office to secure for it the date schedule of the German navy and as much information of the German movements as it could obtain.[81]

Although Nicolson's letter to Grey was not dispatched until July 24, it was indicative of the intense nervousness at London, a nervousness which, we know, had pervaded the admiralty three days earlier. Nicolson wrote: "Please do not think me demented— but Ottley has drawn my attention, once directly and once through Crowe, to the fact that the German High Sea Fleet, cruiser squadron and torpedo flotilla are all concentrated near and about the Norwegian coasts—and in a good position for a 'bolt from the blue,' a contingency which the Defense Committee though considering it most improbable, did not deem that it should be quite ruled out. I have also thought it odd that Kiderlen was so anxious our Fleets should not meet—and it is just possible that he had in his mind that our vessels should not see what the others were doing. . . ."[82] Grey, the same day, expressed his opinion that there was no cause for alarm at that moment, but added that if relations became strained, Germany could take advantage of the fact that her fleet was mobilized and use "mobilization for manoeuvres at full strength for attack. . . ."[83] The British admiralty, in the

[79] Nicolson to Goschen, July 18, 1911, ibid., no. 633.
[80] Goschen to Nicolson, July 22, 1911, ibid., no. 635.
[81] Admiral Bethell to Nicolson, July 21, 1911, ibid., no. 634.
[82] Nicolson to Grey, July 24, 1911, ibid., no. 636.
[83] Grey to McKenna, July 24, 1911, ibid., no. 637.

meantime, was decidedly wrought up over the possible activities of the German fleet; nor did the fact that the German officials were equally nervous relieve the strain.

A glance along the political horizon on the morning of July 21 discovered little to encourage the Asquith ministry as it met in cabinet session. The dock strike was in full swing; the Parliament Bill[84] had the day before faced a third reading in the House of Lords and the bitter struggle between the government and the die-hards was in its intense stage; France had informed England of the German demands and had exerted her persuasive powers to convince the British government that she could not, and would not, yield and that British interests were vitally affected; and the British admiralty was seeking to arouse the foreign office to the danger of a meeting of the British and German fleets and the possibility of a "bolt from the blue." Closely woven into this disturbed pattern was the growing fear of some lurking menace hidden in German silence. The British government had tried to fathom the ultimate purpose of the Swabian secretary but to no avail.

The German notification of her Agadir *coup* had been delivered July 1; the British reply, in which Britain's determination to safeguard her interests and maintain her obligations was asserted, had been given on July 4; and other than Metternich's "curious conversation" with Nicolson on July 12, no further communication had been received from the German foreign office. This continued silence led to increased suspicion of German motives. In his explanation to Parliament, November 27, Grey stated that the foreign office had received information from other quarters that a "partition of Morocco, arrived at by negotiations to which it was not intended we should be a party . . ." was the German objective. He then learned, he said, of the Congo demands, which were so exorbitant and so unacceptable to France that the "negotiations would be thrown back on some other basis and the question of the possible partition would arise again. . . ." [85] Breakdown of negotiations loaded with consequences dangerous to European peace

[84] The Parliament Bill of 1911 gave control of legislation to the House of Commons and relegated the House of Lords to a subordinate position.

[85] *Par. Deb.*, 5th series, House of Commons, vol. XXXII, pp. 47, 48.

might then result. By July 19 Grey was convinced that some
definite information must be secured from Germany to allay the
growing suspicion of her motives. He therefore addressed a request
to Asquith that he be empowered to "make some communication
to Germany to impress upon her that, if the negotiations between
her and France come to nothing, we must become a party to a
discussion of the situation. . . ." He explained to his premier that
fifteen days had passed since he had delivered the British reply to
Metternich, and as the German government had not indicated that
they recognized the British position, he feared Germany would
"assume that we [England] know the demand they have made
upon France and if we give no sign, their attitude will stiffen . . .";
and since the British government did not know what was happening at Agadir, he also feared that the "long ignorance and silence
combined must lead the Germans to imagine that we don't very
much care. . . ." [86] He received the necessary authorization and
summoned Metternich into conference during the afternoon of
July 21.[87]

Grey explained to the German ambassador that the British
government had waited in the hopes that France and Germany
would reach a satisfactory adjustment of their difficulties, but
that he had heard that German demands were so excessive that it
was evident that France could not accept them, and that the
question of German objective in Agadir again loomed large. As
Agadir was a closed port, it was impossible to discover what the
Germans were doing, "whether German troops are landed there,
or whether treaties were concluded there which injure the economic
share of others. . . ." [88] Agadir, well-adapted to become a naval
base, was of peculiar interest to the British. If the negotiations
over the Congo should break down, British interests would become
definitely involved and the British government must, accordingly,
be admitted into the conversations. Metternich, as much in the
dark as Grey, replied that he had no information to deliver; but,
conscientious in his defense of German interests, he asserted that

[86] Grey to Asquith, July 19, 1911, *Br. Docs.,* vol. VII, no. 399.

[87] Grey to Goschen, July 21, 1911, *ibid.,* no. 411; Metternich to Bethmann
Hollweg, July 21, 1911, *G. P.,* vol. XXIX, no. 10617.

[88] Grey to Goschen, July 21, 1911, *Br. Docs.,* vol. VII, no. 411.

Germany had no intention of injuring British rights or interests and that Grey should be willing to wait until such injury had been inflicted. He argued that Germany was not bound by the Anglo-French agreement of 1904 but only by the Algeciras Act and the Accord of 1909, both of which recognized the independence of the sultan, which France had destroyed. He criticized British policy that used "one measure for France, another for Germany," for what France had done in Morocco was infinitely more than what Germany had done; yet England upheld France in her actions but wished to denounce Germany.[89] Grey remarked keenly that "at any rate, whatever France had done had been known to the world. She had not occupied a closed port from which she could operate without anyone else knowing what was happening. . . ."[90] From this conversation Metternich gained the idea that Grey feared the failure of the Franco-German negotiations and, possibly because of French pressure, he sought to inject England into the conferences. He also understood that Grey would support France and grant to Germany "no fulcrum in Agadir," but that outside Morocco he extended "all possible good wishes."[91] The British foreign secretary asserted that he "impressed upon Count Metternich" that England "must join in a discussion of the situation if it continued without any settlement with France being reached. . . ."[92] Later he said that he held this interview because he was afraid the Franco-German negotiations would fail and a solution that would affect British interests and bring into operation British treaty obligations would result.[93] If he specifically urged Metternich to secure definite information from Berlin, neither his nor the German ambassador's reports reveal the fact; but his anxious tones and his insistence that England must be admitted into the discussion should have prompted Metternich to secure instructions at once.

But Grey's maneuvers had no effect. Metternich's despatch of the preceding day, which reported the inflammatory *Times* article

---

[89] Metternich to Bethmann Hollweg, July 21, 1911, *G. P.,* vol. XXIX, no. 10617.
[90] Grey to Goschen, July 21, 1911, *Br. Docs.,* vol. VII, no. 411.
[91] Metternich to Bethmann Hollweg, July 21, 1911, *G. P.,* vol. XXIX, no. 10617.
[92] Grey to Goschen, July 21, 1911, *Br. Docs.,* vol. VII, no. 411.
[93] *Par. Deb.,* 5th series, House of Commons, vol. XXXII, pp. 50, 51.

but did not seek instructions, had not been answered. Although he now sought instructions, he did not consider the situation sufficiently urgent for him to use the telegraph service but merely entrusted his report of the Grey interview to the regular post and then leisurely awaited instructions. The interview had taken place in the afternoon of July 21 and his despatch was dated as of the same day. Under such circumstances, reply from Berlin could not be expected before July 22, unless the home office recognized the urgency of the situation from his report of July 20 and wired its instructions. In the interim events in London were moving with great rapidity.

From the moment the *Panther* appeared before Agadir, Sir Francis Bertie, Sir Arthur Nicolson, and Sir Eyre Crowe watched every German move with increasing apprehension. Sir Edward Grey, more and more convinced of the danger, gradually became converted to their views. Winston Churchill, then in the home office, stated that the question of German motives occupied "repeatedly" the attention of the British cabinet,[94] and that he became convinced that British withdrawal would not help the situation but that "a very decided word would have to be spoken and spoken before it was too late. . . ." Convinced that German intentions "were malignant," he acknowledged that he "read all the papers and telegrams which began to pass with a suspicion and . . . could see beneath the calm of Sir Edward Grey a growing and at some moments a grave anxiety. . . ."[95] Churchill, who before the end of the month experienced a spasm of terror, had become infected with the virus of fear even before July 21.

A more important victim of the epidemic of nervousness which now seemed to plague the British cabinet was the pro-German, pacifist chancellor of the exchequer, David Lloyd George. While the British cabinet was predominantly liberal-imperialist in complexion, Lord Morley, Lord Loreburn, and Lloyd George had tended to keep them in check.[96] The general impression had gained ground that the pro-French proclivities of Sir Edward Grey were best restrained by the pro-German sympathies of David Lloyd George. The attitude of the vigorous Welshman became, there-

[94] Winston Churchill, *The World Crisis*, p. 29.
[95] *Ibid.*, p. 30.   [96] *Ibid.*; Grey, *op. cit.*, vol. I, p. 225; Wolff, *op. cit.*, p. 53.

fore, of peculiar importance in this period of tension. Churchill
stated that for weeks Lloyd George could not make up his mind.
"But on the morning of July 21, when I visited him before the
Cabinet, I found a different man. His mind was made up. He saw
quite clearly the course to take. He knew what to do and how and
when to do it. . . . He told me that he was to address the Bankers
at their Annual Dinner that evening. . . . He showed me what he
had prepared, and told me that he would show it to the Prime
Minister and Sir Edward Grey after the Cabinet. . . ." Churchill
assured him that he approved of his proposed plan.[97]

The deflection of Lloyd George to the opposite wing of the
party was surprising but thorough. His later explanation of his
action bristled with antagonism mingled with fear of his Teutonic
friend. He wrote: "When the rude indifference of the German
Government to our communication had lasted for seventeen days.
. . . I felt that matters were growing tensely critical and that we
were drifting clumsily towards war. It was not merely that by failing even to send a formal acknowledgment of the Foreign Secretary's letter the Germans were treating us with intolerable inso-
lence, but that their silence might well mean that they were blindly
ignorant of the sense in which we treated our obligations under the
Treaty, and might not realize until too late that we felt bound to
stand by France. . . ."[98] He, therefore, decided some action
must be taken to impress upon German officials the seriousness of
British views.[99]

The cabinet meeting took place on the morning of July 21.[100]
In the afternoon, Lloyd George consulted both Asquith and Grey,
since he did not feel that he had the right to meddle in foreign

---

[97] Churchill, *op. cit.,* p. 31.

[98] David Lloyd George, *War Memoirs,* vol. I, p. 41.

[99] Wolfgang Kleinknecht maintains that either Crowe or Nicolson was responsible for the idea of Lloyd George's speech. He believes that, discouraged
over their failure to force Grey into vigorous action, they decided that if the
pacifist pro-German chancellor of the exchequer could be aroused, Grey would
be convinced of the danger. They therefore served Lloyd George with sufficiently
exciting news as to inflame his sense of national pride and arouse him to action.
—*Die englische Politik in der Agadirkrise (1911),* pp. 76-77. But Kleinknecht's
deductions are conjectures based on the known anti-German feeling of the two
members of the foreign office and not on conclusive proof.

[100] Churchill, *op. cit.,* p. 31.

affairs without their consent.[101] He therefore submitted the terms of his speech to the prime minister, who fully approved and sent immediately for the foreign secretary "in order to obtain his views and procure his sanction. My recollection is that when he arrived, he cordially assented to every word of my draft. . . ." [102] Grey[103] and Asquith[104] have confirmed his statement of their approval. Grey stated that "The speech was entirely Lloyd George's own idea. I did nothing to instigate it, but I welcomed it. . . ." [105] Lloyd George himself acknowledged responsibility for the speech and scorned the rumor that he "was merely acting as mouthpiece to read out a statement prepared by the cabinet, and was at most but vaguely aware of its implications. . . . The initiative in this matter was my own, as was the wording of the statement," he stated. "Certainly I secured authoritative approval before I made it, but it was not actually submitted to the whole cabinet in advance. . . ." [106] The consultation between Grey, Asquith, and Lloyd George apparently took place after the Grey-Metternich conversation; for Grey in the course of his account of this interview given to Parliament, stated that "What I had said to the German Ambassador that day as regards Agadir and the negotiations with France was obviously suitable only . . . for diplomatic channels and not for public statement. The Chancellor of the Exchequer therefore made his speech in quite general terms. . . ." [107] This statement indicated that Grey's conversation with Metternich had already taken place before the interview, but there is nothing to show that the foreign secretary made any attempt to modify or withhold Lloyd George's speech until after a reply arrived from Berlin. The evidence seems conclusive that a cabinet meeting took place on the morning of July 21, that Lloyd George knew then what he intended to say, that he had shown his speech to Churchill, that consultation with Grey and Asquith in which their acquiescence was secured took place in the afternoon after the cabinet meeting and after the Grey-Metternich conversation but that no reference

---

[101] Lloyd George, *op. cit.*, vol. I, p. 41.
[102] *Ibid.*   [103] Grey, *op. cit.*, vol. I, p. 225.
[104] H. H. Asquith, *The Genesis of the War*, p. 148.
[105] *Op. cit.*, vol. I, p. 225.   [106] *Op. cit.*, vol. I, p. 42.
[107] *Par. Deb.*, 5th series, House of Commons, vol. XXXII, pp. 49, 50.

was made to the cabinet as a whole, and that no suggestion was made to withhold action until Metternich received a reply from Berlin.

On the evening of July 21, after a day full of perplexing problems, Lloyd George faced the assembled bankers of the city of London at the banquet tendered them by the Lord Mayor.[108] He spoke to them of politics, of insurance bills, and of world prosperity, and then read slowly from his manuscript, as though to show that his words had been weighed carefully, the section relating to foreign affairs. After he stated his sincere devotion to peace as the "first condition of continued prosperity" and his faith in the "common sense of nations" which made possible continued peace, he said with studied deliberation:

> But I am also bound to say this—that I believe it is essential in the highest interests, not merely of this country, but of the world, that Britain should at all hazards maintain her place and prestige among the Great Powers of the world. Her potent influence has many a time been in the past, and may yet be in the future, invaluable to the cause of human liberty. It has more than once in the past redeemed Continental nations, who are sometimes too apt to forget that service, from overwhelming disaster, and even from national extinction. I would make great sacrifices to preserve peace. I conceive that nothing would justify a disturbance of international good-will except questions of the gravest national moment. But if a situation were to be forced upon us in which peace could only be preserved by the surrender of the great and beneficent position Britain has won by centuries of heroism and achievement, by allowing Britain to be treated, where her interests were vitally affected, as if she were of no account in the Cabinet of nations, then I say emphatically that peace at that price would be a humiliation intolerable for a great country like ours to endure. National honour is no party question. The security of our great international trade is no party question; the peace of the world is much more likely to be secured if all nations realize fairly what the conditions of peace must be. . . .[109]

Perhaps that city audience, "whose minds were obsessed with the iniquities of the Lloyd George Budget and the fearful hardships it had inflicted upon property and wealth . . . did not com-

---

[108] London *Times,* July 22, 1911; Churchill, *op. cit.,* p. 31; Asquith, *op. cit.,* p. 148.   [109] London *Times,* July 22, 1911.

prehend in any way the significance or the importance of what they heard. . . ." [110] They may have taken it "as if it had been one of the ordinary platitudes of ministerial pronouncements upon foreign affairs . . . ," [111] but their cheers[112] announced their agreement with this paragraph, which soon became known as the famous Mansion House speech.

[110] Churchill, *op. cit.*, p. 31. [111] *Ibid.*, p. 32. [112] London *Times*, July 22, 1911.

Chapter XII

REPERCUSSIONS: ANGLO-GERMAN RELATIONS

While France and Germany bartered, England remained in the background until the Lloyd George speech forced her into the limelight. From that moment, the English motive became an all-important question. Did she adopt the ruthless tactics of her rival in order to preserve peace or in order to safeguard peculiarly British interests, in order to strengthen the Entente, or in order merely to reduce the price France must pay for her protectorate of Morocco? Was her technique adapted to her purpose? What were her gains and what were her losses? What was her defense, or did she need one?

The British foreign office has been severely criticized for its technique.[1] Grey had waited nearly three weeks for an answer to his communication of July 4, but on July 21 failed to wait twenty-four hours for a reply. He confessed that his earlier statement was not in the nature of a direct question but that "it was unusual for any Government completely to ignore a communication such as I had made. . . ." [2] His critics asked why, if he "judged the German notification and the German ambassador's assertion insufficient, he did not request more definite explanations. . . ." [3] The German foreign office had not offered explanations prior to July 21, but neither had the British foreign office definitely asked for any and to this extent must bear its share of responsibility for the resultant tension.[4] Grey's excuse apparently was that he feared a direct question might complicate the issue, but that when there was imminent danger of a disruption of the Franco-German negotiations he presented his request to the German ambassador in order to stave off disaster. His actions, however, had almost the opposite effect. His weeks of patience had allowed Germany to believe that England understood her procedure, and his sudden

[1] Morel, *op. cit.*, p. 141; Neilson, *How Diplomats Make War*, p. 152; Friedjung, *op. cit.*, p. 32; Valentin, *op. cit.*, p. 102; Lutz, *op. cit.*, p. 130.

[2] Grey, *op. cit.*, p. 223.

[3] Morel, *op. cit.*, p. 153. [4] Kleinknecht, *op. cit.*, pp. 44-46.

haste infuriated her. The statement, "If Lloyd George had waited, the threat would never have been made . . . ," [5] is perhaps justified.

The defense of the British foreign office is based on the fact that Lloyd George was scheduled to speak on the evening of July 21, not July 22 or some later date. If he were to make any statement, it must necessarily be at that time. This criticism resolves itself into another question: Why did the British foreign office approve of Lloyd George's including a statement of foreign policy in his speech? If Grey's object were primarily to force a reduction of German compensation demands,[6] his apparent haste was unnecessary. He knew that he would be facing parliamentary questioning in a few days and would then be in a position to make any statement he wished relative to the German menace. A statement thus made would have the advantage of official status. Moreover, if a satisfactory reply had not been received by that time, his issuance of a warning would have been less subject to criticism than was the policy pursued.

Grey defended his procedure on the grounds that he, Asquith, and Lloyd George "felt that for a Cabinet Minister of first-rate importance to make a speech on a formal occasion and to say no word about Foreign Affairs . . . would be misleading to public opinion here and everywhere." [7] His argument is not convincing. It was customary for the chancellor of the exchequer to be the principal guest at the annual dinner given by the lord mayor to the bankers of the city of London,[8] but it was no iron-clad rule that he would discuss foreign affairs.[9] In fact, Lloyd George had been known on such occasions to restrict "himself to a few observations on the revenue." [10] However, if Grey believed that the chancellor could not speak without reference to foreign affairs, it seems strange that the question was not discussed in the morning cabinet meeting and agreement reached as to what he, a representative of the cabinet, should say. It is true Asquith and Grey

---

[5] Moon, *op. cit.*, p. 213. See also Lutz, *op. cit.*, p. 130; Ward and Gooch, *op. cit.*, vol. III, p. 445.

[6] E. D. Morel, "The True Story of Morocco Negotiations," in *Nineteenth Century*, vol. LXXI (February, 1912), p. 246.

[7] *Par. Deb.*, 5th series, House of Commons, vol. XXXII, p. 50.

[8] Asquith, *op. cit.*, p. 148.   [9] *Cf.* reports given in the *Annual Register*.

[10] *Annual Register*, 1909, p. 165; *ibid.*, 1908, p. 155.

were not informed of the plan until after this meeting, but their failure to present the question voluntarily to the assembled ministers indicates that they grasped the idea of the necessity of the pronouncement only after Lloyd George had presented it to them. Even then a cabinet session could have and should have been called to deliberate on the advisability of the move. Perhaps the presence of such vigorous opponents as Lord Loreburn and Lord Morley deterred the actors.[11] Yet it seems more probable that they were blind to the potential danger involved in their act.[12]

The effect of the speech may have been more drastic than the government expected,[13] but its various members loyally supported their co-worker. The liberal ministers of England seemed to have succumbed to a fear that the German government might interpret omission of any statement of foreign policy from Lloyd George's speech as indicative of weakness and of disunion within the government due to party differences on the tormenting domestic issues.[14] There was some indication that Grey considered that the unusual and indirect manner adopted to present British views to the German government would be less objectionable and less of a threat than any official statement.[15] The idea seemed to have been that the technique employed would give Germany the necessary warning while it left the British government in a position where, in case it seemed advisable, it might withdraw by simply repudiating its chancellor of the exchequer. But after the Grey-Metternich conference of July 25,[16] none entertained any idea of official repudiation. National honor had become too deeply involved. Nevertheless, the British blow lacked finesse and savored greatly of big-stick diplomacy. Such a method can be justified only on the grounds that Grey and his associates believed that a critical stage had arrived where British position must be clearly defined or Germany

---

[11] Kleinknecht, *op. cit.*, p. 67.   [12] Gooch, *Before the War*, vol. II, p. 75.

[13] Metternich to Bethmann Hollweg, July 29, 1911, *G. P.*, vol. XXIX, no. 10636. Metternich here accredited the British cabinet with authorizing Lloyd George's speech.

[14] Churchill, *op. cit.*, p. 33; Grey before the House of Commons, *Par. Deb.*, 5th series, vol. XXXII, p. 50; Schmitt, *op. cit.*, p. 333; Mensdorff to F. O., July 24, 1911, *Ö. U. A.*, vol. III, no. 2570.

[15] *Par. Deb.*, 5th series, House of Commons, vol. XXXII, pp. 50, 52.

[16] See pp. 309-311, *infra*.

might become over-confident and precipitate war. This seems to have been the state of mind of the British government on July 21.

And now we may ask: Why did Kiderlen permit such a state of mind to develop in England? His opponents asserted that he did not recognize the British danger until it was upon him.[17] He, on the contrary, insisted that he had always been cognizant of Great Britain as an interested party in the Moroccan quagmire.[18] Nevertheless, he allowed himself to be bogged down by British opposition. Success of his plan depended upon his keeping England aloof, yet he made no move to pacify British sensibilities. In defense of German policy, Bethmann Hollweg claimed that Metternich's communication of July 1 was sufficient explanation and that, as France was keeping England informed, the British government had no right whatever to suspect German designs. He asserted his willingness at the time to dispel any British doubts if he had been questioned.[19] The question arises as to why he should trust France to keep England aloof. Metternich's original explanation was based on alleged defense of nationals, which was obviously a screen for the true German objectives and which no one took seriously. After July 1 Metternich was not kept informed of the progress of negotiations and was without authorization to answer any questions propounded by the British government. He was, therefore, forced to await instructions from Berlin at a time when a prompt response was essential. However, the German ambassador was justly criticized for not recognizing the urgency of Grey's communication of July 21 and for his failure to wire for an immediate reply.[20] His defense was that he accepted the current belief that Lloyd George was pro-German and that the Mansion House speech came as a surprise to him. Churchill defended him with these words: "How could he know what Mr. Lloyd George

[17] Reventlow, op. cit., p. 228; A. Tirpitz, My Memoirs, vol. I, p. 210; Wolff, op. cit., pp. 55, 56; Benckendorff to Neratov, Aug. 29, 1911, Siebert, op. cit., no. 693.

[18] Note of Kiderlen, Aug. 12, 1911, in Jäckh, op. cit., vol. II, p. 138; Jonescu, op. cit., p. 62.

[19] Stenographische Berichte des Reichstags, XII Legislaturperiode, II session, vol. 268, p. 8348.

[20] Count Metternich was recalled early in 1912 largely because of imperial displeasure with his handling of the Moroccan crisis.

was going to do? Until a few hours before, his colleagues did not know. Working with him in close association, I did not know. No one knew. Until his mind was definitely made up, he did not know himself. . . ." [21] Charges of negligence might just as well be made against Kiderlen. He was apparently blind to the *Times* hint that Metternich had communicated to him on July 20[22] and which probably reached him July 21. If he had understood clearly the British situation, he would have seen therein a need for telegraphic instructions to his London representative regardless of later developments. As it was, he sent no reply until after receipt of the despatch of July 21.

Germany perhaps did not know that British temper was not inclined to tolerate further delay, but German success dictated that British temper should not be severely taxed. Kiderlen may have expected to win his point with France before England became aroused sufficiently to make any move. He repeated many times that he knew that England would stand on the side of France and that he had no hopes of changing her attitude where Morocco was involved. He therefore may have considered it futile to make any friendly overtures to her and thus have adopted the policy of letting Anglo-German affairs drift until Britain applied pressure herself. Spender presents the unique explanation that Kiderlen failed to make any communication to England during the three weeks of silence merely because he was actually wondering what to say.[23] Brandenburg believes that Kiderlen recognized that any assurance sent to London would at once be transmitted to Paris and the effectiveness of his *coup* destroyed.[24] Yet it seems possible that the German secretary might have played his cards more adroitly and prevented the development of any active British hostility. Although Kiderlen recognized Britain as an interested party when he worked out his plans on May 3,[25] he failed to plan for the eventuality of British interference; and that neglect cost him dearly. Popular reception of Lloyd George's speech drove home the full force of its meaning and explains its effect upon the course of the crisis; for just as the foreign offices became more

---

[21] *Op. cit.*, p. 33.

[22] Metternich to Bethmann Hollweg, July 20, 1911, *G. P.*, vol. XXIX, no. 10616.

[23] *Op. cit.*, p. 404.   [24] *Op. cit.*, p. 379.   [25] See Chapter IX, *supra.*

conciliatory, public opinion burst into chauvinistic flames.

The London *Times* not only published the speech in full but carried an editorial in praise of the chancellor's address. "Mr. Lloyd George's clear, decisive, and statesmanlike reference, at the Bankers' dinner last night, to the European situation created by the German demands in West Africa will be endorsed without distinction of party by all his countrymen . . ." was its prophecy. The editorial denounced the German demands as "nothing less than a claim for absolute European predominance. Neither France nor Great Britain could have entertained them for a moment without confessing themselves overborne by German power. . . ." It also predicted that "with the better understanding of British temper which Mr. Lloyd George's speech is calculated to produce those demands will assume a more reasonable form. Mr. Lloyd George is under no suspicion of jingoism, and it may be taken that in what he said he spoke not only for himself, but for the British Government. He spoke, indeed, for his countrymen as a whole. . . ." [26] The *Daily Chronicle* titled its article "England's warning to Germany." [27]

Among the French papers, the *Journal des Débats* announced that Lloyd George, "contrary to British usage," read his speech in order to show that he was "the spokesman of the entire cabinet," and explained that the chancellor of the exchequer was a pacifist involved in troubles at home but above all a British subject who saw clearly in the German propositions "a germ of destruction for the British influence in Africa. . . ." The *Journal* rejoiced that the government and British people were firmly attached to the Triple Entente and declared, "Yesterday's discourse of M. Lloyd George is worth more than the sending of a cruiser into Moroccan waters. . . ." [28] If German public and German statesmen had been inclined to view moderately the British stroke, British and French papers with their jingoistic language destroyed all credence in conservative statements which described the speech as general platitudes that could have been made equally well by any German statesman. The less aggressive of the chauvinists were content to

[26] London *Times*, July 22, 1911.
[27] Metternich to Bethmann Hollweg, July 22, 1911, *G. P.*, vol. XXIX, no. 10621.
[28] *Journal des Débats*, July 22, 1911, in Gauvain, *op. cit.*, vol. III, pp. 39-41.

use the term "warning" instead of the drastic word "threat" employed by their more vigorous compatriots. The text of the speech may have contained no threat, but the interpretation seized by the press and blazoned before the public eye left no doubt in German minds that a threat was intended.

Even the moderate German papers denounced the Mansion House speech as unwarranted interference. They were particularly annoyed by the fact that the spokesman was one whom they had long considered a friend. The *Berliner Tageblatt* regretted Lloyd George's action but placed the heaviest responsibility on the London *Times*, whom it charged with consciously striving to disrupt the Franco-German negotiations since it did not wish to see an improvement in their relations. Wolff, editor of the paper, also criticized Kiderlen for not recognizing the influence of the *Times* and for not keeping in close touch with the British foreign office.[29] The *Kölnische Zeitung* titled its editorial "The Enigma of Lloyd George's Speech" and answered his praise of the peaceful policy of his nation with a panegyric to German service in that field.[30] Another moderate paper, the *Frankfurter Zeitung*, reminded Lloyd George that he had often complained of the excessive nervousness of his countrymen in their fear of Germany, and yet he now delivered a speech that would inevitably alarm the public. The Downing Street habit of judging France in Fez, Spain in Larache, and Russia in Persia by different standards from that used in judging Germany in Agadir was especially irritating to this paper. The one ameliorating point, it stated, was the fact that the speech also contained a warning to France that in her "tête à tête with Germany" she must consider British interests.[31]

The possibilities involved in Kiderlen's diplomacy had excited the Pan-German papers; the German demands for the French Congo had aroused the French press; but it took Lloyd George's speech to inflame the press of all three nations.[32] Jules Cambon

[29] *Berliner Tageblatt*, July 25, 1911 (Editorial).

[30] *Kölnische Zeitung*, July 24, 1911 (Editorial).

[31] *Frankfurter Zeitung*, July 24, 1911 (Editorial).

[32] Goschen to Grey, July 26, 1911, *Br. Docs.*, vol. VII, no. 424; Goschen to Grey, July 27, 1911, *ibid.*, no. 428; Schoen to Bethmann Hollweg, July 22, 1911, *G. P.*, vol. XXIX, no. 10622; Metternich to Bethmann Hollweg, July 22, 1911,

was "aghast at the effect which Mr. Lloyd George's speech has had on the French Colonial Chauvinists. . . ." [33] The French imperialists, swollen with confidence in British support, were in no mood for conciliation, and Cambon's task was made more difficult. The German chauvinists, irritated by British interference in a Franco-German dispute, decried British action as unjustified assumption of interests. More and more did the German people become convinced that England would use every opportunity "in all corners of the world to burden systematically the development of the German Empire. . . ." [34] A wave of indignation that refused to subside swept over Germany but reached its apex in Heydebrand's sensational speech in the Reichstag in which he proclaimed to the world that British action "as a stroke of lightning in the night has shown the entire German people where its enemy stands. . . ." [35] In an atmosphere of mutual taunts and defamation built up by British, French, and German press, the diplomats faced weary months of tedious negotiations. The immediate effect of the Mansion House speech was to increase international tension, to make intercourse between the powers difficult, and to prolong the delay in effecting a settlement.

Public excitement had its counterpart in official agitation. On July 21 Metternich sent an account of that day's interview with Grey to his foreign office, but it did not arrive until the next day. On the twenty-second, he transmitted a summary of Lloyd George's speech and the newspaper comments relative thereto to Bethmann Hollweg. [36] That same day Kiderlen telegraphed to London for the text of the speech, [37] and on the twenty-third, before receiving an answer to his telegram, he mailed his official reply to Metternich's despatch of July 21. [38] Kiderlen had the

ibid., no. 10621; *Kreuzzeitung,* July 26, 1911, in Schiemann, *op. cit.*, p. 241; Carroll, *Germany and the Great Powers,* p. 699.

[33] Goschen to Nicolson, July 27, 1911, *Br. Docs.*, vol. VII, no. 431.

[34] Jenisch to Bethmann Hollweg, Aug. 13, 1911, *G. P.*, vol. XXIX, no. 10639; Goschen to Grey, Aug. 16, 1911, *Br. Docs.*, vol. VII, no. 476. The words quoted are those accredited to William II by Jenisch.

[35] *Stenographische Berichte des Reichstags,* XII Legislaturperiode, II session, vol. 268, p. 7722.

[36] Metternich to Bethmann Hollweg, July 22, 1911, *G. P.*, vol. XXIX, no. 10621.

[37] Kiderlen to Metternich, July 22, 1911, *ibid.*, no. 10620.

[38] Kiderlen to Metternich, July 23, 1911, *ibid.*, no. 10618.

newspaper reports of and comments on the Mansion House speech before he dispatched this reply but did not have the entire text.

On July 24 Metternich delivered to Grey the communication authorized by his superior. His country, the ambassador reported, had landed no troops at Agadir and would land none except in case of extreme necessity. "Germany had never thought of creating a naval port on the Moroccan coast and would never think of it. Such ideas were hallucinations. She had no designs on Moroccan territory. . . ." Germany was willing to make concessions to France in the colonial field, but in return expected France to come to terms with her; otherwise she must insist on the strict maintenance of the Algeciras Act. Kiderlen, through Metternich, labeled as tactics harmful to a peaceful solution of the difficulties the chauvinistic tone of the British and French press which threatened Germany with French allies and friends, and, equally so, the failure of the French government to maintain secrecy.[39] He brusquely denied any designs on French pre-emptive rights to the Belgian Congo with the flat statement, "We have no such intention. . . ."[40] In substance, Germany now officially informed England that she had no designs upon Moroccan territory or upon the Belgian Congo, but that she expected ample compensation from France or a return to the status of the Algeciras Act. Grey, thereupon, sought to discover German attitude toward a conference in case the negotiations broke down; but this prospect had no chance, as Metternich had no authorization to reply to the suggestion. When Grey then asked permission to transmit the German communication to Parliament, the ambassador again pleaded lack of power and requested the British minister to make no public statement until he secured further instructions.[41] But realizing now the need for haste, Metternich the same day telegraphed Grey's last request to Berlin and earnestly sought his superiors to send him telegraphic instructions.[42] The first telegram he received was inflammatory; and the second, a reply to his request for instructions, was equally stiff and indignant.

[39] *Ibid.;* Metternich to F. O., July 24, 1911, *ibid.,* no. 10624; Grey to Goschen, July 24, 1911, *Br. Docs.,* vol. VII, no. 417.

[40] Kiderlen to Metternich, July 23, 1911, *G. P.,* vol. XXIX, no. 10618.

[41] Grey to Goschen, July 24, 1911, *Br. Docs.,* vol. VII, no. 417.

[42] Metternich to F. O., July 24, 1911, *G. P.,* vol. XXIX, no. 10624.

Kiderlen, upon receipt of the text of Lloyd George's speech, wired his protest. He denied that British interests were in any way affected by the Franco-German negotiations; but if they were, Germany expected that England would communicate an expression of her wishes "by the usual diplomatic way. When the English Government, instead of this, had issued a public declaration by one of their members, which at least could be meant as warning in our direction and actually by British as by French papers has been considered a warning bordering on a threat, it is difficult for us to recognize the reason for it. . . ." With the tone of the French and part of the British press as it was, Kiderlen did not doubt that the British government realized the effect that such a maneuver would have on the public mind of each nation. "If the English government had the intention to complicate and entangle the political situation and to lead towards violent explosion it could, it is true, select no better means than the speech of the Chancellor of the Exchequer. . . ." He thereupon instructed Metternich to discuss the matter with the foreign minister; and in case Grey asserted that the meaning of the speech was not that given it by the press, he was "to say to the minister that we then expect an unambiguous public declaration in this sense. . . ."[43]

In his second telegram, Kiderlen asserted that "we have designated our communication to Grey expressly as confidential and expect therefore, that it be treated as such. . . ." He denied to the British minister the right to present the German communication of July 24 to Parliament and justified his refusal upon the grounds that such a statement coming after Lloyd George's speech would leave the impression that Germany had given way before a threat. The question had now become one of national prestige. Germany demanded the same rights to respect from the council of nations as Lloyd George had demanded for England. No conference was needed, he asserted, for Germany was determined to secure respect for her treaty rights.[44]

Armed with instructions from home, Metternich executed his commission with a proud, haughty demeanor which threw the British cabinet into a panic. Immediately after the meeting, Grey

---

[43] Kiderlen to Metternich, July 24, 1911, *ibid.*, no. 10623.
[44] Kiderlen to Metternich, July 25, 1911, *ibid.*, no. 10625.

summoned Churchill and Lloyd George and greeted them with the
words, "I have just received a communication from the German
Ambassador so stiff that the Fleet might be attacked at any moment. I have sent for McKenna to warn him!"[45] Grey reported
that Metternich had declared that Lloyd George's speech had rendered it impossible for the German government to give public
explanations of its intentions,[46] and that Germany denied the need
for a conference and proclaimed her right as one of the signatories
of the Algeciras Act "by herself to vindicate the rights of the
Treaty." Upon what grounds Germany based her right to be sole
guardian of the treaty is not clear; but Metternich continued,
"German dignity as a Great Power would make it necessary to
secure by all means, and if necessary also alone, full respect by
France for German Treaty rights. . . ."[47] Both men, aroused by
implications of injury to their national honor, took refuge in an
extremely provocative reserve, rigidly determined to maintain personal and national dignity. Since Germany "had said that it was
not consistent with their dignity, after the speech of the Chancellor of the Exchequer, to give explanations as to what was taking
place at Agadir," Grey "felt that the tone of their communication
made it not consistent with our [British] dignity to give explanations as to the speech of the Chancellor of the Exchequer. . . ."
He nevertheless reasserted British desire to see Franco-German
negotiations succeed, at the same time insisting upon the safeguarding of British interests.[48] Metternich answered that Germany had no desire to infringe upon British rights and that such
"intentions exist only in the English imagination. . . ."[49] The
German ambassador stated that he concluded the interview with
an "expression of the conviction that the more they imparted
warnings threatening us, the more firmly would we proceed. . . ."
He described the interview as "extremely lively, but he [Grey]
held himself in the bounds of diplomatic etiquette. . . ."[50]

[45] Churchill, *op. cit.,* p. 32.

[46] Kiderlen to Metternich, July 25, 1911, *G. P.,* vol. XXIX, no. 10625; Metternich to F. O., July 25, 1911, *ibid.,* no. 10626; Kiderlen to Treutler, July 26, 1911,
ibid., no. 10628; Grey to Goschen, July 25, 1911, *Br. Docs.,* vol. VII, no. 419.

[47] Grey to Goschen, July 25, 1911, *Br. Docs.,* vol. VII, no. 419.

[48] *Ibid.*   [49] Metternich to F. O., July 25, 1911, *G. P.,* vol. XXIX, no. 10626.

[50] *Ibid.*

The days July 25 to 28 were days of high tension when almost anything might have happened. Benckendorff surmised that "one step further, and a war between England and Germany would have broken out as a result of the Franco-German dispute, although independent of it. . . ." [51] Kiderlen, who had defined Lloyd George's speech as a "colossal bluff," [52] described Grey as "obstinate and prejudiced, but not intriguing and insincere," and explained the British action as one sprung from a fear of injury to British rights plus the greater fear of a breach in the Entente that had been created by French pressure and clamor for support. He charged the French with purposely creating a "chauvinistic din" in an effort to force Germany to give way, but he believed that France would yield when she realized that Germany was determined to stand her ground. He therefore advised the imperial master that the situation only required firmness and insistence upon a strict adherence to the Algeciras Act.[53] With the French and German governments determined not to yield and the British sick with neurotic fear, the peace of Europe was gravely threatened.

As soon as McKenna, first lord of the admiralty, received Grey's communication, he hurried away to give the warning orders.[54] Excitement permeated the admiralty, and every order that issued from its portals aroused conjecture. The anticipated meeting of the German and British fleets, which had occupied the attention of the two governments for several days was settled by a British order, issued July 25, cancelling the cruise of the Atlantic fleet. Nicolson instructed Goschen, July 26, to inform Kiderlen that the change had no other object.[55] The same day, Metternich, apparently unaware of the Anglo-German correspondence on this point, telegraphed that England had ordered the fleet to stay at Cromarty until Friday and then to move to Portsmouth.[56] Newspaper comments attached great significance to the change in the plans

---

[51] Benckendorff to Neratov, Aug. 1, 1911 in Siebert, *op. cit.*, no. 689.

[52] Szögyény to F. O., July 27, 1911, *Ö. U. A.*, vol. III, no. 2572. Of this Lloyd George said, "However it was a bluff he [Kiderlen] was not prepared to call. It was in truth by no means bluff."—Lloyd George, *op. cit.*, vol. I, p. 44.

[53] Kiderlen to Treutler, July 26, 1911, *G. P.*, vol. XXIX, no. 10628.

[54] Churchill, *op. cit.*, p. 32.

[55] Nicolson to Goschen, July 26, 1911, *Br. Docs.*, vol. VII, no. 638.

[56] Kiderlen to Treutler, July 26, 1911, *G. P.*, vol. XXIX, no. 10629.

of the British fleet, and continued official denial that the change had anything to do with the Moroccan situation was not believed.[57] German officials found it difficult to convince the Kaiser that the maneuver was not connected with the Moroccan problem and was in no way an act of courtesy to France.[58]

The state of nerves to which a group of British officials had succumbed was evident in the spasm of terror that gripped Churchill suddenly on the afternoon of July 27 while he attended a garden party. He there learned from the police commissioner that the reserves of naval cordite stored at Chattenden and Lodge Hill were protected by only a few constables and could easily be taken by a group of "twenty determined Germans in two or three motor cars. . . ." Churchill related that he left the garden party and immediately demanded of the admiralty that marines be sent to the defense of the naval stores. Unable to secure his wishes from that office, he then called the war department. Haldane, more amenable to Churchill's program, ordered a company of infantry for each magazine to advance to the allegedly endangered spots. The home secretary concluded his account with a statement, almost a boast, that "by the next day the cordite reserves of the navy were safe." [59] Thoroughly convinced of the menacing intrigues underlying the German program, he saw German spies and German troops on every knoll. His extreme anxiety was only a few shades more intense than the general temper of the British government.

To meet a supposed danger, the British foreign secretary had warned the admiralty that the fleet might be attacked; the war office had strengthened the defenses around the naval stores; and the British fleet had changed its program of a cruise in Norwegian waters. It is not surprising that Germany spoke of British war preparations as intensifying the strain under which the chancelleries of Europe were then working, but the British government believed that Germany might actually attack the fleet and thus

---

[57] *Ibid.* See also editor's footnote, p. 219.

[58] William II to Bethmann Hollweg, July 27, 1911, *ibid.*, no. 10630; Bethmann Hollweg to William II, July 27, 1911, *ibid.*, no. 10631.

[59] Churchill, *op. cit.*, p. 34.

took precautions against an attack that Germany really had no intention of making.

Excitement was also high across the channel. On July 27 the German army was executing its usual maneuvers near Metz and wild rumors spread as to its activities.[60] The French government called in troops from Champagne where they had gone to quiet domestic disturbances, and immediately rumors of French mobilization spread.[61] Until the end of July none of the participants was making aggressive war preparations, but they were each so nervous that even the ordinary military maneuvers excited consternation. Public excitement and official uneasiness made progress in negotiations impossible. Jules Cambon, depressed and excited, bemoaned the newspaper furor and the indiscretions of his own government no less than the intransigence of the German, and saw no hope of success. The mid-summer heat of Berlin added to the inflamed tempers and accentuated the difficulties involved in the delicate negotiations.[62] Berlin papers grew more indignant each day as the foreign press continued its praise of Lloyd George's speech.[63] The air cleared slightly on July 27 when Asquith addressed the House of Commons.

On July 26 Kiderlen had modified his instructions to Metternich sufficiently to authorize a statement in Parliament that Franco-German negotiations did not touch British interests, but he asked that Grey not give any of the confidential details of the German communication. Although he insisted that the negotiations must remain exclusively Franco-German, Kiderlen requested that the British government definitely state its wish for a successful conclusion of negotiations, as such a statement would help to further a peaceful solution.[64]

Grey and Metternich had recovered their composure, and their interview of July 27 proceeded in a friendly atmosphere. Grey expressed his appreciation of the amicable tone of Kiderlen's com-

[60] Goschen to Grey, July 28, 1911, *Br. Docs.*, vol. VII, no. 432.

[61] Schoen to F. O., July 31, 1911, *G. P.*, vol. XXIX, no. 10681.

[62] Goschen to Grey, July 26, 1911, *Br. Docs.*, vol. VII, no. 423; Goschen to Grey, July 26, 1911, *ibid.*, no. 424; Goschen to Grey, July 27, 1911, *ibid.*, no. 429.

[63] Goschen to Grey, July 27, 1911, *ibid.*, no. 428.

[64] Kiderlen to Metternich, July 26, 1911, *G. P.*, vol. XXIX, no. 10627.

munication and smoothed away some of the points of friction, notably German resentment to newspaper comments that he had defined German demands as "obviously impossible." [65] The more cordial relations established by this interview, and not the "energetic and firm procedure of Metternich" [66] on July 25, made for saner counsels and prepared the ground for Asquith's speech.

With more congenial relations already established between the two foreign offices, Asquith appeared before the House of Commons on July 27 and briefly summarized the situation. He said in part: "It is our desire that these conversations should issue in a settlement honourable and satisfactory to both the parties, and which His Majesty's Government can cordially say that it in no way prejudices British interests. We believe that to be quite possible; we earnestly and sincerely desire to see it accomplished. The question of Morocco itself bristles with difficulties, but outside Morocco, in other parts of West Africa, we should not think of attempting to interfere with territorial arrangements considered reasonable by those who are more directly interested. . . ." He then denied the charges that the British government had tried to foment trouble between France and Germany, but made it clear that if the negotiations failed, England must become an active party to a discussion of the situation. Lloyd George's speech, he explained, claimed no "predominant or pre-eminent position," but "it would have been a grave mistake to let such a situation drift till an assertion of our interest in it might, owing to previous silence, cause surprise and resentment at the moment when this assertion became most necessary. . . ." [67]

England's desire for a successful solution of the Franco-German strife was clearly expressed, but was couched in terms that left no doubt of her support of France. She would accept the territorial arrangements "considered reasonable by those who are more directly interested. . . ." Demands which France called unreason-

[65] Metternich to F. O., July 27, 1911, *ibid.*, no. 10634; Grey to Goschen, July 27, 1911, *Br. Docs.*, vol. VII, no. 430.

[66] Aehrenthal to Kiderlen, Aug. 10, 1911, *ö. U. A.*, vol. III, no. 2585; Szögyény to F. O., Aug. 21, 1911, *ibid.*, no. 2599; editor's footnote to Metternich to F. O., July 27, 1911, *G. P.*, vol. XXIX, no. 10633. Schoen stated that the German exception expressed by Metternich forced England to be more conciliatory.— *Op. cit.*, p. 148.   [67] *Par. Deb.*, 5th series, vol. XXVIII, pp. 1827-1828.

able were deemed unacceptable by England. "The Prime Minister's statement should make it finally clear that, while we shall not hesitate to assert our interests or discharge our obligations in the contingency which he named, we interpose no difficulties and only desire a solution creditable to all sides . . ." was the verdict of the London *Times*.[68] The *Journal des Débats* rendered homage to Great Britain for her loyalty to the Entente as expressed in the Asquith and Lloyd George speeches,[69] but official France was not satisfied. Caillaux credited Lloyd George's speech with being of some value, but deplored the fact that, officially, England made no commitments.[70] Sir Francis Bertie expressed his personal opposition to a Franco-German conflict; but when Paul Cambon asked Grey what would be the position of England if the Franco-German negotiations broke down and a conference were rejected by Germany, the British minister shifted the responsibility to the shoulders of his colleagues and avoided a definite reply.[71]

Metternich reported that Asquith's speech revealed British determination to protect British interests in Morocco but also showed that England had no intention of handicapping the negotiations, and he hoped that the words of the prime minister would do much to quiet the public in all directions.[72] Goschen reported that it had an excellent effect in Berlin, and he felt that it would "give Kiderlen a much desired opportunity to climb down a little. Cambon's spirits have risen enormously. . . ."[73] Kiderlen agreed that the statement in the House of Commons should calm public opinion;[74] but the Kaiser later asserted that the Asquith speech, because it was official, was more aggressive than the Lloyd George address.[75] The immediate effect of the prime minister's explanation to Parliament, however, was to cool the excited tempers of Europe and to permit negotiations to proceed; though it was not a panacea for all the ills of Anglo-German relations. Public opin-

[68] London *Times*, July 28, 1911 (Editorial).
[69] *Journal des Débats*, July 28, 1911, in Gauvain, *op. cit.*, vol. III, p. 55.
[70] Caillaux, *op. cit.*, p. 138.
[71] *Ibid.*; Grey to Bertie, July 28, 1911, *Br. Docs.*, vol. VII, no. 433.
[72] Metternich to F. O., July 27, 1911, *G. P.*, vol. XXIX, no. 10635.
[73] Goschen to Nicolson, July 27, 1911, *Br. Docs.*, vol. VII, no. 431.
[74] Kiderlen to Treutler, July 28, 1911, *ibid.*, no. 10679.
[75] Szögyény to F. O., Aug. 21, 1911, *Ö. U. A.*, vol. III, no. 2599.

ion of both countries was too highly inflamed to be quenched by ministerial explanations that gave no details. England had shown her displeasure in a sensational manner, and Germany continued to nurse her resentment of her rival's interference. Renewal of friendly relations was rendered impossible by annoying incidents that arose as negotiations between France and Germany continued to drag at an incredibly slow pace. Sporadic outbursts of wrath were the natural accompaniment of such affairs as, for example, the Cartwright interview.

A little over a month after Lloyd George's speech, the German public was again aroused to fury by the publication in the *Neue Freie Presse* of an article written by Dr. Münz, a journalist, giving an account of an alleged interview with the half-blind, energetic, clever, anti-German, British ambassador at Vienna, Sir Fairfax L. Cartwright.[76] According to this article, Cartwright had denounced German policy in Morocco, had proclaimed British whole-hearted support of France, and had criticized the operation of the German government. "The German Government," he was quoted as saying, "does not, like the English, represent the public opinion of the country. The action of Agadir was obviously inspired by the entourage of the Kaiser. If Germany had a Government which truly expressed public opinion it would not continue the unfortunate policy in Morocco. . . ."[77] Although Cartwright's name was not used, it was so poorly disguised that anyone might have identified the one to whom the article referred. For a British diplomat to issue for publication such statements was, of course, the height of diplomatic impropriety and was so regarded by German officials and the German public. Bethmann Hollweg asked for an official assertion as to the truth of the newspaper article.[78] In the meantime, Cartwright, fully conscious of the fact that the article accredited to him was outside the bounds of diplomatic courtesy, had wired Grey that, although the German embassy wished to hold him accountable for it, he was not in fact

---

[76] Münz has given his version of this affair in an article, "The Cartwright Interview of August, 1911," in *Contemporary Review*, vol. CXXXVII, pp. 308-316. *British Documents*, vol. VII, contains the British version.

[77] Münz, *op. cit.*, p. 313.

[78] Bethmann Hollweg to Metternich, Aug. 27, 1911, *G. P.*, vol. XXIX, no. 10643; Metternich to Grey, Aug. 29, 1911, *Br. Docs.*, vol. VII, App. V, p. 837.

responsible for its publication; and "although some of the views expressed may be mine, I did not express them to Dr. Münz (who is deaf) and the greater part of the article is mere guess-work on his part. . . ." [79] Cartwright continued to deny responsibility for the article[80] and asserted that Münz had waylaid him one morning and requested an interview which Cartwright had refused. As the journalist pursued him, he referred him to Asquith's speech for British views and commented only on the activities of the Pan-Germans.[81]

Grey replied to Metternich's request with the statement that "neither Sir F. Cartwright nor I nor any British diplomatist that I know of had any cognizance of the article in the *Neue Freie Presse* before it appeared. . . ." He then launched into complaints of the German press, which seemed determined to vilify British diplomatists and British policy with only slight justification for their attacks. As the German press seldom accepted British refutation of charges which it had made, he doubted the good of any official denial.[82] Cartwright complained of the campaign against him launched by the German press, but he did not deny that the sentiments expressed in the article corresponded to his own. Grey and Kiderlen, accordingly, worked out the following statement: "'The Imperial Government have from the British Government on inquiry a declaration to the effect that the British Ambassador at Vienna has neither inspired the article published in the *Neue Freie Presse*, nor has the ambassador made the statements ascribed to him by the author of the article. With that the incident is dispatched for the Imperial Government in a satisfactory manner. . . ." [83] This statement was published by the *Norddeutsche Allgemeine Zeitung*, September 15, and officially the incident was

---

[79] Cartwright to Grey, Aug. 26, 1911, *Br. Docs.*, vol. VII, App. V, p. 837.

[80] Cartwright to Nicolson, Aug. 31, 1911, *ibid.*, p. 839; Cartwright to Grey, Aug. 31, 1911, *ibid.*, p. 838.

[81] Cartwright to Nicolson, Aug. 31, 1911, *ibid.*, p. 839.

[82] Grey to Metternich, Aug. 30, 1911, *ibid.*, p. 838.

[83] Grey to Goschen, Sept. 5, 1911, *Br. Docs.*, vol. VII, App. V, p. 841; Grey to Goschen, Sept. 8, 1911, *ibid.*, p. 842; Goschen to Grey, Sept. 14, 1911, *ibid.*, p. 843; Kiderlen to Metternich, Sept. 3, 1911, *G. P.*, vol. XXIX, no. 10645; Metternich to F. O., Sept. 5, 1911, *ibid.*, no. 10646; Kiderlen to Metternich, Sept. 6, 1911, *ibid.*, no. 10647; Metternich to F. O., Sept. 8, 1911, *ibid.*, no. 10648; Kiderlen to Metternich, Sept. 11, 1911, *ibid.*, no. 10649.

closed.[84] Nevertheless, public opinion did not consider the explanation satisfactory. Cartwright was known to hold the views expressed in the article; and the failure of the British government to deny the sentiments herein stated, as well as responsibility for their publication, was taken as additional evidence of British ingrained hostility to the German nation.[85] Aehrenthal had been quick to express his regret that an Austrian newspaper had published an article hostile to Germany and inciting to the German public.[86] Yet enmity to Cartwright remained so pronounced that Austria, without presenting a definite demand, gradually worked for and secured his recall.[87] In sum, the Cartwright interview had the effect of pouring salt into an already open wound. Germany, now thoroughly convinced where her enemy lay, was willing to believe all the charges later made as to British preparations for war during the months of August and September.[88]

The most sensational disclosure of British war preparations was a speech by Captain Faber delivered at a mayoral dinner at Andover on November 17, in which he charged the British government with complete war preparations during the crisis. According to his account, while the British fleet was divided into three divisions, the government lost sight of the German fleet and feared an attack on each division separately. A war board for the admiralty was then formed to meet all emergencies and to arrange for coöperation of army and navy forces.[89]

Grey dodged the issue, when questioned in Parliament, by comparing Faber's speech with Heydebrand's oration, and in this man-

---

[84] Kiderlen to Metternich, Sept. 9, 1911, *G. P.,* vol. XXIX, no. 10649, editor's footnote.

[85] London *Times,* Aug. 31, 1911; Cartwright to Nicolson, Sept. 14, 1911, *Br. Docs.,* vol. VII, App. V, p. 843; Hoyos to F. O., Sept. 15, 1911, *Ö. U. A.,* vol. III, no. 2630; Schwabach to Crowe, Nov. 1, 1911, Schwabach, *op. cit.,* pp. 220-224; Grey to Goschen, Nov. 7, 1911, *Br. Docs.,* vol. VII, no. 663; Goschen to Grey, Nov. 10, 1911, *ibid.,* no. 673; Grey to Goschen, Oct. 10, 1911, *ibid.,* no. 657.

[86] Aehrenthal to Müller, Aug. 28, 1911, *ibid.,* vol. III, no. 2605.

[87] Mensdorff to F. O., Oct. 5, 1911, *Ö. U. A.,* vol. III, no. 2712; Aehrenthal to Mensdorff, Oct. 10, 1911, *ibid.,* no. 2737. The recall was delayed for two years.

[88] See, for example, Kleinknecht, *op. cit.,* pp. 90-113.

[89] *Annual Register,* 1911, p. 258; Bethmann Hollweg to Metternich, Nov. 22, 1911, *G. P.,* vol. XXIX, no. 10657 and editor's footnote.

ner only skirted a denial.[90] British activities during the summer and fall of 1911 gave basis for the captain's statements although the details were not accurate. Nicolson told Hardinge in September that "preparations for landing four or six divisions on the continent have been worked out to the minutest detail." [91] Haldane acknowledged that he had the military organization in such order that if the government decided on action he could "mobilize the Expeditionary Force and send it straight off to the continent. In order to be quite ready I stopped the manoeuvres that were customary at this time of the year, alleging the intense drought which prevailed as a reason. The money so saved was spent in completing mobilization arrangements. . . ." [92] Haldane gave information of his activities to the German military attaché, Major Ostertag, who reported to Berlin that England could throw six infantry divisions on the Belgian frontier with speed. Haldane also claimed that the Berlin office undervalued this information, for it did not believe England was prepared to act.[93] Churchill gave an account of an all-day meeting of the committee of imperial defence on August 23, where reports of suspected German mobilization activities along the Rhine were heard and plans for coöperation between French and British divisions were discussed in full and all points of danger surveyed. After this conference, Churchill reported, "The War Office hummed with secrets. . . . Not the slightest overt action could be taken. But every preparation by forethought was made and every detail was worked out on paper. . . . " [94] British and French military authorities were in close touch during those days. As early as July 20 a meeting was held between General Dubail and General Wilson "with the view of determining the conditions of eventual participation of an English army in operation of French armies of the northeast in a war against Germany. . . ." [95] British military attachés made fre-

---

[90] *Par. Deb.,* 5th series, House of Commons, vol. XXXII, pp. 55-56.

[91] Nicolson to Hardinge, Sept. 14, 1911, in Nicolson, *op. cit.,* p. 253.

[92] R. B. Haldane, *Autobiography,* p. 224.

[93] *Ibid.,* p. 225; Ostertag report, Oct. 24, 1911, *G. P.,* vol. XXIX, no. 10652.

[94] *Op. cit.,* pp. 38-45.

[95] Memorandum of meeting held on July 20, 1911, between General Dubail and General Wilson, Aug. 21, 1911, *Br. Docs.,* vol. VII, no. 640. Hermann Oncken saw a close relation between this conference and the speech of Lloyd

quent reports of the status of the French army and the probable effectiveness of French military organization.[96]

News of British preparations leaked across the channel and excited the German government. Eckardstein reported on August 12 that the railroad strike in England had been settled by governmental appeal to the patriotism of the worker. "The strike is finished, Europe has beaten us . . . ," he reported a representative of the workers as saying. According to his information the government had told the negotiators that "by reason of a secret written treaty concluded within the last fourteen days with France, England at any moment could be called up with her collective war power . . . to take part in an eventual war between France and Germany . . . ," and in the light of the international situation, appealed to the workers and the companies to settle the strike.[97] Churchill told Metternich that Asquith had said nothing "beyond a general appeal to the railway companies to come to terms with their men, considering the uncertainty of the international situation. . . ." This conversation revealed to Metternich Churchill's fear that Germany was determined to press to war.[98]

Although Grey continued to state that he did not believe that the Kaiser wanted war, fear of war was ever present in the minds of the British ministers. Even Grey thought the possibility sufficiently great to warn McKenna and to inquire of Russia what her action would be in case such complications arose. He likewise informed Russia that in case of war England would participate on the side of France and that there really was the possibility that both Russia and Austria would be drawn into the conflict.[99] Lloyd George wrote on September 1, "War is by no means inevitable but it is becoming an increasing probability. It is so much in the reckoning as to render it urgently necessary for us to take every step that would render the issue of war more favourable, always pro-

---

George.—*Das Deutsche Reich und die Vorgeschichte des Weltkrieges,* vol. II, p. 701.   [96] Bertie to Grey, Aug. 25, 1911, *Br. Docs.,* vol. VII, no. 641.

[97] Metternich to Bethmann Hollweg, Aug. 12, 1911, *G. P.,* vol. XXIX, no. 10642. Account of the strike and its settlement is given in most general accounts of English history and also in *Annual Register,* 1911, pp. 204–211.

[98] Metternich to Bethmann Hollweg, Aug. 12, 1911, *G. P.,* vol. XXIX, no. 10642.

[99] Benckendorff to Neratov, Aug. 16, 1911, Siebert, *op. cit.,* no. 691.

vided that such a step does not increase the chance of precipitating war. . . ." [100] This last sentence of the chancellor of the exchequer stated the British policy. All British maneuvers were a result of the growing conviction that the Franco-German negotiations had no hope of success and that war might result. With the bitter enmity which the German press continued to display toward the British foe, the British cabinet expected the opening of hostilities to be marked by a display of force against England. Germany, for her part, apparently had no idea of attacking the British fleet; but fear of such an attack seemed constantly to haunt the minds of the British cabinet. British war preparations did not reach the stage of actual mobilization, but the unusual activities did excite the German people.[101] The fact that these preparations were not at all offensive in nature was recognized by German authorities, but in times of strain the line between the offensive and the precautionary is often difficult to draw.[102] The tension was great in late July, in mid-August, and again in early September, and at each time Britain augmented her military defenses. As the news of these activities reached Germany, increased bitterness arose.

Towards the end of 1911, Anglo-German bitterness found virulent expression in Reichstag and Parliamentary debates[103] and in the newspaper accompaniment to these debates.[104] The foreign offices wished to prevent an explosion of popular feeling and worked in concert in an effort to present the situation as peacefully as possible. Grey and Bethmann Hollweg agreed as to what

---

[100] Lloyd George to Grey, Sept. 1, 1911, *Br. Docs.,* vol. VII, no. 642.

[101] Bethmann Hollweg to Metternich, Nov. 22, 1911, *G. P.,* vol. XXIX, no. 10657; Metternich to Bethmann Hollweg, Nov. 1, 1911, *ibid.,* no. 10653; Kiderlen to Heeringen, Nov. 29, 1911, *ibid.,* no. 10664; Ostertag to Metternich, Dec. 12, 1911, *ibid.,* no. 10670; Reventlow, *op. cit.,* pp. 237-238; Friedjung, *op. cit.,* p. 43.

[102] Kiderlen to Heeringen, Nov. 29, 1911, *G. P.,* vol. XXIX, no. 10664; Heeringen to Kiderlen, Dec. 25, 1911, *ibid.,* no. 10671; Kühlmann to Bethmann Hollweg, Jan. 17, 1912, *ibid.,* no. 10672; Zimmermann to Heeringen, Jan. 26, 1912, *ibid.,* no. 10673; Heeringen to Kiderlen, Dec. 5, 1911, *ibid.,* no. 10665.

[103] *Par. Deb.,* 5th series, House of Commons, vol. XXXII; *Stenographische Berichte des Reichstags,* XII Legislaturperiode, II session, vol. 268.

[104] Goschen to Grey, Nov. 6, 1911, *Br. Docs.,* vol. VII, no. 664; Goschen to Grey, Nov. 10, 1911, *ibid.,* no. 673.

each should say in his respective parliamentary address. The effect of Lloyd George's speech, and not the speech itself, was to form the crux of the reports.[105] Firebrands on both sides of the channel disrupted the plans of the ministers. Heydebrand's speech in the Reichstag, delivered amidst enthusiastic cheers and applause led by the Crown Prince, breathed defiance to the British Empire in its effort to block German expansion.[106] Erzberger, a member of the Center Party, less fiery but no less determined, proclaimed as "the great political lesson from the entire conflict of the summer of 1911" the fact that the power who wished to block German expansion was not France but "the cousin from across the channel." [107] The statement was repeated with ominous frequency that England was the one who disputed German claims to a place in the sun. Germany could understand French opposition to her Agadir *coup* but could not understand British interference. "We will not forget for a long time the arrogance of her attitude," [108] unfortunately expressed the mood of the German people.

Every aggressive statement made by statesmen in the Reichstag and each defiant article carried by the Pan-German press found an echo in British papers and Parliament. The *Times* viewed Heydebrand's speech as very disquieting, and although it recognized the moderation of Bethmann Hollweg's address, it protested against "the unfairness of his references to Lloyd George's speech. . . ." [109] Metternich urged Grey to make no defense of the famous speech in Parliament, for the bitterness was so great in Germany that any action which might reinforce it would lead to war. Grey agreed to avoid all controversial points.[110] Kiderlen, however, was forced in a Reichstag committee to make statements in defense of his British policy that were interpreted by Grey as a violation of

[105] Goschen to Grey, Nov. 7, 1911, *Br. Docs.*, no. 665; Grey to Goschen, Nov. 7, 1911, *ibid.*, no. 667; Grey to Goschen, Nov. 8, 1911, *ibid.*, no. 669; Grey to Goschen, Nov. 18, 1911, *ibid.*, no. 695; Metternich to Bethmann Hollweg, Nov. 18, 1911, *G. P.*, vol. XXIX, no. 10656; Bethmann Hollweg to Metternich, Nov. 17, 1911, *ibid.*, no. 10654.

[106] *Stenographische Berichte des Reichstags*, XII Legislaturperiode, II session, vol. 268, pp. 7718-7721.   [107] *Ibid.*, p. 7797.

[108] Pourtalès to Louis, Jan. 4, 1911, in Louis, *Carnets de Louis*, vol. I, p. 223.

[109] London *Times*, Nov. 10, 1911 (Editorial).

[110] Metternich to Bethmann Hollweg, Nov. 18, 1911, *G. P.*, vol. XXIX, no. 10656.

the arrangement made between the chancellor and himself; and, as a result, the British minister and the German chancellor through the medium of their respective parliamentary debates entered upon a discussion in which each attempted to justify his national policy.[111] Grey's speech on November 27 was moderate in tone, but other speakers were less conciliatory. The Earl of Ronaldshay defended Lloyd George's address as "one of those happy lapses from what I used to regard as a rather anaemic Imperialism to a more robust Imperialism, with which the . . . Chancellor of the Exchequer occasionally electrifies the political atmosphere. . . ."[112] Of course the task of quenching the flames of popular excitement was rendered more difficult by praise of this type. Both British and German statesmen were guilty of indiscreet comments, and those who worked for an Anglo-German *détente* faced the wreckage of their plans and wondered if there was sufficient left for salvage.

Lloyd George's speech came as a result of German disregard for British sensibilities. One point was self-evident; that is, the movement of a German warship to a Moroccan harbor, to the territory concerning which England was pledged to give France support and in which her own interests conceived the erection of a German naval base as dangerous, was bound to bring England into the fray. Kiderlen lost his opportunity when he failed to face the situation frankly and to take all precautions to avoid British suspicions of his actions. Grey and his associates, in a panic, adopted the policy of issuing a warning, if not a threat, to the German government in order to break the menacing silence. In doing this, the British government displayed the same heavy hand in diplomacy for which it criticized its German rival. As a result, Anglo-German relations reached a stage of tension where war might occur at any moment, and the ill will thus engendered remained to burden all efforts at the establishment of a *détente* between the two nations. Justification for Lloyd George's speech rests upon the

---

[111] Goschen to Grey, Nov. 19, 1911, *Br. Docs.*, vol. VII, no. 697, and minute of Crowe attached, Nov. 22, 1911; Grey before House of Commons, *Par. Deb.*, 5th series, vol. XXXII, pp. 43-66. Grey had great respect for Bethmann Hollweg but none for Kiderlen.—Gooch, *Before the War*, vol. II, pp. 75, 226.

[112] *Par. Deb.*, 5th series, vol. XXXII, p. 111.

grounds that the British government was convinced that war was dangerously near, that unless England defined her stand in a firm and irrevocable manner, Germany would force France into a position where she must fight or submit to humiliating demands, and that British interests were so deeply involved that she could not remain aloof. Defenders of Grey's policy claim that the Mansion House speech was an important agent in the maintenance of peace in mid-summer, 1911.[113] Its effect upon the course of Franco-German negotiations formed the basis for its fame as an agent of peace.

[113] See, for example, Grey, *op. cit.*, vol. I, p. 226; Wilson, *op. cit.*, p. 133; Seymour, *Diplomatic Background of the War*, p. 188.

Chapter XIII

DISCORD: FRANCO-GERMAN NEGOTIATIONS

The Mansion House speech momentarily shoved the Franco-German negotiations into secondary place while Anglo-German relations occupied the headlines. The fate of all three nations, however, depended upon the success or failure of the principal negotiators. Three significant conferences had taken place prior to July 21.[1] Basis for negotiations—a free hand for France in Morocco in exchange for colonial compensation to Germany, perhaps in the Congo—had been established on July 9 only to be disrupted six days later when Kiderlen named the entire Congo as the ransom price. His threat of "extreme lengths" issued in the interview of July 20 and Cambon's defiant reply increased the electric tension which permeated the atmosphere of the foreign offices. At this crucial moment, Lloyd George slung the British warning into the maelstrom and churned the foam into an angry roar, a roar which did not subside but remained ever present to affect the course of all further conferences between the interested parties. The negotiators must tread warily if a harmonious settlement were to be reached in the council room while cries of injured national prestige and national honor filled the streets. Against this background tumult Kiderlen and Cambon on July 23 resumed negotiations.

Cambon reported that this first conversation after the Mansion House speech was of a different tone from the two preceding ones. "My interlocutor showed to me, as he had never done up to the present, his desire for an entente with us . . ."[2] was his summation of Kiderlen's attitude. The change, however, was one of tone and not of terms. Kiderlen repeated his demand for the entire Congo, amplified his offer of Togo and a frontier adjustment along the north Camerun border, but denied any intention of asking for French pre-emption rights on the Belgian Congo. He feared that the pourparlers would be broken off if France continued to talk

[1] See Chapter X, *supra*.
[2] Cambon to Selves, July 24, 1911, *Affaires du Maroc*, 1910-1912, no. 467.

only of frontier rectification. Cambon recognized the danger and did not dispute the value of German offers, but confessed that no French parliament would ratify a treaty that alienated the entire Congo.[3] This view was upheld by the French foreign office in its announcement that it did not want Togo, and that if that colony were omitted from the exchange, German offers were not commensurate with her demands.[4] France saw no reason for considering Togo, since the German colonial secretary had already made clear his opposition to the cession of that colony, an opposition strongly supported by the German press.[5]

The moderate tone of the first conference disappeared in the second when Kiderlen tenaciously declared his determination not to modify his demands. The French ambassador pointed out that such an attitude constituted an ultimatum and not a basis for negotiation; but this statement, plus all further efforts to soften the German's obstinacy, brought only repetition of the threat of a return to the Act of Algeciras. The German secretary had again taken the position that France must yield or Germany would go to "extreme lengths."[6]

Pessimism took possession of the foreign offices and a feeling of dismay gripped German as well as French and British officials. Kiderlen wrote that after the conversation with Cambon he saw things "a little dark";[7] but this apparently did not lessen his resolve, much to the consternation of his chancellor, who consistently complained of the secrecy which veiled the plan of the foreign secretary. On the evening of the twenty-eighth, Bethmann Hollweg invited himself to dinner with Kiderlen in the hopes that he would "tell the plain truth about the state of the conversation with the French ambassador. . . . The result of the conversation at and

[3] *Ibid.;* Oppenheimer to Crowe, July 25, 1911, *Br. Docs.,* vol. VII, no. 420.

[4] Selves to Cambon, July 25, 1911, *Affaires du Maroc,* 1910-1912, no. 470.

[5] Lindequist to Bethmann Hollweg, July 22, 1911, *G. P.,* vol. XXIX, no. 10674.

[6] Cambon to Selves, July 28, 1911, *Affaires du Maroc,* 1910-1912, no. 476; Bertie to Grey, July 29, 1911, *Br. Docs.,* vol. VII, no. 440. There is no record of this interview in the German documents.—Kiderlen to Treutler, July 28, 1911, *G. P.,* vol. XXIX, no. 10679, editor's footnote. Kiderlen's impression of the conference is given in his letter of July 29, 1911, published in Caillaux, *op. cit.,* p. 320.   [7] *Ibid.*

after dinner was a sleepless night for the chancellor. . . ." [8] Kiderlen informed him that Cambon had refused the German demands and had suggested unsatisfactory frontier adjustments as a counter-proposal, which he in turn had rejected. The question was now one of prestige. Bethmann Hollweg was greatly upset by his subordinate's remark that "when our prestige in foreign lands is lowered we must fight. . . ." [9] On the trip to Swinemünde, whither the two adjourned to consult the Kaiser, the chancellor was relieved by the assurance that the threatening phrase meant only that Germany must be prepared for the worst.[10]

During the five days from July 23 to July 28, Kiderlen's attitude had changed from cordiality to truculency, a change that might be accounted for in several ways. At first glance, the explanation seems to be that the obstinate leader of German foreign policy had been subdued by Lloyd George's speech but again encouraged to aggressive action by Asquith's conciliatory address to Parliament. It must be remembered, however, that Kiderlen did not have the text of the Mansion House speech when he conferred with Cambon on July 23 and that he, on the same day, had sent the British government an amicable explanation of German intentions; but that on the following day after receiving the text of the oft-quoted speech, he assumed a resentful attitude, defined the issue as one of national prestige, and refused Grey's request that his earlier statements be given to Parliament.[11] His change of attitude had taken place prior to the Asquith speech. It seems more probable that Lloyd George's action stirred him to obstinacy and rancorous humor, rather than to a calm and friendly consideration of his opponent's views, and that he used the conference of July 28 to inform France of his resentment of the unwarranted interference of her British friend; for in this interview he complained bitterly of Lloyd George's speech, as he did of the indiscretions of the French press.[12] Because he did not believe that

---

[8] Otto Hammann, "Aufzeichnungen," July 30, 1911, in *Archiv für Politik und Geschichte*, 1925, p. 547.   [9] *Ibid.*, p. 548.

[10] *Ibid.*   [11] See Chapter XII, *supra*.

[12] Cambon to Selves, July 28, 1911, *Affaires du Maroc*, 1910-1912, no. 476; Bertie to Grey, July 29, 1911, *Br. Docs.*, vol. VII, no. 440.

France would fight, this astute German diplomat felt that he could reveal his irritation to the French ambassador and through this official channel impress upon France the necessity of yielding. This deduction was the outgrowth of the intricate maneuvers for which Caillaux must bear the responsibility; for the behind-the-scene activities of the French premier encouraged Kiderlen in the belief that, if he only remained firm, France would yield.

Out of the repercussions in France following the Mansion House speech came Caillaux's so-called intrigues. On July 23, the French chauvinists, assured of British diplomatic support, were impatient with any suggestion of compromise; and this impatience, according to Lancken, accounted for the "stiff neck" displayed by Caillaux and his "harsh declaration that cession of the entire Congo coast absolutely would not be considered. . . ." [13] Imperialist and nationalist groups strengthened the French foreign office in its refusal to consider the German demands, but the more conciliatory groups were made uneasy by the chauvinist clamor. Cambon was distressed by the situation and warned his government of the need for "more largesse of spirit" if the pourparlers were to continue.[14] He feared that if a rupture in the direct negotiations occurred, the English proposal for an international conference would necessarily result and the international cords which bound French action in Morocco would be tied more firmly than ever.[15] Caillaux, convinced that in case of war France could not depend on aid from England or Russia but must face Germany alone,[16] and disgusted with the incompetence of his foreign minister, entered into a series of maneuvers which he claimed had the sole purpose of securing for his native land an honorable settlement and of preserving the peace of Europe,[17] but which brought down upon him charges of duplicity, trickery, chicanery, even treason,

---

[13] Lancken to Langwerth von Simmern, July 26, 1911, *G. P.*, vol. XXIX, no. 10676.

[14] Cambon to Selves, July 24, 1911, *Affaires du Maroc,* 1910-1912, no. 468; Caillaux, *op. cit.,* p. 160.

[15] Cambon to Selves, July 24, 1911, *Affaires du Maroc,* 1910-1912, no. 468.

[16] Selves to Cambon, July 26, 1911, *ibid.,* no. 471; Selves to Paul Cambon, July 27, 1911, *ibid.,* no. 473; Paul Cambon to Selves, July 28, 1911, *ibid.,* no. 475; Caillaux, *op. cit.,* pp. 138-147; Fabre-Luce, *op. cit.,* p. 63.

[17] Caillaux, *op. cit.,* pp. 155, 165.

and ultimately drove him from office. Perhaps the truth lies hidden somewhere between the two extremes.

A maze of charges, counter-charges, denials, and refutations becloud the non-official negotiations which began on July 25 and continued at broken intervals until the major points of the Franco-German agreement had been reached; but piercing the maze is clearly discernible the fact that through the medium of intermediaries the French premier revealed to the German secretary a more conciliatory attitude than that adopted by his foreign office. Responsibility for initiating these interviews rests upon Lancken, a member of the German embassy in Paris, who acted with the approval of Kiderlen.[18] On July 25, according to Caillaux, Fondère reported that Lancken had sent for him, but that he awaited official approval before acting. Caillaux, thereupon, advised him to see what the German embassy wanted, and if the question of the Moroccan negotiations were broached, he was to say that although the premier viewed the situation pessimistically, he was determined not to yield.[19] Fondère thus became the non-official agent through whom the French premier and the German embassy carried on an exchange of views without the knowledge of the French foreign minister. Caillaux maintained that through this source the German embassy let him understand that the empire would be willing to accept a part instead of the entire Congo and would cede to France a large part of Togo and the Bec of Canard. The intermediary was then sent to sound the German embassy on the question of further reductions in return for adjustments of the Bagdad railroad question and for advantages in the Turkish Empire. To these suggestions the German reply was an abrupt "nothing doing." [20] Caillaux says that he, knowing Fondère would repeat his statements, then spoke of his conviction that a general solution of problems between the two nations would not only be more advantageous but also more likely to succeed than any negotiation limited to one field. These statements were not definite offers but only expressions of general opinion.[21]

A different view of the Fondère-Lancken affair is presented by

[18] *Ibid.*, p. 163; Lancken, *op. cit.*, p. 101; Carroll, *Germany and the Great Powers,* p. 674, footnote 1.   [19] Caillaux, *op. cit.*, p. 163.
[20] *Ibid.*, p. 164.   [21] *Ibid.*, p. 165.

Schoen's telegrams to his foreign office dispatched July 26 and 27, which were evidently in Kiderlen's hands at the time of his arrogant interview with Cambon on July 28. In the first telegram Schoen stated that Fondère, after a conversation with Caillaux, had reported to the German embassy that the French could not concede all of the Congo, but that they would, "even against the wish of England," cede that part of the French Congo east of Camerun with the Sangha River to its junction with the Congo River as the southern frontier. He even mentioned the possibility of a secret treaty in which France would grant to Germany her preëmption rights on the Belgian Congo and left the impression that Caillaux would be willing to form a compromise even more favorable to Germany.[22] The French premier flatly denied that he had made any comment relative to the Belgian Congo or to any opposition which England might make, but accepted the substance of the remainder of Schoen's report.[23] According to the second telegram, Fondère, as the agent of the French premier, suggested to the German embassy that France and Germany adjust all their difficulties, as a general settlement would be easier to justify before public opinion than a trade narrowed to Morocco and the Congo. He presented as points that France might concede: a German president of the Ottoman debt commission, a retrocession of 30 per cent in the Bagdad railroad, admission of all Bagdad stock to the Paris bourse, and an agreement about the railroads of the Orient. He also considered the possibility of ceding Germany some French island possessions.[24] These offers, if made by Caillaux, were presented without the approval of the foreign office.

After France and Germany had reached an agreement, accusations, which charged him with crimes ranging from disrespect towards his foreign minister to trifling with French honor were flung at the wily French premier.[25] When the treaty was before the sen-

---

[22] Schoen to F. O., July 26, 1911, *G. P.*, vol. XXIX, no. 10675, also published in Caillaux, *op. cit.*, p. 303.   [23] *Ibid.*, p. 305.

[24] Schoen to F. O., July 27, 1911, *G. P.*, vol. XXIX, no. 10678, also published in Caillaux, *op. cit.*, p. 307.

[25] See debates in the chamber of deputies, *Annales de la chambre des députés*, session extraordinaire, 1911; and in the senate, *Annales du senat*, session ordinaire, 1912. See also *Journal des Débats*, Dec. 13, 1911, Jan. 11, 1912, in Gauvain, *op. cit.*, vol. III, pp. 237, 279-282; memorandum by Sir Eyre Crowe, Jan. 14, 1912,

ate committee, Caillaux, apparently annoyed by insinuations made by the press, lost his cunning and hastened the downfall of his cabinet by the abrupt statement, "I give my word that there was never political nor financial transactions of any sort other than the diplomatic and official negotiations." [26] Clemenceau pounced upon the issue and forced a crisis by asking Selves to substantiate this statement. Selves refused to answer and before the end of the day tendered his resignation, not to his immediate superior but to the president of the republic.[27] Unable to reconstitute his cabinet or to give a satisfactory explanation of the situation, on January 14, 1912, Caillaux was forced out of office.[28] His tactless and useless denial of a fact known to many of his enemies opened the floodgates; and in the deluge of accusations which swirled about him, Schoen's telegrams of July 26 and July 27 did most to condemn him.

Since the first days of July, Selves had been irritated by the fact that his advice was seldom observed and his counsel was seldom sought, and this irritation was to grow when, in late August, Caillaux removed all control from the hands of his foreign minister and took over direct management of affairs.[29] Selves was in no mood to support his superior in any ministerial crisis, and the so-called "Green Memoranda" furnished him ample ammunition.

Br. Docs., vol. VII, App. III, pp. 821-826; Nicolson, *op. cit.*, p. 254; letter of Walter Roch, *Spectator*, Nov. 25, 1932, p. 752; Albin, *op. cit.*, pp. 237-239, 246; Stuart, *French Foreign Policy*, p. 316; Isvolski to Sazonov, Jan. 4, 1912, Isvolski, *op. cit.*, vol. II, no. 181; Steed, *op. cit.*, p. 342; Fabre-Luce, *op. cit.*, p. 91.

[26] Raymon Poincaré, *Au Service de la France*, vol. I, pp. 5, 6; Roch, *op. cit.*; Caillaux's Rejoinder, in *Spectator*, Dec. 9, 1932, p. 829; Pierre Baudin before the senate, Feb. 7, 1912, *Annales du senat*, session ordinaire, 1912, pp. 210-220. Poincaré stated that he advised Caillaux, prior to the meeting of the commission, to acknowledge that as chief of the government he had used agents he deemed necessary for the public interests. His voluntary denial, therefore, came as a surprise to Poincaré.—*Au Service de la France*, vol. I, p. 7.

[27] *Ibid.*, vol. I, pp. 8, 9; Pierre Baudin before the senate, *Annales du senat*, session ordinaire, 1912, pp. 210-220; Roch, *op. cit.*; Caillaux's Rejoinder, *Spectator*, Dec. 9, 1932, p. 829.

[28] Schoen to Bethmann Hollweg, Dec. 30, 1911, *G. P.*, vol. XXIX, no. 10792; Schoen to Bethmann Hollweg, Jan. 10, 1912, *ibid.*, no. 10793; Schoen to Bethmann Hollweg, Jan. 11, 1912, *ibid.*, no. 10795; *Journal des Débats*, Jan. 11, 1912, in Gauvain, *op. cit.*, pp. 273-278; Poincaré, *Au service de la France*, vol. I, pp. 9-12.

[29] See p. 344, *infra*.

Schoen's telegrams of July 26 and 27 had been sent in a code which the secret service attached to the French foreign office had earlier deciphered.[30] The telegrams with their condemning statements were thus made known to the foreign office. According to Caillaux's account, Selves brought the translations to him on the morning of July 28 and replied to his remark that the reports were exaggerated with the statement: "There is only one thing important in these memoranda, that is the last phrase. . . ."[31] The objectionable last sentence of Schoen's second telegram read: "Caillaux urgently requests that Cambon be not informed of these overtures. . . ."[32]

In all his statements made at that time and later, the accused minister has consistently maintained that he kept Cambon fully informed of all his activities and even employed great caution in seeing that all information which might come to his hands was transmitted as rapidly as possible to the ambassador in Berlin.[33] Caillaux not only denied the statement attributed to him, but he also charged the German embassy with purposefully using the cipher known to the French in order to sow discord between the various branches of the French department and garner the harvest while its opponents were busy with quarrels among themselves.[34] The deciphered telegrams played such a large part in the debates in the senate[35] that Lancken was led to protest to the French foreign minister, and in his protest declared that the statements in the telegrams were exaggerated.[36] However, Lancken in his report of July 26, a report which was not deciphered by the French, stated that Fondère had remarked to him that there was less confidence in Cambon in Paris and that he would probably be

[30] Caillaux, *Agadir*, p. 303; Schoen to F. O., July 26, 1911, *G. P.*, vol. XXIX, no. 10675, editor's footnote; Bertie, *The Diary of Lord Bertie*, vol. II, pp. 275-276.   [31] Caillaux, *Agadir*, p. 168.

[32] Schoen to F. O., July 27, 1911, *G. P.*, vol. XXIX, no. 10678, also published in Caillaux, *Agadir*, p. 307.

[33] Caillaux's answer to Crowe, Oct. 12, 1932, *Br. Docs.*, vol. VIII, Addendum, pp. 795-797; Caillaux, *Agadir*, pp. 308-309, 168.

[34] *Ibid.*, pp. 310-312.

[35] For example, see Jenouvrier before the senate, Feb. 5, 1912, *Annales du senat*, session ordinaire, 1912, pp. 156-168.

[36] Poincaré, *Au service de la France*, vol. I, p. 70.

recalled as soon as the current negotiations were completed.[37] Such a statement coming from Caillaux's confidence man does not indicate that the premier had that complete trust in his ambassador which he would have one believe. Kiderlen's informal report to the baroness repeated the incriminating statement that the French premier wished to keep his ambassador in ignorance of his overtures.[38]

If Caillaux had planned originally to operate without informing Cambon, he changed his plans and on July 29 sent M. Pietri, a member of the finance department, to Berlin to give the ambassador a full account of the Fondère-Lancken conversations.[39] Pietri's report of his mission,[40] confirmed by Kiderlen's acknowledgment that Cambon made him the same offers as Lancken had brought,[41] shows that the French ambassador was given a full account of the situation on July 31. There is no way of determining whether the premier's decision to send Pietri was made before or after he learned of the deciphered telegrams. He, of course, maintained that he planned from the beginning to keep Cambon informed, but that the disgruntled mood of the foreign office made it impossible to use the customary channels in transmitting the information and the unusual method of sending a special agent was necessary.[42] Caillaux does not discuss his later use of Fondère, but the German documents show that he was employed frequently throughout the month of August.[43] Schoen, on August 8,

[37] Lancken to Langwerth von Simmern, July 26, 1911, *G. P.*, vol. XXIX, no. 10676.   [38] Letter of Kiderlen, July 29, 1911, in Caillaux, *Agadir*, p. 322.
[39] *Ibid.*, pp. 165, 322; Tardieu, *op. cit.*, p. 473.
Lancken also went to Berlin to give an oral report of the situation to Kiderlen. His activities while in the capital were veiled in secrecy and are still shrouded in mystery. Only an extract from a private letter to Langwerth von Simmern after his return to Paris is given in *G. P.* In this extract he stated his conviction that Germany would not modify her demands and Fondère's equally strong belief that France would not yield.—Schoen to F. O., July 27, 1911, *G. P.*, vol. XXIX, no. 10678, editor's footnote, pp. 303-304. Pietri complained that Lancken "gave no signs of life while in Berlin. . . ."—Caillaux, *Agadir*, p. 324. His commission was to inform Kiderlen of the situation, and that he apparently did. If his mission involved further activities, they have as yet not come to light.—Lancken, *op. cit.*, p. 102.   [40] Caillaux, *Agadir*, pp. 323-330.
[41] Kiderlen's letter, Aug. 2, 1911, *ibid.*, p. 333.   [42] *Ibid.*, p. 165.
[43] Schoen to F. O., Aug. 4, 1911, *G. P.*, vol. XXIX, no. 10686; Kiderlen to Schoen, Aug. 5, 1911, *ibid.*, no. 10688; Schoen to F. O., Aug. 8, 1911, *ibid.*, no.

again quoted Fondère as saying that Caillaux requested that Cambon be ignored in these negotiations.[44] There is also evidence that Fondère was not the only intermediary employed by the French premier. Through such men as the financiers Spitzer, Günzbourg, and Schwabach, he relayed news to Kiderlen in preference to using the official diplomatic channel.[45] Caillaux has yet to clear himself from the charge of readiness to handicap his ambassador's work by operating behind his back.

Although Caillaux, speaking before the senate commission, denied the existence of non-official negotiations, he later openly acknowledged the Lancken-Fondère conversations and conceded that in general the disputed telegrams were accurate. Finally he came to speak with pride of the fact that he was willing to offer large concessions in order to maintain the peace of Europe.[46] Nevertheless, on two points he remained obdurate. He insisted that at no time did he attempt to circumvent Cambon, nor did he at any moment waver in his steadfast loyalty to the entente with England. He designated as palpably false all charges that he was willing to sacrifice British friendship on the altar of German promises. That he did sponsor a movement for a rapprochement between his native land and her historic enemy, he willingly acknowledged; but he did not see in that any disloyalty to England.[47] British officials were dubious of Caillaux's reasoning. Bertie complained that the premier one day remarked to him that "alliances and friendships are things which one can modify. . . ." Both Selves and Poincaré soothed him with assurances of French loyalty to the entente and asked that the remark not be transmitted to the British government.[48] Bertie's reports during the

---

10693; Schoen to F. O., Aug. 10, 1911, ibid., no. 10703; Schoen to F. O., Aug. 18, 1911, ibid., no. 10713.   [44] Schoen to F. O., Aug. 8, 1911, ibid., no. 10693.

[45] Lancken to Simmern, Aug. 21, 1911, ibid., no. 10717; conversation between Schwabach and Caillaux, Sept. 16, 1911, in Schwabach, op. cit., pp. 209-212, also published in Berliner Monatshefte, May, 1931, pp. 475-479; Fabre-Luce, op. cit., pp. 62-64. Paul Schwabach managed the business of the court banker, Bleichroder, and the salon of his mother, an intimate friend of Princess Radzewill.—Tabouis, op. cit., p. 177.

[46] Caillaux, Agadir, pp. 305-312; Caillaux's answer to Crowe, Br. Docs., vol. VIII, Addendum, pp. 795-797.   [47] Ibid.; Fabre-Luce, op. cit., p. 60.

[48] Poincaré, Au service de la France, vol. I, p. 149; Fabre-Luce, op. cit., p. 68.

entire course of the crisis revealed profound distrust of the
French friend,[49] and his diaries show almost an antipathy to the
premier of the day.[50]

The chief assailant whom Caillaux had to face was Sir Eyre
Crowe, who made of the Frenchman an arch-conspirator willing
to use any means necessary to secure the coveted German friendship.[51] He charged Caillaux with plotting as early as 1908 for the
acquisition of all Morocco, including the Spanish sphere, and in
return offering to Germany all the French Congo and in addition
forming "large and important schemes for a Franco-German control of Turkish finance and for pushing the Bagdad Railway
on in its advance to the Gulf with the assistance of the French
money and the French money-market. There seem also to have
been discussions of a very large loan to Austria-Hungary to
be negotiated in Paris, which was to be employed mainly for
the purpose of considerably increasing the armaments of the
Triple Alliance. . . ."[52] British interest would be injured by such
schemes, nor could these be harmonized with "the Anglo-French
understanding for action on parallel lines and reciprocal consideration for one another's interests in the East. . . ."[53] Crowe believed that Kiderlen, "having M. Caillaux's concessions as it were
in his pocket, and seeing that the French Government were not
active or prompt in redeeming their Finance Minister's pledges,
thought the dispatch of the ship would make an impression in
Paris sufficient to strengthen M. Caillaux's hands in getting his
Cabinet to accept the policy of a general understanding with
Germany. . . ."[54] German anger at British interference was consequently not surprising, for to them it indicated that England
prevented the execution of the Franco-German plan of coöperation. Crowe resented French trickery in using British friendship
to turn German anger against England instead of using it to combat the arch-offender, Germany.[55] Caillaux's answer to these accusations may be summed up in the three sentences: "No more

---

[49] See Bertie's reports in *Br. Docs.*, vol. VII.

[50] Bertie, *op. cit.*, vol. I, pp. 35-36, 63, 224, 259, 276, 290, 349, 351; vol. II,
pp. 34, 186, 202.

[51] Memorandum by Sir Eyre Crowe, Jan. 14, 1912, *Br. Docs.*, vol. VII, App.
III, pp. 821-826.   [52] *Ibid.*, p. 821.   [53] *Ibid.*   [54] *Ibid.*, p. 822.   [55] *Ibid.*, p. 823.

incredible story could be imagined";[56] "I had no contact of any sort, at any moment, neither with Berlin nor with the German representatives in Paris before May, 1911 . . .";[57] and "Sir E. Crowe had not a shadow of proof for the incredible mass of canards he accumulates in his Memorandum. . . ." [58]

Crowe's memorandum is largely conjecture and presents no proof of Caillaux's duplicity. A confidential report of Goschen to Grey on August 25, 1911, quoted Zimmermann as saying that the entire crisis arose "from the fact that it was not recognized in England that the dispatch of a ship to Agadir, which had been the Emperor's idea, was really meant to make it easier for the French Government to defend any compensation they might be ready to give, and which they had expressed readiness to give, before the French Parliament. . . ." [59] One could more readily accept the above statement if it were not for the fact that an accusation which the German documents prove false is included. The German documents show clearly that the sending of the ship to Agadir was Kiderlen's idea and not the Emperor's and that the German secretary had difficulty in convincing his master of the advisability of the plan.[60] The German documents reveal no indication of any collusion between the astute Kiderlen and the shrewd Caillaux. Neither do Kiderlen's private letters make any revelations. Crowe's suspicions of everything non-British seemed to have led him to build an elaborate plot from a few facts. Paul Schwabach, the German financier used by Kiderlen as his intermediary during the crisis, was in frequent correspondence with Sir Eyre Crowe.[61] He seemed to have consulted his chief, Kiderlen, before dispatching any letter[62] and to have used his friendship with the British senior clerk in order to present the German cause and to instil suspicion of France in British circles. Through frequent letters to Crowe[63] and to Baron Rothschild,[64] he kept the British informed of all gaps

[56] Caillaux's answer to Crowe, Oct. 12, 1932, *Br. Docs.*, vol. VIII, Addendum, p. 795.   [57] *Ibid.*   [58] *Ibid.*, p. 796.   [59] *Br. Docs.*, vol. VII, no. 518.
[60] See Chapter IX, *supra.*   [61] Schwabach, *op. cit.*
[62] For example, see Schwabach to Kiderlen, Aug. 11, 1911, *ibid.*, p. 205.
[63] See, for example, Schwabach to Crowe, July 28, 1911, *ibid.*, pp. 199-201; Schwabach to Crowe, Aug. 16, 1911, *ibid.*, pp. 206-208.
[64] See, for example, Schwabach to Alfred von Rothschild, July 28, 1911, *ibid.*, pp. 201-204,

that the French diplomats left in their report of the status of the
Franco-German pourparlers. If he knew of any plot between Kiderlen and Caillaux, his letters do not reveal it.

The case against Caillaux is built upon several facts. He was a
financier in touch with international financiers of all countries.
These men, in the public mind, were willing to barter anything for
the chance of securing economic profit. On May 7, 1911, while he
was finance minister, he instituted non-official negotiations with
German entrepreneurs on the question of a Congo-Camerun railroad project.[65] When this maneuver leaked into the parliamentary
debates, suspicion of all his tactics was aroused. His useless denial
of the Fondère-Lancken conversations and the incriminating evidence of the "Green Memoranda" increased this suspicion. His
removal of the direction of affairs from the hands of Selves and
assumption of control himself were then viewed, not as the exercise of his responsibility as premier to secure a satisfactory solution of all difficulties, but as a move designed to facilitate the execution of his sinister conspiracies.

Forasmuch as the overthrow of his cabinet followed closely
upon the resignation of his foreign minister, Caillaux refused to
give to the chamber a full and satisfactory explanation of all his
devious tactics. He claimed that he had prepared a dossier in his
defense and had wished to present his case to the public but that,
upon the request of his successor, Poincaré, he had agreed to remain silent.[66] Poincaré, although he opposed Caillaux's policy of
conciliation towards Germany, substantiated this statement and
declared that he deposited in the Quai d'Orsay the dossier prepared by his predecessor along with the letters which Cambon had
sent him. He further asserted that Cambon had disapproved of
the Congo-Camerun railroad project of May but had supported
Caillaux in his conduct of the Agadir crisis. Poincaré believed
that if the accused ministers introduced their defense into the parliamentary debate, national temper would increase its furor and
lamentable repercussions would arise. Delcassé, Caillaux, Briand,
and Cruppi were "on fire to answer" the attacks made against

---

[65] See Chapter V, *supra*.

[66] Caillaux, *Agadir*, p. 240; Caillaux's Rejoinder, *Spectator*, Dec. 9, 1932,
p. 829.

them; but he asked them to be silent and they agreed.[67] He then secured closure of the debate and parliamentary acceptance of the treaty.[68] Debates on the accusations continued rampant in the press, and exaggerated rumors then current might have served to feed Crowe's suspicions. That Caillaux was anxious to nurture friendly relations between France and Germany was freely acknowledged, but that he was willing to barter British friendship to secure this aim is not proven. Although the French premier used devious and questionable means to foster his ends, the charge that the dispatch of the *Panther* was for the purpose of aiding him to deliver concessions already promised is not supported by any evidence available.

When the Franco-German treaty was under debate in parliament, many of its opponents, forced to vote for the treaty due to the exigencies of international affairs, turned their wrath upon the ministers involved and upon the secrecy with which foreign affairs were conducted. Before the issue became a domestic one, however, the two chief actors, Kiderlen and Cambon, made many moves and counter-moves and faced periods of tension that almost ended in disaster before they finally worked to a solution which their respective countries were willing to accept. After the acrimonious conference of July 28, Kiderlen, with Bethmann Hollweg, adjourned to Swinemünde to consult with the Kaiser, who had recently returned from his Norwegian cruise.[69] Some circles hoped that the Emperor would restrain his subordinate and recommend a more conciliatory attitude, while others pointed out that plans had been made prior to the Kaiser's departure and that he was in constant telegraphic communication with Berlin.[70] What took place at Swinemünde has not been revealed. Kiderlen wrote that both the Emperor and the chancellor gave him *carte blanche* to conduct the negotiations entirely as he saw fit.[71] Tirpitz stated that William II agreed to a reduction of demands and to the ac-

[67] Poincaré, *Au service de la France,* vol. I, pp. 71-75.
[68] *Annales du senat,* session ordinaire, 1912, p. 287.
[69] Kiderlen to Treutler, July 28, 1911, *G. P.,* vol. XXIX, no. 10679, editor's footnote, pp. 304-305.
[70] Schwabach to Rothschild, Aug. 2, 1911, in Schwabach, *op. cit.,* p. 204; *Journal des Débats,* July 31, 1911, in Gauvain, *op. cit.,* vol. III, p. 60.
[71] Letter of Kiderlen, Aug. 2, 1911, in Caillaux, *Agadir,* p. 332.

ceptance of a part instead of the entire Congo.[72] The official reports speak only of William's anger at the attacks made against him in the French press.[73] Whatever may have taken place, Kiderlen returned to Berlin in a more pleasant frame of mind, and, as a result, a more congenial atmosphere pervaded the interview of August 1.

While Kiderlen was in conference with his superiors at Swinemunde, Cambon was meeting Pietri and also receiving new proposals from the foreign office. Selves, on July 30, defined the part of equatorial Africa that France would be willing to concede in return for a free hand in Morocco and for the Bec of Canard. He offered Germany access to the Sangha and an extension of the southern frontier of the Camerun to a point on the coast midway between Libreville and Rio Muni. If Togo were again offered, France would give in exchange certain islands in the Indian and Pacific oceans.[74] Thus fortified, Cambon undertook to secure an agreement on the basis of instructions received from the foreign office and information imparted by Pietri.

The conference of August 1, conducted in a cordial manner, resulted in the establishment of a basis of negotiations. The conferees spoke first of the Congo and the island proposals; and although Kiderlen consented to modify his demand for the entire Congo, he insisted upon access to the sea between Rio Muni and Libreville and upon territorial access to the Congo River. Germany did not wish to renew the Togo offer and agreed only to study this proposed island concession.[75] Kiderlen feared that France made this offer only to embroil him further with England.[76] They then turned to Morocco. In this field the German secretary

<hr/>

[72] Kiderlen to Treutler, July 28, 1911, *G. P.*, vol. XXIX, no. 10679, editor's footnote, pp. 304-305.

[73] Isvolski to Benckendorff, Aug. 2, 1911, Isvolski, *op. cit.*, vol. I, no. 104.

[74] Selves to Cambon, July 30, 1911, *Affaires du Maroc*, 1910-1912, no. 479. Vollenhoven, an expert from the colonial office, was sent to Berlin to advise Cambon on technical matters and was entrusted with the delivery of this despatch.

[75] Cambon to Selves, Aug. 1, 1911, *Affaires du Maroc*, 1910-1912, no. 480; Kiderlen to Schoen, Aug. 2, 1911, *G. P.*, vol. XXIX, no. 10683; Isvolski to Benckendorff, Aug. 2, 1911, Isvolski, *op. cit.*, vol. I, no. 104; Szögyény to F. O., Aug. 1, 1911, *Ö. U. A.*, vol. III, no. 2578.

[76] Letter of Kiderlen, Aug. 2, 1911, in Caillaux, *Agadir*, pp. 332-334.

placed no restrictions upon French political action; but as the consent of other powers would be necessary, he advised that the word "protectorate" should not appear in the treaty. When Cambon asked if it were merely a question of drafting, he remarked, "You write the agreement. . . ." [77]

The French ambassador set to work to formulate a satisfactory accord relative to Morocco at the same time that he was troubled by conflicting orders from home concerning the Congo. On August 2, Selves had agreed to territorial access to the Congo;[78] but on August 3, after he had apparently discussed the situation with Caillaux, he withdrew his consent and stated that any access to the Congo River which cut French possessions must not be granted.[79] Caillaux stated that the telegram of August 2 had been sent without his knowledge or consent and that Cambon's private letter to him was his first inkling of the offer. He, thereupon, rebuked Selves for his action and reminded him that the cabinet must deliberate upon all proposals of such a drastic nature.[80] This led to the telegram of August 3 withdrawing the French offer; yet both ministers were even then disposed to concede Germany territorial connection with the Congo River.[81] The difference lay in the fact that Caillaux, more experienced in diplomatic technique, simply wished to play his cards with more reserve.

The conference of August 4 progressed not at all. Kiderlen refused to discuss further the question of Togo and declared that the islands France offered had no value. He was willing to continue negotiations on the basis of acquisition of a part of the Congo, but asked for a further extension to the south to the Ogowe-Alima line, and withdrew his offer of the Bec of Canard. He again stressed the fact that the crux of the matter lay in German need for access to the coast and to the Congo River.[82]

---

[77] Cambon to Selves, Aug. 1, 1911, *Affaires du Maroc,* 1910-1912, no. 480.

[78] Selves to Cambon, Aug. 2, 1911, *ibid.,* no. 483.

[79] Selves to Cambon, Aug. 3, 1911, *ibid.,* no. 486.

[80] Caillaux, *Agadir,* pp. 172-174.

[81] *Ibid.,* p. 173; Bertie to Grey, Aug. 3, 1911, *Br. Docs.,* vol. VII, no. 454.

[82] Cambon to Selves, Aug. 4, 1911, *Affaires du Maroc,* 1910-1912, no. 489; Kiderlen to Schoen, Aug. 4, 1911, *G. P.,* vol. XXIX, no. 10685; Isvolski to Benckendorff, Aug. 6, 1911, Isvolski, *op. cit.,* vol. I, no. 106. The question of

Before further progress could be made, the sensitive combatants were struggling at each other's throats with cries of national honor and national prestige. The game of bluff came dangerously near wrecking all that had been accomplished. Caillaux, as early as July 30, sent orders to the generals and admirals concerning possible mobilization. He told Bertie that he hoped the German spies would learn of these orders and recognize that France could not be pushed too far. Bertie commented that the same German spies would probably discover that the orders were bluff.[83] Newspapers played up the rumor of mobilization, and the tension became so great that Caillaux felt it necessary to deny all warlike preparations.[84] German temper was in no mood to parley when news of another maneuver reached German ears.

Fondère, on August 4, informed Schoen that Caillaux, disturbed by the feverish state of French public opinion, declared that France could make no additional concessions and that if signs of a possible agreement were not evident within eight days, French and British men-of-war would move to Agadir.[85] Upon receipt of this news, Kiderlen classified it as a threat and first instructed Schoen to have no further contact with either official or non-official agents of the French government;[86] then he later ordered him to inform Fondère that unless the threat was withdrawn he would break off negotiations.[87] When the matter was brought to the attention of William II, he heartily supported his secretary's action; and when the French reply was delayed, he urged the foreign office to demand of Caillaux that he, within twenty-four hours, withdraw the threat, make a suitable apology, and pledge himself to offer a satisfactory project for the completion of the negotiations, or a rupture would occur.[88] The Kaiser considered the fact that Caillaux left Paris on August 5 and did not think the German protest was sufficiently

---

French option of Spanish Guinea was mentioned, but apparently not discussed at this time.   [83] Bertie to Grey, July 31, 1911, *Br. Docs.*, vol. VII, no. 447.

[84] Kiderlen to Schoen, July 30, 1911, *G. P.*, vol. XXIX, no. 10680; Schoen to F. O., July 31, 1911, *ibid.*, no. 10681.

[85] Schoen to F. O., Aug. 4, 1911, *ibid.*, no. 10686.

[86] Kiderlen to Schoen, Aug. 5, 1911, *ibid.*, no. 10687.

[87] Kiderlen to Schoen, Aug. 5, 1911, *ibid.*, no. 10688.

[88] William II to Kiderlen, Aug. 9, 1911, *ibid.*, no. 10696; Jenisch to F. O., Aug. 6, 1911, *ibid.*, no. 10689.

important to hasten his return an added insult.[89] The Emperor's ire was aroused not only by the effrontery of the French but by the attacks made against him in the Pan-German press and especially in an article in the *Post*, which contrasted the bravery of the earlier Hohenzollerns with the craven air of the present "William the Timid" and accredited the ruler with making concessions to France without his secretary's knowledge. The official papers, especially the *Norddeutsche Allgemeine Zeitung*, gave a vigorous defense of the Emperor and denied all implications of discord between the foreign secretary and his master.[90] William was too irritated by the incessant clamor to move cautiously. Free discussion in the French press of the possibility of war[91] and the German fleet maneuvers increased the tension.[92]

Meanwhile, Fondère had reported that the French premier undoubtedly wished to secure a peaceful solution of difficulties;[93] and on the same day, August 8, Schoen telegraphed that Caillaux declared the idea of a threat was a misunderstanding. In fact, Caillaux claimed that he had merely remarked that a nervous public opinion made negotiations difficult. If he had said anything about sending ships, it was that "hot-heads could demand sending ships." He assured the German ambassador that he had no intention of issuing a threat.[94] Upon receipt of this telegram, William agreed that there was no necessity for transmitting his ultimatum, and once more the explosive atmosphere cleared.[95] The French premier seemed to have been playing a rather dangerous game of bluff, and Kiderlen, in turn, successfully called his hand.

From August 9 to August 17, first one proposal and then another was presented only to be rejected, modified, or withdrawn by

[89] William II to Kiderlen, Aug. 9, 1911, *ibid.,* no. 10696.

[90] Jenisch to F. O., Aug. 9, 1911, *ibid.,* no. 10699; Goschen to Grey, Aug. 6, 1911, *Br. Docs.,* vol. VII, no. 463; Carroll, *Germany and the Great Powers,* pp. 676-678.

[91] Major von Winterfeldt's Report, Aug. 7, 1911, *G. P.,* vol. XXIX, no. 10705; *Journal des Débats,* Aug. 3, 1911, in Gauvain, *op. cit.,* pp. 63-67.

[92] Admiral staff to William II, Aug. 8, 1911, *G. P.,* vol. XXIX, no. 10692; Kiderlen to Jenisch, Aug. 8, 1911, *ibid.,* no. 10691.

[93] Kiderlen to Jenisch, Aug. 8, 1911, *ibid.,* no. 10694; Schoen to F. O., Aug. 8, 1911, *ibid.,* no. 10693.

[94] Kiderlen to Jenisch, Aug. 9, 1911, *ibid.,* no. 10697; Kiderlen to Jenisch, Aug. 9, 1911, *ibid.,* no. 10700.   [95] Jenisch to F. O., Aug. 9, 1911, *ibid.,* no. 10698.

one side or the other. The continual shifting of position made it difficult for the various parties to keep in touch with events. Cambon and Kiderlen argued over guarantees for economic equality in Morocco, cession of French preëmption rights on Spanish Guinea, the right of passage between the ceded portions of the Congo, and, constantly, the delimitation of the southern frontier of the Congo cession.[96] At the same time, Kiderlen, through Fondère, reminded Caillaux of his early offers and urged that he grant Germany access to the Congo River and a portion of the coast section.[97] Through the same intermediary he was reassured that the French premier desired a peaceful solution of difficulties and that financial circles would press him to a satisfactory solution. Caillaux, however, unfailingly replied that his proposals were only a suggestion, and that though they might have formed a basis for negotiations at the time they were made, the excited temper of the public now made it impossible to secure their acceptance.[98] France wished to secure complete freedom in Morocco with as little cost as possible and to present the territorial cession as an exchange, while Germany wished to restrict French action through economic guarantees and to secure the lion's share in any territorial exchange. Consequently each offer was weighed with national interest in mind and each new proposal called for compensatory demands from the opposing side.

The frayed nerves of Europe had reached the stage where every incident seemed sinister. On August 13 Cambon reported to Selves that rumors were current in Germany that the government planned to land troops at Agadir,[99] since news from Tangier claimed that

---

[96] Cambon to Selves, Aug. 9, 1911, *Affaires du Maroc,* 1910-1912, no. 494; Selves to Cambon, Aug. 11, 1911, *ibid.,* no. 496; Cambon to Selves, Aug. 14, 1911, *ibid.,* no. 504; Cambon to Selves, Aug. 13, 1911, *ibid.,* no. 498; Selves to Cambon, Aug. 14, 1911, *ibid.,* no. 503; Selves to Cambon, Aug. 16, 1911, *ibid.,* no. 509; Selves to Cambon, Aug. 16, 1911, *ibid.,* no. 508; Kiderlen to Schoen, Aug. 9, 1911, *G. P.,* vol. XXIX, no. 10701; Kiderlen to Jenisch, Aug. 11, 1911, *ibid.,* no. 10704; Kiderlen to Schoen, Aug. 14, 1911, *ibid.,* no. 10709; Kiderlen to Bethmann Hollweg, Aug. 12, 1911, *ibid.,* no. 10708; Schoen to F. O., Aug. 16, 1911, *ibid.,* no. 10710.

[97] Kiderlen to Schoen, Aug. 17, 1911, *G. P.,* vol. XXIX, no. 10711.

[98] Schoen to F. O., Aug. 10, 1911, *ibid.,* no. 10703; Schoen to F. O., Aug. 18, 1911, *ibid.,* no. 10713.

[99] Cambon to Selves, Aug. 13, 1911, *Affaires du Maroc,* 1910-1912, no. 500.

two agents of the Mannesmanns were endangered.[100] On the same date he also reported that Kiderlen informed him that a conference between the chancellor, the colonial minister, and an agent from the admiralty was to take place on the sixteenth, after which he would visit the Kaiser and then leave for a six days' vacation.[101] This combined news threw Selves into a panic. He feared that Kiderlen planned an interruption in the negotiations while Germany made further advances into Morocco and would return with the idea of holding the Sous.[102] Selves notified his superior of the situation and informed him that he was calling the ministers of war and navy into consultation. That Selves would take such action on his own initiative was highly irritating to the premier. He had been away from Paris since August 5, but he decided to return to the city on August 17 and transfer control of affairs into his own hands.[103]

Before Caillaux returned, Selves had sought to discover the British attitude toward the dispatch of French and British ships to Agadir in case Germany effected a debarkation of troops. Grey suggested that a conference be tried first, warned France that the sending of ships might be followed by mobilization of German troops on the French frontier, and advised her to consider such a contingency before taking any drastic action.[104] On August 20 Caillaux repeated the inquiry and suggested that the ships be sent to Mogador and Saffi instead of to Agadir.[105] He received no encouragement in his hope for British support. In fact Grey consid-

---

[100] Isvolski to Benckendorff, Aug. 14, 1911, Isvolski, *op. cit.*, vol. I, no. 108. Several Europeans arrived in Agadir in mid-July. Among these were two agents of the Mannesmanns, anxious to "provide an incident." Their presence rendered more difficult the task of the captain of the *Berlin.*—Pick, *Searchlight on German Africa*, pp. 29-31.

[101] Cambon to Selves, Aug. 13, 1911, *Affaires du Maroc*, 1910-1912, no. 501; Isvolski to Benckendorff, Aug. 14, 1911, Isvolski, *op. cit.*, vol. I, no. 108; Isvolski to Benckendorff, Aug. 15, 1911, *ibid.*, no. 109; Kiderlen to Bethmann Hollweg, Aug. 12, 1911, *G. P.*, vol. XXIX, no. 10708.

[102] Selves to Cambon, Aug. 15, 1911, *Affaires du Maroc*, 1910-1912, no. 506; Isvolski to Benckendorff, Aug. 14, 1911, Isvolski, *op. cit.*, vol. I, no. 108; Caillaux, *Agadir*, p. 175.

[103] *Ibid.*, pp. 175-178.

[104] Grey to Bertie, Aug. 16, 1911, *Br. Docs.*, vol. VII, no. 475; Selves to Paul Cambon, Aug. 22, 1911, *Affaires du Maroc*, 1910-1912, no. 515.

[105] Bertie to Grey, Aug. 20, 1911, *Br. Docs.*, vol. VII, no. 485.

ered such an action futile yet dangerous.[106] Throughout the trying days of late August, he insisted upon a conference before any drastic action was taken, and never did he approve sending warships to any Moroccan port.[107]

While the French government was trying to decide what to do in case German troops were landed at Agadir, other isolated incidents inflamed the popular mind and revealed how easily the excited tempers of the time might force the governments to serious measures. The *Matin,* on August 16, published a report that two French officers had torn down the German flag in Aix-les-Bains. The foreign office immediately informed Schoen that investigations were under way and later reported that the incident was the action of discontented workers and not that of French soldiers.[108] The German public, already greatly excited, became enraged and spoke freely of the eventuality of war.[109] The incident was closed; but, as the Kaiser remarked, it was a "symptom," a danger signal.[110]

An incident which shaded from the tragic to the ludicrous arose in connection with Kiderlen's vacation. After his consultation with the Kaiser he departed for Chamonix to visit his friend, the Baroness. Caillaux stated that, with the excited state of the public temper, he feared that some hot-heads, angered by the arrogance of the German secretary in interrupting negotiations while he took a vacation on French soil, might create a scene which could lead to disastrous results. As soon as he learned of the proposed visit, he instructed the prefect of the department to give M. Kiderlen an official reception when he arrived at the station. This was done. Kiderlen received the prefect, thanked him, and immediately left for Geneva.[111] Schoen attempted to defend his chief for his tactless action with the rather lame excuse that Kiderlen "had inadvertently overlooked the fact that Chamonix was on French soil." [112]

[106] Grey to Bertie, Aug. 21, 1911, *ibid.,* no. 487.

[107] See Chapter XII, *supra,* and Grey to Bertie, Aug. 23, 1911, *Br. Docs.,* vol. VII, no. 511; Paul Cambon to Selves, Aug. 23, 1911, *Affaires du Maroc,* 1910-1912, no. 517.

[108] Kiderlen to Jenisch, Aug. 17, 1911, *G. P.,* vol. XXIX, no. 10712.

[109] Cambon to Selves, Aug. 20, 1911, *Affaires du Maroc,* 1910-1912, no. 513; Zimmermann to Schoen, Aug. 19, 1911, *G. P.,* vol. XXIX, no. 10714.

[110] Marginal note of Kaiser's to despatch, Kiderlen to Jenisch, Aug. 17, 1911, *G. P.,* vol. XXIX, no. 10712.

[111] Caillaux, *Agadir,* pp. 342-345.   [112] Schoen, *op. cit.,* pp. 150-151.

The incident left an impression that did not further the cause of peaceful negotiations.

The mere fact that Cambon had gone to Paris and Kiderlen had left Berlin excited the popular imagination and aroused conjecture in diplomatic circles. The report spread that Kiderlen remarked to Cambon before he left for Paris, "You return to Berlin on the 28th and then we will both decide whether war or peace. . . ." [113] Germany complained of French press propaganda, of the Aix-les-Bains incident, and of Lloyd George's speech, and asserted that under such circumstances she must "unconditionally insist on acceptance of her proposals. . . ." [114] In like manner France complained that the activities of the Pan-German press and the colonial league were more objectionable than the indiscretions of her own papers.[115]

German public opinion became more and more excited as the Pan-German press became more aggressive.[116] As early as April, 1911, Dr. Class, president of the Pan-German league, wished to publish a pamphlet advocating German annexation not only of Morocco but also of the Rhone department. Kiderlen simply called such a suggestion "nonsense." [117] Nevertheless, in August, the league insisted stubbornly on acquisition of the Sous territory and published the pamphlet, *West Marokko Deutsch*, which served to excite the cupidity of the interested circles in Berlin and to stir the national spirit of France to fury. The rich mineral section of the Sous was, according to this publication, the necessary complement to German industrial development. They had cheered Kiderlen's Agadir *coup* because they expected to gain therefrom the coveted region, and they called upon him to uphold the prestige of his land —a thing which could be done only if the Sous became German.[118] To add to the tension, came reports from the other side of the

---

[113] Isvolski to Benckendorff, Aug. 18, 1911, Isvolski, *op. cit.,* vol. I, no. 112.

[114] Zimmermann to Schoen, Aug. 19, 1911, *G. P.,* vol. XXIX, no. 10714.

[115] Cambon to Selves, Aug. 20, 1911, *Affaires du Maroc,* 1910-1912, no. 513.

[116] Osten Sacken to Neratov, Aug. 18, 1911 in Siebert, *op. cit.,* no. 692; Cambon to Selves, Aug. 20, 1911, *Affaires du Maroc,* 1910-1912, no. 513; Letter of Kiderlen, Aug. 12, 1911, in Jäckh, *op. cit.,* vol. II, p. 138.

[117] Letter of Kiderlen, April 19, 1911, *ibid.,* vol. II, p. 122.

[118] Hammann, *World Policy of Germany,* p. 222; Caillaux, *Agadir,* pp. 184-186; Wertheimer, *op. cit.,* pp. 169-173.

Rhine that the French army maneuvers had been adjusted to meet the strained political situation, that officers and men on leave were called to the garrisons on the frontier, and that Caillaux had called a meeting of the ministers of war, navy, and foreign affairs.[119] Both German and French papers spoke of the eventuality of war "as a contingency regrettable but possibly unavoidable. . . ."[120] Cambon brought the news that public opinion in Berlin was so excited that unless Kiderlen presented some gains to the Reichstag it would be difficult to maintain peace.[121] Caillaux recognized that the interim before Cambon's return to Berlin must be used to clarify French proposals, to fortify her ambassador in the difficult task that awaited him, and to prepare for contingencies that might arise. To accomplish his ends, he did not rely entirely upon official agencies but continued to employ in addition various non-official intermediaries.

Lancken reported that Fondère, Günzbourg, a Russian banker in Paris, Conty, subdirector in the foreign office, and Tardieu, editor of the *Temps*, came to the embassy unsummoned. All these had the impression that Germany would yield if France remained firm in her position, but the German officials gave them to understand that such impressions were dangerous to follow. They were especially insistent that the Moroccan treaty should be written in such definite terms that no further possibility of misunderstanding might arise. Lancken understood that Caillaux wanted to arrange matters satisfactorily, but that the deciphered telegram episode had surrendered him to his enemies—a fact which made it more difficult for him to grant concessions than it had been three weeks before.[122] In every contact with one of Caillaux's intermediaries, the German agents received the impression that the premier was more conciliatory than his foreign minister and that he was willing to remove Selves from office if it were not for the fear of an ex-

---

[119] Report of Major von Winterfeldt, Aug. 24, 1911, *G. P.,* vol. XXIX, no. 10723; William II to Bethmann Hollweg, Aug. 28, 1911, *ibid.,* no. 10724; Report of Major von Winterfeldt, Aug. 19, 1911, *ibid.,* no. 10715.

[120] Corbett to Grey, Aug. 20, 1911, *Br. Docs.,* vol. VII, no. 486.

[121] Bertie to Grey, Aug. 22, 1911, *ibid.,* no. 510.

[122] Lancken to Langwerth von Simmern, Aug. 21, 1911, *G. P.,* vol. XXIX, no. 10717.

cited public reaction.[123] Selves was quoted as saying that German demands might prevail, but at the expense of a French ministerial crisis which would drive out of office both himself and the colonial minister, Lebrun. Schoen hoped, for his part, that such a crisis would not occur, for the tendency of the public would be to make martyrs of the two ministers and render Caillaux's task even more difficult.[124] Although presumably official negotiations were at a standstill, Germany constantly reminded her rival that she would insist upon access to the sea and to the Congo River and would maintain her claim to the southern frontier on the Ogowe-Alima line.[125] As France was working out her definite proposals during these days, these reminders were sent with the expectation that they would affect the decision of the French government. Germany hoped that in the ministerial conflict in progress Caillaux would win over his foreign minister, but Schoen warned his superiors of the possibility of the premier's overthrow and the installation of a more nationalistic government.[126] Germany must not be obdurate enough to provoke this eventuality.

From August 22 to August 29 the French government examined in detail the various points at issue, worked out a project of an accord, and gave to her ambassador definite instructions as to procedure. On August 22, Cambon first reported to his immediate superior, Selves, and afterward to the premier.[127] Caillaux summoned to this meeting Selves; Lebrun, minister of colonies; Messimy, minister of war; Delcassé, minister of marine; Cruppi, minister of justice; Paul Cambon, ambassador to London; and Barrère, ambassador to Rome.[128] Paul Cambon and his brother Jules had been working in close touch on all points in the Moroccan project, and the first proposal, which Selves had approved, had been sent to the

[123] Schoen to Bethmann Hollweg, Aug. 30, 1911, ibid., no. 10731; Schoen to F. O., Aug. 25, 1911, ibid., no. 10722; Bethmann Hollweg to William II, Aug. 27, 1911, ibid., no. 10727.

[124] Schoen to Bethmann Hollweg, Aug. 30, 1911, ibid., no. 10731.

[125] Schoen to F. O., Aug. 27, 1911, ibid., no. 10729; Schoen to F. O., Aug. 29, 1911, ibid., no. 10730; Bethmann Hollweg to Schoen, Aug. 24, 1911, ibid., no. 10720; Bethmann Hollweg to Schoen, Aug. 25, 1911, ibid., no. 10721.

[126] Schoen to Bethmann Hollweg, Aug. 30, 1911, ibid., no. 10731.

[127] Tardieu, op. cit., p. 483.

[128] Caillaux, Agadir, p. 180; Tardieu, op. cit., p. 484; Bertie to Grey, Aug. 22, 1911, Br. Docs., vol. VII, no. 510.

ambassador in London for his observations.[129] He criticized the proposed treaty as being indefinite and ambiguous and suggested various changes.[130]

The chief points of conflict in these meetings were the articles that demanded the renunciation of the capitulations and the abrogation of the protégé system. Paul Cambon pointed out that these items affected nations other than Germany and were likely to arouse serious objections, especially from the British. Such modifications of the Madrid convention[131] would necessitate consultation with all its signatory powers.[132] Although Selves was inflexible, the cabinet agreed to renounce or modify these points if outside pressure became great. The Congo treaty provoked more anger. The frontier as proposed by Germany involved the injection of a wedge that would sever the French colony of Gabun from the Chari-Tchad province and thus split French Equatorial Africa. The rumor that the government might cede the province of Gabun had brought forth a strong nationalistic clamor which deterred official action, but the Moroccan prize had to be paid for, and the ministers must discover a province that could be sacrificed with the least possible public resentment. The principle of the coupure was accepted, but Cambon was to strive to make it as minute as possible and to safeguard French right of transit.[133]

The first cabinet conference was followed by an interview between Jules Cambon and Caillaux on the twenty-third, one between the ambassador and President Fallières on the twenty-fourth, and a new cabinet meeting on the twenty-fifth.[134] Through these various meetings the work begun on the twenty-second was carried to completion. Cambon carried with him to Berlin a draft for a treaty and specific instructions as to procedure. He was first to secure full recognition of French political rights in Morocco, arrange for the economic guarantees deemed necessary, and only then discuss the

---

[129] Selves to French representatives in London, Berlin, and St. Petersburg, Aug. 13, 1911, *Affaires du Maroc,* 1910-1912, no. 502.

[130] Paul Cambon to Selves, Aug. 14, 1911, *ibid.,* no. 505.

[131] See Chapter I, *supra.*

[132] Paul Cambon to Selves, Aug. 14, 1911, *Affaires du Maroc,* 1910-1912, no. 505; Caillaux, *Agadir,* p. 180.

[133] *Ibid.,* pp. 181-183; Tardieu, *op. cit.,* pp. 486-489.

[134] Caillaux, *Agadir,* p. 183; Tardieu, *op. cit.,* p. 484.

question of the Congo territory.[135] France wanted to be assured first that her ambitions in Morocco were really satisfied before she entered on a discussion of compensation, for only to the degree that she attained her goal in the Sherifian empire would she be willing to grant concessions in another field.

Kiderlen, Bethmann Hollweg, and Cambon returned to Berlin to pick up again the threads of negotiations.[136] The air hung heavy with suspense. Nine weeks of fruitless bargaining had exhausted the public patience, and the unexplained and unexpected cessation of negotiations called forth endless speculation. By the time Cambon reached Berlin, rumors had filtered back to Paris that Germany would not accept the French proposals and that the situation was serious.[137] The Pan-German meeting of August 30, although more hostile to England than to France, aggravated the tension. Openly demanding the same rights for Germany in western Morocco that France secured in the remainder of the territory, the Pan-Germans pressed their arguments with grim warnings of the danger of black troops from Morocco becoming a threat to their homeland.[138] The possibility of war was freely discussed in the press and diplomatic circles.[139] Bertie declared that France did not want war but was not afraid of it.[140] Tittoni, Italian minister, was convinced war would come; for, although all parties wanted peace, the force of events would drag them into war.[141] The French army succumbed to the war spirit.[142] German military authorities sought the advice of the chancellor on all maneuvers, as they feared to move troops far from the western frontier.[143] Anxiously the public on both sides of the Rhine awaited the resumption of conferences scheduled to begin on September 1. On that day the news appeared that resumption of negotiations had been postponed until Monday,

---

[135] *Ibid.*, p. 485.

[136] Bethmann Hollweg to William II, Aug. 29, 1911, *G. P.*, vol. XXIX, no. 10725.

[137] Isvolski to Benckendorff, Aug. 31, 1911, Isvolski, *op. cit.*, vol. I, no. 115; Somssich to F. O., Aug. 30, 1911, *Ö. U. A.*, vol. III, no. 2606.

[138] Goschen to Grey, Aug. 31, 1911, *Br. Docs.*, vol. VII, no. 523.

[139] Carroll, *French Public Opinion and Foreign Affairs*, p. 246.

[140] Bertie to Grey, Sept. 2, 1911, *Br. Docs.*, vol. VII, no. 643.

[141] Somssich report, Sept. 2, 1911, *Ö. U. A.*, vol. III, no. 2611.

[142] Somssich to F. O., Sept. 2, 1911, *ibid.*, no. 2612.

[143] Note of Von Heeringen, Aug. 31, 1911, *G. P.*, vol. XXIX, no. 10726.

September 4. Kiderlen's reticence and his ignorance, or disdain, of folk psychology prevented him from making the simple explanation that the postponement was due to a slight illness of Cambon. As conjectures ran rampant, and even the suggestion that Cambon feigned illness in order to prevent resumption of negotiations gained currency, the Berlin bourse, unable longer to stand the strain, crashed.[144]

Heavy selling on Saturday, September 2, checked up unprecedented losses,[145] but the liquidations pouring in from the provinces precipitated a veritable "Black Monday" on September 4. Government bonds and industrials sank to record lows; many speculators and investors suffered heavy losses, and some faced ruin.[146] The downward slump was checked on September 5 by an official announcement published in the *Norddeutsche Allgemeine Zeitung* to the effect that negotiations had been resumed and would likely pursue an "easier course than before their interruption. . . ." [147] Throughout the month of September the Berlin bourse remained hypersensitive to every move in the diplomatic field. Unfavorable news on September 9 brought a "very bad tone" to the exchange, especially in industrials and bank shares, but the crash of that day was in no degree as severe as that of September 4.[148] By September 22, financial circles were reassured; the exchange became more firm; and the danger of a panic passed.[149]

The financial crisis on the Berlin bourse cannot be explained entirely from the standpoint of political uncertainty. A general economic decline was evident during the fall of 1911. Short agricultural crops, labor troubles, and a speculative wave had upset

---

[144] *L'Afrique française*, Sept., 1911, p. 341; Tardieu, *op. cit.*, p. 497.

[145] *L'Afrique française*, Sept., 1911, p. 341; Oppenheimer to Grey, Oct. 21, 1911, *Br. Docs.*, vol. VII, App. I, p. 799.

[146] Oppenheimer to Grey, Oct. 21, 1911, *Br. Docs.*, vol. VII, App. I, p. 799; Tardieu, *op. cit.*, p. 492; Caillaux, *Agadir*, p. 194; London *Times*, Sept. 5, 1911; Albin, *op. cit.*, p. 258; Oncken, *op. cit.*, p. 707.

[147] *L'Afrique française*, Sept., 1911, p. 341; Albin, *op. cit.*, p. 260; *Journal des Débats*, in Gauvain, *op. cit.*, p. 75.   [148] London *Times*, Sept. 11, 1911.

[149] Oppenheimer to Grey, Oct. 21, 1911, *Br. Docs.*, vol. VII, App. I, p. 803; Goschen to Nicolson, Sept. 22, 1911, *ibid.*, no. 564; Schwabach to Otto Joel, Sept. 22, 1911, Schwabach, *op. cit.*, p. 213; London *Times*, Sept. 18, 1911 (Editorial); Bethmann Hollweg to William II, Sept. 16, 1911, *G. P.*, vol. XXIX, no. 10742, editor's footnote, pp. 379-380.

the markets in London, New York, Paris, and Berlin. This speculative wave following the crisis of 1907 had spread widely among
the German middle class. The fight on the trusts in the United
States had cut short orders for iron and steel, and industrials on
the New York exchange suffered severe losses. American selling on
foreign exchanges caused uneasiness on the European bourses, but
Berlin apparently remained comparatively steady until the fall
movement of crops necessitated adjustments on the money markets. Early in the year the Paris bourse showed signs of strain;
and to safeguard their own markets, French financiers began to
call in funds from Berlin, Brussels, London, Geneva, and elsewhere.[150]

The British consul-general in Berlin, Oppenheimer, reported
that French capital had been withdrawn from Germany to the
amount of 10,000,000 pounds by September 25 and that there was
a "very strong suspicion in Germany that this withdrawal of French
capital was effected as the result of broad hints thrown out by the
French government. . . ." He explained that this withdrawal had
been effected over a long period of time, and that although French
and British money had been curtailed, other foreign money remained and even increased because of the raise in the German dis-
count rate.[151] Caillaux at one time boasted that he had caused the
panic on the Berlin bourse by influencing French financiers to withdraw funds entrusted to German enterprises;[152] but the German
financier, Schwabach, on September 16, 1911, quoted the French
premier as spontaneously denying any such charges. Schwabach
assured him that none really suspected him of such trickery because a weak bourse, evident in other countries as well as in Germany, was the result of many reasons not associated with politics.[153] Schwabach insisted that French money had been withdrawn

[150] Oppenheimer to Grey, Oct. 21, 1911, Br. Docs., vol. VII, App. I, pp. 796-805;
Raphael-Georges Levy, "Les Crises financières de 1907 et 1911," in Revue des
deux mondes, series 6, January, 1912, pp. 153-191; New York Times, Aug. and
Sept., 1911; London Times, Sept. 2-Sept. 22, 1911; E. R. Turner, "The Morocco
Crisis of 1911," in South Atlantic Quarterly, vol. XI, p. 31.

[151] Oppenheimer to Grey, Oct. 21, 1911, Br. Docs., vol. VII, App. I, p. 799.

[152] Caillaux, Agadir, p. 197.

[153] Conversation between Schwabach and Caillaux, Sept. 16, 1911, in Schwabach, op. cit., pp. 209-212, also published in Berliner Monatshefte, May, 1931,
pp. 475-479.

from the Berlin exchange much earlier and that at the time of the "Black Monday" affair not a sufficient amount remained to disturb the exchange even if it were entirely withdrawn.[154] The incorrigible French press took a different tone and during September openly bragged about the share France had in bringing about the crash.[155]

That all the exchanges were affected by the disturbances was evident. Government bonds were quoted in Paris, Berlin, and London at about the same per cent reduction. Exchange rates on sterling, reichsmarks, and Belgian francs showed the effect of French withdrawals. The reductions seemed most marked in the period of crisis—that is, from August 31 to September 22—indicating that the withdrawal of French funds at that time was a result, and not a cause, of the crash. Moreover, the sterling quotations seemed as seriously affected on the Paris bourse as did the reichsmark.[156] French funds weakened the Berlin bourse at the time of its need by their absence and consequent failure to come to the aid of the distressed exchange, but the movement seemed to be the natural economic response to a disturbed market and not the result of government pressure.[157] The further bragging of the French press that French financiers came to the rescue of the Berlin exchange and saved Germany from bankruptcy[158] has even less foundation. The French government issued an official statement repudiating the charge that it had exercised any influence upon French financiers in connection with the Berlin bourse,[159] and Caillaux consist-

---

[154] *Ibid.;* Schwabach to Otto Joel, Dec. 28, 1911, Schwabach, *op. cit.,* p. 235; Schwabach to Otto Joel, Sept. 22, 1911, *ibid.,* p. 213; Oncken, *op. cit.,* p. 707. Benac takes the same view. He wrote Georges Louis, Nov. 18, 1911:

"French money in Germany—There was none of it in Germany and there has not been for six months, or so little that it does not count.

"When I needed money for my little bank of Saloniki, quite recently, the Ottoman Bank was not able to give it to me. It is Gwinner who came to my aid!"—Louis, *op. cit.,* vol. I, p. 214.

[155] Schwabach to Otto Joel, Sept. 22, Schwabach, *op. cit.,* p. 213; *Kreuzzeitung,* Sept. 27, 1911, in Schiemann, *op. cit.,* p. 264.   [156] Levy, *op. cit.,* p. 172.

[157] Tardieu, *op. cit.,* pp. 493-495; Schwabach to Otto Joel, Sept. 22, 1911, Schwabach, *op. cit.,* p. 213; Levy, *op. cit.,* p. 175.

[158] Goschen to Nicolson, Sept. 22, 1911, *Br. Docs.,* vol. VII, no. 564; London *Times,* Oct. 3, 1911 (Paris correspondent); Oppenheimer to Grey, Oct. 21, 1911, *Br. Docs.,* vol. VII, App. I, p. 803.

[159] London *Times,* Oct. 3, 1911 (Paris correspondent).

ently denied rendering any aid to the German market.[160] French funds did gradually return to Germany, but only in that degree expected by a steadier bourse.

The action of German financiers more than that of their French brothers occupied the position of prime importance in the financial maneuvers of those fateful days. Economic factors were sufficient to provoke a weak bourse in the early fall of 1911, and when these were accentuated by the uncertainty of the political situation, the makings of a crisis were at hand. The blatant cries of war and fears of war which rent the air caused the postponement of the interview of September 1 to be interpreted as an advanced notice of a rupture in negotiations. Small investors, already upset by the steady American selling, became frightened and began to unload their holdings upon the market. Oppenheimer and Schwabach agreed that the large German banks had sufficient funds to stop the inroad if they had cared to do so.[161] The fact that they did not intervene frightened prospective investors, and a run on savings banks resulted. The German bankers, annoyed by the secrecy of the foreign office and unable to determine from the meagre information dished out to them whether war was imminent or not, refused to take action until sufficient news was issued to make it possible for them to judge the future with some degree of accuracy.[162] High financiers and small investors alike responded to the publication of reassuring statements and checked the downward plunge of securities. Oppenheimer was convinced that German finances were sufficiently strong to face the eventualities of financial strain even to the extent to which war might subject them, and that the financiers were exercising their economic strength to force the government to put an end to the political uncertainty.[163] A period of uncertainty, indecision, and conjecture works the greatest hardship on financial operations, for the game depends upon ability to guess with a degree of certainty. The British consul-general gave no credence to the theory that the financial

---

[160] Caillaux, *Agadir,* p. 199, footnote 1.

[161] Oppenheimer to Grey, Oct. 21, 1911, *Br. Docs.,* vol. VII, App. I, p. 800; Schwabach to Joel, Dec. 28, 1911, Schwabach, *op. cit.,* p. 235.

[162] Oppenheimer to Grey, Oct. 21, 1911, *Br. Docs.,* vol. VII, App. I, p. 800.

[163] *Ibid.;* Goschen to Nicolson, Sept. 22, 1911, *ibid.,* no. 564.

leaders of Germany forced the foreign office to yield to French demands because they were not financially prepared for war,[164] but he believed their action was taken to compel the government to unmask its secretive mien.[165]

The financial crisis had its influence upon the course of Franco-German negotiations, but the extent to which it affected the decisions of the foreign secretary lies in the realm of conjecture. There seems to be no shred of evidence to substantiate the rumor that German financial leaders, called into conference by government officials, had declared they were not able to finance a war of two months' duration and that this decision of the money lords forced Kiderlen to yield in his demands.[166] The German government, however, could not ignore the distress signals thrown out by the disturbed economic order and must necessarily have taken these facts into consideration. The course of events following the crash of September 9 indicated a greater harmony of views than had existed previously between the two interlocutors. Points of differences continued to appear, but they were thrashed out in the council room without reaching a point of crisis. This might lead to the assumption that the black days of September 4 and September 9 had preserved the peace of Europe by convincing the German government that it was not financially prepared for war. Such an assumption ignores the fact that the large German banks proved themselves sound enough to check the crash when they decided to throw their resources into the breach and also ignores the other factors aligned against war. Significant among these forces was the cautious attitude of the other powers.

The Agadir crisis, primarily a conflict between Germany and France, could easily have been transformed into a violent struggle between the Triple Entente and the Triple Alliance. Each potential combatant viewed the situation with alarm and in the interest of peace exerted discreet pressure upon the principal contenders. Since Lloyd George's speech, the world knew that if it came to war England would be arrayed on the side of France and suspected her

---

[164] Halévy, *op. cit.*, p. 25; Ward and Gooch, *op. cit.*, p. 452; Seymour, *op. cit.*, p. 190.

[165] Oppenheimer to Grey, Oct. 21, 1911, *Br. Docs.*, vol. VII, App. I, p. 800.

[166] Caillaux, *Agadir*, p. 196.

of strengthening her forces in preparation for any emergency. Although she kept herself in readiness and well informed on the military strength of her friends,[167] she insisted that a rupture in negotiations must be followed by a conference; and only if Germany refused to accept this overture and made it clear that she "meant war and has forced it," would England enter.[168] The British Empire would not favor a war over Morocco, but the persistent anti-British clamor in the German press threatened to change the situation into one affecting British honor and prestige. Therein lay the danger; and Kiderlen had to reckon with the fact that although the British government might urge moderation upon France, he dared not press it too far, for in that instance England would stand firm in defense of her Gallic friend. Moreover, he could count none too strongly upon his own ally.

Austria had consistently maintained the attitude that her interests in the Moroccan imbroglio was limited to two phases, maintenance of the open door and preservation of peace.[169] The Hungarian minister, Khuen Héderváry, had earlier assumed an aggressive air in his opposition to Kiderlen's policy[170] and again in September impressed upon Aehrenthal that Hungary would not be willing to go to war over Morocco.[171] Aehrenthal couched his communications to the German government in terms of perfect loyalty to the alliance, but at the same time he insisted that Austria laid upon Germany the task of maintaining peace.[172] His attitude had established a feeling of cordiality between the French and Austrian governments; and, taking advantage of this friendly atmosphere during the trying days of September, he, at the request of Germany, exercised "a light, friendly pressure on Paris." [173] He spoke to the French ambassador, Crozier, of the disastrous effect that the prolonged tension might have upon the tranquility

---

[167] Bertie to Grey, Sept. 8, 1911, *Br. Docs.*, vol. VII, no. 644, enclosure, Col. Fairholme to Bertie, Sept. 7, 1911.

[168] Grey to Bertie, Sept. 8, 1911, *ibid.*, vol. VII, no. 540.

[169] See Chapter X, *supra;* Crozier to Selves, Sept. 9, 1911, *Affaires du Maroc, 1910-1912*, no. 540.

[170] See Chapter X, *supra*.

[171] Khuen Héderváry to F. O., Sept. 4, 1911, *Ö. U. A.*, vol. III, no. 2613.

[172] See Chapter X, *supra*.

[173] Aehrenthal to Somssich, Sept. 9, 1911, *Ö. U. A.*, vol. III, no. 2619, footnote.

of Europe and of Austrian urgent desire to maintain peace.[174] He also instructed Somssich, Austrian ambassador in Paris, to announce to the French government that Austria, having no interest in Morocco other than the open door, had refrained from interference, but that she laid "great value on it that no serious complications result from the pourparlers." [175] He then notified Germany[176] and England of the action taken.[177] His purpose seemed to have been to urge moderation upon both nations in order to avoid the ultimate contingency of fulfilling his pledges under the bonds of the Triple Alliance. His strategy followed close upon the heels of the Russian démarche, and for a few days the international pressure upon France was more weighty than that exerted upon Germany.

When the *Panther* first anchored off Agadir, France had been uneasy as to the attitude of her eastern ally because of the apparent close relationship developing between Russia and Germany after the Potsdam Agreement.[178] Just as the Austrian attitude had brought forth expressions of gratitude from the French government, the Russian restraint had called forth appreciative statements from the German government. Kiderlen commented that "if England had followed the Russian example, our negotiations with France would have made further progress . . . ,[179] and the Emperor declared that the friendly feeling between Russia and Germany had not been "disturbed in the least by the Moroccan difficulty." [180]

After its assuring France in early July of Russia's loyalty to the alliance, the tsar's government assumed an aloof air of quiet and watchful waiting until long delay with its recurring periods of acute crisis seemed likely to plunge Europe into war. As she did not wish to become embroiled in a conflict for which she was not

---

[174] Crozier to Selves, Sept. 9, 1911, *Affaires du Maroc,* 1910-1912, no. 540.

[175] Aehrenthal to Somssich, Sept. 9, 1911, *Ö. U. A.,* vol. III, no. 2619; Somssich to F. O., Sept. 16, 1911, *ibid.,* no. 2633; Aehrenthal to Somssich, Sept. 23, 1911, *ibid.,* no. 2643.

[176] Aehrenthal to von Flotow, Sept. 12, 1911, *ibid.,* no. 2623; Von Flotow to F. O., Sept. 13, 1911, *ibid.,* no. 2625.

[177] Cartwright to Grey, Sept. 10, 1911, *Br. Docs.,* vol. VII, no. 542; Mensdorff to F. O., Sept. 25, 1911, *Ö. U. A.,* vol. III, no. 2648.

[178] See Chapter X, *supra.*

[179] Osten Sacken to Neratov, Aug. 16, 1911 in Siebert, *op. cit.,* no. 690.

[180] Szögyény to F. O., Aug. 21, 1911, *Ö. U. A.,* vol. III, no. 2599.

prepared and in which she saw no profit for herself, Russia, in the late summer, dropped her passive demeanor and injected into the discussion an astounding proposal. The first indication of a change of policy of the Russian government came on August 22 when Isvolski commented to Selves that "he could not see what harm the Germans at Agadir and in the Sous country could do to France supposing that the French government could not get them out of Agadir by compensations elsewhere. German occupation of Agadir might affect British interests but not those of France. . . ." Selves did not take seriously this comment, which had been dropped in an informal manner at a public reception, and he informed Bertie that Isvolski's personal opinions did not correspond with the official attitude of the Russian government.[181] As this subtle warning failed to take effect, Isvolski a few days later spoke again to Selves of the state of negotiations, deplored the possibility of war, and asked whether, if the negotiations failed, the French government would accept arbitration. Selves commented that Russia, as the ally of France, could hardly offer her mediation, whereupon the Russian ambassador, to the utter amazement of diplomatic circles, proposed as a suitable arbiter, the Emperor of Austria.[182]

The French foreign minister still seemed to think that Isvolski was acting without authority from St. Petersburg; but on September 1, in a formal interview, which he declared was conducted according to instructions from his home office, Isvolski repeated his proposal. He argued that "the extent of cessions of colonial territory to be made by France could not be of importance to her when it became, as it might, a question of avoiding war. A war would be a great danger to recently established liberal institutions in Russia, and it would be difficult to make Russian people realize the necessity of war for a few kilometres more or less of colonial territory. . . ." In case negotiations broke down, Isvolski asked, would France accept the arbitration of the Austrian Emperor, Francis Joseph?[183] Selves told him that French offers were the

<hr>

[181] Bertie to Grey, Aug. 23, 1911, *Br. Docs.*, vol. VII, no. 495.

[182] Bertie to Grey, Aug. 29, 1911, *ibid.*, no. 497. Later the suggestion arose that Taft might be a suitable arbiter.—Grey to Bertie, Sept. 11, 1911, *ibid.*, no. 544; Grey to Bertie, Sept. 20, 1911, *ibid.*, no. 561.

[183] Bertie to Grey, Sept. 1, 1911, *ibid.*, no. 499.

limit of her concessions and that if Germany did not agree, she would be responsible for the rupture. The question, moreover, was not one merely of a few acres of colonial territory, but one of the dignity of the nation.[184] The French government suspected that this move had been made at the suggestion of the German government,[185] but the Russian court denied this implication and insisted that the action had been taken only as a means to preserve peace.[186]

Buchanan, British ambassador to St. Petersburg, taken by surprise by this démarche,[187] expressed his astonishment to Neratov, who stated that Isvolski had been instructed to point out "the grave consequences that would ensue were France to approach this final stage of the negotiations in an unconciliatory spirit. . . ." Buchanan remarked that "there was at the present moment more need to counsel moderation at Berlin than at Paris and that if Germany heard that representations were being made at Paris she might think that Russia was wavering in her support of her ally and become more intransigeant. . . ." Neratov replied that Berlin knew that if war broke out it would be a European one and that Russia had maintained a firm tone towards Germany.[188] Benckendorff, who received the news from Paul Cambon, assured Grey that Russia was bound by her treaty of alliance and had no intentions of withdrawing, but that at the same time she did not wish to fight a war solely "for reasons of high diplomacy" that were "incomprehensible to public opinion." He asserted that, "in this case more than in any other, Russia must take into consideration all possible proposals, and leave nothing undone to make possible the preservation of a just peace. . . ."[189]

Selves had no faith in Isvolski and sought, through his ambassador in St. Petersburg, to discover if the move had been an authorized one.[190] Neratov confessed that he had commissioned Isvolski to counsel moderation, but he did not mention the pro-

[184] Selves to Georges Louis, Sept. 1, 1911, *Affaires du Maroc*, 1910-1912, no. 524.

[185] Bertie to Grey, Sept. 1, 1911, *Br. Docs.*, vol. VII, no. 499.

[186] Buchanan to Grey, Sept. 7, 1911, *ibid.*, no. 504.

[187] Buchanan to Nicolson, Sept. 7, 1911, *ibid.*, no. 506.

[188] Buchanan to Grey, Sept. 7, 1911, *ibid.*, no. 504.

[189] Benckendorff to Neratov, Sept. 8, 1911 in Siebert, *op. cit.*, no. 698.

[190] Selves to Louis, Sept. 3, 1911, *Affaires du Maroc*, 1910-1912, no. 528; Louis to Selves, Sept. 3, 1911, *ibid.*, no. 527; Goschen to Nicolson, Sept. 8, 1911, *Br. Docs.*, vol. VII, no. 508.

posed Austrian arbitration.[191] Selves was not able to determine whether that proposal was an official or a personal one of the Russian ambassador, but its obvious impracticability lent color to the view that the idea was Isvolski's. Georges Louis reported that, although Russia would take all precautions to avoid war, he was convinced that she would "not back out of the categorical assurances which she has given, and that if the negotiations break down, she will come to France's assistance. . . ." [192] Although Isvolski continued to prate among his society friends that Russian aid need not be expected, the French government paid only slight attention to him.[193] Reports from St. Petersburg gave the needed assurances that in case of war, however much it might be deplored, Russia would remain true to her alliance. This fact was as well known in Berlin as in Paris and London.

Russia's attitude may have been due to the situation within her foreign office. Since Sazonov had not as yet left Switzerland whither he had gone to recuperate,[194] Neratov, whom the French ambassador in St. Petersburg considered as a henchman of Isvolski's,[195] was still in control of foreign affairs. Both Neratov and Isvolski were absorbed in pet projects of their own from which they did not wish to be deflected by serious complications in a field as remote to their interests as was Morocco. Anglo-Russian relations at this time were none too cordial as a result of the acting minister's aggression in Persia,[196] while Russo-German relations were bettered by the completion of their Near Eastern agreement signed August 19, 1911,[197] less than a month before the Russian démarche in Paris. While Neratov was belligerently pushing Russian interests in Persia, Isvolski, his confidant in Paris, was again scheming to secure the opening of the Straits; and in fact, in November, he wished to barter Russian consent to the Franco-German treaty (as finally concluded) for

[191] Buchanan to Grey, Sept. 7, 1911, Br. Docs., vol. VII, no. 504.

[192] Buchanan to Nicolson, Sept. 7, 1911, ibid., vol. VII, no. 506; Louis to Selves, Sept. 19, 1911, Affaires du Maroc, 1910-1912, no. 554; Louis to Selves, Sept. 27, 1911, ibid., no. 540.

[193] Bertie to Grey, Sept. 17, 1911, Br. Docs., vol. VII, no. 554.

[194] Serge Sazonov, Fateful Years, 1909-1916, p. 39.

[195] Langer, op. cit., p. 336. See also Louis, op. cit., vol. I, pp. 31-32.

[196] See p. 246, footnote 40, supra.   [197] Fay, op. cit., vol. I, p. 275.

French consent to his plot relative to the opening of the Straits.[198] Russia's intrigues in the Balkans had begun to stir not only at Constantinople but also at Belgrade and Sofia, where her ministers were interested in the creation of a Balkan league.[199] The tsarist government, busy with its schemes in Persia, the Balkans, and even in the new revolution-torn Chinese Republic wherein lay the valuable Manchurian sphere of influence, and disturbed by insurrectionary rumblings within its own domain, did not wish to use its slim military resources in a war merely for the sake of its ally's ambitions in Morocco.

Although it was evidently true that Russia's military preparedness had not reached a stage where she could risk a war[200] and that domestic safety made war a dangerous expedient, Neratov apparently did not even consider that Russia, as an ally of France, owed her strong moral support. As a matter of fact, he remained consistently indifferent to suggestions from Paris, and at no time during the crisis did he offer France any effective assistance. France had every reason to be discontented with the attitude of her ally, especially when she compared it with the staunch support given by Great Britain. Sazonov would like to give Russia some credit for exercising "a pacificatory influence on the attitude of Berlin," [201] but he acknowledged that "impartiality obliges me to recognize, however, that the deciding factor in the political crisis of 1911 was the firm announcement by the English Government of its solidarity with France. . . ." [202] While the Entente Cordiale paid handsome dividends, the Russian alliance yielded none, or, at best, only meagre returns.

On the same day that Isvolski made his démarche before the French government, Pourtalès, the German ambassador to St. Petersburg, sent a summary of Russian views to the Berlin office. He acknowledged the friendly attitude which Russia had maintained throughout the crisis but insisted that, although France had not as yet persuaded her ally to take a strong stand against Germany,

---

[198] For a full discussion of the Straits question and the part played by Isvolski, Neratov, and Charykov in the maneuver, see Langer, *op. cit.*

[199] Langer, *op. cit.*, p. 339.

[200] Fay, *op. cit.*, vol. I, p. 293; Caillaux, *Agadir*, p. 144; Buchanan to Grey, Sept. 3, 1911, *Br. Docs.*, vol. VII, no. 501.

[201] Sazonov, *op. cit.*, p. 39.   [202] *Ibid.*, p. 40.

only Russian need for peace prevented an outbreak of anti-German feeling. A policy friendly to Germany was unpopular, he asserted, and, unless different leaders came into power, Russia would continue to subordinate Russo-German friendship to the closer ties which bound her to France and England.[203] So far as the evidence reveals, the German government did not know of the Russian démarche made at Paris; and its judgment of possible Russian action rested upon the report of its ambassador, a report that gave it no encouragement to hope for Russian friendship or even neutrality in case of war. Kiderlen must have recognized that if it came to war, he would find France, England, and Russia allied against him, while Austria offered him only reluctant support, and Italy brusquely rebuffed him.[204] The international terrain was not favorable for either side to assume an intransigeant attitude. They must struggle through to a peaceful solution; but months of work still lay before them.

---

[203] Pourtalès to Bethmann Hollweg, Sept. 1, 1911, *G. P.,* vol. XXIX, no. 10732.

[204] Italy intended to profit from the French protectorate in Morocco and was not interested in supporting Germany in this particular crisis. See Chapter XIV, *infra.*

FRANCO-GERMAN TREATY, NOVEMBER 4, 1911

From the beginning of the century French imperialists had had their eyes fastened on Morocco, and now in the fall of 1911 they were to win their prize. Before they were assured of victory, the drama of the march to Fez, the *Panther's* Spring, and the Mansion House speech faded into months of wearisome dickering over acres of swamp lands or reef-strewn coast. While the financial crisis and the continuous clamor of the Pan-Germans, matched by the cries of the French imperialists, held the public mind engrossed,[1] Cambon and Kiderlen resumed their interrupted conferences on September 4 and settled down to a minute, point by point bargaining.

The French ambassador had returned to Berlin armed with a project of an accord relative to Morocco which he presented to his opponent in their first interview.[2] He had expected trouble over the articles relating to abolition of the protégé system and revision of consular jurisdiction, not only from Germany, but also from the other powers; yet he had been instructed to be unwavering in this regard, for German consent would be of great advantage in later negotiations with the other powers.[3] As it was expected, Kiderlen vigorously protested these points; but he also objected to the restriction of economic equality to thirty years. It was agreed, however, that the protocol relative to Morocco should be tentatively settled before the question of compensation was discussed and the French proposed draft was accepted as a basis of negotiations.[4] Informed of the German attitude, Selves reminded

[1] *L'Afrique française*, Sept., 1911; *Journal des Débats*, Sept. 5, 1911, in Gauvain, *op. cit.*, vol. III, p. 73.

[2] Cambon to Selves, Sept. 4, 1911, *Affaires du Maroc*, 1910-1912, no. 529; Kiderlen to Bethmann Hollweg, Sept. 4, 1911, *G. P.*, vol. XXIX, no. 10733.

[3] Selves to Cambon, Sept. 1, 1911, *Affaires du Maroc*, 1910-1912, no. 523; Cambon to Selves, Sept. 2, 1911, *ibid.*, no. 525; Selves to Cambon, Sept. 2, 1911, *ibid.*, no. 526; Cambon to Selves, Aug. 31, 1911, *ibid.*, no. 522.

[4] Cambon to Selves, Sept. 4, 1911, *ibid.*, no. 529; Kiderlen to Bethmann Hollweg, Sept. 4, 1911, *G. P.*, vol. XXIX, no. 10733.

the ambassador that Kiderlen had promised France complete sway in Morocco but now wished to limit her power materially through retention of protégé rights.[5] Through an extension of her list, Germany could draw under her protection such a large section of the population that all other points granted France would be of no value. France must win complete freedom in Morocco. Caillaux, at the same time, sent an intermediary to the German embassy to express his sincere desire for an agreement and suggested that the Ouenza mines dispute might be solved to the satisfaction of Germany.[6]

In the meantime, the German foreign office studied the French project more in detail,[7] disapproved of several points, and drew up a counter-project which was presented to Cambon on September 7.[8] These German proposals sketched in sharp lines the chasm that separated German and French views and strengthened the belief that the aim of the Wilhelmstrasse was the same as that of the Pan-Germans. Interpreted at St. Petersburg, London, and Paris as nothing less than the establishment of a Franco-German economic condominium in the Sherifian empire, this projected treaty aroused the opposition of all whose own economic interest would be threatened by a privileged position granted to Germany.[9] France was thus placed in the favored position of defending the rights of Europe against the cupidity of Germany. She made the most of her advantage in her contacts with the foreign offices and through the leaks which gave to the press sufficient reason to cry out against the faithlessness of the Teuton. It was rumor of these proposals that again brought forth the cry of the inevitableness of war and precipitated a second crash on the Berlin bourse.[10]

[5] Selves to Cambon, Sept. 5, 1911, *Affaires du Maroc,* 1910-1912, no. 534.

[6] Schoen to F. O., Sept. 5, 1911, *G. P.,* vol. XXIX, no. 10736. Germany desired a share in the development of the Ouenza mines in Algeria.

[7] Note of Langwerth von Simmern, Sept. 5, 1911, *ibid.,* no. 10735.

[8] Cambon to Selves, Sept. 7, 1911, *Affaires du Maroc,* 1910-1912, no. 536.

[9] Cambon to Selves, Sept. 8, 1911, *ibid.,* no. 537; Isvolski to Benckendorff, Sept. 8, 1911, Isvolski, *op. cit.,* vol. I, no. 118; Isvolski to Benckendorff, Sept. 12, 1911, *ibid.,* no. 120; Isvolski to Benckendorff, Sept. 13, 1911, *ibid.,* no. 121; Benckendorff to F. O., Sept. 11, 1911, Benckendorff, *Diplomatischer Schriftwechsel,* vol. II, no. 453; Lucius to F. O., Sept. 13, 1911, *G. P.,* vol. XXIX, no. 10740; Zimmermann to Schoen, Sept. 10, 1911, *ibid.,* no. 10737; *Journal des Débats,* Sept. 9 and Sept. 10, 1911, in Gauvain, *op. cit.,* vol. III, pp. 80, 83.

[10] See Chapter XIII, *supra.*

The chief differences between the projected German and French treaties arose over the questions of judicial reform, of foreign relations, of protégés, and of economic guarantees within the Sherifian empire. The French text stated definitely that German interest in Morocco was purely economic, but the German text omitted this article. France wished the treaty to grant her the right, on her own initiative, to intervene in matters relating to administrative, economic, financial, and military reform within the Sherifian empire, while Germany insisted that this intervention should come only upon the petition of the sultan. Protected by the Madrid Convention, Germany refused to renounce her protégé rights and asserted that the judicial reform suggested by France to replace consular jurisdiction should be on the model of the mixed tribunals used in Egypt. The German text revised the article in which France promised equality of tariffs and taxes on railroads so as to include all means of transit, and omitted entirely the time limit of thirty years that she had imposed. The Moroccan State Bank, omitted in the French draft, remained in the German as instituted by the Act of Algeciras.[11]

The uproar against the German proposals arose, not over any of the above mentioned articles, but over the suggested arrangement relative to public works. The French text had briefly stated that the construction of roads was to be by adjudication, but the operation of these roads would be entrusted to Morocco or to the country to whom she willingly delegated this trust. Germany elaborated this article in the following fashion. France in cooperation with the Society of Public Works was to be conceded the right to build as military roads the Casablanca-Settat and Oudjda-Taourirt lines. She was to influence the *maghzen* to build the Tangier-Fez line before any other road except the two military roads. If Germany secured the concession for the construction of this line, she was to retain a 30 per cent share and grant 70 per cent to France. All roads constructed north of the Tensift River were to be distributed on the same percentage; but all roads south

[11] Note of Langwerth von Simmern, Sept. 5, 1911, *G. P.*, vol. XXIX, no. 10735; Cambon to Selves, Sept. 8, 1911, *Affaires du Maroc*, 1910-1912, no. 539; Selves to Cambon, Aug. 30, 1911, *ibid.*, no. 520; note of Zimmermann, Sept. 10, 1911, *G. P.*, vol. XXIX, no. 10738; French and German draft conventions, Sept. 4-8, 1911, *Br. Docs.*, vol. VII, no. 539.

of that river, that is, in the coveted Sous section, were to be allotted in the reverse ratio, 70 per cent German and 30 per cent
French, and two-thirds of all officials on these southern roads were
to be German. In addition, France and Germany were to urge
Morocco to open the port of Agadir, after which opening of other
ports would be according to German wishes in the Sous region
and according to French wishes north of Tensift. In this manner,
Kiderlen proposed to mark off southern Morocco as a German
economic sphere of interest and leave to France only the section
that lay between the Tensift River and the Spanish sphere.[12] If
this arrangement were to operate, assertions of loyalty to the system of adjudication and the régime of the open door would be
meaningless, and the economic privileges of other powers would
be crushed between the French and German grants.

French officials agreed that this section of the German proposals
must be renounced;[13] and although Germany through various
intermediaries kept in touch with Caillaux, she was unable to detect any signs of weakening on these points. Caillaux, however,
continued to show himself inclined to conciliation and ready to
offer further compensation objects, perhaps in the Orient.[14] German authorities denied that an economic partition or even a
privileged position to German industry was intended but declared
that their sole object was to prevent the extrusion of German investments from Morocco.[15] Their denial gained no credence in the

---

[12] *Ibid.* According to Dr. Pick, the Hamburg group on August 20 had proposed
a German governor for South Morocco, a French governor for North Morocco.
He also states that *en route* to Mogador Dr. Otto Mannesmann told Regendanz
that they had submitted a railroad proposal to the foreign office.—*Searchlight
on German Africa,* pp. 36, 45. Both these reports may have influenced Kiderlen
in preparing the demands of September 7.

[13] Cambon to Kiderlen, Sept. 16, 1911, *G. P.,* vol. XXIX, no. 10743; Schoen
to F. O., Sept. 12, 1911, *ibid.,* no. 10739; Cambon to Selves, Sept. 10, 1911,
Affaires du Maroc, 1910-1912, no. 542; Selves to Cambon, Sept. 13, 1911, *ibid.,*
no. 547; Isvolski to Neratov, Sept. 14, 1911, Isvolski, *op. cit.,* vol. I, no. 122.

[14] Schoen to Bethmann Hollweg, Sept. 13, 1911, *G. P.,* vol. XXIX, no. 10741;
Schwabach to Kiderlen, Sept. 13, 1911, Schwabach, *op. cit.,* pp. 208-209;
conversation between Schwabach and Caillaux, Sept. 16, 1911, *ibid.,* pp. 209-212.

[15] Neratov to Benckendorff, Sept. 14, 1911 in Siebert, *op. cit.,* no. 701; Louis to
Selves, Sept. 15, 1911, *Affaires du Maroc,* 1910-1912, no. 549; Zimmermann to
Schoen, Sept. 10, 1911, *G. P.,* vol. XXIX, no. 10740; *Kreuzzeitung,* Sept. 13,
1911, in Schiemann, *op. cit.,* pp. 247-248.

face of the elaborate distribution of economic concessions. Kiderlen, who had posed as the defender of economic equality in Morocco, had let this advantage slip from his hands into those of his opponents. France now took up the rôle and played it to a fruitful end; but although she stressed the need of maintaining the economic rights of all powers, her interest was in truth more personal. The Franco-German Accord of 1909 had shown that economic cooperation between France and Germany led only to endless disputes, for the line between economic and political interests was too faintly drawn. The question would arise again. Germany, controlling 70 per cent of all the railroads in the south, regulating the opening of the ports in the region, and retaining her protégé rights, would be in an excellent position to transform her privileged economic position into political control. This counter-proposal of the German government did not harmonize with Kiderlen's promise to grant France a free hand in Morocco. The task was now one of working out a compromise between the divergent views.

On September 16 Kiderlen agreed to a revision of the protégé system if the other powers signatory of the Madrid Convention would accept the same restrictions,[16] but he did not give way on the railroad question until September 19. On that date he renounced the article relating to the 70 and 30 per cent distribution of railroad construction but asked that "proprietors of mines and other industrial or agricultural concessions without distinction of nationality . . . be permitted to build by their private means railroads . . . destined to join their centers of production with trunk lines or with ports. . . ." [17] Upon this basis negotiations continued. Cambon frequently complained that the indiscretions of the French press and the attitude of the Paris cabinet rendered his task more difficult. He approached both the Russian and British ambassadors in Berlin with the suggestion that their respective governments exert pressure upon the Paris cabinet to persuade it to approach the German proposal in a conciliatory

---

[16] Cambon to Selves, Sept. 16, 1911, *Affaires du Maroc*, 1910-1912, no. 550; Bethmann Hollweg to William II, Sept. 16, 1911, *G. P.*, vol. XXIX, no. 10742.

[17] Cambon to Selves, Sept. 19, 1911, *Affaires du Maroc*, 1910-1912, no. 552; Bertie to Grey, Sept. 19, 1911, *Br. Docs.*, vol. VII, no. 556; Isvolski to Benckendorff, Sept. 20, 1911, Isvolski, *op. cit.*, vol. I, no. 123.

manner.[18] After each conference, modified proposals were presented in answer to objections raised, but this constant shifting of the terrain aroused suspicions as to the motives of both parties.[19] Nevertheless, by October 9 the newspapers began to publish the information that the Moroccan agreement had practically been completed;[20] and on October 12 Cambon reported that he and Kiderlen had "initialed *ne varietur* the accord relative to Morocco," [21] and on the fourteenth announced that they had likewise initialed the interpretative letters which accompanied the project.[22]

---

[18] Schoen to F. O., Sept. 20, 1911, *G. P.*, vol. XXIX, no. 10745; Osten Sacken to Neratov, Sept. 12, 1911, Siebert, *op. cit.*, no. 703; Cambon to Selves, Sept. 21, 1911, *Affaires du Maroc*, 1910-1912, no. 556; Goschen to Nicolson, Sept. 28, 1911, *Br. Docs.*, vol. VII, no. 570; Goschen to Nicolson, Sept. 22, 1911, *ibid.*, no. 564. Leaks continued to permit the press to publish details of the negotiations at times prior to their discussion in conference. At one instance, Kiderlen refused to discuss new proposals which Cambon brought because he had already read them in the papers, and stated that the attitude of the press made it impossible for Germany to entertain the project.—Kiderlen to Schoen, Oct. 3, 1911, *G. P.*, vol. XXIX, no. 10753; Schoen to F. O., Oct. 4, 1911, *ibid.*, no. 10756; Bertie to Grey, Oct. 6, 1911, *Br. Docs.*, vol. VII, no. 577; Goschen to Grey, Oct. 6, 1911, *ibid.*, no. 578; Goschen to Grey, Sept. 1, 1911, *ibid.*, no. 526.

[19] Selves to Cambon, Sept. 23, 1911, *Affaires du Maroc*, 1910-1912, no. 557; Cambon to Selves, Sept. 26, 1911, *ibid.*, no. 558; Cambon to Selves, Sept. 27, 1911, *ibid.*, no. 559; Selves to Cambon, Sept. 29, 1911, *ibid.*, no. 561; Selves to Cambon, Sept. 30, 1911, *ibid.*, no. 562; Cambon to Selves, Sept. 30, 1911, *ibid.*, no. 563; Selves to Cambon, Sept. 30, 1911, *ibid.*, no. 564; Selves to Cambon, Oct. 2, 1911, *ibid.*, no. 565; Cambon to Selves, Oct. 4, 1911, *ibid.*, no. 568; Selves to Cambon, Oct. 5, 1911, *ibid.*, no. 569; Cambon to Selves, Oct. 6, 1911, *ibid.*, no. 570; Cambon to Selves, Oct. 8, 1911, *ibid.*, no. 572; Cambon to Selves, Oct. 8, 1911, *ibid.*, no. 573; Selves to Cambon, Oct. 9, 1911, *ibid.*, no. 574; Somssich to F. O., Oct. 6, 1911, *Ö. U. A.*, vol. III, no. 2721; Kiderlen to Schoen, Oct. 4, 1911, *G. P.*, vol. XXIX, no. 10755; Kiderlen to Schoen, Oct. 4, 1911, *ibid.*, no. 10754; Schoen to F. O., Sept. 29, 1911, *ibid.*, no. 10748; Schoen to Bethmann Hollweg, Sept. 28, 1911, *ibid.*, no. 10749. These negotiations are summarized in Tardieu, *op. cit.*, pp. 483-498, and Caillaux, *Agadir*, pp. 200-213.

[20] Schoen to F. O., Oct. 9, 1911, *G. P.*, vol. XXIX, no. 10579; *Journal des Débats*, Oct. 9, 1911, in Gauvain, *op. cit.*, vol. III, pp. 132-135.

[21] Cambon to Selves, Oct. 11, 1911, *Affaires du Maroc*, 1910-1912, no. 580; Lord Granville to Grey, Oct. 11, 1911, *Br. Docs.*, vol. VII, no. 587; Szécsen to F. O., Oct. 11, 1911, *Ö. U. A.*, vol. III, no. 2743; Bethmann Hollweg to William II, Oct. 11, 1911, *G. P.*, vol. XXIX, no. 10761.

[22] Cambon to Selves, Oct. 14, 1911, *Affaires du Maroc*, 1910-1912, no. 588. France was entrusted with the task of securing the adherence of the sultan. His formal adhesion was given November 9.—*Docs. dip. français*, series 3, vol. I, no. 78; Mulay Hafid to Selves, Nov. 9, *Affaires du Maroc*, 1910-1912, no. 657.

The completed treaty gave to France sufficient guarantees that the establishment of her protectorate over Morocco would meet no opposition from Germany. German exclusive economic interest in the Sherifian empire was definitely stated. French intervention was to depend upon French discretion, and not upon petition of the sultan. The two governments agreed to a revision "in accord with the other powers and on the basis of the Convention of Madrid, [of] the lists and condition of foreign protégés and agricultural associates in Morocco . . . ," and also agreed to try to secure the consent of the other powers to a modification of the convention. The question of consular jurisdiction was left indefinite in the treaty itself; but the interpretative letters included a statement that, when a new judicial system had been formed, Germany would renounce her rights at the same time as the other powers. French power was restricted to some extent in the economic guarantees awarded to Germany. Economic equality in tariffs and taxes on all means of transit was accorded with no time limit; the state bank was retained with supervision over adjudication of public works and the operation of railroads; fishing rights were guaranteed; the exploitation and export of iron were not to be subjected to any special taxes but only to a fixed royalty on production according to the mining law; and although the partition of Morocco into railroad spheres of influence was renounced, proprietors of mines and other industrial and agricultural enterprises were granted the right to construct roads from their plants to trunk lines or to ports. All disputes were to be settled by The Hague court.[23]

These restrictions were not of such nature as to handicap the establishment of French political preponderance in Morocco. The Franco-German Accord of 1909 with its vague, ambiguous terms was now superseded by an accord that definitely placed control in French hands. The period of uncertainty was over. It remained only to be seen whether France was willing to pay the price necessary to make effective the initialed treaty. The Congo accord had yet to be written.

---

[23] Cambon to Selves, Nov. 4, 1911, *Affaires du Maroc*, 1910-1912, no. 644; *G. P.*, vol. XXIX, nos. 10772, 10773, 10774, 10775, 10776.

On October 15 the two disputants entered the last lap of their long and tedious journey.[24] The compensation that France was to pay Germany for her renunciation of all political rights in Morocco, including her withdrawal from Agadir, became the vital point of discussion. During the August conferences in Paris, the French government had accepted the principle of compensation and laid down in general the lines that the Congo accord was to follow. A frontier rectification on the Togo-Dahomey border and the cession of the Bec of Canard were to form French gains in the territorial bargain and thus make it possible for the ministry to submit the Congo agreement as an exchange of territory and not as the purchase price for freedom in Morocco. Germany's gain lay in the Congo. Cambon was instructed to grant German demands for access to the ocean and to the Congo River rather than break off negotiations, but he was to restrict the coupure as much as possible. Germany was to agree to the free passage of French troops and merchandise through the territory ceded east of the Sangha River; and each nation was to renounce all authority over natives living in the ceded lands.[25] At his conference of September 4, Cambon gave Kiderlen a general survey of the Congo project, and the German secretary reported that these were not satisfactory but could serve as a basis for negotiations.[26]

For six weeks France and Germany disputed, article by article, the projects that gradually fused into the agreement over Morocco. While the negotiators were thus busy, the press of each country was aggressive in its attacks upon concessions made by its government. The French newspapers were bold in their assertions that a government which yielded to pressure and paid for German renunciation of Morocco would be faithless to its trust.[27] The Comtesse de Brazza published an open letter to the president of the republic in which she recounted the exploits of her husband

---

[24] Cambon to Selves, Oct. 15, 1911, *Affaires du Maroc*, 1910-1912, no. 590. These negotiations are summarized in Tardieu, *op. cit.*, pp. 498-518.

[25] See Chapter XIII, *supra*.

[26] Cambon to Selves, Sept. 4, 1911, *Affaires du Maroc*, 1910-1912, no. 523; Bethmann Hollweg, Sept. 4, 1911, *G. P.*, vol. XXIX, no. 10733.

[27] *L'Afrique française*, Sept., 1911, pp. 309-311; *Journal des Débats*, Sept. 17, 1911, Oct. 12, 1911, in Gauvain, *op. cit.*, vol. III, pp. 94, 141; Carroll, *French Public Opinion and Foreign Affairs*, p. 224.

and besought the government not to sacrifice the territory which had cost him his life.[28] Her emotional appeal, only the most dramatic of the letters of explorers, added to the continuous trumpeting of the colonial and imperialistic press, aroused such a popular furor that the French ministry was afraid it would not be able to carry through parliament the original offers.

On October 3 Caillaux sent three intermediaries to Lancken to explain the situation and to suggest that a slight strip along the Ubangi and assurances of French aid in the acquisition of Spanish Guinea and the Belgian Congo be substituted for the Congo wedge.[29] When he repeated his overtures on October 8, he urged upon the German ambassador the need for a speedy conclusion of negotiations; for otherwise his ministry would be overthrown in favor of the Tiger, Clemenceau, with whom it would be difficult to form any kind of agreement.[30] Agitation stimulated by Clemenceau and Briand, master technicians, who in the art of destroying ministers had no equal, threatened the life of the Caillaux cabinet even before the completion of negotiations.[31]

Almost daily from October 8 to October 15, the premier, operating through non-official channels, strove to convince the German government of the danger involved in further delay and tried to persuade it to accept, in lieu of the Congo strip, territory that would not cut into two parts any French colony. He also tried to induce Germany to yield on one other point, the cession of French option rights on the Belgian Congo.[32] This proposal, which had been mentioned in an indirect fashion by the French press, looked upon with favor by the British government, first denied and then embraced by Germany, had become a thorny problem, since the Belgian government viewed with disfavor this unwarranted trafficking in property of hers which she had no in-

---

[28] Letter of Comtesse de Chambrun-Brazza, in *L'Afrique française*, Sept., 1911, pp. 310-311.

[29] Lancken to Langwerth von Simmern, Oct. 3, 1911, *G. P.*, vol. XXIX, no. 10757.   [30] Schoen to F. O., Oct. 8, 1911, *ibid.*, no. 10758.

[31] Selves to Cambon, Oct. 10, 1911, *Affaires du Maroc*, 1910-1912, no. 577; Schwabach to Kiderlen, Oct. 11, 1911, *G. P.*, vol. XXIX, no. 10763.

[32] Schoen to F. O., Oct. 10, 1911, *G. P.*, vol. XXIX, no. 10760; Kiderlen to Schoen, Oct. 11, 1911, *ibid.*, no. 10762; Schoen to F. O., Oct. 12, 1911, *ibid.*, no. 10764; Schwabach to Kiderlen, Oct. 11, 1911, *ibid.*, no. 10763.

tention of releasing.[33] Despite his efforts, Caillaux's pleadings fell on barren ground; for, at the same time that the French premier was trying to reduce the compensatory offers, the Pan-German and German colonial leagues were crying for larger and more luscious morsels, while they scoffed at the tiny, unsavory tidbit which promised to be their reward for their much vaunted Bismarckian stroke. Consequently, when Cambon and Kiderlen turned to the question of the Congo, their course still lay over a rocky terrain.

At their first interview on the topic, Kiderlen informed the French ambassador that on the question of access to the Congo River he must remain adamant; and upon this point he did not waver.[34] Rights of concessionaire companies, who had long held almost monopoly privileges in the Congo strip, formed another point of dispute as well as a point of resentment among the German imperialists. A strong campaign against the acceptance of the Congo accord arose in the Reichstag and in the German press.[35] Cambon interpreted the movement as one determined to force a failure of the negotiations in order to return to the question of Morocco and secure its partition.[36] On October 21 he reported that the campaign against the Moroccan accord had borne its fruit and that Kiderlen, in a heated discussion, had refused the French proposals.[37] On the same day Caillaux wrote a personal letter to him, which he suggested might be shown to the German secretary. In this he asked for further concessions along the north Camerun frontier and for a more favorable rectification of the Togo border so that he could present the agreement as a territorial exchange instead of a price paid for Morocco. He granted all

---

[33] Schoen to F. O., Oct. 14, 1911, *ibid.,* no. 10765; Schoen to F. O., Oct. 12, 1911, *ibid.,* no. 10764; N. E. Beyens, *Germany before the War,* p. 236. Albin stated that Caillaux, through Fondère, tried to treat with Davignon, Belgian minister of foreign affairs, but that Davignon refused to deal except through official channels.—*Op. cit.,* p. 313.

[34] Cambon to Selves, Oct. 16, 1911, *Affaires du Maroc,* 1910-1912, no. 591.

[35] Isvolski to Benckendorff, Oct. 18, 1911, Isvolski, *op. cit.,* vol. I, no. 144; Cambon to Selves, Oct. 18, 1911, *Affaires du Maroc,* 1910-1912, no. 594; Cambon to Selves, Oct. 18, 1911, *ibid.,* no. 595; Cambon to Selves, Oct. 20, 1911, *ibid.,* no. 598; Schoen to F. O., Oct. 18, 1911, *G. P.,* vol. XXIX, no. 10766.

[36] Cambon to Selves, Oct. 19, 1911, *Affaires du Maroc,* 1910-1912, no. 596.

[37] Cambon to Selves, Oct. 21, 1911, *ibid.,* no. 601.

other German demands and pleaded with the German government
to form a treaty so mutually satisfactory that no rancor would
remain.[38] Kiderlen replied that he too sought a treaty which would
increase friendship between the two nations but that such a treaty
could not be formed unless Germany received adequate compensation.[39] France yielded and granted the Congo coupure.[40]

The Belgian Congo remained to perplex the negotiators.[41]
Kiderlen insisted that French option rights be ceded to Germany
and pressed his demands in such an aggressive fashion that Cambon again warned his government that there was grave danger of
a rupture.[42] Evidently the German secretary had no intentions of
carrying his demands to that extreme point; instead, as he recognized the international complications involved in this issue, he
agreed to a general statement that all the powers signatory to
the Treaty of Berlin should be consulted before any territorial
change within the Congo basin was to be effective.[43] With this
problem adjusted, negotiations moved rapidly to a conclusion,
and on November 2 the Congo accord was initiated.[44] The Moroccan and Congo agreements were then officially signed on November 4.[45]

For four months the astute, capable French ambassador had
matched wits with the brusque, shrewd German secretary while

[38] Caillaux to Cambon, Oct. 21, 1911, Caillaux, *Agadir*, pp. 359-360.
[39] Kiderlen to Cambon, Oct. 23, 1911, *G. P.*, vol. XXIX, no. 10769.
[40] Selves to Cambon, Oct. 24, 1911, *Affaires du Maroc*, 1910-1912, no. 606.
[41] Cambon to Selves, Oct. 26, 1911, *ibid.*, no. 607; Cambon to Selves, Oct. 26,
1911, *ibid.*, no. 608; Selves to Cambon, Oct. 27, 1911, *ibid.*, no. 609; Cambon to
Selves, Oct. 27, 1911, *ibid.*, no. 611.
[42] Cambon to Selves, Oct. 27, 1911, *ibid.*, no. 612; Neratov to Isvolski, Oct. 31,
1911, Isvolski, *op. cit.*, vol. I, no. 150; Selves to Cambon, Oct. 28, 1911, *Affaires
du Maroc*, 1910-1912, no. 615; Selves to French representatives at St. Petersburg and London, Oct. 28, 1911, *ibid.*, no. 617.
[43] Cambon to Selves, Oct. 31, 1911, *Affaires du Maroc*, 1910-1912, no. 626;
Cambon to Selves, Oct. 30, 1911, *ibid.*, no. 622; Cambon to Selves, Nov. 1, 1911,
ibid., no. 629.
[44] Bethmann Hollweg to William II, Nov. 2, 1911, *G. P.*, vol. XXIX, no. 10771;
Selves to French representatives at London, Brussels, The Hague, Stockholm,
St. Petersburg, Vienna, Rome, Madrid, Lisbon, Washington, Nov. 3, 1911,
Affaires du Maroc, 1910-1912, no. 639.
[45] Cambon to Selves, Nov. 4, 1911, *Affaires du Maroc*, 1910-1912, no. 644.
The treaty is published also in *G. P.*, vol. XXIX, nos. 10772, 10773, 10774,
10775, 10776 and in *Br. Docs.*, vol. VII, pp. 831-836.

Europe waited in breathless suspense expecting in any moment to be plunged into war. The fruit of this agony was not worth the bother. France won Morocco and a small section along the northeast frontier of the Cameruns lying between the Chari and Logone Rivers. If she had shown a little more wisdom and vision in her foreign policy, she could have won the prize with less of a tempest. Germany gained a narrow strip on the south of her Camerun colony that brought her to the coast slightly north of Libreville and a section of French Congo to the east delimited in such fashion as to touch the Congo and Oubangi Rivers, and thus injected as a festering splinter a slice of German territory between the two parts of French Equatorial Africa. Kiderlen's bold *coup* had brought his country a few acres of undeveloped tropical land infested with the dread sleeping sickness.[46] She probably would have gained more, certainly no less, if the *Panther* had never cast anchor off the reefs at Agadir.

As the Franco-German treaty of November 4 destroyed the Act of Algeciras, the two signatories undertook as their first task to secure the consent of the other signatory powers. Their respective representatives were instructed to inform the governments to which they were accredited of the terms of the treaty and to ask their adherence thereto.[47] Grey as early as September 5 accepted in principle the project relative to Morocco,[48] and when the final draft was submitted to him, he only asked for specific assurances that the economic provisions did not establish a special position for French and German nationals.[49] Upon receipt of the French guarantee that not a privileged position but equality of trade was

---

[46] H. Wichmann, "Das deutsch-französische Kamerun-Kongo-Abkommen vom November 4, 1911," in Petermann, *Mitteilungen,* 1911, vol. II, pp. 332-333; debates in the Reichstag, *Stenographische Berichte des Reichstags,* vol. 268.

[47] Kiderlen to Metternich, Nov. 4, 1911, *G. P.,* vol. XXIX, no. 10777 (similar telegrams to ambassadors in Vienna, Rome, Madrid, and St. Petersburg); Selves to French representatives in London, Brussels, The Hague, Stockholm, St. Petersburg, Vienna, Madrid, Rome, Lisbon, Washington, Nov. 3, 1911, *Affaires du Maroc,* 1910-1912, no. 639.

[48] Paul Cambon to Selves, Sept. 5, 1911, *Affaires du Maroc,* 1910-1912, no. 533.

[49] Grey to Bertie, Oct. 4, 1911, *Br. Docs.,* vol. VII, no. 576; Selves to Bertie, Oct. 15, 1911, *ibid.,* no. 588; Metternich to F. O., Nov. 6, 1911, *G. P.,* vol. XXIX, no. 10781.

the purpose of the agreement,[50] he expressed his approval.[51] British interest was now centered on the task of alleviating the intense anti-British feeling which gripped Germany, and her officials were hopeful that the removal of Morocco as a cause of friction in the international field might prove helpful. Other powers took the opportunity to bargain their consent against some coveted project of their own. The French ally, Russia, expressed her joy over the completion of the treaty but took the occasion to ask for French support in Manchuria and in the Straits question.[52] She, however, did not press her point but soon issued the desired approval.[53] Austria was more persistent in her request.

When Aehrenthal was notified of the accord, he indicated that he would barter Austrian consent in return for a French loan.[54] He informed his ambassadors that Spain had asked Austria to delay recognition so as to make the Spanish position more favorable. He refused joint action with Spain,[55] but replied, when he was officially presented with the text of the treaty, that he found it necessary to study the agreement in detail in order to assure himself that the open door was protected.[56] On November 16 he authorized Szécsen to question the French government on the economic guarantees awarded to Austrian subjects and on the future revision of the Madrid Convention, and to seek French consent to a loan of a milliard of francs.[57] Crozier was inclined to

---

[50] Selves to Daeschner, Nov. 16, 1911, *Affaires du Maroc,* 1910-1912, no. 671; also in *Docs. dip. français,* series 3, vol. I, no. 137.

[51] Daeschner to Selves, Nov. 15, 1911, *Docs. dip. français,* series 3, vol. I, no. 127.

[52] Neratov to Isvolski, Oct. 5, 1911, Isvolski, *op. cit.,* vol. I, no. 132; Isvolski to Neratov, Nov. 8, 1911, *ibid.,* no. 154; Lucius to F. O., Nov. 6, 1911, *G. P.,* vol. XXIX, no. 10782, footnote.

[53] Lucius to F. O., Nov. 6, 1911, *G. P.,* vol. XXIX, no. 10782; Panafieu to Selves, Nov. 15, 1911, *Docs. dip. français,* series 3, vol. I, no. 130.

[54] Crozier's note, Nov. 4, 1911, *Ö. U. A.,* vol. III, no. 2870; Crozier to Selves, Nov. 4, 1911, *Docs. dip. français,* series 3, vol. I, no. 10.

[55] Aehrenthal to ambassadors in Madrid, Berlin, London, and Paris, Nov. 4, 1911, *Ö. U. A.,* vol. III, no 2869.

[56] Aehrenthal to ambassadors in Paris, Berlin, London, Rome, Madrid, Constantinople, and St. Petersburg, Nov. 6, 1911, *ibid.,* vol. III, no. 2877.

[57] Aehrenthal to Szécsen, Nov. 16, 1911, *ibid.,* no. 2938; Aehrenthal to Szécsen, Nov. 20, 1911, *ibid.,* no. 2954; Crozier to Selves, Nov. 19, 1911, *Docs. dip. français,* series 3, vol. I, no. 152.

interpret this move as an effort on the part of Austria to free herself from German domination and to win the friendship of the Entente.[58] Many British and French circles, however, did not see in the Austrian request a friendly hand extended to the Entente but instead a wily trick by which she could secure funds to finance the military preparations of the Central Powers.[59] Although Aehrenthal might promise that the funds thus secured would not be used for military purposes, they could easily be indirectly applied by settling other Austrian obligations and freeing her resources for military expenses. The French government considered the possibility too dangerous and refused the loan.[60] Aehrenthal continued his policy of delay until January 4, 1912, when he sent Berlin and Paris a formal notice of Austrian acceptance of the treaty.[61] France was annoyed but not greatly worried over Aehrenthal's tactics. She trusted Germany to exert the necessary pressure to secure ultimately the Austrian consent.[62] The Spanish problem was of a different nature.

Notified of the treaty, Spain agreed to approve it when her own problems had been satisfactorily arranged.[63] The secret clauses of the Anglo-French treaty of 1904 and the various treaties between France and Spain had guaranteed to her Ifni in the south and the northern section of the Sherifian empire,[64] but Spain did not trust her alleged friends and watched with jealous eyes the gradual French penetration of Morocco. When France moved to Fez, Spain occupied Larache and El Ksar and later greeted the Agadir *coup* with joy, for she hoped to be included in the negotiations. Her constant importunities to the various foreign offices annoyed them without securing much attention for her claims. When France and

---

[58] Cartwright to Grey, Nov. 19, 1911, *Br. Docs.,* vol. VII, no. 696.

[59] Cartwright to Nicolson, Nov. 23, 1911, *ibid.,* no. 708; Poincaré, *Au service de la France,* vol. I, pp. 239-241; Steed, *op. cit.,* pp. 345-347.

[60] Szécsen to F. O., Dec. 9, 1911, *Ö. U. A.,* vol. III, no. 3080.

[61] Saint-Aulaire to Selves, Jan. 4, 1912, *Docs. dip. français,* series 3, vol. I, no. 43; Aehrenthal to Paris and Berlin, Dec. 27, 1911, *Ö. U. A.,* vol. III, no. 3167.

[62] Selves to Berckheim, Nov. 22, 1911, *Docs. dip. français,* series 3, vol. I, no. 190; Crozier to Selves, Nov. 29, 1911, *ibid.,* no. 243.

[63] Bunsen to Grey, Nov. 8, 1911, *Br. Docs.,* vol. VII, no. 630; Geoffray to Selves, Nov. 6, 1911, *Docs. dip. français,* series 3, vol. I, no. 35.

[64] See Chapter II, *supra.*

Germany opened negotiations, she was shoved aside and told to wait until the two chief antagonists had settled their dispute, after which she might present her brief.[65] Throughout the summer and fall France was in touch with Spanish officials; various proposals were tentatively entertained; but serious consideration was postponed until after the conclusion of the Franco-German treaty. England constantly admonished Spain to trust to her British friend to safeguard her interests and to do nothing that might accentuate the international tension.[66] Spain fretted but, deserted by Germany, waited her turn in the council room.

In the final settlement, Germany agreed to stand aloof while France made her settlement with Spain, and after November 4 the French government seriously undertook the task. Upon the invitation of France and Spain, Sir Maurice Bunsen, the British ambassador in Madrid, joined Señor Garcia Prieto, Spanish foreign minister, and Geoffray, the French ambassador, in the conduct of negotiations.[67] France took the position that since she had purchased German renunciation, as a result of which Spanish control within her allotted sphere could be consolidated, the Madrid government should be willing to reward its neighbor for the service rendered. The extreme French view was embodied in the Regnault proposal presented in early November. France asked for the cession of Ifni and a frontier demarkation that would leave to her, with the exception of the Tangier section, the entire Atlantic coast of Morocco from Cape Spartel to Ceuta.[68] England refused to accept this delimitation; and, despite the stubborn resistance of Caillaux, she insisted that the coast section of the territory promised Spain in the treaty of 1904 be allowed her.[69] She much preferred to have

[65] See Chapter X, supra.

[66] Bunsen to Grey, Aug. 30, 1911, Br. Docs., vol. VII, no. 521; Bunsen to Grey, Sept. 3, 1911, ibid., no. 527; Bertie to Grey, Sept. 1, 1911, ibid., no. 525; Bunsen to Grey, Sept. 19, 1911, ibid., no. 559.

[67] Grey to Bunsen, Dec. 4, 1911, ibid., no. 734; Grey to Bunsen, Dec. 6, 1911, ibid., no. 735.

[68] Bertie to Grey, Oct. 21, 1911, ibid., no. 598. The internationalization of Tangier was agreed upon.

[69] Bertie to Grey, Oct. 21, 1911, ibid., no. 598, Crowe's note; Bertie to Grey, Nov. 2, 1911, ibid., no. 614; Bertie to Grey, Nov. 3, 1911, ibid., no. 618; Bertie to Grey, Nov. 26, 1911, ibid., no. 716.

Spain rather than France on the northwest coast of Morocco, but she accepted the principle of compensation to France for the sacrifice she had made to Germany.

According to Spain, her task was to safeguard herself from being compelled to pay both France and Germany. The danger lay in the absorption of Spanish Guinea by the Cameruns. Consequently, she refused to accept the idea of a modification of zones established in 1904 until she had been assured that her agreement with France would constitute the full total of her obligations. Supervision of customs, regulation of railroad construction, especially the priority claims of the Tangier-Fez line, the correlation of Spanish and French advisory power over the sultan, and the many interrelated administrative problems perplexed the negotiators and, coupled with the problem of delimiting the zones, plagued the foreign offices for over a year.[70] Not until November 14, 1912, were the numerous problems adjusted and the Franco-Spanish treaty initialed.[71] France gained the hinterland around Ifni and extended the frontier of her sphere in the north, but Spain retained the coast section practically as drawn in 1904. The Franco-Moroccan treaty establishing the French protectorate was signed[72] and the work of making that protectorate effective was well advanced before the Franco-Spanish negotiations were completed.

France and Italy had made their bargain in 1901. The Agadir crisis gave Italy the chance to collect, and she took the opportunity to filch from Turkey her Tripolitan province. As she was busy with that task when the treaty was presented to her, she approved without demurrer.[73]

In November, 1911, France and Germany submitted their treaty to the various powers and asked for their approval, but the court before which the treaty was to face its most severe trial was the tribunal of Franco-German public opinion. Internal strife complicated the issue in both countries. The German public received simultaneously the news of the initialing of the treaty and the

[70] The documents relative to the lengthy and tedious negotiations are given in *Docs. dip. français,* series 3, vols. I, II, III, and IV.

[71] Geoffray to Poincaré, Nov. 14, 1912, *ibid.,* series 3, vol. IV, no. 238.

[72] Traité conclu entère la France et le Maroc, 30 mars, 1912, pour L'Organisation du Protectorat Français dan L'Empire Cherifien, *ibid.,* series 3, vol II, no. 278.   [73] Legrand to Selves, Nov. 9, 1911, *ibid.,* series 3, vol. I, no. 71.

resignation of the colonial secretary, Lindequist.[74] This minister had consistently protested against the compensation objects under discussion. His objection to the cession of Togo was so violent that the foreign secretary was forced to withdraw this territory from consideration. He considered the Congo as a worthless strip of swamplands which had been stripped of its sole resource, caoutchouc, by the various concessionaire companies and whose value was not equal to the vast expense necessary to develop it. He wished instead to secure the French colony of Dahomey, which, added to the already fruitful Togoland, would give to Germany adequate returns for her investments.[75] Convinced that he could not support the government policy and resentful of Kiderlen's disdain, the colonial secretary on August 9 tendered his resignation. The Kaiser was, however, persuaded by Kiderlen not to accept it, because the state of negotiations was such that the inevitable clamor excited by this action might prove disastrous.[76] Lindequist was, therefore, persuaded to retain his portfolio until negotiations were completed; but as soon as he received a copy of the text of the treaty, he wrote a lengthy analysis of the disadvantages involved and with this tendered his resignation,[77] which the Emperor now accepted.[78] Official papers severely criticized the colonial secretary for his behaviour and explained it on the basis of personal pique, while non-official papers praised in eulogistic terms the courage of an official who refused to support a treaty of which he disapproved. This rift within the government circle added personal bitterness to the attacks made upon Kiderlen's Moroccan policy.

German reception of the Franco-German treaty was marked by general dissatisfaction and rancor.[79] The crushing disappointment of the German imperialists and the bitter humiliation of German patriots aroused a tempest comparable in intensity to the storm

---

[74] Cambon to Selves, Nov. 3, 1911, *Affaires du Maroc,* 1910-1912, no. 638.

[75] Lindequist to Bethmann Hollweg, Aug. 5, 1911, *G. P.,* vol. XXIX, no. 10690.

[76] Kiderlen to Jenisch, Aug. 9, 1911, *ibid.,* no. 10722.

[77] Lindequist to Kiderlen, Oct. 31, 1911, *ibid.,* no. 10770.

[78] *Ibid.,* editor's footnote.

[79] Schoen, *op. cit.,* pp. 152, 153; Rachfahl, *op. cit.,* p. 337; Wolff, *op. cit.,* pp. 62-64; Tirpitz, *op. cit.,* vol. I, pp. 212, 213; Bülow, *op. cit.,* vol. III, p. 125; Goschen to Grey, Nov. 6, 1911, *Br. Docs.,* vol. VII, no. 664; *Kreuzzeitung,* Nov. 8, 1911, in Schiemann, *op. cit.,* p. 322; *Berliner Tageblatt,* Nov. 2, 1911.

provoked by the *Daily Telegraph* interview.[80] Four months of ex-
pectancy, fanned to fever pitch by passionate propaganda led by
the Pan-Germans, had culminated in meagre gains. The desires of
the German imperialists had been inflamed by visions of the fabulous wealth that would revert to them with the acquisition of southern Morocco. The Sous was their El Dorado. In their eyes, Kiderlen's action could have no other motive. Instead of this land of
vast riches, which they had held almost within their grasp, the
foreign secretary offered them a fever-infested, concession-plagued
marshland in the Congo. Private interests encouraged them in their
outcry against the secretary.[81] The treaty stood before them as a
testimony of the weakness of the German government, of its undue yielding to British pressure, and as a mark of national humiliation. They successfully turned their disappointment into a question of national prestige and added to their cohorts the intense
national patriots. The government papers were hard pressed in
their efforts to capture the public attention and to explain the
numerous advantages accruing to Germany. Their greatest efforts
were centered upon refutation of the charge that Germany had
any intention of acquiring territory in Morocco. They argued that
since 1909 Germany had renounced all political interests in the
Sherifian empire, that she had never held any territory in Morocco
and therefore had not sacrificed any. They also pointed out that
the improved relations with France expected from the agreement
and the territorial acquisitions in the Congo represented concrete
gains for the German nation.[82] The nearness of the Reichstag elec-
tions, which made of the treaty a political issue, the agitation fos-
tered by private interests, and the tendency among the foreign
press to describe the agreement as a victory for France and the
Entente transformed the official utterances into a feeble cry
scarcely heard above the din. To the accompaniment of the press
clamor the battle opened in the popular chamber.

On November 9, Bethmann Hollweg defended the treaty before

---

[80] Hammann, *The World Policy of Germany*, p. 222; Carroll, *Germany and
the Great Powers*, pp. 690-694.

[81] Wichmann, *op. cit.*, p. 333; Bebel before the Reichstag, Nov. 9, 1911, *Stenographische Berichte des Reichstags*, vol. 268, p. 7723.

[82] *Journal des Débats*, Oct. 29, 1911, in Gauvain, *op. cit.*, vol. III, pp. 151-153;
Goschen to Grey, Nov. 6, 1911, *Br. Docs.*, vol. VII, no. 664.

the Reichstag.[83] He denied all charges of weakness, renounced any intention of securing any territory in Morocco, pointed out that German economic interests had been safeguarded, and described the Congo compensation as of real value. Germany, he insisted, had won that which she set out to gain and therefore had not yielded before any type of pressure. Hertling, leader of the Center Party, answered the chancellor's speech. He reminded his audience that the rumor still existed that the *Panther* had had in mind a territorial exchange in Morocco and that Germany had drawn back before an English threat. He denied that the treaty brought any advantages to Germany, for he had no faith in French economic guarantees or in the possible value of the Congo.[84] His speech was forgotten in the uproar created by his successor, Herr von Heydebrand, leader of the Conservative Party, whose fiery speech shifted the ground from Franco-German to Anglo-German relations.[85] Conservative, Center, and National Liberal leaders criticized the government for its weakness, but the Socialist Bebel charged it with warlike designs. In a typical socialist speech, he attacked the capitalist cliques—the Mannesmanns, the Krupp-Bohlen, and the Schneider-Creuzot syndicates—who to gain profit for themselves drove the government to an aggressive action pregnant with possibilities of war.[86] Debates continued through November 12; but the low value of the Congo, the advisability of the Agadir act, the resignation of Lindequist, Lloyd George's speech, and the possible danger of war hung as questions unsatisfactorily answered. The Reichstag registered its protest but then approved the treaty.[87]

After ratification, a new debate arose over the policy of the foreign secretary. As early as November 11, Kiderlen-Waechter denied the charges that he had assured press representatives that the foreign office wished to acquire land in Morocco. He asserted that a meeting of fifty representatives of the press had taken place and that they, among themselves, decided on annexation of southern Morocco, but that he told the "chief matador, take care, you alone will not be able to accomplish it and the government does not

---

[83] *Stenographische Berichte des Reichstags,* vol. 268, pp. 7708-7713.

[84] *Ibid.,* pp. 7713-7718.   [85] *Ibid.,* pp. 7718-7722.

[86] *Ibid.,* pp. 7723-7730.   [87] *Ibid.,* pp. 7730-7807.

stand behind you. . . ." [88] A more vigorous campaign against the
foreign secretary arose in the Reichstag at the beginning of the
next year, provoked by a suit between the conservative weekly,
Grenzboten, and the Pan-German *Post.*

The *Grenzboten* called the *Post, Rhenisch-Westfälische Zeitung,*
and *Tagliche Rundschau* "the Mannesmann press" and "accused
them of wilfully leading the public astray about German intentions
in Morocco, and threatened to expose the relations between the
three journals and the Messrs. Mannesmann." This statement
aroused the ire of the *Post,* which in reply spoke of these insinuations as "a base calumny." The *Grenzboten* then brought suit
against the *Post* for slander. The *Post* won the case. The court
decided that the accusations of the *Grenzboten* justified a sharp
reply.[89] Testimony brought into the trial included statements of
Pan-Germans that Kiderlen had assured them that southern Morocco was his ultimate purpose. Class, president of the League,
insisted that prior to the *coup* the foreign secretary had twice
stated his approval of the Pan-German program (openly one of
acquisition of South Morocco) and of the Pan-German press
agitation. Furthermore Kiderlen had remarked that he [Class]
"would be delighted with our Moroccan policy. . . ." [90] On the day
the *Panther* approached Agadir, Class had a conversation with
Zimmermann, who exuberantly announced the *Panther's* move and
asserted that the government intended to take hold of this territory and not get out.[91] This leader of the League was, and remained, convinced "that Kiderlen had intended territorial acquisition in West Morocco. . . ." [92]

On February 17, 1912, the Social Democrat Ledebour introduced the question and the Pan-German testimony before the
Reichstag. He charged the government with welcoming, if not encouraging, the Pan-German agitation, and thus exciting the public while Franco-German negotiations were in progress.[93] Kiderlen
rose to answer these charges. He explained that the entire program
had been worked out before the ship had left for Agadir. He acknowledged that a few days before the *coup* he had said to Dr.

[88] *Ibid.,* p. 7807.   [89] London *Times,* Jan. 4, 1912 (Berlin correspondent).
[90] Class, *op. cit.,* pp. 182, 203-204.   [91] *Ibid.,* pp. 206, 223.
[92] *Ibid.,* p. 222. [93] *Stenographische Berichte des Reichstags,* vol. 283, pp. 96-98.

Class, "We will shortly do something in order to bring the Moroccan affair to a head. I beg you, however, that not too much noise be made about it. Be careful, it is only a beginning of negotiations. . . ." In answer to the charge against Zimmermann, he stated that the under-secretary told Class that no German settlements would be made in Morocco. Kiderlen confessed, however, that in September he told the president of the Pan-German League that, due to the chauvinistic spirit in the French press, "it would be good if a patriotic feeling were shown among us. . . ." [94] He consistently denied that he had ever told anyone that he wished to take a part of Morocco. Class as consistently insisted that the foreign secretary told him that that was his original plan. Kiderlen's known sympathy with the Pan-Germans, his frequent conferences with them, and his failure to check the agitation of their press were offered as arguments strengthening the Pan-German claim; but the dispute was allowed to rest with no conclusive evidence presented by either side.

The Franco-German treaty of November 4, 1911 was viewed by the Germans as a national humiliation, inflicted upon them by the aggressive action of the British and the weak, vacillating, dilatory policy of their own government. When one of the signatory nations greets a treaty with such an outburst of resentment, it might be expected that the other would acclaim it as a national victory and rejoice over her conquest. Quite otherwise was the reception accorded the Franco-German treaty in France. The German style of diplomacy that anchored a gunboat in a Moroccan harbor and kept her there throughout the negotiations resembled too much a gunman's technique, the extraction of a ransom at the point of a pistol. The French patriots resented the mailed-fist diplomacy of their neighbor, and their resentment turned against their own government, which had submitted to such treatment. The four months of fractious delay had increased their irritation and wiped out all the benefits that might have accrued to a peaceful and judicious settlement of the Moroccan question. They argued that France had no need to make an additional bargain with Germany in order to secure her approval of French political rights in Morocco, since

[94] *Ibid.*, pp. 102-104; *Journal des Débats*, Feb. 18, 1911, in Gauvain, *op. cit.*, vol. III, p. 361; Wertheimer, *op. cit.*, p. 158.

she had recognized the preponderance of French political interests
in 1909. The economic terms of the treaty of 1911 held France
in economic tutelage. For what then, they asked, did the French
government, without a struggle, surrender a strip of territory won
by the exertions, the lives, and the financial investments of French
subjects? The wedge, which cut French Equatorial Africa, was
looked upon as a mutilation that stood as a symbol of French
weakness. Even after the sacrifices had been made, peace was in
no way assured, for the frontiers were so involved that future disputes might easily arise.[95]

The opposition papers were given new fuel when on November
8 the *Matin* published the secret treaty of 1904 between France
and Spain.[96] This was soon followed by the publication of the
Franco-Spanish treaties of 1902 and 1905 and, on November 21,
by the publication of the secret terms of the Anglo-French Accord
of 1904.[97] The press now added to their denunciation of the Franco-
German treaty an indictment against secret diplomacy with all its
disastrous results. The French public were made to realize that the
purchase price had bought only a decapitated land. Spain, who
had rendered no aid but had handicapped France in her efforts to
free the land from German interference, was now to share in the
reward.[98] Public hostility was so great prior to the parliamentary
debates that the ministry feared for its life and, indeed, for the
life of the treaty. For this reason Caillaux sought and secured
from the German government the prompt recall of the *Panther*.[99]
As he did not wish to see the conciliatory Caillaux cabinet replaced
by that of an intransigent Clemenceau prior to a ratification of

---

[95] Tardieu, *op. cit.*, pp. 593-595; Schoen to F. O., Nov. 5, 1911, *G. P.*, vol.
XXIX, no. 10779; *Journal des Débats*, Nov. 5, 6, 1911, in Gauvain, *op. cit.*, vol.
III, pp. 167, 171, 174; *Temps*, Dec. 20, 1911; *Le Matin*, Dec. 21, 1911;
Fabre-Luce, *op. cit.*, pp. 64-70; Carroll, *French Public Opinion and Foreign
Affairs*, pp. 247-249.

[96] Stuart, *French Foreign Policy*, p. 327; Bertie to Grey, Nov. 9, 1911, *Br.
Docs.*, vol. VII, no. 670.

[97] Bertie to Grey, Nov. 11, 1911, *Br. Docs.*, vol. VII, no. 675.

[98] Carroll, *French Public Opinion and Foreign Affairs*, pp. 249, 250.

[99] Cambon to Kiderlen, Nov. 14, 1911, *G. P.*, vol. XXIX, no. 10784; Selves to
Cambon, Nov. 4, 1911, *Affaires du Maroc*, 1910-1912, no. 645; note of Schwabach,
Nov. 23, 1911, Schwabach, *op. cit.*, pp. 226-228, also published in *Berliner Monat-
shefte*, May, 1931, pp. 479-481.

the treaty, Kiderlen arranged for the recall of the ship on November 28.[100] Caillaux needed this vantage point when he submitted the newly created treaty for the ratification of the French parliament.

The debates in the chamber of deputies lasted from December 14 until December 20, upon which date this body ratified the accord.[101] Chief opposition arose over the restrictions on Morocco, the cleavage in the Congo, the Spanish demands, and the vicious character of secret diplomacy. The speech of the aged Count Albert de Mun, December 11, aroused the greatest excitement in its emotional appeal to the former courage of the French nation, which had never before surrendered a colony without defending it with her arms.[102] Selves had to face severe charges of incompetence and weakness, and his replies failed to convince his opponents. Jaurès, as usual, attacked the policy of the government and the method by which it had secured the protectorate of Morocco.[103] Jules Delahaye bitterly criticized Caillaux and charged him with intrigues with international financiers to secure the protectorate for their advantage.[104] Relatively little personal animosity was shown in the debates in the chamber and approval was secured with a minimum of difficulty. The senate proved to be a more serious obstacle in the path of ratification.

The senate commission first took up the consideration of the treaty, and in the testimony taken before that group Caillaux's non-official negotiations were aired in such manner as to effect the overthrow of his cabinet.[105] Revelations about dissension in the cabinet and its lack of unity in foreign policy made, of course, a very bad impression both within parliament and in the press.[106] Public suspicion was aroused by the publication of the secret treaties and by the half-told tale of Caillaux's intrigues, and faith in each minister who had tinkered with the Moroccan problem was

---

[100] Von Hornhardt to Kiderlen, Nov. 18, 1911, *G. P.*, vol. XXIX, no. 10785, editor's footnote; Kiderlen to Schoen, Nov. 25, 1911, *ibid.*, no. 10787; Schoen to Bethmann Hollweg, Nov. 28, 1911, *ibid.*, no. 10789.

[101] *Annales de la chambre des députés*, session ordinaire, 1911, p. 1564; Schoen to Bethmann Hollweg, Dec. 21, 1911, *G. P.*, vol. XXIX, no. 10791.

[102] *Annales de la chambre des députés*, session ordinaire, 1911, pp. 1350-1354.

[103] *Ibid.*, pp. 1511-1518.   [104] *Ibid.*, pp. 1401-1408.   [105] See Chapter XIII, *supra*.

[106] Kühlmann to Bethmann Hollweg, Jan. 11, 1912, *G. P.*, vol. XXIX, no. 10794.

thereby weakened. Delcassé, Pichon, and Cruppi were suspected
of designs as unsavory even as those of Caillaux. The debates in
the senate retold the entire history of the Moroccan problem,
stressed the formation of the Accord of 1909, blamed the successive governments for their failure to make this Accord effective,
and denounced the treaty of 1911 in terms now tinctured with bitter personal animosities.[107] Pichon denied the innate defects in the
Accord of 1909 and placed the responsibility for its death upon
his successors.[108] He later declared that "Agadir" with its mani-
fold results would not have occurred if he had remained in office
because then the march to Fez would not have taken place.[109] He
failed, of course, to explain how he would have avoided it. Cruppi
was blamed for the advance to Fez and for the failure of the economic collaboration planned in the Accord of 1909. Delcassé was
criticized because he had instituted the policy of bargaining whose
natural fruit was the Agadir crisis. If England, Spain, and Italy
were to be paid for their consent to a French protectorate of Morocco, the historic enemy of the Republic, Germany, must also be
appeased. The senators, therefore, criticized the successive governments because they had failed to recognize and give attention
to this cankerous necessity before it became dangerous. Clemenceau, not only the most capable, but the bitterest foe of the treaty,
fought its ratification with all his force. The appeals of the government defenders that, despite the imperfections of the Accord
and the obnoxious conduct of the ministers, the treaty must be
ratified in order to preserve the peace of Europe, had no effect
upon this enraged senator, who consistently cast his vote against
its adoption.[110] Poincaré, as premier, sponsored the agreement,
not because it was perfect, but because it was indispensable that it
be ratified; and he successfully rallied the necessary votes on February 10.[111] The Franco-German treaty of November 4, 1911
emerged as a final settlement of the delicate Moroccan question.

The debates in the senate had their repercussions in public opin-

---

[107] Debates in the senate, Feb. 5-10, *Annales du senat,* session ordinaire, 1912,
pp. 155-283.   [108] *Ibid.,* pp. 228-239.

[109] Schoen to Bethmann Hollweg, April 10, 1912, *G. P.,* vol. XXXIX, no. 15642.

[110] *Annales du senat,* session ordinaire, 1912, pp. 272-281.

[111] *Ibid.,* pp. 264-273. The final vote was 222 for to 48 against the treaty.—
Ibid., p. 283.

ion. Personal animosities, suspicion, and distrust played a large part in the activities of all parties; but national resentment against the enemy across the Rhine held the foreground. All parties except the Socialists stirred up enmity against her, and the conviction spread that "Germany sooner or later will fall upon its weaker western neighbor. . . ." [112] France must, therefore, prepare for the inevitable. This feeling had its counterpart in Germany. Although the immediate crisis had happily passed, the general impression remained that the inevitable conflict had only been postponed.

---

[112] Lancken to Bethmann Hollweg, Feb. 14, 1912, *G. P.*, vol. XXIX, no. 10797; Schoen to Bethmann Hollweg, Jan. 12, 1911, *ibid.*, no. 10796.

Chapter XV

MOROCCO: LAND OF SIROCCOS

Greedy imperialism and egoistic nationalism combined to bring forth the Agadir crisis. Hypocritical protestations of respect for the independence and territorial integrity of the Sherifian empire and declarations of a desire to save the decadent country from its fate were employed with equal facility by all the powers when national interest dictated, but were forgotten at the moment when self-interest required a wholly different technique. In like manner, the Act of Algeciras was quoted by both France and Germany as the legal basis for their policy when it conformed to peculiarly French or German interest but was declared impracticable by those same powers when it failed to justify their acts. The game was an imperialistic one with the stakes geared high, since national prestige required of each player that he win a prize worthy of his name. When such forces as private investments, national self-interest, and national prestige coalesce, the resulting compound is an explosive that requires careful handling if disaster is to be avoided. Yet it was with just such forces that England, France, and Germany were playing in 1911, and the pushful or blustering methods there employed almost brought about a disastrous conflagration.

The ardent French imperialist, Delcassé, had designed and carried to partial completion a program of international bargains and peaceful penetration with complete absorption of Morocco as the ultimate objective; but, having once introduced the policy of bargaining, he failed signally by not recognizing the need for buying German consent to his program as he had bought British, Spanish, and Italian.[1] He consequently left to succeeding ministeries a heavy heritage, that of satisfying the bitterest opponent of French policy. His successors, frequently less imperialistic than he, and tied by the restraining influence of the Act of Algeciras, sought to restrict their action to the limits legally set by that Act, at the same time endeavoring to maintain French predominant

---

[1] See Chapter II, *supra.*

position within the Sherifian empire.[2] France argued that the police powers conceded to her by the Act formed an international mandate which justified her occupation of Casablanca and the Chaouya on the ground of her special interest in the maintenance of order within the realm[3] and thus imposed upon her the duty of protecting Europeans even within the interior.[4] If she could move to Fez, rescue the beleaguered Europeans, withdraw and leave an independent sultan, the Act of Algeciras would not be violated; but if the disintegration of the Sherifian empire compelled recurring expeditions of this nature or permanent occupation of the capital by French troops, the independence of the sultan would become mere fiction. Germany did not wait to see if France could achieve her announced program, the first of these possibilities; but, convinced that her rival only awaited a favorable opportunity to grab the coveted prize, she planned her action on the basis of the latter contingency.[5] The uncertain nature of French policy strengthened rather than weakened her conviction.

Frequent cabinet changes, coupled with the French custom of appointing the foreign secretary for political rather than diplomatic reasons, had resulted in a series of weak ministeries which apparently saw only immediate issues without correlating them to a larger view of general policy. Stephen Pichon alone seemed to recognize the essential elements involved in the Moroccan question and to seek a solution in line with those elements, but even he failed to make the most of his opportunity. Under his guidance, Jules Cambon sought to remedy the chief defect in the French program by securing German consent to that program; but, apparently with the hope that he might gain his coveted objective with little cost, Pichon contented himself with the general phrases embodied in the Accord of 1909 and failed to take the opportunity to bargain with Germany as France had formerly bargained in 1904 with England and Spain.[6] It is true that she might have found Germany intractable at this time, but Bülow in 1909 was certainly more pliable than was Kiderlen in early 1911. Moreover, if France met a refusal, her share of responsibility for the crisis of 1911

---

[2] See Chapter III, *supra.*

[3] See Chapter III, *supra.*   [4] See Chapter VIII, *supra.*

[5] See Chapter IX, *supra.*   [6] See Chapter IV, *supra.*

would have been less. The Accord of 1909 won for her only one
advantage, German recognition of her predominant political position in Morocco; but it saddled her with economic pledges that
Pichon's successor, the inexperienced Cruppi, was unable to uphold. Faced simultaneously with the task of making operative an
inherently impracticable agreement and with the task of reconciling
international obligations with the chaotic conditions of Morocco,
Cruppi bogged down[7] and bequeathed to his even more inexperienced
successor, Selves, the job of extricating his country from the quagmire. Selves, ignorant of the intricate details which befogged the
Moroccan issue and inexperienced in diplomatic technique, was
bewildered by the magnitude of his task and unable to evaluate
any proposal with soundness of judgment.[8] On the other hand,
Premier Caillaux, whose contacts had been more international
than had those of his foreign minister, knew what he wished to
attain and with native French shrewdness set to work to drive a
close bargain with his opponent, at the same time determined that
a bargain should be reached. Diplomatic finesse, backstairs negotiations, and utter disregard for conventional procedure were his
stock in trade. He therefore shoved Selves aside when, in his judgment, the need arose, and conducted affairs as he deemed best.[9] He
accepted as his own the objective of his predecessors, the acquisition of Morocco with as little cost as possible, and with masterly
dexterity sought to outmaneuver his stolid German opponent. If,
as his critics claimed, he had previously made a bargain with Kiderlen,[10] he had no scruples in ignoring it completely as he saw
the chance to drive home a deal more favorable to his native land.
He was, however, consistently more conciliatory than his foreign
minister and was determined that no incident should occur that
might precipitate a conflict. Left to himself, Selves would probably
have blundered into war before he realized whither his actions
might be leading him. Caillaux was a strong agent for peace
throughout the crisis, so much so, in fact, that he called down upon
his head the bitter recriminations of the French nationalists. The
conflict within the French cabinet, however, made for delay in

---

[7] See Chapters V and VI, *supra*.   [8] See Chapter IX, *supra*.
[9] See Chapter XIII, *supra*.   [10] See pp. 335-337, *supra*.

negotiations, increased international suspicion and ill will, and weakened France's position.

Of all the French actors, only Jules Cambon, ambassador to Berlin, merits special recognition for his consistency of purpose, his sagacity, and his diplomatic skill; but encumbered by Selves' inexperience and Caillaux's duplicity, he lost the chance of many moves that should have been played to his advantage. Although France emerged the victor, the sharp practice pursued by her leaders did not redound to her credit. Her strategy was more successful but hardly less reprehensible than was the German.

The singleness of purpose underlying French policy stands in marked contrast to the multiplicity of motives that determined German action. In one respect the policies of the two nations were alike. Each wished to secure colonial territory, not only for the economic returns which that territory might bring, but also for the increased prestige that would result from the development of colonial empires. For these reasons, Germany felt she could not afford to see her rivals add choice morsels to their domains and gain nothing for herself. In the Moroccan imbroglio, her leaders saw an opportunity through which they might appease the craving for colonies that possessed her people. In truth, Kiderlen, when he stated that he saw in Morocco the last chance for Germany, without war, to secure desirable territory,[11] expressed the opinion of most of his countrymen. The prime motive underlying German action was the acquisition of territory the possession of which would benefit her economic development and enhance her prestige.

Kiderlen, conscious of the fact that bulking bigger in the colonial world carried with it added respect from the great powers, wished to use the Moroccan situation as a medium through which he might strengthen the international position of his homeland. Over Morocco Germany had suffered a diplomatic defeat in 1906, and she still wished to enforce the point that France could not gain her protectorate until German consent was granted. Her *amour-propre* seemed to demand that the earlier defeat be wiped out by a marked victory. Kiderlen also recognized the growing

[11] First resignation petition of Kiderlen's, July 17, 1911, in Jäckh, *op. cit.*, vol. II, p. 129.

strength of the Triple Entente, and yet he believed Great Britain
might be lured away from the hostile circle. If he could only solve
the Moroccan problem, he could free Germany from the continual
annoyance of British opposition in all parts of the world and might
even win for her British friendship.[12] Thus he might weaken the
Triple Entente while he strengthened the Triple Alliance.[13] He
apparently hoped at one stroke to acquire territory and to gain
British friendship. But because of the territory he desired, he was
unable to do both. The two objectives were incompatible.

What territory did Kiderlen hope to gain when he executed his
coup? In an overture made to Spain in 1903, Germany had proposed that she be permitted to take southern Morocco in case a
partition of that empire were effected.[14] Nothing came of this overture, significant only because indicative of German official interest
in the territory. The foreign office refrained from further moves
in this direction; but Pan-German propaganda,[15] the Mannesmanns' activities,[16] and statements from court circles[17] heralded
abroad that southern Morocco with its rich promise of mineral
wealth and its fruitful valleys was the region needed to fulfil German colonial aspirations. There is evidence which indicates that in
1911, despite his denial, the brusque leader of German foreign affairs had adopted the policy of these colonial enthusiasts and
originally planned to name the Sous as the price France must pay
for German consent to her acquisition of northern Morocco. His
frequent consultations with Pan-German leaders throughout the
course of the crisis and his encouragement of their chauvinistic
propaganda strengthened their belief that in Morocco he was as
good a Pan-German as Dr. Class himself. Moreover, the fact that
Agadir, the port that they had long named as their legitimate
prey, was chosen as the strategic point where the German demonstration was to take place stimulated their faith in his ultimate
aim. Leaders of the organization charged Kiderlen with actually

---

[12] *Ibid.,* p. 66.

[13] For similar views, see Asquith, *op. cit.,* p. 146; Jonescu, *op. cit.,* p. 66;
Hammann, *Bilder aus der letzten Kaiserzeit,* p. 84; Schmitt, *op. cit.,* p. 319;
Turner, *op. cit.,* p. 32.   [14] See p. 39, *supra.*

[15] See Chapters VI, XIII, and XIV, *supra.*   [16] See Chapter VI, *supra.*

[17] For example, see the statement of the Crown Prince at Grunewald,
p. 208, *supra.*

stating to them his intention of taking the Sous, and his close association with the group provoked doubt in the minds of many as to the sincerity of his denial.[18] This somewhat indirect evidence is substantiated by several documents and by the course of Kiderlen's actions, which at times was in variance with his statements.

The German plan of action was worked out in Kiderlen's note of May 3 and in that of Zimmermann's dated June 12.[19] Both notes stressed the importance of southern Morocco to the development of German industry; and the note of Zimmermann, to which his chief gave his hearty approval, played with the idea of transforming this region into German territory. The sequence of events tied to the Kissingen interview points to the conclusion that the German foreign secretary hoped to play his cards so well that the Sous would fall into his hands. Cambon, in his letter to Poincaré, definitely stated that Kiderlen had asked for Mogador but that he had refused, and added the comment that the sole cause for the Agadir crisis was the fact that German designs on southern Morocco were blocked by French refusal.[20] At Kissingen the French ambassador left open the entire colonial field as a basis for negotiation and only closed the door to Morocco; yet Kiderlen immediately decided that he must grab his "clenched pledge," and without waiting for the interview to bear fruit, executed his plan in a highly provocative manner.

If he had no designs on Morocco, why did Kiderlen consider that he must act before a reply from Paris could be delivered? Was it because he did not think the French government would offer adequate compensation; or was it because he was afraid that, although adamant on the question of Morocco, the notoriously conciliatory Caillaux ministry would make a proposition so favorable to German interests that he would be forced to consider it seriously and risk losing the chance of securing Moroccan territory? His known Pan-German sympathies, his interest in the Sous, and his hurried actions in late June seem to indicate that the latter contingency disturbed him more than the former. His demands made in early September strengthened that view. Although in July he had expressly stated his willingness to renounce Morocco completely in

---

[18] See Chapter XIV, *supra*.

[19] See Chapter IX, *supra*.   [20] See pp. 213-214, *supra*.

exchange for adequate compensation in the Congo, he all but disrupted the negotiations in September when he presented the German demand for a partition of Morocco into economic spheres of
influence in which control of railroads and ports in the region
south of the Tensift River was to fall to Germany.[21] He apparently still cherished a faint hope that his country might keep alive
in this region incipient rights which, properly nourished, would
grow into future possession of the land. Since economic imperialism as represented by control of railroads can easily transform
itself into political domination, France was justified in her assumption that Kiderlen's demands were incompatible with his renunciation of all political interest in the Sherifian empire. For these reasons it seems that Kiderlen sent the *Panther* on its historic journey
primarily for the purpose of securing colonial territory, preferably
the Sous,[22] an objective he did not completely renounce until September. However, he did not begin his program until he had an alternative to offer in case he failed in his original purpose. That
alternative was the French Congo.

Suggestions that territory in the French Congo might form an
acceptable compensation to Germany for her renunciation of Morocco were made as early as 1905.[23] They continued to appear from
time to time in newspapers of both lands and formed the basis for
a newspaper debate during June and early July, 1911. Although
some authorities state that when the comment, "One may seek elsewhere," was made at Kissingen the Congo was meant,[24] and although the Kaiser later stated that in May German officials had
decided upon that region as the prospective compensation,[25] that

---

[21] See Chapter XIV, *supra*.

[22] For similar views, see Pinon, *France et Allemagne*, p. 219; Schmitt, *op. cit.*,
p. 319; Stowell, *op. cit.*, p. 24; Pick, *Searchlight on German Africa*. In fact,
the thesis of Dr. Pick's publication is that Kiderlen, convinced by the Hamburg group of the value of the Sous, sought to acquire it. This objective he
renounced only when reports from Regendanz began to question the fertility of
the area. Other factors, however, must have influenced Kiderlen in his renunciation; for he had given way on all vital questions by September 19, the day
Regendanz wrote his first report from Agadir that questioned the "suitability"
of the area for German colonists. Regendanz' letter of October 3, which expressed
his disappointment in the land, could have had little or no effect upon the negotiation; as it probably reached Berlin after Kiderlen had decided to recognize
French control of Morocco.   [23] Caillaux, *Agadir*, p. 25.

[24] See Chapter IX, *supra*.   [25] See Chapter X, *supra*.

basis of negotiation was not recognized officially until the conferences of July 7 and July 9.[26] From that date until the completion of the treaty the negotiations took the form of dickering between the two traders, with Germany striving to gain the maximum and France attempting to reduce to a minimum the territory she must relinquish. With shrewd bargaining in progress and a skilled technique required, the blunt, secretive, churlish manner adopted by the German foreign secretary operated to his disadvantage.

In early July the time appeared favorable to the German plan. France[27] and England[28] were both torn by domestic disturbances. The two governments had little time for consideration of foreign policy. The Kaiser's visit to London in May gave him the impression that British sympathy was definitely swinging to the side of Germany.[29] Russia had not forgotten the lukewarm attitude of her friends in the Bosnian crisis, and the Potsdam Agreement gave the German foreign office courage to hope that she would not oppose the German move.[30] When, for a few days in late June, chaos reigned in the French government as the ministerial crisis disrupted governmental business,[31] the opportune moment seemed to have arrived. With the cards apparently stacked in his favor, Kiderlen threw the game away by his failure to consider the psychological effects of his tortuous tactics.

The legal case for Germany rested upon her fight to defend her nationals and her obligations under the Act of Algeciras.[32] Her position as defender of the internationalization of Morocco was, however, seriously weakened by the Accord of 1909. In that Accord, she had recognized French political preponderance in the Sherifian empire in exchange for a Franco-German economic condominion, both of which were in direct contradiction to the provisions of the Algeciras Act. Only when the Accord failed to produce the economic results that she desired did she become concerned over the destruction of the international agreement. Her argument that France had violated the Act of Algeciras seemed beside the point when both nations had connived at its abrogation in 1909. She

---

[26] See Chapter X, *supra.*
[27] See Chapter X, *supra.*
[28] See Chapter XI, *supra.*
[29] See p. 226, *supra.*
[30] See Chapter X, *supra.*
[31] See Chapter IX, *supra.*
[32] See Morel, *Morocco in Diplomacy,* pp. 126-129; Nicolson, *op. cit.,* p. 249.

further weakened her case when she stated that the *Panther* had gone to Agadir to defend German nationals. If there were Germans in the closed port of Agadir, they had no legal right to be there; and if there were none present, German claim that she must defend her nationals lost validity. Kiderlen would have done better to have chosen Mogador as the scene for his dramatic entrance into the arena.

France's gradual absorption of Morocco despite her protests of allegiance to the Act of Algeciras had placed her in the position of having to defend her actions, but the brutal manner in which Germany injected herself into the imbroglio transformed the situation. Kiderlen's action alienated international good will[33] and turned the sympathy of the world to France, who now occupied the position of one unwarrantedly attacked. Germany must now defend her action. As news of the Kissingen interview spread, the conviction grew that the truculent German secretary had acted hastily and unwisely. If France were willing to negotiate without pressure, why should he risk throwing all Europe into war? The original feeling, that Germany as a signatory of the Act of Algeciras had the right to demand its preservation and that as a colonial power she had a just claim to compensation, changed to one of resentment at the gunman tactics employed by her leader in foreign affairs. Kiderlen was thus forced to negotiate with the sympathy of the world against him.

The adoption of a mailed-fist diplomacy was in itself unwise, but Kiderlen's choice of ground upon which to stage his *coup* and his failure to clarify the situation to the British government were nothing short of foolhardy. If, as he asserted, part of his ambition was to win British friendship, his tactics appear stupid; for he should have known that any action capable of being interpreted as one designed to establish a German base on the Atlantic coast of northwest Africa would arouse suspicion and indignation throughout the British Empire. Anglo-German naval rivalry was the most disturbing factor in their relationship; yet he chose as his weapon a naval demonstration in the one spot recognized as

---

[33] J. Ellis Barker, "The Morocco Crisis and the European Situation," in *Fortnightly Review,* vol. XCVI, pp. 590-603; Gooch, *Franco-German Relations,* p. 249.

the best natural harbor on the Moroccan Atlantic littoral. He might have offset the disadvantages accruing to his unwise choice if he had from the first clarified the situation to the British government. In the light of British sensitiveness on the question of naval power, self-interest dictated that he take the utmost caution to assure her that Germany had no intention of establishing a naval base on the west coast of Morocco. Moreover, since he knew that in Moroccan affairs England was bound by her pledge to France, and if, as he later claimed, Germany had no desire to secure Moroccan territory, he would have been wise to have convinced Great Britain of that fact. Instead of consciously striving to turn British sympathy to Germany, he adopted the highly irritating policy of leaving to the British government the task of fathoming the riddles of a sphinx. With apparently no conception of the effect his actions might have on British psychology, Kiderlen selected exactly those methods that would incur that country's enmity instead of winning its friendship.[34] His ambition in this respect failed signally, largely because he did not foresee the difficulties involved in his program and consequently did not take the precautions necessary to counteract their destructive influences. He seemed blind to the warning note of the *Times* and was unprepared when British ministers aped his own blustering mien.

Sir Edward Grey inherited his obligations to France from his predecessor, Lord Lansdowne, and these so bound him not to oppose French policy in Morocco that he was in no position to demand as the price of British support that France, before she went to Fez, come to an agreement with Germany.[35] His loyalty to the Entente, added to his meagre knowledge of European countries, tended to becloud his judgment of continental politics and of issues on which he must determine British alignment. As a result he secured the reputation of being blindly pro-French and stubbornly anti-German,[36] a fact Kiderlen should have pondered upon before he ordered the *Panther* to move to Agadir. Despite this reputation, Grey's tendency to let matters drift produced a policy that bewildered both friend and foe.

During the first three weeks of July, the British government

---

[34] For similar views, see Reventlow, *op. cit.*, p. 229, and Kleinknecht, *op. cit.*, p. 64.   [35] See Chapter II, *supra.*   [36] See Chapter, XI, *supra.*

consistently vetoed all suggestions for aggressive action that came from her French friend, and proposed as the alternative to direct negotiations an international conference which nobody wanted. Throughout the same period, no effort was made to unravel the German plan by direct contact with that government. Grey allowed matters to drift for three weeks and only took the initiative when he became frightened because of the imminent breakdown of Franco-German negotiations. He then apparently threw discretion to the winds, and failing to scrutinize the possible effects of his acts, he permitted Lloyd George to assume, in effect, the duties of the foreign secretary.[37]

The Mansion House speech represented the same tactless, blundering type of mailed-fist diplomacy as did the *Panther's* Spring. It was a threat to Germany just as the *Panther* was a threat to France. In each instance the aggressor nation was vociferously demanding that its opponent talk, and in each instance it could have gained its objective without the use of such dangerous weapons. With the same undue haste that Kiderlen displayed after Kissingen, Grey had failed to await a reply from Berlin after his interview with Metternich on the afternoon of July 21. In fact, in the clutches of a panicky fear, he had sanctioned the proposal of the pro-German, pacifist chancellor of the exchequer, who in a highly irregular fashion had then proclaimed British policy. As the regular course of diplomatic intercourse was open, the adoption of an irregular medium emphasized to the German public that a threat was intended, and no amount of diplomatic palaver could remove that impression.

A mailed-fist, whether brandished by a British or a German arm, carries with it all the elements of danger. The immediate effect of the Lloyd George speech was to increase the international tension, to encourage French chauvinists, to excite public opinion on both sides of the channel, and to render more difficult the task of those who wished to secure a peaceful solution.[38] It did make clear to Kiderlen that, if the Franco-German negotiations broke down, he could not reckon on British indifference but must count on active British participation on the side of France. It therefore be-

---

[37] See Chapter XI, *supra.*　　　[38] See Chapter XII, *supra.*

came one of the forces that influenced him in his decision to modify his demands. Perhaps the final settlement of the Agadir crisis would have been different if Lloyd George's speech had not been delivered. France would probably have had to pay a higher price for German consent to her program, but Anglo-German relations would not have suffered such a severe blow. British policy sacrificed to the cause of France its prime motive, preservation of peculiarly British interests. Germany gathered from her plunge into ruthless diplomacy a few acres of swampland; England reaped a harvest of malignant enmities.

Mutual suspicion of bellicose intentions fed the already excited tempers, and on several occasions the danger of war hung perilously close. If, on any one of these occasions, Kiderlen had refused to yield, war would probably have resulted. To no one force can the sole credit for the modification of his program be attributed. Neither the Kaiser nor the chancellor wanted war, and although they were frequently overpersuaded by their foreign secretary, they besieged him with pacific advice. Before he consented to the Agadir *coup*, the Kaiser had been convinced that no serious complications would arise, and until the German press dubbed him "William the Timid," [39] he fretted over Kiderlen's boldness and consistently urged him to avoid war. The financial crisis of early September[40] forced even the bold Swabian to weigh the probabilities of a general economic and financial depression and to realize that a false move might convert the situation into a panic. A survey of the international situation brought him no encouragement. Of his allies, Austria granted only lukewarm support and plentiful advice to keep the peace, while Italy announced her support of France. Although Russia was not hostile to Germany,[41] he could not hope to draw her from the enemy camp that was, after July 21, as much British[42] as French. Kiderlen consequently modified his proposals to meet the exigencies of peace; and though encouraged by British support, France, held in restraint by her conciliatory premier and the sagacious Cambon, matched the German moderation until an agreement was reached. The cataclysm had to await a new crisis.

[39] See p. 342, *supra.*

[40] See Chapter XIII, *supra.*

[41] See Chapter XIII, *supra.*

[42] See Chapter XII, *supra.*

Thus the hopes of the optimistic that, now, since the Moroccan problem had presumably been removed from the field of international friction, improvement would come in Franco-German and Anglo-German relations, were soon to prove a mirage. The march to Fez, the *Panther's* Spring, the Mansion House speech, and the long months of tedious negotiations had created in each land an atmosphere which bred discontent, suspicion, and hatred. Germany, disappointed with her meagre gains, saw in the entire situation proof of the encirclement policy of the Entente Powers. France, annoyed by German bullying, felt that she had been forced to relinquish to her hated enemy a French colony won by French money and French blood, in return for which she had secured only ephemeral German rights in Morocco. Great Britain, suspicious of Germany and none too confident of France, girded her forces against the evil day. The excitation of patriotic fervor had stultified all sense of international rights. Each nation strove to bind more closely its allies and friends and to strengthen its military equipment so that the ultimate crash would find it fully prepared. The diplomats who claimed that in 1911 they preserved the peace told only half the story, for they did nothing to check the sirocco's onward rush.

The Agadir crisis was, in fact, one of the milestones on the road to the Great War. Italy interpreted the incident as the signal for her to collect her prize, Tripoli, and upon the slightest of pretexts declared war upon Turkey. The consequent embarrassment to the Ottoman empire offered to the Balkan league the desired opportunity to give vent to their nationalistic aspirations in the Balkan wars of 1912 and 1913. The bedlam herein created was only the preliminary storm before the crisis of 1914 threw the world into flames.

The crisis of 1911, although presumably one between France and Germany, was in reality one between the Triple Entente and the Triple Alliance. The maintenance of that delicate equilibrium in European affairs depended upon a balance of power between these groups. That balance had been seriously threatened; and each group, determined to swing the equilibrium of forces in its favor, began to prepare for the conflict it deemed inevitable. With accelerated tempo, the nations sped their armament construction.

Wolff declared that the real victor in the Agadir crisis was Tirpitz, who won support for his naval program;[43] for none dared deny the latent danger to the fatherland. The Entente Powers, on the other hand, drew steadily closer together,[44] and strove to match or surpass the military preparations of their rivals. Consequently, a new navy or army bill in one land brought forth a flood of similar bills throughout Europe, and efforts to check the deluge proved futile. The Triple Entente and Triple Alliance stood face to face in battle array.

[43] *Op. cit.*, p. 92.

[44] Franco-British Informal Agreement of September, 1912.—Fay, *op. cit.*, vol. I, pp. 317-323; Ward and Gooch, *op. cit.*, vol. III, pp. 437-440.

BIBLIOGRAPHY

Primary Authorities

Documents: Official Publications

Belgische Aktenstücke, 1905-1914. Auswärtigen Amt. Berlin.
Die Belgischen Dokumente zur Vorgeschichte des Weltkrieges, 1855-1914. Edited by Bernard Schwertfeger, 5 vols. 2 supplements. Berlin, 1925.
British Documents on the Origins of the War, 1898-1914. Edited by George P. Gooch and Harold Temperley, London, 1927-
Documents diplomatiques: Affaires du Maroc. Ministère des affaires étrangères, Paris, 1901-1912.
Documents diplomatiques français, 1871-1914. Ministère des affaires étrangères, commission de publication des documents relatifs aux origines de la guerre de 1914. Three series, Paris, 1929-
Documents diplomatiques: Question de la protection diplomatique et consulaire au Maroc. Ministère des affaires étrangères, Paris, 1880.
Entente Diplomacy and the World. Translated by B. de Siebert, edited by G. A. Schreiner, New York, 1921.
Die Grosse Politik der Europäischen Kabinette, 1871-1914. Edited by Johannes Lepsius, Albrecht Mendelssohn-Bartholdy, and Friedrich Thimme, Berlin, 1922-1927.
Österreich-Ungarns Aussenpolitik von der Bosnischen Krise 1908 bis zum Kriegausbruch, 1914. Edited by Ludwig Bittner and Hans Übersberger, Vienna, 1930—
Verhandlungen des Reichstags. Nr. 189. Weissbuch: Denkschrift und Aktenstücke über deutsche Bergwerksinteressen in Marokko. Issued by Theobald von Bethmann Hollweg, January 17, 1910.

Treaties

Martens, Georg Fr. de, *Nouveau Recueil général de traités et autres actes relatifs aux rapports de droit international.* Second series. Goettingue, Dieterich, 1885-

Annuals

Annual Register. London, 1758-
British Foreign and State Papers. London, 1812-
Débats parlementaires: Annales de la chambre des députés. Paris, 1876-
Débats parlementaires: Annales du senat. Paris, 1876-

Journal officiel de la Republique française. Paris, 1881-

Parliamentary Debates. Fifth series, London, 1909-

Verhandlungen des Reichstags. Stenographische Berichte des Reichstags. Berlin, 1870-

Other Correspondence, Memoirs, and Secondary Works Containing Source Materials

Ashmead-Bartlett, E., *The Passing of the Shereefian Empire.* London, 1910.

Asquith, Herbert Henry, *The Genesis of the War.* New York, 1923.

———, *Memoirs and Reflections, 1852-1927.* 2 vols., Boston, 1928.

Barclay, Sir Thomas, *Thirty Years, Anglo-French Reminiscences, 1876-1906.* Boston, 1914.

Benckendorff, Graf Alexander, *Diplomatischer Schriftwechsel.* Edited by B. von Siebert, 3 vols. Berlin, 1928.

Bertie, Lord of Thane, *Diary of Lord Bertie.* Edited by Lady Algernon Gordon Lennox, 2 vols. New York, 1924.

Bethmann Hollweg, Theobald von, *Betrachtungen zum Weltkriege.* 2 vols. Berlin, 1919.

Blunt, W. S., *My Diaries, 1888-1914.* 2 vols. London, 1919.

Bülow, Prince Bernhard H. M., *Memoirs of Prince von Bülow.* Translated by F. A. Voight, 4 vols. Boston, 1931-1932.

Caillaux, Joseph, *Agadir, ma politique extérieure.* Paris, 1919.

———, "Agadir: M. Caillaux's Rejoinder," in *Spectator,* December 9, 1932.

Cambon, Jules, *Le Diplomate.* Paris, 1926.

Churchill, Winston Leonard Spencer, *The World Crisis.* New York, 1927.

Class, Heinrich, *Wider den Storm.* Leipzig, 1932.

Eckardstein, Hermann F. von, *Persönliche Erinnerungen an König Eduard.* Dresden, 1927.

Grey, Edward, Viscount of Fallodon, *Twenty-five Years, 1892-1916.* 2 vols. London, 1925.

Haldane, Lord Richard Burdon, *Autobiography.* London, 1929.

Hammann, Otto, *Bilder aus der letzten Kaiserzeit.* Berlin, 1922.

Harris, Lawrence, *With Mulai Hafid at Fez, Behind the Scenes in Morocco.* London, 1909.

Isvolski, Alexander, *Der Diplomatische Schriftwechsel, 1911-1914.* Edited by Friedrich Stieve, 4 vols. Berlin, 1924.

Jäckh, Ernest, *Kiderlen-Wächter, der Staatsmann und Mensch.* 2 vols. Stuttgart, 1924.

Jonescu, Take, *Some Personal Impressions.* London, 1919.

Lancken Wakenitz, Oscar von der, *Meine Dreissig Dienstjahre, 1888-1918*. Berlin, 1931.

Lloyd George, David, *War Memoirs*. 5 vols. Boston, 1933-

Louis, Georges, *Les Carnets de Georges Louis*. 2 vols. Paris, 1926.

Nicolson, Harold, *Portrait of a Diplomatist*. New York, 1930.

Pick, F. W., *Searchlight on German Africa: The Diaries and Papers of Dr. W. Ch. Regendanz*. London, 1939.

Poincaré Raymon, *Au Service de la France—neuf années de souvenirs*. 10 vols. Paris, 1926-

Sazonov, Serge, *Fateful Years, 1909-1916*. London, 1927.

Schoen, Wilhelm Edward, *Memoirs of an Ambassador*. Translated by Constance Vesey, London, 1922.

Schwabach, Paul H. von, *Aus Meinen Akten*. Berlin, 1927.

————, "Unterredungen mit Caillaux," in *Berliner Monatshefte*, May, 1931.

Steed, Henry Wickham, *Through Thirty Years*. New York, 1925.

Tardieu, André Pierre Gabriel, *Le Mystère d' Agadir*. Paris, 1912.

Tirpitz, Alfred von, *My Memoirs*. 2 vols. New York, 1919.

Newspapers, 1911 et passim, *and Magazines*

Berliner Tageblatt.

Bulletin mensuel du Comité de l'Afrique française et du Comité du Maroc. Paris, January 1, 1891-

Frankfurter Zeitung.

Gauvain, Auguste, *L'Europe au jour le jour*. Paris, 1917-

Journal des Débats.

Kölnische Zeitung.

Le Matin.

Morning Post.

New York Times.

Questions diplomatiques et coloniales. Paris, 1897-1914.

Revue des deux mondes. Bureau de la *Revue des deux mondes*. Paris, 1829-

Schiemann, Theodor, *Deutschland und die grosse Politik, 1901-1914*. 14 vols. Berlin, 1902-1915.

Temps.

Times (London).

SECONDARY AUTHORITIES

Books

Albin, Pierre, *La Querelle franco-allemande. Le "Coup" d' Agadir; Origines et developpement de la crise de 1911*. Paris, 1912.

Alengry, Jean, *Les Relations franco-espagnoles et l'affaire du Maroc.* Paris, 1920.

Anderson, Eugene N., *The First Moroccan Crisis, 1904-1906.* Chicago, 1930.

Bakeless, John, *The Economic Causes of Modern War.* New York, 1921.

Balch, Thomas W., *France in North Africa.* Philadelphia, 1906.

Bérard, Victor, *L'Affaire marocaine.* Paris, 1906.

Bernard, Augustin, *Le Maroc.* Paris, 1922.

Bernard, François, *Le Maroc économique et agricole.* Paris, 1917.

Beyens, Napoleon E., *Germany before the War.* New York, 1916.

Brandenburg, Erich, *From Bismarck to the World War.* Translated by E. Adams, London, 1927.

Carroll, Eber Malcolm, *French Public Opinion and Foreign Affairs, 1870-1914.* New York, 1931.

——, *Germany and the Great Powers, 1866-1914.* New York, 1938.

Cecil, Algernon, *British Foreign Secretaries, 1807-1916.* London, 1927.

Chisholm, George G., *Handbook of Commercial Geography.* London, 1928.

Cruickshank, Earl Fee, *Morocco at the Parting of the Ways.* Philadelphia, 1935.

Davis, W. S., *The Roots of the War.* New York, 1918.

Dawson, W. H., *The German Empire, 1867-1914.* 2 vols. London, 1919.

Débidour, Antonin, *Histoire diplomatique de l'Europe depuis le Congrès de Berlin jusqu'á nos jours.* 2 vols. Paris, 1916-1917.

Dictionary of National Biography. Supplement. London, 1901.

Diplomate, Un, *Paul Cambon, Ambassadeur de France.* Paris, 1937.

Dubois, Marcel, and Terrier, Auguste, *Les Colonies françaises.* 6 vols. Paris, 1900.

Dupuy, E., *Comment nous avons conquis le Maroc.* Paris, 1929.

Enthoven, Henri Émile, *Von Tanger Tot Agadir.* Utrecht, 1929.

Fabre-Luce, Alfred, *Caillaux.* Paris, 1933.

Fay, Sidney B., *The Origins of the World War.* 2 vols. New York, 1929.

Feis, Herbert, *Europe, The World's Banker, 1870-1914.* New Haven, 1930.

Fidel, Camille, *Les intérêts économiques de la France au Maroc: le commerce du Maroc en 1900 et 1901.* Paris, 1903.

Flournoy, Francis Rosebro, *British Policy towards Morocco in the Age of Palmerston.* Baltimore, 1935.

Friedjung, Heinrich, *Das Zeitalter des Imperialismus, 1884-1914.* 3 vols. Berlin, 1919.

Gooch, G. P., *Before the War: Studies in Diplomacy.* 2 vols. New York, 1936, 1938.

————, *Franco-German Relations, 1871-1914.* New York, 1923.

————, *Recent Revelations on European Diplomacy.* London, 1930.

Grelling, Richard, *Belgian Documents.* New York, 1919.

Der Grosse Brockhaus. Leipzig, 1933.

Hale, Oron James, *Germany and the Diplomatic Revolution.* Philadelphia, 1931.

Halévy, Elie, *The World Crisis of 1914-1918: An Interpretation.* Oxford, 1930.

Hallgarten, Wolfgang, *Vorkriegs Imperialismus. Die Soziologischen Grundlagen der Aussenpolitik Europaeischer Grossmaechte bis 1914.* Paris, 1935.

Hammann, Otto, *The World Policy of Germany, 1890-1912.* London, 1927.

Hardy, George, "Le Maroc," in Hannotaux, Gabriel, *Histoirie des colonies françaises et de l'expansion de la France dans le monde.* 6 vols. Paris, 1929.

Harris, Norman Dwight, *Intervention and Colonization in Africa.* New York, 1914.

Kleinknecht, Dr. Wolfgang, *Die Englische Politik in der Agadirkrise, (1911).* Berlin, 1937.

Leclerc, Charles René, *Situation économique de Maroc, 1908-1909.* Oran, 1910.

Lutz, Hermann, *Lord Grey and the World War.* London, 1928.

Martin, Alfred G. P., *Le Maroc et L'Europe.* Paris, 1928.

————, *Quatre siècles d'histoire marocaine, au Sahara de 1504 à 1902, au Maroc de 1894 à 1912, d'après archives et documentations indigènes.* Paris, 1928.

Maurice, Louis Bompard, *La Politique marocaine de l'Allemagne.* Paris, 1916.

Meakin, Budgett, and Meakin, K. A., "Morocco," in *Encyclopedia Britannica,* eleventh edition.

Michon, Georges, *The Franco-Russian Alliance.* Translated by Norman Thomas. New York, 1929.

Moon, Parker Thomas, *Imperialism and World Politics.* New York, 1926.

Morel, Edmund Deville, *Morocco in Diplomacy.* London, 1912.

Neilson, Francis, *How Diplomats Make War.* New York, 1916.

Neumann, Kurt, *Die Internationalität Marokkos.* Berlin, 1919.

Noël, Pierre, *Les Rapports de la France et du Maroc.* Paris, 1905.

Oncken, Hermann, *Das Deutsche Reich und die Vorgeschichte des Weltkrieges.* 2 vols. Leipzig, 1933.

27

Pinon, René, *France et Allemagne, 1870-1913*. Paris, 1913.

Piquet, Victor, *Le Maroc*. Paris, 1917.

Poincaré, Raymon, *The Origins of the War*. London, 1922.

Rachfahl, Felix, *Kaiser und Reich, 1888-1913*. Berlin, 1915.

Reclus, Élisée, *The Earth and Its Inhabitants*. 19 vols. New York, 1882-95.

Reventlow, Ernst, *Politische Vorgeschichte des Grossen Krieges*. Berlin, 1919.

Roberts, S. H., *History of French Colonial Policy, 1870-1925*. 2 vols. London, 1929.

Rohrbach, Paul, *Deutschland unter den Weltvolkern: Materialen zur Auswärtigen Politik*. Stuttgart, 1921.

Sabin, Mony, *La Paix au Maroc*. Paris, 1933.

Schmitt, Bernadotte E., *England and Germany, 1740-1914*. London, 1918.

Schuman, Frederick L., *War and Diplomacy in the French Republic*. New York, 1931.

Seymour, Charles, *Diplomatic Background of the War*. New Haven, 1916.

Shuster, W. Morgan, *The Strangling of Persia*. New York, 1912.

Sloans, W. M., *Greater France in Africa*. New York, 1929.

Sontag, R. J., *European Diplomatic History, 1871-1932*. New York, 1933.

Spender, J. A., *Great Britain: Empire and Commonwealth, 1886-1935*. London, 1936.

Stichel, Bernhard, *Die Zukunft in Marokko*. Berlin, 1917.

Stowell, E. A., *The Diplomacy of the War of 1914*. New York, 1915.

Stuart, Graham H., *French Foreign Policy from Fashoda to Serajevo, 1898-1914*. New York, 1921.

———, *The International City of Tangier*. Stanford, 1931.

Tabouis, Geneviève, *The Life of Jules Cambon*. Trs. C. F. Atkinson. London, 1938.

Terrier, Auguste, *Le Maroc*. Paris, 1931.

Valentin, Veit, *Deutschlands Aussenpolitik von Bismarck's Abgang bis zum Ende des Weltkrieges*. Berlin, 1921.

Ward, A. W., and Gooch, G. P., *Cambridge History of British Foreign Policy*. 3 vols. Cambridge, 1922.

Werner, Lothar, *Der Alldeutsche Verband 1890-1918*. Berlin, 1935.

Wharton, Mrs. Edith Newbold, *In Morocco*. New York, 1920.

Wilson, H. W., *The War Guilt*. London, 1928.

Wolff, Theodor, *The Eve of 1914*. London, 1935.

Zabel, Rudolf, *Marokko*. Altenburg, 1905.

Zeys, Paul, *Agadir: Conflits immobiliers des confins Sud-Marocains, 1911-1932*. Paris, 1933.

Articles, Monographs, and Reports

Andreas, W., "Kiderlen-Waechter," in *Historische Zeitschrift*, vol. CXXXII.

Barker, J. Ellis, "Anglo-German Differences and Sir Edward Grey," in *Fortnightly Review*, vol. XCVII.

———, "Germany, Morocco, and the Peace of the World," in *Fortnightly Review*, vol. XCVI.

———, "The Morocco Crisis and the European Situation," in *Fortnightly Review*, vol. XCVI.

Beazley, C. Raymond, "Die Verantwortlichkeit für den Weltkrieg, 1911," in *Berliner Monatshefte*, vol. VIII, January, 1930.

Bensusan, S. L., "Morocco, the Powers, and the Financiers," in *Contemporary Review*, vol. C.

Bernard, Augustin, "Touat et Maroc," in *Questions diplomatiques et coloniales*, June, 1900.

Blache, Jules, "Modes of Life in the Moroccan Countryside," in *Geographical Review*, vol. XI.

Caix, Robert de, "Le Gouvernement allemand et l'affaire Mannesmann," in *L'Afrique française*, 1910; "La Politique française et l'affaire d'Agadir," in *L'Afrique française*, July, 1911; "Dans L'Attente d'un accord franco-allemand," in *L'Afrique française*, August, 1911; "La Crise franco-allemand," in *L'Afrique française*, September, 1911.

Clariond, Louis, et Mauchaussé, Paul, "Le Charbon au Maroc," in *L'Afrique française*, 1934.

Clarjean, Bernard, "Petrole Nord-Africain et défense nationale," in *L'Afrique française*, April, 1937.

Deschanel, Paul, "Budget of Foreign Affairs," in *L'Afrique française*, 1912.

Dillon, E. F., "Morocco and Germany," in *Contemporary Review*, vol. C.

Dorobantz, Jacques, "M. de Kiderlen-Waechter," in *Questions diplomatiques et coloniales*, 1910, Part II.

Fidel, Camille, "Les intérêts français et les intérêts allemands au Maroc," in *L'Afrique française*, 1905.

Fischer, Theobald, "Morocco," in Smithsonian Institute *Annual Report*, 1904. Washington, 1905.

Hammann, Otto, "Aufzeichnungen," in *Archiv für Politik und Geschichte,* 1925.

Hartung, Fritz, "Die englische Politik in der Marokkokrise des Jahres, 1911," in *Berliner Monatshefte,* vol. X, August, 1932.

———, "Die Marokkokrise des Jahres 1911," in *Archiv für Politik und Geschichte,* 1926, Part II.

Hoffherr, René et Mauchaussé, Paul, "Industrialisation minière et politique complementaire franco-marocaine," in *L'Afrique française,* 1934.

Jacqueton, G., "Les Mines de L'Afrique française," in *L'Afrique française,* 1933.

Johnston, Sir Harry H., "The Aftermath of Agadir: Suggestions for a Settlement of Territorial Ambitions," in *Nineteenth Century,* vol. LXXI.

Lacharrière, Ladrette de, "Dans le Sud et L'Ouest de Maroc," in *L'Afrique française,* 1912.

Langer, William L., "Russia, the Straits Question, and the Origins of the Balkan League, 1908-1912," in *Political Science Quarterly,* vol. XLIII.

Leclerc, René, "L'Année administrative marocaine en 1910," in *L'Afrique française,* 1911.

Levy, Raphael-Georges, "Les Crises financières de 1907 et de 1911," in *Revue des deux mondes,* series 6, January, 1912.

MacLeod, J. M., "The Achievements of France in Morocco," in *Geographic Journal,* vol. LII.

Millet, Philippe, "The Truth about the Franco-German Crisis of 1911," in *Nineteenth Century,* vol. LXXI.

Morel, Edmund Deville, "The Franco-German Dispute," in *Nineteenth Century,* vol. LXX.

———, "The True Story of Morocco Negotiations," in *Nineteenth Century,* vol. LXXI.

———, "The 'Truth' about the Franco-German Crisis: A Reply to M. Philippe Millet," in *Nineteenth Century,* vol. LXXII.

Münz, Sigmund, "The Cartwright Interview of August, 1911," in *Contemporary Review,* vol. CXXXVII.

Ogilvie, Alan G., "Morocco and Its Future," in *Geographic Journal,* vol. XXXIX.

Pick, F. W., "New Light on Agadir," in *Contemporary Review,* September, 1937.

Pinon, René, "Jules Cambon," in *Revue des deux mondes,* series 8, vol. XXIX.

Riker, Thad W., "British Policy in the Fashoda Crisis," in *Political Science Quarterly*, vol. XLIV.

Roch, Walter, "Agadir: M. Caillaux and Sir Eyre Crowe," in *Spectator*, November 25, 1932.

Staley, Eugene, "Mannesmann Mining Interests and the Franco-German Conflict over Morocco," in *Journal of Political Economy*, vol. XL.

Tarde, Alfred de, "The Work of France in Morocco," in *Geographical Review*, vol. VIII.

Tardieu, André, "France et Espagne (1902-1912)," in *Revue des deux mondes*, series 6, vol. XII.

Thomasson, Commandant de, "La Crise marocaine," in *Questions diplomatiques et coloniales*, 1911, Part II.

Turner, Edward Raymond, "The Morocco Crisis of 1911," in *South Atlantic Quarterly*, vol. II.

Wendel, Hugo C. M., "The Protégé System in Morocco," in *Journal of Modern History*, vol. XI.

Wertheimer, Mildred, *The Pan-German League, 1890-1914*, in "Columbia University Studies in History, Economics, and Public Law," vol. XCII. New York, 1924.

Wichmann, H., "Das deutsch-französische Kamerun-Kongo-Abkommen vom November 4, 1911," in Petermann's *Mitteilungen*, 1911.

Williamson, Francis Torrance, *Germany and Morocco before 1905*, in "Johns Hopkins Studies in Historical and Political Science." Baltimore, 1937.

INDEX

A bd-el-Kader, 23-24

Abdul Aziz, 15, 27, 30, 31, 48, 49, 53, 53-56, 58, 61, 72, 90, 124-125, 144

Act of Algeciras, 44-47, 51, 53, 56, 61, 70, 72, 73, 75, 78, 81, 82, 83, 97, 100, 101, 103, 104-106, 108, 111, 124, 126, 131, 137, 144, 150-151, 153-155, 170, 171, 172, 178, 180-183, 188, 189, 190-196, 200-205, 210, 211, 220, 221, 228, 229, 231, 232, 234, 240, 248, 253, 266, 270, 272, 274, 276, 280, 286, 294, 308, 310, 311, 326, 365, 374, 388, 389, 395, 396

Act of Berlin, 113, 115

Aehrenthal, Count Aloys, 1; on return of Loehr to Fez, 60; reception of the Franco-German Accord of 1909, 78; on the *Panther's* Spring, 249-250; reception of Asquith's speech of July 6, 276; and the Cartwright affair, 318; support of Germany, 356-357; pressure on France, 356-357; acceptance of the November treaty, 375-376

Agadir, 143, 145, 155, 156, 217, 220, 221, 222, 223, 224, 225, 226, 229, 231, 232, 234, 235, 238, 240, 241, 242, 246, 247, 253, 254, 255, 266, 268, 273, 274, 275, 280, 283, 286, 287, 289, 292, 293, 294, 295, 297, 306, 308, 310, 316, 322, 336, 341, 343, 344, 345, 346, 355, 358, 366, 370, 376, 381, 382, 386, 388, 392, 396, 398, 399, 400, 401

Algeciras conference, 42, 44-46, 59

Algeria, 6, 23, 29-30, 33, 88, 95-96, 105, 154

Amande, General, 85

Angad, plan of, 8

Anglo-French Entente, 42, 46, 77, 209, 271, 283, 285, 287, 288, 300, 305, 311, 315, 334, 355, 361, 376, 397, 400, 401

Anglo-French treaty, 1904, 37, 209, 294, 376, 384, 389

Anglo-Russian Entente, 46

Arab, 12

Army (in Morocco), composition of, 17; French instructors in, 17, 30-31; in loan of 1910, 89, 92, 94; Turkish instructors in, 92, 94, 159-160; French

military mission, 157; danger to French instructors, 157-158; proposed reforms, 158-163

Ashmead-Bartlett, Ellis, criticism of the Casablanca bombardment, 49-50

Asquith, Herbert H., speech in the House of Commons, July 6, 276-277, 289; naval maneuvers, 290; cabinet meeting of July 21, 292; Grey-Metternich conference of July 21, 293; and Lloyd George's speech, 296-297, 301-302; speech in the House of Commons, July 27, 314-316, 317, 327; and the railroad strike, 320

Atlas, 4, 123, 142

Austria, at the Algeciras conference, 44; attitude toward recognition of Mulay Hafid, 60; and the Casablanca deserter affair, 66; reception of the Franco-German Accord of 1909, 78; and the loan of 1910, 93; and the expedition to Fez, 190, 193, 200; reaction to the Agadir *coup*, 236; press attitude toward the German *coup*, 249-250; and the possibility of war, 320; support of Germany, 356-357, 362, 399; acceptance of the November treaty, 375-376

B agdad railway, 81, 180, 329-330, 335

Balkan League, 361, 400

Bassermann, Ernest, a National Liberal and Pan-German, 135

Baudin, Pierre, 82

Bebel, August, 381

Belgian Congo, 265, 286-288, 308, 325, 330, 371, 373

Benckendorff, Graf Alexander, Russian ambassador to London, on the expedition to Fez, 195; and the proposed conversations à *quatre*, 243-244; on Russian attitude, 245, 247, 359; on British attitude, 279, 311

Beni M'Tir, revolt of, 174, 176; of the boulevards, 188

Berbers, 13-15

Berckheim, French chargé, 61, 93

Berlin bourse crash, 350-355, 363, 364

Berteaux, French minister of war, 117, 227

Bertie, Sir Francis, and the railroad